Mexican Philosophy
in the 20th Century

Oxford New Histories of Philosophy

Series Editors
Christia Mercer and Eileen O'Neill

Advisory Board
Jacqueline Broad, Marguerite Deslauriers, Karen Detlefsen, Don Garrett,
Robert Gooding-Williams, Andrew Janiak, Marcy Lascano, Lisa Shapiro,
Tommie Shelby

*

Oxford New Histories of Philosophy provides essential resources for those aiming to diversify the content of their philosophy courses, revisit traditional narratives about the history of philosophy, or better understand the richness of
philosophy's past. Examining previously neglected or understudied philosophical figures, movements, and traditions, the series includes both innovative new
scholarship and new primary sources.

*

Published in the series
Mexican Philosophy in the 20th Century: Essential Readings
Edited by Carlos Alberto Sánchez and Robert Eli Sanchez, Jr.

Mexican Philosophy in the 20th Century

Essential Readings

EDITED BY CARLOS ALBERTO SÁNCHEZ

and

ROBERT ELI SANCHEZ, JR.

OXFORD
UNIVERSITY PRESS

OXFORD
UNIVERSITY PRESS

Oxford University Press is a department of the University of Oxford. It furthers
the University's objective of excellence in research, scholarship, and education
by publishing worldwide. Oxford is a registered trade mark of Oxford University
Press in the UK and certain other countries.

Published in the United States of America by Oxford University Press
198 Madison Avenue, New York, NY 10016, United States of America.

© Oxford University Press 2017

CIP data is on file at the Library of Congress
ISBN 978–0–19–060130–0 (pbk)
ISBN 978–0–19–060129–4 (hbk)

9 8 7 6 5 4 3 2 1
Paperback printed by Webcom, Inc., Canada
Hardback printed by Bridgeport National Bindery, Inc., United States of America

Para México, sus filósofos, y a quienes no conocen fronteras.

For all would-be students of philosophy who could not find anything in the library resembling their own experience.

THE HORSEMAN

In the far-off mountains rides a horseman,
Wandering alone in the world and wishing for death.
In his breast he carries a wound, his soul is destroyed.
He loved her more than his own life,
And he lost her forever.
That's why he is wounded, that's why he seeks death.
He spends whole nights singing with his guitar,
Man and guitar weeping by the light of the stars.
Then he loses himself in the night, and although the night is very beautiful,
He asks God to bear him away to her,
The woman he loved more than his own life,
And lost forever.
That's why he is wounded, that's why he seeks death.

—José Alfredo Jiménez, the great Mexican philosopher-mariachero[1]

---

[1] "El jinete," translation in Gilbert M. Joseph and Timothy J. Henderson, eds., *The Mexico Reader: History, Culture, Politics* (Durham, NC: Duke University Press, 2002), 53.

CONTENTS

SERIES EDITORS' FOREWORD

Oxford New Histories of Philosophy (ONHP) speaks to a new climate in philosophy.

There is a growing awareness among many that philosophy's past is richer and more diverse than previously understood. It has become clear that canonical figures are best studied in a broad context. More exciting still is the recognition that our philosophical heritage contains long-forgotten innovative ideas, movements, and thinkers. Sometimes these thinkers warrant serious study in their own right; sometimes their importance resides in the conversations they helped reframe or problems they devised; often their philosophical proposals force us to rethink long-held assumptions about a period or genre; and frequently they cast well-known philosophical discussions in a fresh light.

There is also a mounting sense among philosophers that our discipline benefits from a diversity of perspectives and a commitment to inclusiveness. In a time when questions about justice, inequality, dignity, education, discrimination, and climate (to name a few) are especially vivid, it is appropriate to mine historical texts for insights that can shift conversations and reframe solutions. Given that philosophy's very long history contains astute discussions of a vast array of topics, the time is right to cast a broad historical net.

Lastly, there is increasing interest among philosophy instructors in speaking to the diversity and concerns of their students. Although historical discussions and texts can serve as a powerful means of doing so, finding the necessary time and tools to excavate long-buried historical materials is challenging.

ONHP is designed to address all these needs. It will contain new editions and translations of significant historical texts. These primary materials will make available, often for the first time, ideas and works by women, people of color, and movements in philosophy's past that were groundbreaking in their day, but left out of traditional accounts. Informative introductions will help instructors and students navigate the new material. Alongside its primary texts, *ONHP* will also publish monographs and collections of essays that offer philosophically subtle analyses of understudied topics, movements, and figures. In combining primary materials and astute philosophical analyses, *ONHP* will make it easier for philosophers, historians, and instructors to include in their courses and research exciting new materials drawn from philosophy's past.

ONHP's range will be wide, both historically and culturally. The series plans to include, for example, the writings of twentieth-century Mexican philosophers, formerly enslaved Americans, early modern and late medieval women, Islamic and Jewish authors, and non-western thinkers. It will excavate and analyze problems and ideas that were prominent in their day but forgotten by later historians. And it will serve as a significant aid to philosophers in teaching and researching this material.

We are proud to contribute to philosophy's present and to a richer understanding of its past.

Christia Mercer and Eileen O'Neill
Series Editors

ACKNOWLEDGMENTS

When we agreed to take on the task of representing Mexican philosophy outside of Mexico and in English, we knew that we could not do it alone, and that, even if we could, we should not. We knew that we would need help translating, both to translate the number of texts we wanted to in the time we had, and with the inexplicably difficult task of rendering certain Mexicanisms into English. We were also acutely aware that since this anthology was meant to represent *Mexican* philosophy, the decision about what and whom to include should not be left entirely to two Mexican-Americans. The project of representing Mexican philosophy—we continue to believe—ought to be genuinely bi-national. Thus, we are sincerely grateful to the community of philosophers and scholars, both in the United States and Mexico, who through countless readings and conversations have not only saved us from innumerable errors in translation but who have also assured us of the significance of our selection of texts. Their assurance has given us the confidence to continue with the project when it seemed the most challenging or, on occasion, beyond our capabilities. In particular, we would like to thank the original group of philosophers who met with us in Williamsburg, Virginia, in the spring of 2014 to discuss the future of Mexican philosophy in the United States: Alejandro Tomasini Bassols, Amy Oliver, Aurelia Valero Pie, Guillermo Hurtado, and Kim Díaz. Not only did they convince us of the need for this anthology, but each of them has generously advised us until the very end. We would also like to thank the College of William & Mary, particularly the Latin American Studies program, for providing financial support to host the first of what is now a bi-annual and bi-national symposium on Mexican philosophy.

We are especially grateful to Aurelia Valero Pie and Guillermo Hurtado, who campaigned on our behalf before the many powers that be in Mexico, and whose knowledge and dedication to promoting Mexican philosophy were crucial to producing this text.

We would also like to acknowledge other institutions whose support helped us to realize this project. For the opportunity to pursue this project full-time for a year, as well as the opportunity to live in Mexico City for three months, Robert Sanchez would like to thank the University of California Institute for Mexico and the United States (UC MEXUS). It is impossible to overstate the value of being able to scour countless bookstores and libraries in Mexico, especially when one does not know what one is looking for. And, as a bi-national project, we benefited from the many face-to-face conversations with our Mexican colleagues. An especially valuable gathering took place at the Second Bi-annual Symposium on Mexican Philosophy at San Jose State University in April 2016. Carlos Sánchez would like to thank San Jose State University for sponsoring this event through a Global Initiatives Grant. We would also like to thank the *Universidad de Guanajuato* and the *Instituto de Investigaciones Filosóficas* at UNAM for inviting us to their national symposium on Mexican philosophy in Mexico in June 2016. We are grateful for their generosity and hospitality and for their sincere faith in our work and its urgency. For relieving us of some of the financial burdens associated with this project, we are especially grateful to Dean Lisa Vollendorf in the College of Humanities and Arts at San Jose State University. Carlos would also like to thank Laura Plunkett from the Department of Philosophy for her tireless administrative work. Finally, many thanks are due to series editors Christia Mercer and Eileen O'Neill, and to Peter Ohlin at OUP, who were willing to complicate the philosophical landscape.

Although some of the texts we have translated are now part of the public domain, many of them are not. And so we want to thank the *Fondo de Cultura Económica* for granting us permission to translate the essays by Rosario Castellanos, Jorge Portilla, and Alfonso Reyes, and Ediciones ERA for the rights to translate Jose Revueltas. But we are especially thankful for (and honored by) the trust and faith of the authors' families, who have given us access and permission to works that helped to define not only Mexican culture, but also their family names and histories. Specifically, we would like to thank Juan Villoro, Samuel Ramos Palacios, Dr. Silvestre Villegas, Cecilia Uranga, and Leonor Ortiz Monasterio.

Last, we would like to thank our loved ones for their patience, support, and encouragement over the last two years. As with many a worthwhile project, it is not until the project is complete that one realizes that it was probably too ambitious (in the time allowed) and that it would cost much more than one could anticipate. Nevertheless, the editors are grateful for a support system they are not sure they deserve. In particular, Robert would like to thank his mother, father, and Terry, whose love and honesty continue to ground him and remind him who he is; his grandmother, who has always supported him, especially throughout this project; Neal Tognazzini, for his enduring friendship and confidence;

Angela Camarena for her patience; and his newborn daughter, Sofía Belén, for the light she has brought into his world.

Carlos would lack the focus and discipline necessary without the love and laughter of his three boys, Julian, Pascual, and Ethan. But he is especially grateful for the love, support, and selfless sacrifice of Tricia Ryan, who has held steady for many, many years, and in spite of countless difficulties. Finally, Carlos would like to dedicate this book to his father, Patricio Jiménez Sánchez, who every day longs for the day in which he will return to his *tierra*, Acuitzeramo, Michoacán, and live out the rest of his days.

PERMISSIONS

The following is a list of permissions we secured to translate and publish the corresponding essays. The other essays included in our anthology are now considered part of the public domain in Mexico.

Rosario Castellanos, "Sobre Cultura Femenina," in *Sobre Cultura Femenina,* © 2005, Fondo de Cultura Economica. All rights reserved. Mexico City.

José Gaos and Francisco Larroyo, "Dos ideas de la filosofia," in José Gaos, *Obras Completas III. Ideas de la filosofía,* México, UNAM, 2003. José Gaos, "Cuatro espadas," in *Obras Completas VI. Pensamiento de lengua española. Pensamiento español,* México, UNAM, 1990. Translated and published by permission of the family of Jose Gaos, c/o Angeles Gaos de Camacho.

Edmundo O'Gorman, "El arte o de la monstruosidad," originally published by Universidad Veracruzana in 1960. Translated and published by permission of Leonor Ortiz Monasterio.

Jorge Portilla, "Comunidad y grandeza del mexicano," in *Fenomelogia del relajo y otros ensayos,* © 1984, Fondo de Cultura Economica. All rights reserved. Mexico City.

Samuel Ramos, *Historia de la filosofía en Mexico,* originally published by Imprenta Universitaria in 1943; *Veinte años de educación en México,* originally published by Imprenta Universitaria in 1941. Translated by permission of Samuel Ramos Palacios.

José Revueltas, "Posibilidades y limitaciones del mexicano," in *Ensayos sobre Mexico,* © 1985, Ediciones Era. All rights reserved. Mexico City.

Alfonso Reyes, *La x en la frente,* © 1959, Fondo de Cultura Economica. All rights reserved. Mexico City.

Emilio Uranga, "Ensayo de una ontologia del mexicano," originally published by *Cuadernos Americanos* 57, no. 3 (1951). Published by permission of Cecilia Uranga.

TRANSLATORS

Minerva Ahumada, PhD, is a full-time Lecturer of Philosophy at Arrupe College of Loyola University, Chicago. She specializes in Latin American Philosophy and Narrative Ethics.

Cecilia Beristáin teaches philosophy in Mexico City and is the author of *I Say "I": A Philosophical Investigation of the Word "I" and What We Can Say about Ourselves (Ich sage "ich": eine sprachphilosophische Betrachtung des Wortes "ich" und dessen, was wir über uns selbst sagen, 2012)*.

David W. Bird is an Associate Professor of Spanish Literature at Saint Mary's College in Moraga, California. His research concentrates on philosophy and history of ideas in Spain during the fifty years before the Spanish Civil War (1936–1939).

Roberto Cantú is Emeritus Professor in the Department of Chicana/o and Latina/o Studies and jointly in the Department of English at California State University, Los Angeles. He is the editor of *The Reptant Eagle: Essays on Carlos Fuentes and the Art of the Novel* (2015), and of *The Forked Juniper: Critical Perspectives on Rudolfo Anaya* (2016).

Kim Díaz is an adjunct Professor of Philosophy at El Paso Community College in El Paso, Texas and Visiting Professor of Philosophy at Jawaharlal Nehru University, Centre for Philosophy, School for Social Science. She works for the United States Department of Justice and is the Managing Editor for the *Inter-American Journal of Philosophy*, specializing in Latin American Philosophy. And she is co-editor of the *Philosophy of the Americas Reader* (Bloomsbury, forthcoming).

Amy A. Oliver is Associate Professor in the Department of Philosophy and Religion and jointly in the Department of World Languages and Cultures at

American University in Washington, DC. She is the editor of *The Role of the Americas in History* (1992), and of *Feminist Philosophy in Latin America and Spain* (2007).

Jose G. Rodriguez, Jr., is an MFA student, specializing in Creative Writing at the University of Texas, Rio Grande Valley.

Alexander V. Stehn is an Associate Professor of Philosophy at the University of Texas, Rio Grande Valley. He specializes in US-American and Latin American philosophy.

Aurelia Valero Pie is a Research Professor at the *Universidad Nacional Autónoma de México* in Morelia, Michoacán. She is the author of *José Gaos in Mexico: An Intellectual Biography* (*José Gaos en México: una biografía intelectual, 1938–1969*) (2015).

INTRODUCTION

1. Background and Rationale

In the spring of 2014, scholars from the United States and Mexico gathered at the College of William & Mary to discuss the possibility and the challenges of making Mexican philosophy widely available in the United States. Although the participants had been working independently on various themes, questions, and aspects of Mexican philosophy for years, and although they were not the first to raise questions about the history of Mexican philosophy, this meeting was the first bi-national gathering at an American university to discuss the future of Mexican philosophy in, and for, the United States. There have been several meetings to discuss the nature, history, and future of "Latin American" philosophy as an option for academic study in the United States, but none that had focused specifically on the nature, history, and future of "Mexican" philosophy.

That this was a first might come as a surprise, given the large Mexican and Mexican-American population in the United States, as well as the continual growth of Mexican and Chicano/a studies in recent decades. So the first question one might ask about Mexican philosophy in the United States is simply, *what took so long?*[1] It is not that North American philosophers were completely unaware of a Mexican philosophical tradition,[2] or that there was not was not enough material to sustain interest in it,[3] or that they had no contact with

---

[1] Similar questions have already been asked about Latin American philosophy. See Jorge J. E. Gracia, *Latinos in America: Philosophy and Social Identity* (Malden, MA: Blackwell, 2008).

[2] See, for example, O. A. Kubitz, "Humanism in Mexico," *Philosophy and Phenomenological Research* 2, no. 2 (1941) and John H. Haddox, "Philosophy with a Mexican Perspective," *Philosophy and Phenomenological Research* 24, no. 4 (1964). The dates of these studies are revealing, as they suggest that not much has been published in a mainstream journal in quite some time.

[3] See two important works by John H. Haddox: *Vasconcelos of Mexico, Philosopher and Prophet* (Austin: University of Texas Press, 1967) and *Antonio Caso, Philosopher of Mexico* (Austin: University

Mexican philosophers.[4] In fact, scholars in other disciplines have been taking an active interest in several major Mexican philosophers for quite some time, such as Sor Juana Inés de la Cruz, Samuel Ramos, José Vasconcelos, Alfonso Reyes, and Miguel León-Portilla, which again makes one wonder why *philosophical* investigation into these thinkers has been so rare.

One obvious explanation—and, by contrast, what in part explains why scholars *have* written much about a few specific texts, such as Ramos's *Profile of Man and Culture in Mexico* or Vasconcelos's *The Cosmic Race*—is that the vast majority of the more influential texts in the Mexican philosophical tradition are not available in English.[5] That is, although scholars and students are able to read *about* Mexican philosophers,[6] they are often not able to read them directly, and thus are not able to respond to them or incorporate them into their own research. So, at this first meeting in Williamsburg, Virginia, the consensus was that the primary task for the future of Mexican philosophy in the United States was to translate its most representative texts into English. This anthology is the first installment of that project.

Of course, there is more to translating than simple translation—the task does not boil down to simply *carrying terms across* from one language to another. In our case, translating also meant selecting and editing, and thus making certain decisions about what ultimately counts as Mexican philosophy; that is, as we undertook this task, we realized that to decide which texts are the most representative is to take a stance on what it is that they represent. And if Patrick Romanell, who has written what is arguably the single best introduction to Mexican philosophy in English, is right, and a "philosopher's philosophy" (i.e., the articulate conception of certain ideals of culture, such as the good or the true or the beautiful) always reflects a "people's philosophy" (i.e., the unarticulated *pre*-conceptions or attitudes or worldview of a people), then producing an anthology of texts that represent "Mexican philosophy," what philosophers have written, is also to take a

---

of Texas Press, 1971). Another important resource for English readers is A. Robert Caponigri, trans., *Major Trends in Mexican Philosophy* (Notre Dame, IN: University of Notre Dame Press, 1966).

[4] See Rudolph Carnap, "Notes and News," *The Journal of Philosophy* 67, no. 24 (1970), in which Carnap discusses visiting a Mexican jail to converse with Mexican philosophers who had been incarcerated by the Mexican government in 1968.

[5] Samuel Ramos, *Profile of Man and Culture in Mexico* (Austin: University of Texas Press, 1962) and José Vasconcelos, *The Cosmic Race* (Baltimore, MD: Johns Hopkins University Press, 1997). We mention these two texts in particular because they are the most severely criticized outside of philosophy. It remains to be seen how they will fare in areas such as Chicano or Mexican Studies when these works are put in their *philosophical* context.

[6] See, for instance, one of the latest efforts to introduce classic texts of Mexican philosophy to an English-speaking readership: Carlos Alberto Sánchez's *The Suspension of Seriousness: On the Phenomenology of Jorge Portilla* (Albany: State University of New York Press), which includes a translation of Jorge Portilla's *La Fenomenología del relajo* as an Appendix.

stance on the Mexican "people's philosophy," what Romanell calls "the Mexican mind" (i.e., the unwritten philosophy of the Mexican people).[7] Ultimately, then, to select, edit, and translate what we take to be the most representative texts of Mexican philosophy, written and unwritten, is to take a stance on and interpret *what it means to be Mexican*. In short, we quickly understood that there is no way to reconstruct the history of Mexican philosophy through its texts, which appears to be a purely descriptive task, without taking a stance on what Mexican philosophy is, or, more generally, on what counts as Mexican, which is clearly a normative task.

Like all "what is it?" questions, there are two ways of looking for a definition of Mexican philosophy: moving from the particular to the general, and from the general to the particular. In the end, we found that the most accurate and helpful answer requires a combination of both approaches.

1A. FROM PARTICULAR TO GENERAL

The inclusion of several of the readings in this anthology does not require much justification. That is, there are certain texts in the history of philosophy in Mexico that ought to be part of *any* anthology of Mexican philosophy, either because of the influence they have had so far on the history of the tradition, such as Antonio Caso's *Existence as Economy and as Charity*; or because of their role in helping to define Mexican philosophy as it is currently understood, such as Samuel Ramos's *History of Philosophy in Mexico*; or because of their contribution to the question of what it means to be Mexican, such as Emilio Uranga's "Essay on an Ontology of the Mexican." In that respect, if the goal is to introduce the reader to some of the best offerings of Mexican philosophy—the most insightful, penetrating, challenging, influential, or provocative—the choice of several of the texts included here simply was not up to us.

What does require some explanation is not why we included many of the texts we chose, but why we did not include other obvious choices. For instance, those with some familiarity with the history of philosophy in Mexico will want to know why we did not include works by Sor Juana Inés de la Cruz or Benito

---

[7] Patrick Romanell, *Making of the Mexican Mind: A Study in Recent Mexican Thought* (Notre Dame, IN: University of Notre Dame Press, 1952), 13–15. As Mexican-Americans, this project of interpretation is especially complex for us. Although our parents, grandparents, or great-grandparents are Mexican by birth, we were born into and grew up in a *different* culture via processes of displacement and migration. This different culture is neither the so-called "American" culture promoted in political and cultural narratives, but neither is it "Mexican" culture. Rather, it is a hybrid culture distinct from the one we now endeavor to interpret through the careful selection and translation of philosophical texts.

Díaz de Gamarra or Nezahualcoyotl.[8] Even those without any familiarity with Mexican philosophy will wonder why there is not more representation of female authors, indigenous thought, or contemporary Mexican philosophy. The simple, unproblematic answer is that we chose authors and texts that clearly frame a tradition and simultaneously provide a point of entry for those who are willing to engage with it critically, especially those who will offer feminist, indigenous, or contemporary critiques. The more complicated answer is that the authors and texts that have been left out of our collection were also excluded from the philosophical conversation by those structures of exclusion and marginalization that have been widely prevalent in Mexico since the Mexican Revolution of 1910. Our goal is not to deny or justify these exclusions. Instead, our hope is that the work we have undertaken here begins a conversation in the United States, where marginalized voices are now encouraged to emerge and proclaim their place and historical identity. Nevertheless, it is with the realization of inevitable limitations that we began to rely less on particular texts and more on a general approach to the meaning of "Mexico" and "Mexican philosophy."

1B. FROM GENERAL TO PARTICULAR

There are at least two ways of proceeding: one historical and one philosophical, and again we found that the best answer is a combination of both. First, the historical.

In giving shape to this anthology, we wanted to present Mexican philosophy as a *tradition*, as opposed to presenting a history of philosophy in the geographical territory of what is now Mexico. Moreover, instead of focusing on a group of individual philosophers from a different part of the world, who we are convinced ought to be included in the global history of philosophy, our aim was to present a roughly unified set of thinkers, whose philosophy is grounded in and represents a defining set of social, political, cultural, and philosophical circumstances; who are self-critical, that is, who are philosophers and not ideologues serving Church or State; who mutually and directly influence one another, that is, who are in dialogue with one another; and who share a set of questions, concerns, methods, styles, or who expressly opposed them. This, we think, is best way to do the history of philosophy.[9]

---

[8] This list could be extended to include any or all of the philosophers cited by Guillermo Hurtado in his entry "Philosophy in Mexico" in the *Stanford Encyclopedia of Philosophy*.

[9] One of our models for approaching the history of philosophy is Bertrand Russell, who writes, "My purpose is to exhibit philosophy as an integral part of social and political life: not as the isolated speculations of remarkable individuals, but as both an effect and a cause of the character of various communities in which different systems flourished. [. . .] The great age of the scholastic philosophy was an outcome of the reforms of the eleventh century, and these, in turn, were a reaction against

With the goal of presenting a tradition and working with what has become a relatively standard history of Mexican philosophy, we have decided to focus on the first half of the 20th century. This is not to suggest that Mexican philosophy "begins" in the 20th century, though one would be hard-pressed to identify a tradition as defined in the preceding before the 20th century;[10] or that there are no philosophers during this period who are Mexican but outside of this tradition (e.g., indigenous philosophers). We are simply presenting what we are confident does count as a tradition and one that deserves more attention in the United States.

Several factors help to explain what distinguishes the 20th century from the previous five centuries of Mexican history, but any survey of Mexican philosophy must mention at least the following three. First, and most important, is the Mexican Revolution of 1910. Not only was the Revolution, by all accounts, the most significant event in modern Mexican history, but, as the Mexican poet Octavio Paz writes in his celebrated *The Labyrinth of Solitude*, there is a sense in which Mexicans "had discovered the true character of Mexico" in the Revolution.[11] Second is the founding of the National University in Mexico City, also in 1910, which helps to explain the "normalization" of philosophy in Mexico, to borrow a phrase from the Argentine philosopher Francisco Romero.[12] And third is an intellectual movement among young middle-class intellectuals who criticized what they considered the "official philosophy" of the State, or the official philosophy of the *Porfiriato*, both for being official or ideological and for demoralizing and alienating the Mexican people.[13] This small

previous corruption. Without some knowledge of the centuries between the fall of Rome and the rise of the medieval Papacy, the intellectual atmosphere of the twelfth and thirteenth centuries can hardly be understood." Bertrand Russell, *The History of Western Philosophy* (New York: Simon & Schuster, 1945), ix.

[10] See Romanell, *The Making of the Mexican Mind*, chapter 2.

[11] Octavio Paz, *The Labyrinth of Solitude and Other Essays* (New York: Grove Press: 1985), 160.

[12] According to Samuel Ramos in the essay included in this volume, Romero's "happy expression" means that philosophy has moved beyond the walls of academia. Ramos says about Mexican philosophy: "a general interest in philosophy has been awakened in all cultural media. Books about philosophy can count on an increasing number of readers. A multitude of articles about philosophical themes are appearing in specialized and non-specialized journals." It is also worth pointing out that for Romero, the two main requirements of "normalization" were that the practice of philosophy in Latin America be current or up to date and that it be produced with a certain amount of rigor or discipline and regularity. So, for Romero, the *normalización* of philosophy might better be translated as the "professionalization" of philosophy. However, although Ramos, like many other historians of Latin American philosophy, slightly misconstrues Romero's meaning, both interpretations apply to Mexican philosophy in the first half of the 20th century.

[13] The *Porfiriato* refers to the dictatorial regime of Porfirio Díaz, president of Mexico from 1876 to 1911. For the intellectual significance of *Porfiriato*, see Leopoldo Zea's "Positivism and Porfirism in Mexico," in Susana Nuccetelli and Gary Seay, eds., *Latin American Philosophy: An Introduction with Readings* (London: Pearson: 2003).

group, which included Antonio Caso, José Vasconcelos, Alfonso Reyes, Diego Rivera, and Pedro Henriquez Ureña, referred to themselves as the *Ateneo de la juventud* (Athenaeum of Youth). So strong and influential was their objection to the prevailing scientism and materialism in Mexico that we might speak of two rebellions, as Leopoldo Zea does,[14] one political and one intellectual.

This introduction is not the place to consider the many controversies surrounding the causes and the lasting significance of, or connection among, these historical events.[15] We only want to point out that historically the first half of the 20th century (1910–1960) is a "decisive" moment in Mexican history, as Luis Villoro, one of the most important Mexican philosophers and historians of the 20th century, characterizes it. Writing in 1960, he says:

> The last half century has been decisive for our spirit: it will remain, without doubt, a major moment in which a community tried to describe its true being and liberate itself from all manner of deception.

He continues:

> The central theme [of culture during this period] has two aspects: on the one hand, to break alienating forms [of culture]; on the other, to bring culture back to life, grounding it once again in a national tradition and reality. A double movement is sketched: the negation of forms imposed [from without] and a return to our true reality hidden by those forms.[16]

[14] Leopoldo Zea, "Positivism and Porfirism in Mexico," 218. See also Elizabeth Flower, "The Mexican Revolt against Positivism," *Journal of the History of Ideas* 10, no 1 (1949). For a helpful summary of early 20th-century intellectual and moral discontent in Mexico (in Spanish), see Alfonso Reyes, "Pasado Inmediato," in *Obras Completas de Alfonso Reyes* XII (Mexico City: Fondo de Cultura Económica, 1960), 174–278.

[15] One particular controversy, however, is worth mentioning. Despite the striking correlation among these major historical events, historians doubt that there is any connection among them. For instance, Fernando Salmerón, who represents a relatively standard historical account of Mexican philosophy, claims that "[t]he members of the Ateneo were, in 1910, too young and too lacking in sufficient social influence for their doctrines to go beyond the cultured groups of the middle classes. Moreover, those doctrines did not exist except as projects of philosophical creation in the heads of young thinkers." He adds in a footnote that, despite all the language in the literature about these twin rebellions that suggests otherwise—"parallel," "essential correspondence," "coetaneous phenomena"—"[t]he decisive point is to eliminate any expression which might, even metaphorically, suggest a relation of causality." Fernando Salmerón, "Mexican Philosophers of the Twentieth Century," in *Major Trends in Mexican Philosophy* (Notre Dame, IN: University of Notre Dame Press, 1966).

[16] Luis Villoro, "La cultura mexicana de 1910 a 1960," *Historia Mexicana* 10, no. 2 (1960), 197, 198. The translation is our own.

Following Villoro and others, we have tried to capture the philosophical contribution to this cultural project of self-discovery and affirmation that began in Mexico roughly around 1910 and culminated in the 1940s and 1950s. Not only does this period of philosophy in Mexico mark the emergence of a philosophical program preoccupied by cultural and historical identity and authenticity, but insofar as it insists on the relevance of cultural or national identity in philosophy, it presents a challenge to the Western conception of philosophy, which typically asserts that philosophy is a disinterested discipline whose truths transcend cultural differences. If Western philosophy—to whatever extent it makes sense to speak of it as a unified tradition—denies the possibility of *Mexican* philosophical truths, this is precisely what the majority of the authors included here aimed to disprove.

It is worth repeating that our decision to focus on the first half of the 20th century is not without well-established precedent. In addition to the article by Villoro referred to in the preceding paragraph, several other historians have concluded that Mexican philosophy, understood as an original (i.e., non-imitative or non-derivative) preoccupation with or *from* Mexican cultural and historical reality, begins roughly at the turn of the 20th century. This is true of Romanell's *Making of the Mexican Mind*, Ramos's *The History of Philosophy in Mexico*, José Gaos's *En torno a la filosofía mexicana* (Concerning Mexican Philosophy) and Antonio Ibargüengoitia's *Filosofía Mexicana: En sus hombres y sus textos* (Mexican Philosophy: Its Philosophers and Texts).[17] Gabriel Vargas Lozano, who also endorses this historical account of Mexican philosophy, articulates what distinguishes the 20th century particularly well: "if we consider that our country was subjected to *colonial dependency* during three hundred years, and that only in the 19th century did it have the real possibility of constructing an *independent* nation, then we can see that *it is only* in the 20th century when the conditions for the possibility and development of modern philosophical thought are found."[18] Of course, this historical account of Mexican philosophy has been challenged and will continue to be,[19] but we are confident that it serves as a useful (if not

[17] Antonio Ibargüengoitia, *Filosofía Mexicana: En sus hombres y sus textos* (México, DF: Editorial Porrua, S.A., 1967), 177ff.

[18] Gabriel Vargas Lozano, "Esbozo histórico de la filosofía Mexicana del siglo xx," *Filosofía de la cultura en México*, ed. Mario Teodoro Ramírez (México, DF: Plaza y Valdéz, 1997), 81–121. See also, Aureliano Ortega Esquivel, "Pensamiento, cultura, y politica en México hacia 1934," *Ensayos sobre el pensamiento mexicano*, eds. Aureliano Ortega Esquivel and Javier Corona Fernandez (Guanajuato: Universidad de Guanajuato, 2014), 9–48.

[19] Some argue that the philosophy that merits the qualifier "Mexican" does not emerge until 1934. Aureliano Ortega, for example, argues that "philosophy, in the strict sense, enters the post-Revolutionary Mexican cultural scene in 1934 with the publication of Samuel Ramos's seminal work, *Profile of Man and Culture in Mexico.*" In "Pensamiento, cultura, y politica en México hacia 1934," 32. Even Vasconcelos, who in pushing the birthdate of Mexican philosophy forward would exclude himself, claims that there was no authentic philosophy in Mexico until 1930. In Augusto Salazar Bondy,

mostly accurate) point of departure for more inclusive philosophical discussions yet to come.

Insofar as *México como problema* (the problem of Mexico) constitutes a common denominator among the essays in this volume,[20] Mexico appears as an all-encompassing reality that grounds and gives them a sense of identity. The philosophers represented here thus ask about the Mexicanness of Mexican identity, culture, and history (and sometimes about the lack of Mexicanness[21]). The period between 1910 and 1960 introduces *la filosofía de lo mexicano*, or the "philosophy of Mexicanness," which is one way of characterizing the most contentious period in Mexican philosophy, namely, the period represented by the *Ateneo de la juventud* just before the Revolution and lasting until 1925, *los Contemporáneos* who see their influence wane in the early 1940s, and concluding with the successes and failures of *el grupo Hiperión* (the Hyperion group) in the late 1950s. Although there are drawbacks with focusing on the philosophical questions concerning Mexico and Mexican identity—no single anthology can include everything it might include—this theme and period are marked by an originality that merits consideration, preservation, and revision as we think about and many futures of philosophy in the 21st century.

2. From General to Particular: Philosophical Considerations

Aside from *historical* considerations that recommend focusing on the 20th century, there are also philosophical considerations concerning the reality of Mexico and what would make philosophy "Mexican" that guided our selection.

¿Existe una filosofía de nuestra América? (México, DF: Siglo XXI Editores, 1968), 36. Other historians argue that by fixing the birthdate of Mexican philosophy at 1934 (or 1910 for that matter), we fail to acknowledge crucial antecedents without which Mexican philosophy would not be possible. See, for example, Henry C. Schmidt, *The Roots of Lo Mexicano: Self and Society in Mexican Thought, 1900–1934* (College Station: Texas A&M University Press, 2000). And still other historians, such as Aurelia Valero Pie, one of our translators, argue that the whole discussion of the history of "Mexican philosophy" that takes Ramos's history as its starting point is a self-serving narrative that all but beatifies a small handful of philosophers in the story of Mexican philosophy and purposefully neglects anyone who challenges the legitimacy of this narrative.

[20] See Carlos Illades and Rodolfo Suárez, eds., *México como problema: esbozo de una historia intelectual* (México, DF: Siglo Veintiuno, 2012) and José Gaos, "México, tema y responsabilidad" in *En torno a la filosofía mexicana* (México, DF: Alianza Editorial Mexicana, 1980).

[21] On the idea of Mexicanness and for more context, see Amy Oliver's introduction to *The Role of the Americas in History* by Leopoldo Zea (Savage: Rowman & Littlefied, 1992).

2A. WHAT DO WE MEAN BY "MEXICO" WHEN WE TALK ABOUT "MEXICAN" PHILOSOPHY?

The following question arises: how can we talk about Mexican philosophy when Mexico itself is an imaginary construction, arbitrarily created in the process of conquest and colonialism by individuals intent on exploiting the people and resources encountered within its arbitrarily drawn and historically contingent national borders? One might also object that as a matter of fact, there is no such thing as a unified Mexican culture that philosophy might represent. Moreover, "Mexico" refers to a historical location that is not defined by territory or sameness or essence, but only by history and, in particular, by a history of struggle and overcoming experienced differently by different groups, and to varying degrees.[22]

In addressing these worries, it is helpful to think about the manner in which "American philosophy" is often defined.[23] When one hears "American" philosophy, one immediately thinks of philosophy produced by "Americans," that is, by citizens or residents of the United States. So "America" refers to the United States of America. But in talking about American philosophy, we do not question the arbitrariness of what counts as "American" as opposed to what does not, nor do we wonder whether "America" represents *all* of its different cultural and social groups. (It does not.) And we do not question the validity of this phrase, in part because we do not typically think of "American philosophy" as referring to a well-defined set of concerns or methods that a specific group of people adheres to, but rather to a heterogeneous set of different philosophical approaches to questions that are relevant to a general historical community, one understood as sharing in the struggles and the vision of the nation.

The same can be said of "Mexican philosophy." Mexicans are a historical people and their commonalities extend only as far as they share in a common history. This means that different cultural, social, and racial groups, who share in some elements of that history, will fall under the identifying term "Mexican."

---

[22] An astute reader might object that Mexico is, in fact, defined by territory. After all, we can build walls around it or fight wars over violations of its sovereignty, which usually involve territorial disputes. Our point is that the *idea* of Mexico is one that transcends territory, so that if its borders were somehow moved, the people displaced as a consequence of this action would still identity *as* Mexican or *with* Mexico. This was the case after the Treaty of Guadalupe Hidalgo of 1848, which ceded almost half of Mexico to the United States, including the territories that would become the states of Arizona, New Mexico, Colorado, and California. While those who remained on the US side were legally supposed to be granted US citizenship, they still retained their Mexican identity, thus giving rise to Mexican Americans and their descendants.

[23] For a sense of the Americanness of American philosophy, see Cornel West, *The American Evasion of Philosophy: A Genealogy of Pragmatism* (Madison: University of Wisconsin Press, 1989), or Russell Goodman, *American Philosophy and the Romantic Tradition* (Cambridge: Cambridge University Press, 1991).

Ultimately, and precisely because of the heterogeneity of the Mexican community or the Mexican people, one of the principal obsessions of Mexican philosophy in the first half of the 20th century was the nature of Mexican individual identity ("*el* mexicano") or Mexican cultural identity ("*lo mexicano*" or Mexicanness). It is important to clarify at the outset that Mexican philosophers by and large did not seek what they thought would be the *essence* of Mexican identity. They tried, first, to make sense of the social, racial, ethnic, and economic heterogeneity of the Mexican people by examining the innumerable differences within the Mexican community, and they did so in order to generate a sense of unity, mutual understanding, and respect.[24] And, second, they sought to affirm those differences as inalienable human differences that reflect the human condition itself, not just an accidental history of marginalization—political, economic, social, and philosophical.

2B. WHAT IS MEXICAN PHILOSOPHY?

To begin, it should be clear that any attempt to define Mexican philosophy is at best tentative, a hypothesis to be tested by future readers, in part because Mexican philosophy is not an accomplished fact, but continues to be produced, defined, and redefined. Nevertheless, based in part on the particular cases that are central to the period under discussion, we would like to offer what we take to be some common features of 20th-century Mexican philosophy.

Broadly, Mexican philosophy can be understood as

(1) self-reflective in a double sense, (a) as a return to the self, (b) as a return to the origins, history, and identity of Mexican culture;[25]
(2) critical; and
(3) affirmative or positive.

Let us look first at (1). By self-reflective, we mean that in its postulates, objects of reflection, and prescriptions, Mexican philosophy persistently returns to (i.e., *reflects back into*) the Mexican circumstance as its ground. It represents

---

[24] Whether they succeeded is a different, more contentious story. However, for the sake of how future readers—a different community with different advantages and disadvantages—might adopt or apply this project in the United States, its aim is more important than whether it was successful 100 years ago. Nevertheless, to understand its potential today and in the future, both aim and success should be considered.

[25] We can also say that its aim is "autognosis," following a term used by Abelardo Villegas. See Villegas, *Autognosis* (México: Fondo de Cultura Economica, 1985). Uranga used the term "auscultatory," however, because it implies a *careful attending to*, which need not be implicated in the *über*-rationality of autognosis, or a "knowledge of self." But this distinction we leave for another time.

José Ortega y Gasset's claim that "[o]ne reaches one's full capacity when one acquires complete consciousness of one's circumstances. Through them," says Ortega, "one communicates with the universe."[26] By this Ortega means that self-knowledge, as well as knowledge of the universe, does not begin either with a return to the ego (as Descartes had suggested) or with knowledge of the a priori structures of intuition and understanding (as Kant suggested), but with an intimate knowledge of one's specifically historical, cultural, and social situation. While a good portion of 20th-century Mexican philosophers were influenced by, or were reacting to, Ortega (especially those who came after José Gaos and the arrival of the Spanish exiles after 1938), even those who did not find his philosophy particularly attractive began with the Mexican circumstance as the starting point for philosophy.

The second feature (2) is that Mexican philosophy is critical. What we mean by this is that, as the texts we have collected reveal, 20th-century Mexican philosophers are always willing to challenge the positions of their contemporaries through rigorous dialogical critique (see Portilla). Because it is an internal critique (a critique of one another and not only, say, a critical examination of philosophical currents in England or France), it is both destructive and productive. Unlike earlier philosophical traditions in Mexico (particularly positivism, the Enlightenment philosophy, and Scholasticism), it is never content with simply imitating or repeating old ideas, methods, or traditions, but aims instead to detect and deconstruct inherited modes of thought and modes of being in its effort to establish an honest conception of itself, at the level of individual and society.

And (3), in saying that Mexican philosophy is self-affirmative or positive, what we mean is that, self-consciously aware of its status as historically derivative of European philosophy, it seeks to affirm and justify itself *as genuine philosophy*, not merely an unoriginal imitation, and to "define . . . its 'place' [within] a larger world civilization."[27] This project of self-affirmation grows out of a negative project of resisting the authority of European culture and it evolves into a positive project of affirming the history of Mexican life and thought. This project reaches its culmination in a sense of responsibility among artists and intellectuals to affirm Mexican culture in response to what was perceived as a "crisis" in European culture between the two World Wars. Thus, shortly after World War II, Octavio Paz writes:

[26] José Ortega y Gasset, *Meditations on Quixote*, trans. Evelyn Rugg and Diego Marín (Chicago: University of Illinois, 2000), 41.

[27] Aureliano Ortega, "Pensamiento," 30.

And suddenly we have reached the limit: in these few years we have exhausted all the historical forms Europe could provide us. There is nothing left except nakedness or lies. After the general collapse of Faith and Reason, of God and Utopia, none of the intellectual systems—new or old—is capable of alleviating our anguish or calming our fears. We are alone at last, like all men, and like them we live in a world of violence and deception, a world dominated by Don No One. [. . .] For the first time in our history, we are contemporaries of all mankind.[28]

Now, as several of the philosophers represented here claim, self-affirmation and justification extend not only to philosophy and culture, but to Mexican individuals who, given their historical consciousness of marginality and otherness to the European (and, more recently, the North American), likewise seek validation for their thoughts, life, and cultural productions before the rest of humanity.

Based on these general features, we can say that *Mexican philosophy can be defined as a self-critical investigation of Mexican being (el "ser" de lo mexicano), one born out of and for the sake of the Mexican circumstance, undertaken in order to reveal that being despite a history of colonialism, and to affirm it in an increasingly global understanding of universal culture.*[29]

---

[28] Paz, *The Labyrinth of Solitude*, 194.

[29] Of course, this is only one way of defining the period of Mexican philosophy under discussion, and our definition is not meant to be totalizing or exclusive. For instance, others might place the emphasis on the development of Mexican philosophy and education reform, or on the fact that the majority of the philosophers included here were curiously exercised by the problems of aesthetics. Still others might argue that our definition is overly intellectual and doesn't pay enough attention to the material and political situation in the first half of the 20th century, or that it is lamentable that we didn't include anything by anarchists such as the Flores Magón brothers. Along similar lines, the contemporary Mexican philosopher Guillermo Hurtado offers a slightly different definition of Mexican philosophy. According to Hurtado, Mexican philosophy aimed to be "transformative," in the sense that it reveals the Mexican in his present situation so as to project the possibilities of his future, and "liberatory," in the political sense that it aimed to emancipate the Mexican from a history of colonialism. (For a fuller account of this definition, see Guillermo Hurtado, *El búho y la serpiente: ensayos sobre la filosofía en México en el siglo XX* (Mexico: Unversidad Nacional Autónoma de México, 2007), especially chapters 1 and 2). We have tried to capture the transformative character of Mexican philosophy by referring to it as critical and positive, and its liberatory character by emphasizing the desire to affirm Mexican existence and philosophy after a history of marginalization. Still, Hurtado would place a greater emphasis on thinking of Mexican philosophy as a political philosophy and a philosophy of history aligned with, and able to reveal, significant social movements in the history of the Mexican people, especially the Mexican Revolution of 1910. Rather than think of these as different ways of defining Mexican philosophy, however, we prefer to think of them as different lenses for different purposes.

3. The Philosophy of *lo mexicano*

On the basis of similar observations as those provided in the preceding paragraphs, some historians of philosophy have characterized Mexican philosophy from Antonio Caso through Samuel Ramos, Emilio Uranga, and Leopoldo Zea as *la filosofía de lo mexicano* (the philosophy of *lo mexicano*).[30] But what is meant by the *philosophy of lo mexicano*?

During and after the Revolution, the fine arts, as well as poetry, literature, and political ideology, each in its own way, sought to portray the Revolution as a moment of rupture and disintegration and to portray the post-Revolutionary era as an opportunity for unity and cohesion. Thus, their products (paintings, poems, novels, and political parties) reflected those aspects of the social imaginary considered peculiarly Mexican. What was sought and promoted was that which could *unite* the divisions and hierarchies that led to, and that were eventually revealed by, the Revolution. What was sought was *that which was characteristically Mexican*.[31] But as philosophy began to play an increasingly influential role in the formation of national identity, it resisted the tendency to do so for the sake of narrow patriotism. While the philosophical project of *lo mexicano* begins with the assumption that there is a national circumstance, circumscribed by a common history of conquest and colonialism, the unity that it sought is a universal unity, or an affirmation of its own place within a universal history of thought. This affirmation *depends on* a philosophical conception of what it means to be

---

[30] As we point out, *lo mexicano* refers to "Mexicanness" or *what it means to be Mexican*. However, in the majority of cases throughout this volume, we have decided *not* to translate *lo mexicano* because by not translating it we retain some of the original force of the concept (its original tone, and its distinctive literary feel) and, also, because "Mexicanness" connotes an essentialism that we maintain does not completely describe the concept. In some cases, when considerations of flow and coherence demand it, we have translated the term. These cases are rare.

[31] Examples of this movement abound. In literature, for instance, there was the "Revolutionary novel," which sought to reveal the violence and ideological currents underlying the Revolution, or, more often than not, the *lack* of a unifying ideology. Mariano Azuela's *The Underdogs* and Nellie Campobello's *Cartucho* and *My Mother's Hands* are perhaps the most famous examples. The Campobello sisters are also famous for coordinating efforts to define a national dance, what is now known as the ballet folklorico. This nationalist movement even extended to food and drink, as Mexicans sought unity in their diverse cuisine and as tequila became a symbol of national identity. See Jeffrey M. Pilcher, *¡Que Vivan los Tamales! Food and the Making of Mexican Identity* (Albuquerque: University of New Mexico Press, 1998), and Marie Sarita Gaytán *¡Tequila! Distilling the Spirit of Mexico* (Stanford, CA: Stanford University Press, 2014). But perhaps the most consequential expressions of this movement are Mexican muralism, the establishment of the *Partido Revolucionario Institucional* or the PRI, the Mexican political party in power for the rest of the majority of the 20th century, and *indigenismo* (Indigenism)—each of which deserves a much fuller explanation than we could possibly hope to offer in a footnote.

Mexican (*lo mexicano*), but to the extent that it is philosophical, it aims at what it means to be human.

The notion of *lo mexicano* is perhaps the most controversial notion in 20th-century Mexican philosophy, if not in Mexican culture; thus our interpretation of the *philosophy* of *lo mexicano*, rather than attempting to be definitive, is meant to invite critical engagement with the idea and possibility of a philosophy grounded in something like national identity or historical circumstances. That said, it is important to distinguish a narrow and wide interpretation of the phrase *lo mexicano*. On a narrow reading, *lo mexicano* is a metaphor for that which is *essentially* Mexican (i.e., for that which represents *true* Mexicanness). The problem with this superficial reading, however, is that it invites the immediate question as to *who* or *what* decides what is truly Mexican. (José Revueltas addresses this worry in his essay included in this volume).[32] Moreover, under the assumption that "Mexico" is a historical construct, saying that *x* represents *lo mexicano* while *y* does not seems arbitrary, especially given the diversity of peoples, ethnicities, languages, geographies, and perspectives found within Mexico's borders. Simply put, this superficial reading suggests the following objections (which we present in the form of questions). If certain characteristics are manifestations of *lo mexicano*—for example, *machismo*, inferiority, religiosity, melancholy (see analyses that follow, particularly those of Ramos and Uranga)—do *all* Mexicans possess them? If some, say members of an indigenous community or women or any individual, do not possess them, are they *not* Mexican? And since the vast majority of Mexican philosophers—including those here—were educated men, a privilege that put them in an elite class of their own, does it follow that insofar as they were speaking about themselves, *lo mexicano* automatically excludes the majority of people who make up the historical, geographical, and existential space that is Mexico? In other words, is *la filosofía de lo mexicano* not subject to exactly the same criticisms that were leveled against the many other cultural expressions of the search for *lo mexicano*?[33]

---

[32] Aside from Revueltas, Mexican Marxists argue that the discourse of *lo mexicano* is meant to replace, or conceal, more important discussions about race and class. Other critiques, such as that Roger Bartra, locate the origin of *la filosofía de lo mexicano* in a political movement, one tied to the ideology of the State, which appealed to such unifying narratives in order to justify its power.

[33] One potential objection to identifying Mexican philosophy with *la filosofía de lo mexicano* is that we are lumping it together with tequila, the murals of Diego Rivera and self-portraits of Frida Kahlo, *china poblana*, the *charro*, *Cinco de Mayo*, the legend of Pancho Villa, ballet *folklorico* or *the Concheros* dance, and various other products that have become synonymous with, and symbolic of, Mexican identity—packaged and ready for export. Excluded from this national "self"-representation were mezcal and *pulque*, linguistic and ethnic diversity, and other cultural products that were not useful (or profitable) in a narrowing and simplifying conception of Mexican identity. In other words, the search for *lo mexicano* contributed to the ongoing and systematic erasure and oppression of innumerable Mexican nationals, mostly indigenous, Afro-Mexican, and women. So, this view of Mexican philosophy, like the historical search for *lo mexicano* itself, is at best false and misleading, at worst dangerous and immoral, and either way, unhelpful. What follows, then, is the beginning of a response to this kind of objection.

The general criticism underlying these questions is that the philosophical conception of *lo mexicano* meant to unify Mexicans into one essential category which would exclude whoever did not fit its criteria. And so to suggest that Mexican philosophy is somehow synonymous with *la filosofía de lo mexicano* would be to endorse a national project that was, in the vast majority of its cultural expressions, exclusive, racist, sexist, and unjustified. But this is an erroneous and simplistic view of *la filosofía de lo mexicano*, one that demeans Mexican philosophers by assuming that they were not themselves aware of the tensions and historical exclusions that characterize Mexican history and identity. This is not to say that some, if not many, Mexican philosophers were not racist or sexist. We know that some were. It is also not to say that many of them did not indirectly condone the perpetuation of these practices. Some did. It is simply to say that the suggestion that Mexican philosophers were uncritically engaged in a narrow project of petty nationalism or of looking for the essence of Mexican identity is false, and that there is a way of understanding *lo mexicano* that has greater philosophical potential for students of Mexican philosophy today, in particular, and for students of philosophy more generally.

A broader or more philosophical interpretation of *lo mexicano* suggests that for the *philosophy* of *lo mexicano* the goal was not merely to *unify* but to *affirm*, as our general feature (3) points out. That is, as several of the texts in this anthology demonstrate, Mexican philosophy in the 20th century was not satisfied with pure description of national identity. Instead, the unveiling and clarifying of Mexican being was a response to a history of exclusion and silencing. In particular, it was a response to the history of European culture and philosophy that had historically suppressed both Mexican culture and the Mexican individual through various forms of power and authority. Thus the goal of *la filosofía de lo mexicano* was the affirmation of the Mexican difference, not just an attempt to unify the nation on the basis of that difference. This is an important way of reinterpreting *lo mexicano* because if unity excludes, affirmation proclaims and demands. And it offers students a chance to re-read the philosophy of *lo mexicano* as something potentially broader than the narrow project of identifying cultural products or practices as uniquely Mexican or of looking for the necessary and sufficient conditions for what counts as being Mexican—two projects that, we agree, are destined to fail.

Essential to this broader philosophical interpretation of *lo mexicano* is that the aim of investigating what it means to be Mexican has universal aspirations. Even for some critics of the project, such as Abelardo Villegas and José Revueltas (whose criticism are included in this volume), there is value in making the Mexican experience and perspective available to others. As Emilio

Uranga writes toward the end of his celebrated *Análisis del ser del mexicano*, "We have a lesson to teach, we owe the world a lesson of a vital crisis ... of what is radically human."[34] Uranga's point is that, as rooted in the concrete experience of Mexicans, the lessons to be taught will contribute to a global understanding of *a* radical experience of humanity; that is, communication with the universe of radical humanity—which is *owed* or is a philosophical obligation—can only take place from one's situated, concrete, or radical existence. In his essay included in this collection, Leopoldo Zea emphasizes this need when he says, "Committing ourselves to the universal and the eternal, without making a single concrete commitment, does not commit us to anything." Thus, the effort to *affirm* the existence of the Mexican is not simply a reminder to the rest of humanity that the Mexican exists and should not continue to be ignored; it is a statement that to understand what it means to be human, it is necessary (for Mexicans in particular) to understand what it means to be Mexican, what we might call "the Mexican difference" or *lo mexicano*.

Ultimately, as a philosophical insight, *lo mexicano* captures what Fernando Salmerón refers to as a "[non-]static ... modifiable reality ... filled with possibilities."[35] The task, then, is not to totalize this reality or essentialize it, stripping it of its possibilities, but rather to reveal it as non-static and modifiable, accidental and contingent. Thus, when philosophers of *lo mexicano* arrive at certain descriptions of the Mexican as *macho*, melancholic, or suffering from an inferiority complex, delusions of grandeur, carelessness, violence, and so on,[36] this is merely an exercise of revelation, one grounded in descriptions of historical circumstances, which are constantly in tension, evolving, being remembered or forgotten. Thus *la filosofía de lo mexicano* emerges from an impulse to understand a circumstance that history, politics, and geography has determined as Mexican. It is descriptive in that it necessarily attempts to present and reconstruct the object of analysis, but it is philosophical in that it constantly understands or interprets what counts as Mexican in terms of, or in view of, what the Mexican can or ought to be. And it is *Mexican* philosophy, the philosophy of *lo mexicano*, in that it affirms its own

[34] Emilio Uranga, *Análisis del ser del mexicano* (México, DF: Bonilla Artigas, 2013), 108.

[35] He says, "What I am calling here a post-revolutionary humanism refers to Samuel Ramos's 'new humanism,'" which "presented itself as an adequate reflection of the aspirations of the Mexican Revolution. [It was] the study of the Mexican individual and the educational efforts that aimed to correct his vices of character ... [while] defining a type of man that was more human and more dignified than what was realized during *porfirismo*. But above all, a type of man that is not a fixed entity but a modifiable reality filled with possibilities to constitute a common responsibility." See Fernando Salmerón, "Los filosofos mexicanos del siglo xx," 290.

[36] According to critics such as Roger Bartra, these stereotypes defined an oppressive picture of the Mexican that, Bartra claims, philosophy helped to foster (33–40). See Roger Bartra, *La jaula de la melancholía* (México, DF: Consejo Nacional para la Cultura y los Artes, 2002).

existential and philosophical possibilities—and thus, indirectly, the existential and philosophical potential of historically marginalized peoples—as worthy of general, universal, and human consideration and respect.

4. Summaries and Other Common Themes

In the previous sections, we have sought to present the rationale for this anthology, as well as the interpretive strategy behind our selection of readings and what we mean more generally by the phrase "Mexican philosophy." In summary, we have chosen those texts that consider the *idea* of Mexico and Mexican identity as a vital reality, a problem, and a possibility. In this section, we offer brief summaries of each reading to illustrate our claim that together they constitute a relatively coherent tradition, to provide more historical context, and to identify other common themes and questions for consideration. We begin with Vasconcelos.

JOSÉ VASCONCELOS

As we have mentioned, Vasconcelos was a member of the *Ateneo de la juventud* (Athenaeum of Youth), which was officially established in 1909. The *Ateneo* was founded by young intellectuals who, despite differences in personality and professional goals,[37] shared a common purpose at the turn of the century: to challenge the "official philosophy" of the *Porfiriato* (1876–1911) and to revitalize a nation that they felt had been demoralized by the technocratic rule of a small minority. So, to commemorate the centennial of Mexican independence, the *Ateneo* offered a series of lectures, which they hoped would help to disseminate new ideas for a new century.[38] Vasconcelos's essay included in this volume, "Gabino Barreda and Contemporary Ideas," was the last of the lectures and is said to capture the spirit of the series as a whole.

Gabino Barreda, the titular subject of the essay, was the founder of the *Escuela Nacional Preparatoria* (National Preparatory School or ENP), which, according to Vicente Lombardo Toledano (in the essay included in this collection), "shook the entire country at its foundations." Barreda was a student of the French positivist Auguste Comte, and the founding of the ENP in 1868 was one of many

[37] For example, Vasconcelos was famously much more political than Caso. He had worked closely with Francisco I. Madero on the newspaper *Antireeleccionista* and would eventually run for president (unsuccessfully) in 1929.

[38] Juan Hernández Luna and Fernando Curiel, eds, *Conferencias del Ateneo de la juventud* (Mexico: UNAM, 2000).

attempts to reform Mexican culture through education reform. (The relation between education reform and cultural reform is a common theme throughout this anthology, particularly in the selections by Sierra, Caso and Lombardo, and Ramos.) By 1910, however, positivism in Mexico had become more complex,[39] and it would be a mistake to think of the *Ateneo's* criticism of it as a wholesale rejection or to think of Vasconcelos's essay as a criticism only of Barreda.[40] Instead, it is also a response to Herbert Spencer's theory of social evolution, various strains of egoism and utilitarianism, as well as contemporary views on science, and it is often as respectful or appreciative as it is critical.

Overall, Vasconcelos (and the *Ateneo*) criticized the view that knowledge is based only on what can be observed and that the world appears to us as a series of phenomena that move from the simple to the complex and from the particular to the general. Like the selection of Caso included here, Vasconcelos is opposed to reducing psychology to biology, as well as reducing ethics to solidarity, altruism, and legacy (the three fundamental ideas of ethics that Barreda borrowed from Comte). Instead, and leaning heavily on the philosophy of Henri Bergson, Arthur Schopenhauer, and artists such as Richard Wagner, Vasconcelos faults the Mexican positivist for not being able to see beyond his immediate world, and for failing to appreciate the potential of life, the spirit, or the ideal, which cannot be reduced to the material. But again, and importantly, Vasconcelos's essay is not a flat-out rejection either in content or tone. Two of Vasconcelos's three criteria for the new philosophy are that it cannot *contradict* scientific laws or violate the laws of logic. (The third is that it must prove itself in its moral vitality.) And in terms of tone, he ends on an optimistic note: "The world that a well-intentioned but narrow philosophy [i.e. Mexican positivism] wanted to close is open, thinkers! We are ready to embrace every great innovation; but let's habituate ourselves to be exacting in the name of the seriousness of the ideal."

JUSTO SIERRA

Although the standard account of 20th-century Mexican philosophy is that the *Ateneo* did not—could not—directly influence political life in Mexico at the

---

[39] See Zea, "Positivism and Porfirism in Mexico"; Meri L. Clark, "The Emergence and Transformation of Positivism," in Susana Nuccetelli, Ofelia Schutte, Otávio Bueno, eds., *A Companion to Latin American Philosophy* (Malden, MA: Wiley-Blackwell, 2010).

[40] For a challenge to the claim that the Ateneo rejected positivism outright, see A. Stehn, "From Positivism to 'Anti-Positivism' in Mexico: Some Notable Continuities," in G. Gilson and I. Levinson, eds., *Latin American Positivism: New Historical and Philosophic Essays* (Lanham, MD: Lexington Books, 2012), and Guillermo Hurtado, "The Anti-Positivist Movement in Mexico," in Susana Nuccetelli, Ofelia Schutte, Otávio Bueno, eds., *A Companion to Latin American Philosophy* (Malden, MA: Wiley-Blackwell, 2010).

turn of the century, we agree with Guillermo Hurtado that several of the correlations among these major events in Mexican history are too striking to be completely unconnected. At the very least, they share in what Hurtado calls a "climate of ideas."[41] And Justo Sierra's "Discourse at the Inauguration of the National University" expresses what was in the air as well as any other single document.

Although Sierra was himself one of the *científicos* (scientists), a party of scientists that served as Porfirio Díaz's cabinet and whom Vasconcelos criticizes, and although he had subscribed to Spencer's theory of social evolution,[42] Sierra had himself evolved and, like the *Ateneo*, began to question the limits of science and entertain the need for speculative metaphysics as an essential part of intellectual, and perhaps spiritual, training. And, not unlike Francisco I. Madero, who called the Mexican people to arms against Porfirio Díaz in his famous *Plan of San Luis Potosí*, Sierra offers not-so-subtle suggestions that national education should be autonomous, not an official instrument of the State—a theme we find again in the selections by Lombardo Toledano and Ramos—and that the University should be "tasked with achieving a social and political ideal that can be summarized thus: 'democracy and liberty.' "[43]

Without question, Sierra's address is one of the most eloquent expressions of Mexican culture in the 20th century and deserves a place in this anthology on its literary merit alone. But it is particularly relevant here because, besides suggesting how ideas and reality are related in early 20th-century Mexican history, it helps to coordinate many of the common themes and features noted earlier. Sierra suggests that many of the problems of government are problems with national education: "The University, then, will have sufficient power to coordinate the guiding principles of national character." Like Caso, he believes that "[t]o cultivate wills in order to harvest egoists would be the bankruptcy of pedagogy." For Sierra, one's education should be grounded in or attentive to national circumstances: "No, the University is not a person destined never to

---

[41] Guillermo Hurtado, *La Revolución creadora. Antonio Caso y José Vasconcelos en la revolución mexicana* (Mexico: UNAM, 2016).

[42] His best-known work is an application of this theory to Mexican history. Justo Sierra, *The Political Evolution of the Mexican People*, trans. Charles Ramsdell (Austin: University of Texas Press, 1969).

[43] Again, we do not mean to suggest that there was a direct causal connection between Madero's anti-re-election campaign and Sierra's inaugural address, or even between the founding of the *Universidad Nacional Autónoma de México* (UNAM) and the beginning of the Mexican Revolution. Again, taking a cue from Hurtado's *La revolución creadora*, we are only suggesting that, given the dates (i.e., Sierra delivered his "Discourse" on September 22 and Madero called México to arms on November 20 of the same year) and the language, they are not completely unconnected. And we believe that future historians of ideas in Mexico will continue to use documents like Sierra's "Discourse" to articulate the many connections between intellectual and political life in Mexico at the turn of the 20th century.

turn its eyes away from the telescope or microscope even if the nation is falling apart around it." And he suggests that the production of knowledge should be affirmative and original: "I imagine it like this: a group of students of all ages adding up to a single age, the age of full intellectual proficiency, forming a real personality through solidarity and a consciousness of mission, which, drawing from every source of culture, wherever it springs forth, provided the spring is pure and diaphanous, sets out to acquire the means of nationalizing science and Mexicanizing knowledge." Finally, despite his earlier sympathy with positivism, which dismisses speculative metaphysics as a source of knowledge, Sierra suggests that the success of national education requires reintroducing philosophy or metaphysics into the national curriculum: "There is nothing like that kind of intellectual training to elevate the soul, to better satisfy the spirit, even though, as often happens, it leads to tragic disappointment."

ANTONIO CASO

Another member of the *Ateneo*, Caso, once referred to as the "Mexican Socrates,"[44] influenced Mexican education and cultural life perhaps more as a teacher and orator—he was a famous public speaker—than as a systematic philosopher. That is, though he cultivated and was well respected by an entire generation of philosophers, and wrote widely on many topics, ranging from history, anthropology, psychology, and sociology, he did not produce a systematic philosophy, as did José Vasconcelos.[45] That said, the essay included in this collection, *Existence as Economy and as Charity: Essay on the Essence of Christianity*, is one of Caso's earliest contributions to Mexican philosophy and one his most systematic single texts, and it is certainly his most highly regarded.

Like Vasconcelos, Caso rejects the effort of biologists, and biologically minded philosophers, to reduce life to the organic world, a sphere of existence that is defined by economy and egoism and best summarized in the following formula: *Life = Minimum Effort* x *Maximum Gain*. The problem with this tendency, according to Caso, is that it cannot explain what he calls—again, like Vasconcelos at the end of his essay—"disinterested activity," such as play, art, and self-sacrifice. Simply put, if *life* is exclusively defined by interested or self-interested activity (how does this action benefit me, my survival, or the survival of my species?), how can one explain aesthetic contemplation, or more to the point, the heroic willingness to give one's life for another? Influenced largely by

---

[44] Romanell, *Making of the Mexican Mind*, 71.

[45] Vasconcelos referred to his philosophical system as "aesthetic monism." See, for example, John H. Haddox, "The Aesthetic Philosophy of José Vasconcelos," *International Philosophical Quarterly* 4, no. 2 (1964), 283–296.

the philosophy of Schopenhauer and Bergson, Caso argues that there must be another aspect or dimension of life besides what can be subsumed under purely economic terms.

Caso is not simply arguing for his own version of metaphysical dualism. His primary example of disinterested or selfless activity is the life of Jesus Christ, which Caso also believes is the height of human dignity. In other words, Caso does not argue only that there is more than one order of life or existence; he argues that selfless activity is ultimately what distinguishes *human* life, the best expression of which is found in the essence of Christianity: to go out of oneself, to give oneself to others, to make oneself available "without fear of exhaustion." Thus, Caso is also endorsing a moral principle, *charity*, which is not merely different from the economic principle of survival; it is radically opposed to it. To be human is to be able and willing to sacrifice oneself, a view best expressed in the following formula: *Sacrifice = Maximum Effort* x *Minimum Gain*.[46]

JOSÉ ROMANO MUÑOZ

José Romano Muñoz was a student of Caso and, along with Samuel Ramos, belonged to the second major self-anointed group of Mexican philosophers, *los contemporáneos*, who, under the influence of Ortega's *vitalism* and Edmund Husserl's eidetic phenomenology, began to challenge the anti-intellectualism and irrationalism of Caso's and Vasconcelos's philosophy.[47] However, in his short article included in this collection, published in 1928, Muñoz defends Caso's "intuitionism" against one of Ramos's criticisms, which Ramos had published in the same periodical (*Ulysses*) the year before. Historically, Muñoz's response represents a seminal confrontation between the next wave of Mexican philosophers who, like the previous generation of philosophers, took their task to be that of moving Mexican philosophy forward, but who, unlike the first generation, began to look for the solutions to Mexico's problems within the Mexican mind. Luis Villoro refers to this next generation as inaugurating the second major movement of Mexican culture, a process of *ensimismamiento* (or "withdrawal into the self"[48]). It is also an important confrontation because it illustrates how Mexican

[46] For more on these concepts, see Michael Weinstein, *The Polarity of Mexican Thought* (University Park: Pennsylvania State University Press, 1976), especially chapter 3.

[47] Romano Muñoz was first to introduce the ideas of José Ortega y Gasset to a Mexican audience. His best-known work is *El secreto del bien y del mal*, which offers a moral theory in the phenomenological tradition of Max Scheler and Nicolai Hartmann. In his *History of Philosophy in Mexico*, Samuel Ramos offers this vague analysis of his compatriot: "Romano Muñoz does not have a professional concept of philosophy, even if he knows exactly what it is . . . he is guided, above all, by a vital sense of his own life." Ramos, *Historia de la filosofía en México*, 151.

[48] Villoro, "La cultura mexicana," 207.

philosophy in the period after the Revolution was the product of philosophers *critically* engaging with one another.

In his dismissal, not entirely unlike that of Lombardo Toledano, Ramos had argued that Caso's intuitionism is a form of irrationalism that has no place in philosophy understood as a rational practice. In Caso's defense, Muñoz proposes that intuition has epistemological value, that it alone can penetrate the reality of things that are hidden by concepts and obscured by perception, and that Caso's philosophy shows us how this is so. This article is both a defense of philosophy as traditionally conceived—as rational and critical—and an attempt to broaden its scope to include invention, intuition, and instinct. Muñoz's article perfectly anticipates la *filosofía de lo mexicano* in its reluctance to uncritically employ traditional philosophical methodology and its acceptance of other ways of knowing that are not entirely in tune with Western tradition, a tradition that has often deemed such alternatives as inferior or non-philosophical. "To make philosophy a purely critical labor," writes Muñoz, "would be to condemn it to an irremediable infertility." A true critical philosophy cannot rely merely on reason as its source, but must involve, and depend on, intuition and the non-rational clarity that this brings.

SAMUEL RAMOS

Ramos was one of Caso's most influential students and critics and wrote what is widely considered the first major work of the philosophy of *lo mexicano*: *Profile of Man and Culture in Mexico*. In this work, Ramos offers what he calls a "characterology" of the Mexican by identifying defining characteristics of what it means to be Mexican, specifically those that help to explain Mexico's social, political, and cultural instability. In an unflattering portrait of Mexican behavior, he argues that the Mexican suffers from an "inferiority complex," a phrase he borrows from the psychoanalyst and student of Freud, Alfred Adler. Ramos insists that he is not claiming that the Mexican *is* inferior, just that he has always *felt* inferior, a feeling that explains his proclivity for excessive imitation. And he argues, again borrowing from psychoanalytic therapy, that the cure for this diagnosis begins with self-awareness. Thus, he says, in a line reminiscent of Sierra's "Discourse," "The proper study of the Mexican is the Mexican."[49]

Six years after the publication of the *Profile*, as part of his effort to continue studying the Mexican, Ramos offered a series of courses on the history of philosophy in Mexico at the National University. The result of these classes is the first of the two selections included here, *The History of Philosophy in Mexico*. More than a survey of schools and doctrines of Mexico, which begins with the

---

[49] Ramos, *Profile of Man and Culture*, 178.

Aztecs, Ramos attempts to articulate what would make a philosophy Mexican, in part by demonstrating what has made the majority of philosophy *in* Mexico either un-philosophical (e.g., Aztec thought) or un-Mexican (e.g., Mexican Scholasticism). In short, for Ramos a philosophy is not Mexican if it is imitative or uncritical, unoriginal, and/or unresponsive to Mexican circumstances. And he argues that although there are a few scattered antecedents—notably Benito Díaz de Gamarra—it is not until the 20th century that Mexican philosophers identify the "epistemological justification of a national philosophy," which Ramos claims (somewhat controversially) is based largely on the philosophy of Ortega y Gasset.

In the next selection, "Twenty Years of Education in Mexico," Ramos offers a brief survey of education reform from 1920 to 1940. Like his *History*, the aim of this text is not purely historical. In it he discusses the role of education in the formation of national character and philosophy, paying homage particularly to the education reform of José Vasconcelos, who understood the simple truth that "what most urgently has to be taught to the Mexican people is how to live." Ramos calls Vasconcelos's education reform "the most Mexican," in part because Vasconcelos taught Mexicans to celebrate themselves. And he offers a criticism of the later attempt to implement "socialist education" (which Lombardo Toledano defends in the following selection). One value of this piece is that it exhibits one way in which Ramos's earlier view in the *Perfil* continued to inform his philosophy throughout his career. He concludes:

> Of one thing I am convinced: we will not make it through our crisis with imported doctrines, with ready-made formulas. There is a difficult, but inevitable, task ahead of us: that of creating our own standards and doctrines. [. . .] As long as we live plagiarizing and imitating the foreigner, we are lost. A nation's destiny depends on nothing other than itself, on the potential of its own mind and well-practiced and disciplined will.

ANTONIO CASO AND VICENTE LOMBARDO TOLEDANO

In September 1933, Abelardo Rodriguez (then president of Mexico) and Narciso Bassols (secretary of public education) organized *el Primer Congreso de Universitarios Mexicanos* (the First Congress of Mexican Members of the University), a national meeting to decide, among other things, "the ideological position of the University concerning urgent issues" and "the social importance of the University today." One important practical result of this Congress was that in December 1934, based largely on the recommendation of the Second Commission of this Congress, the *Partido Nacional Revolucionario* (or PNR, or what would come to be renamed the

PRI), Article 3 of the 1917 Constitution was amended, declaring that "[e]ducation provided by the State will be socialist and, in addition to removing all religious doctrine, will combat fanaticism and prejudice, for the sake of which the school will organize its instruction and activities in such a way that builds in the youth a rational and exact concept of the universe and social life."

The debate between Caso and Lombardo Toledano, like many in 20th-century Mexican philosophy, was at once both political and philosophical, and it was public. To decide whether to reform public education, particularly under-graduate education, Caso and Lombardo Toledano argued over the third of five theses recommended by the Second Commission, which reads: "The courses that constitute the curriculum for the Bachelor degree will obey the principle of essential identity regarding the different phenomena of the Universe and will culminate with the teaching of philosophy based on nature."

Naturally, the *identity* of the different phenomena of the Universe is in direct opposition to Caso's dualism, and a teaching based on nature, especially the teach-ing of moral philosophy, is the opposite of his Christian spiritualism, which Ramos was also very critical of (see earlier discussion of Romano Muñoz). Thus Caso argued that despite violating the autonomy of the University and academic freedom, protected under the Constitution, the education reform proposed by the Second Commission was based on a false philosophical thesis: historical materialism. For Caso, again, life is both material and immaterial, and so if the University *were* to endorse a philosophical creed, it should be one based on nature *and* on culture.

Since both Caso and Lombardo agree that the University is defined as a "cul-tural community," much of the debate is focused on the nature of community, culture, history, and ethics. Caso and Lombardo also agree that the essence of the community is to subordinate individual interests to those of the commun-ity and that culture is the creation of values, but they agree on little else. For Caso, the study of history is the study of heroic and exceptional individuals (as he argues in his *Existence*); for Lombardo, it is the study of institutions. While Lombardo defends an ethics that aims for a classless society, Caso argues that an ethics based on economy is at best partial. Although Lombardo agrees with Caso's definition of culture, he does not agree that all values are equally valuable. In a country and world in which children are starving, how can we compare the value of economics to the value of aesthetics?

Aside from the quality of philosophical theses defended and rejected in this debate, we include it here because it presents an important contribution from one of the most influential "Mexican Marxists,"[50] who, like Ramos, was a student of Caso who would later become very critical of his teacher's philosophy. It is

---

[50] About this debate and Lombardo Toledano's life and work, see Robert Paul Millon, *Mexican Marxist: Vicente Lombardo Toledano* (Chapel Hill: University of North Carolina Press, 1966).

also a good example of how Mexican philosophy is grounded in the Mexican circumstance, which as Lombardo makes clear, is also the world's circumstance.

JOSÉ GAOS AND FRANCISCO LARROYO

In 1938 the Mexican government invited José Gaos and other Spaniards to continue their work in Mexico until the Spanish Civil War came to end. Because Francisco Franco and the Nationalists won the war, Gaos (who referred to himself as a *transterrado* or transplant) and several other Spaniards made Mexico their permanent home. In October of that same year, Gaos gave a series of lectures at the National University, his first public appearance in Mexico City. It was, according to one of the attendees, "quite an event because there had been few occasions to hear from a foreigner on, of all things, a philosophical problem."[51] Francisco Larroyo's review, published in a journal of Mexican culture a few months later, is more evidence of the interest in Gaos's lectures. Thus began their debate of several months, which was ultimately published as a single volume, *Dos ideas de la filosofía: pro y contra la filosofía de la filosofía* (Two Ideas of Philosophy: For and Against Metaphilosophy).

We chose to include this debate for a few reasons. First, as is seen more clearly in the other selection of Gaos included here ("My Two Cents"), a common theme among several of these essays is the possibility and meaning of a Mexican or Spanish-American philosophy, which we would categorize as a metaphilosophical discussion. However, as is illustrated in the debate between Larroyo and Gaos, not all Mexican philosophers agreed on the legitimacy of the distinction between metaphilosophy and philosophy. Larroyo, for one, dismissed the idea of metaphilosophy—a higher order reflection on the nature of philosophy, as Gaos speaks of it—as an absurdity, one that is either a contradiction in terms or one that leads to an infinite regress. For Larroyo, the task of defining philosophy is as old as philosophy itself and does not require the "new" discipline of metaphilosophy.

Second, as part of our effort to include some dissidents of *la filosofía de lo mexicano*, we wanted to include a selection from a Mexican Neo-Kantian, since Neo-Kantians presented one of the strongest criticisms of the effort to historicize philosophy à la Ortega and his student Gaos, who, as much as any other philosopher in Mexico, encouraged the idea of Mexican philosophy as characteristically different from philosophy *sin mas* (philosophy *as such*). A student of Caso, Larroyo studied in Germany in the 1930s and embraced many of the tenets

---

[51] Adolfo Menéndez Samará, "Reseña de José Gaos y Francisco Larroyo, *Dos ideas de la filosofía*," *Letras de México* 2, no. 15 (1940), 4.

of the Marburg School, which he brought back to Mexico in his effort to found, along with Guillermo Héctor Rodríguez, the Mexican Neo-Kantian Circle, the most prominent school of thought in Mexico at the turn of the decade. Much of the debate, then, reflects a difference in philosophical schools and the interpretation of those schools.

Finally, like the Caso-Lombardo debate, this selection illustrates how the question about the definition and scope of philosophy was increasingly becoming a subject of public debate, thus contributing to the normalization of philosophy, as Ramos refers to it. And it is not hard to see why that might be. To question whether philosophy is a science, as Larroyo thought, or a personal confession, as Gaos thought; to place the emphasis on philosophizing and take into account the historical circumstances and psychology of the philosopher, as Gaos does, or deny that the truths of philosophy are concrete; to ask whether the essence of the psychology of the philosopher is arrogance or humility—these are questions that are relevant not just to the possibility of Mexican philosophy, but to deciding on the value or relevance of philosophy in Mexican society at large.

LEOPOLDO ZEA

German and French philosophy took hold of the Mexican philosophical imagination in the 1940s and early 1950s, when existentialism, especially in its French variety, became especially popular.[52] Members of *el grupo Hiperión* were particularly drawn to the work of Maurice Merleau-Ponty, Gabriel Marcel, and Jean-Paul Sartre. In "Philosophy as Commitment," Leopoldo Zea, the presumptive leader of the Hiperión group, appeals to Sartrean existentialism in order to make his case for the idea that philosophy represents a form of responsibility. Our "thrownness," he writes, commits us to a world that we did not create and places us in the presence of others for whom we are now responsible. Just as Sartre had announced that we were condemned to be free, Zea here proclaims that we are condemned to this commitment and this responsibility. This is a call to all Mexican and Latin American philosophers who might believe that the labor of philosophy is of little consequence or that the responsibilities they assume as philosophers are only provisional. He writes: "Philosophizing is not simply doing philosophy, but serving one's community, which needs its philosophy as much as it needs policy from lawmakers, strategy from military thinkers, and the art of making shoes from shoemakers." Indeed, philosophy as commitment is a philosophy for one's world, one's circumstance, and one's fellows.

---

[52] For a fuller account, see Carlos Alberto Sánchez, *Contingency and Commitment: Mexican Existentialism and the Place of Philosophy* (Albany: State University of New York Press, 2016), especially chapter 2.

LUIS VILLORO

As a fellow Hiperión, Luis Villoro was also looking at the phenomenological tradition in Europe for inspiration.[53] In the first of two essays included here, Villoro, offering Max Scheler's phenomenology of sympathy as a point of departure, proposes that communion, not solitude, is the natural state of our being. Solitary consciousness, he argues, is unsatisfied in its solitude and seeks, constantly and perpetually, Absolute Transcendence, which Villoro finds in the form of the human other and which he here calls the "you." Having established early a distinction between the "you" and the non-human "other," between *tú* and *él* (the latter of which refers to the mute things that constitute our circumstance or circum-stare), Villoro suggests that it is the *tú* which calls on my solitary Ego and demands recognition; but it is also this *tú*, or "you," which, once approached, speaks to me, engaging me in a conversation, or dialogue, that is the ultimate basis of community. Readers will find in Villoro's treatment echoes of both Scheler and Martin Buber, especially with the latter's distinction between the "I" and "thou." We have decided to translate *tú* as "you," however, because it aligns better with the Spanish distinction between *tú* and *usted*, which is the formal "you," and would have more directly referred to "thou." Moreover, "thou" carries a certain formality and sacredness that we do not find in Villoro's treatment.

In the second selection by Villoro, *The Major Moments of Indigenism in Mexico: Conclusion*, written in 1949 and published in 1950, Villoro relates a history of indigenism in Mexico. Importantly, the aim of this seminal book was not directly to incorporate Mexico's indigenous population into a national identity, or to offer an ethnographic account of indigenous culture, or to participate in *indigenismo*, an earlier state-sponsored effort to valorize Mexico's indigenous with varying degrees of success (or, more to the point, failure). Instead, Villoro wants to understand the Indigenist's consciousness, and particularly how the history of Mexican consciousness of the Indian resulted in the severely problematic 20th-century movement of *indigenismo*, which Villoro argues is "merely a stage in a historical process that leads Mexican culture to reflect on itself."

In a book that, like much of Villoro's (and O'Gorman's) work, makes impressive use of history and other social sciences, Villoro divides the history of

---

[53] Although there was not a very significant difference in age, Zea and Villoro are usually considered as belonging to different generations (although they were both members of *el grupo Hiperión*). Zea was one of the first professional philosophers formed in Mexico and was Villoro's teacher (although Villoro should not be considered as Zea's disciple). Villoro would eventually move away from the issues of *lo mexicano* and create an impressive oeuvre that includes writings on critical Marxism, Anglo-Analytic philosophy, and, toward the end of his life, social political philosophy, especially focused on issues related to the Indigenous rebellion in Chiapas. He is considered by many Mexico's "universal philosopher." See, for instance, Mario Teodoro Ramirez, ed., *Luis Villoro, Pensamiento y Vida: Homenaje en sus 90 años* (México, DF: Siglo XXI Editores, 2014).

Indigenism into three major *momentos* (moments), of which the second and third movement each have two *etapas* (stages). The "Conclusion," included here, is a summary of these moments, which demonstrate how the Spanish, criollo, and mestizo consciousness of the Indian have unfolded in a Hegelian dialectic of thesis, antithesis, and synthesis—a historical process of distancing, appropriating, and evaluating the indigenous element of Mexican culture and society.

EMILIO URANGA

In this important essay published during the Hiperión group's most active period, Emilio Uranga challenges the underlying assumptions of Samuel Ramos's popular and controversial thesis regarding the "Mexican inferiority complex." His basic claim, influenced as he was by Heidegger, is that Ramos's analysis overlooks a more foundational "difference," namely, the difference between *ontological* sufficiency and insufficiency. Ramos's analysis, that is, remains always at an ontic, or philosophically superficial, level of explanation, attributing "inferiority" to the Mexican character without explaining that on which it is grounded. The clue to its grounding lies in *fragility, unwillingness*, and *melancholy*, seemingly essential characteristics that define Mexican existence. Thus, fragility is not related to a simple feeling of inferiority, which is itself related to actual intersubjective relationships between Mexicans and their European colonizers, but rather to a much more complex emotive life predicated on an unconscious awareness of a primordial relationship to nothingness and non-being. Unwillingness, likewise, is not a simple lack of will, but a refusal to externalize, a refusal to be part of the world. We repel back into ourselves and away from the world in unwillingness. Ultimately, inferiority is merely a "symbol" or a "psychological expression" of a deeper ontological condition; as ontic, it is a choice for one who suffers from the ontological mode of insufficiency.

In this essay, the reader will quickly notice what appears to be a certain indignation that Uranga expresses for his Mexican contemporaries. The negative psychological characteristics attributed to Mexicans, grounded as they are in an ontological insufficiency, appear to be criticisms of the Mexican personality—they all suffer from indignation, unwillingness, sentimentality. Even dignity and honor are criticized for what they hide: a fear of destruction or nothingness. This indignation, or critique, however, circles back to his critique of Ramos's psychological assessment of the Mexican character. That is, if we remain on the plane of psychology, the Mexican person and Mexican culture can be easily relativized. But when we move to the ontological realm, we can deal with foundational issues, issues that might clarify the confusion that psychological treatments produce, and that apply both to Mexicans and to humanity in general. Thus, melancholy, unwillingness, and so on, are seen in relation, not to a social or cultural persona, but to *being*: the "Mexican," he says, "is a being without a ground," which, due to his proximity, is the only being for which Uranga may speak. Take away the limitations of proximity, and we can say that the *human being*, Mexican or otherwise, is a being without a ground.

JORGE PORTILLA

Along with Zea, Villoro, Uranga, and Ricardo Guerra, Portilla makes up the core of the famed *el grupo Hiperión*, who, in 1949, organized a series of lectures titled "What is the Mexican" (*¿Que es el mexicano?*), for which Portilla presented "Community, Greatness, and Misery in Mexican Life." In this essay, Portilla introduces the idea of a dialogical community, which he considers an alternative to conceptions of community popular in sociology and certain philosophical circles (and an alternative to the conception of *community* that Caso and Lombardo Toledano agree on in the earlier selection). The aim is to think of community from a Mexican perspective, showing how thinking retains "aspects of the national character" or *lo mexicano* in the process of its philosophical articulation.

Portilla criticizes the practicality of sociological notions of community, which conceive of it as an "organic association" in which one finds oneself at birth, and ties one "by a solidarity of which [one] is not the author," by an "unconscious emotional ground" of those who make it up. These conceptions seem to think of society in terms of its instrumental reality, or lack thereof, and thus do not reflect social reality. He suggests that one think of community in its everydayness or pre-ontologically. When thought of in this way, the community is seen to be an entity that behaves much like a person and which we can hold accountable, much like a person. Thus, to get to the essence of community, we must look at it directly as "vaguely" resembling a person, and we must treat that person not as a stranger, but as what is most familiar to us (i.e., as someone we know and who is in constant dialogue with us).

For Portilla, the community functions much like Edmund Husserl's transcendental ego, laying the conditions for the possibility of our actions. It is, he says, a horizon against which our actions make sense. In Mexico, he argues, this horizon is weak and ineffective. Several useful examples are presented: the bribe, the haggle, and the *casa chica*. The bribe, for instance, a national epidemic, is the result of the weakness of the transcendental structure that ought to regulate it, or prohibit it as unacceptable behavior. In this case, the transcendental structures that would produce communal solidarity are replaced by subjective structures of individual interests. The haggle shows that there is simply no horizon that regulates everyday market exchanges: *everything* is up for negotiation. And if there is some regulating rule, it is not respected, because the community, thought of vaguely as a person, is not respected.

Ultimately, for Portilla, the only account of community that resonates with the Mexican experience is one in which the community, like a person, has a face, that responds and can be held accountable—not a static, descriptive account that merely situates people with, and next to, one another. In this sense, the Mexican is neither a collectivist nor an individualist about community, since he seeks a responsive concept of community, a dialogical community. As he puts it toward the end of the essay, "a society without a face or warmth allows us to grow cold and distrustful."[54]

EDMUNDO O'GORMAN

Though O'Gorman received a master's degree in philosophy, he earned his PhD in history and is better known for his contributions as a historian, particularly for his work redefining the way we ought to think about "America," namely as the object of "invention," not "discovery." But it is precisely O'Gorman's ability to move across disciplines—a skill we find among several philosophers included here, but particularly in the case of Caso, Vasconcelos, and Villoro—that makes his philosophical contribution so compelling, and in many ways, original. For instance, it is in part in view of the question about the possibility of Mexican philosophy that O'Gorman produced his novel approach to the question of America. In a wonderful essay (available in English), he says:

> It seems to us then, that in order to understand the course of Mexican philosophical thought thoroughly, it will not be amiss to review the investigations we have made concerning the being of America, concerning what American is. In this way we will become aware that this philosophical thought reflects the manner whereby the possibility in which this being consists has been realized, and, aware consequently, that in this process one finds the most authentic and definitive meaning of America, its true originality.[55]

Likewise, the essay included here, which we believe is an important contribution to aesthetics, leans heavily on O'Gorman's vast knowledge of art history, art criticism, and Mesoamerican culture.

---

[54] Of note in this essay is Portilla's understanding of Martin Heidegger's conception of time and being-with, which represent some of the earliest analyses of Heidegger's *Being and Time* in the Americas.

[55] Edmundo O'Gorman, "America," in *Major Trends in Mexican Philosophy* (Notre Dame, IN: University of Notre Dame Press, 1966), 61.

On one level, "Art or Monstrosity" explores the issues that arise when the art critic or historian attempts to make sense of a work of art from an "exotic" culture. Even to examine it as a work of art, to call it an "object of art," is to invoke a set of presuppositions, moods, expectations, practices, ideas, and so on, that the original "artist" simply may not have shared. By what right, then, do we speak of—what do we mean when we speak of—"Aztec *art*, of Mayan *art*, of Tarascan *art*"? Perhaps what we take to be artists and works of art, according to our own standards, are something else entirely. On another level, however, and to the extent that Mexicans cannot but view artifacts of Aztec, Mayan, or Tarascan culture through the lens of their dominantly European culture, O'Gorman raises a question about the ability to identify the origins of Mexican identity in pre-Conquest indigenous culture. Perhaps there is a sense in which that culture is forever lost, and *a fortiori*, a sense in which 20th-century *indigenismo* in Mexico (see Villoro) is somehow inauthentic, fabricated, or a missed opportunity.[56]

One reason we chose to include this essay is that it suggests that, to the extent that we are *not* entirely closed off to ancient Mexican culture, there is the possibility that what we learn from it affirms a Mexican *difference* of universal import. As O'Gorman reflects on the famous Aztec statue Coatlicue, now housed in the National Museum of Anthropology in Mexico City, he argues that it captures "the monstrous," a concept he attributes to mythological peoples. He says that in a mythological world where one does not distinguish between the vegetable, animal, or mineral worlds—where flowers bark and minerals lament—there is a fluidity that is lost in a rational world, one inspired by Aristotle's neat, logical classifications. Rather than think of Coatlicue, then, either as an approximation or aberration of Greek standards of beauty, which aim at the mathematician's idea of perfection and symmetry, as it is embodied in the human form, it might be worth reflecting on this impressive statue as representing something completely different—a different world. It may turn out, O'Gorman suggests, that the purpose of what we call art is not to capture *logos* in stone or on canvas, but

[56] Consider, for example, the work of Miguel León-Portilla, who did more than anyone to introduce Aztec thought and culture into mainstream philosophical discussions. One problem with León-Portilla's work, however, is that in trying to answer the question concerning whether the Aztecs did philosophy in the affirmative—in the first chapter of his *Historia*, by contrast, Ramos concludes that although they had a worldview, they did not produce philosophy—León-Portilla invokes a Greek and Western conception of philosophy. León-Portilla's question, then, was whether the Aztecs did what the Greeks did. This leads one to wonder whether, or to what extent, León-Portilla attributes an interpretation of Aztec thought to a people who would not have recognized it as their own. And it is also a missed opportunity to question, as O'Gorman does, the authority of the Greek or Western conception of philosophy by asking how *it* measures up to what may be a radically different approach to the universe and humanity. See Miguel León-Portilla, *Aztec Thought and Culture* (Norman: University of Oklahoma Press, 1963), particularly the introduction.

to remind us of the fundamental fluidity and ambiguity that define human existence, and as it was so monstrously expressed in mythology.

ROSARIO CASTELLANOS

Written in 1950 when she was only twenty-five years old, *Sobre cultura femenina*
is Castellanos's first attempt to champion a woman's right to participate in the
production of culture via certain forms of personal expression. Her argument
centers on the notion that culture is the refuge for those who have been exiled
from maternity. Simply, she means that the realm of cultural production had been
reserved for those who are incapable (men) or have chosen not to participate in
the giving of human life (women), that is, in the birthing and raising of children.
Culture requires egoism and, since maternity is the ultimate rejection of egoism,
representing complete giving of oneself for another, women can participate in
either one or the other, but, she suggests, not both. Her immediate concern, however, seems to be with those who have a choice between maternity and producing
culture and have chosen the latter. But women who have chosen the latter, she
says, have been devalued and marginalized from those opportunities that contribute to meaningful cultural production in one way or another, a marginalization
owed to those structures of patriarchy that have existed since antiquity.

However, as she sees it, modern (industrial) labor culture represents an
opportunity for women to be part of cultural production without having to
choose between maternity and the production of culture. Women, she points
out, are as able as men and have already proven that no kind of work is beyond
their capabilities (especially during times of war) or interests. This includes the
area of cultural production in the arts, especially literature. The conclusion of her
essay is a call for women to take up the pen with courage and delve into themselves, into their own experiences, and write their stories. As introspective, she
says, these literary efforts will lack the objectivity and abstraction that is usually
characteristic of philosophy, which is seen as more technical. But rather than
view this interpretation of literary life and activity as deficient, as less noble or
valuable or sophisticated as philosophy, as "women's work," she suggests that it
may be a virtue. So, although she says that women were not *historically* given the
"gift" of objectivity, and that they are typically denied the kind of training necessary to be successful in fields like philosophy, she does not despair, for literature,
which, as Virginia Woolf reminds us, has never been denied to women, provides
its own, equally legitimate forms of producing knowledge and culture.

Aside from representing one of the early female contributions to
Mexican philosophy—for the most part, women in Mexico were not encouraged to produce original philosophy until after 1960—we have chosen to
include this piece by Castellanos because what she says about the virtues of

literature (in part in opposition to philosophy) is closer to how we have defined Mexican philosophy: as placing a greater value on commitment, historical and personal experience, and cultural impact. So we read Castellanos's encouraging women to pursue literary careers as a call to pursue Mexican philosophy.

JOSÉ REVUELTAS

José Revueltas's "Possibilities and Limitations of the Mexican," published in 1959, represents the anti-essentialist critique that had been leveled against the philosophy of *lo mexicano* in the previous two decades. In his own Marxist-inspired intervention into this tradition, Revueltas accomplishes two things: one, he provides a brilliant history of the emergence of the idea of Mexican national identity, an idea that, given the complex economic and political history of Mexico, has been impossible to realize. Tracing this impossibility to the Aztec Empire's failures to unify its various tributaries, which ultimately led to the empire's downfall at the hands of the Spanish, Revueltas suggests that the idea of a common national identity has always been a dream of those seeking political and economic power. The second accomplishment is that he offers a brutal critique of the idea of *lo mexicano* itself, which, in his interpretation, states that there is or can be a unified national identity that depends on finding those essential commonalities that tie all Mexican people together. However, he insists, those commonalities exist neither in history nor in the Mexican individual himself, who historically has experienced different realities and different struggles, depending on time, place, and class. Ultimately, *lo mexicano*, or what Revueltas calls "the national" [*lo nacional*], is an ideological construction, rooted in the desire to resolve certain historical and economic contradictions that have existed since Spanish colonialism. As he says by way of conclusion, "the Mexican is not a single type for whom unique laws and definitions exist or ought to be invented, because such a type is to be found nowhere under any circumstances within the modern human conglomeration." Despite its overall negative and critical tone, Revueltas ends on a positive note, suggesting that a new political consciousness (one beholden to socialism[57]) can allow the Mexican to overcome the shortcomings of his history and achieve contemporaneousness with the modern, developed, world.

[57] Vicente Lombardo Toledano held a similar view. See the Caso–Lombardo Toledano debate included in this volume.

ALFONSO REYES

In 1952, after four years of conferences on the theme of *el mexicano* and *lo mexicano*, Leopoldo Zea was invited to coordinate a new book series on Mexican identity for the popular editorial Porrúa y Obregón. The purpose of the series was to compile short works, past and present, on the theme of Mexico and Mexican identity. Alfonso Reyes's *La x en la frente. Algunas páginas sobre México* (The X on the Brow: Some Reflections on Mexico) was the first in the series that would eventually include twenty books, including Zea's own *Conciencia y posibilidad del mexicano*, also published in 1952.

Reyes's *The X on the Brow* was a strange but obvious choice for the first title of a series on Mexico and Mexican identity. Strange because Reyes, who had lived the bulk of his life outside Mexico and who wrote largely on classically "Western" themes and authors, was often criticized for not being concerned enough with the particular problems of Mexico, and strange because he was somewhat critical of "imitative existentialists, a group of literary patriots who are inventing 'the Mexican' in the 11th hour of history,"[58] referring to *el grupo Hiperión*. But it was an obvious choice, too, because rather than view Western culture as an alternative or obstacle to the development of Mexican identity, Reyes's constant concern with Mexican identity was one of elevating it to the level of universal culture, alongside the best that Western culture had previously offered. More than anyone else in the tradition of *lo mexicano*, perhaps, Reyes's authorship saw the process of self-discovery Mexico was undergoing as an opportunity to situate it in universal culture.

The title is, in Reyes's typical style, a combination of puns that reflects the tension between the universal and particular of Mexican identity and philosophy. Instead of *con el nopal en la frente* (with a *nopal* on the forehead)—a way of referring to Mexicans of indigenous ancestry who deny their Mesoamerican or Mexican identity—Reyes's title indicates a challenge to the Real Academia that insisted on changing the Nahuatl "x" in "Mexico" to a Spanish "j," which would have resulted in "Mejico."[59] For Reyes, though the pronunciation of his country's name recommends a "j"—keeping the Nahuatl "x" would require Mexicans to pronounce "Mexico" as "meh-SHEE-coh," how the Mexica (meh-SHEE-ca) or Aztecs referred to themselves. But this was precisely the tension and unity that define Mexican identity, and that makes Reyes's reflections on Mexico an obvious choice for a series on Mexican identity. About the "x," Reyes said, "Oh, *x* of

---

[58] Alfonso Reyes, *Mexico in a Nutshell and Other Essays*, trans. Charles Ramsdell (Berkeley: University of California Press, 1964), 12.

[59] We thank the translator for pointing this out to us.

mind, tiny in yourself, but immense in the cardinal directions you indicate: you were a point of intersection of destiny."[60]

The X on the Brow is a compilation of essays on the theme of Mexico and Mexican identity. Though Reyes had been preoccupied with philosophy since the very beginning of his career, none of these essays, nor the collection of them, amounts to a philosophical analysis or system or stance on its theme. Reyes's style, like that of many other authors included here, fused history, literature, philosophy, and poetry into small provocative essays, which were subtle, suggestive, poetic, ironic, and always insightful and challenging. And each essay approaches its theme from a different point of view. In "Alphabet, Bread, and Soap," Reyes questions the root of the problems of Mexico (education or soap) and more generally the problem with appearances in Mexico. In "Mexico's Three Kingdoms," he points the importance of understanding geography in the attempt to understand Mexican identity. All are reflections "in search of the national soul"; all are at the same time deeply cosmopolitan; and all strain (and potentially enlarge) a traditional notion of the possibilities of philosophical prose. Thus we place Reyes at the end as a kind of synthesis of the various tensions, contradictions, and themes that tug our authors in the four cardinal directions of their destiny.

ABELARDO VILLEGAS

The text from Abelardo Villegas is the most recent in the present collection. Published in 1960, it is the conclusion to his seminal work, *La filosofía de lo mexicano*, an attempt to offer a panoramic view as well as a critique of what had been, up to that time, Mexican philosophy itself, that is, *the philosophy of lo mexicano*. With his conclusion, Villegas closes the book on that period in the history of philosophy that had dared to question the meaning of specifically situated human beings—that is, Mexicans. Though a critique of *la filosofía de lo mexicano*, Villegas does not dismiss it outright. His conflict is with the method underscoring that philosophical project: historicism. Historicism, or the view that truth is dependent on history, offers Mexican philosophers an opportunity to articulate their philosophies as historical beings, thus contributing their historical difference to the philosophical conversation. (The Gaos-Larroyo debate offers another discussion of historicism.) However, historicists face a fundamental "aporia," as their project calls for defining an essentially historical being (the Mexican) using ahistorical categories (e.g., solitude, accidentality, melancholy, etc.). Thus, Villegas chastises Uranga for his "essentialism," for looking for essences while attempting to ground his approach in history.

[60] Quoted in Alfonso Reyes, *The Position of America and Other Essays*, trans. Federico de Onís (New York: Alfred A. Knopf, 1950), viii.

However, he does not think that the answer is to dismiss historicism altogether (although he rejects perspectivism outright, which for philosophers such as Ortega y Gasset, is solipsistic and relativistic), since one needs generic terms in order to speak, and especially in order to speak about historically singular events and objects. He proposes that we must understand historicism as that idea that history is continuous, with each moment dependent on a previous moment. It is this continuity that makes communication and intersubjectivity possible. We must also understand the historical event as dictating its own narrative, or at least limiting what can be said about it. In that sense, then, what can be said of a thing, event, or person need not be an essence, but a description agreed upon by individuals that then "transcends its moment" and reaches other peoples and other times. Additionally, he says that identifying what is Mexican need not be a matter of finding essential characteristics in the Mexican spirit, but rather one of identifying experiences that can be communicated from one moment to the next. He concludes that a philosophy of *lo mexicano* is possible insofar as it is grounded, not on the essential uniqueness of the Mexican experience, but rather on the possibility of communicating that uniqueness to other peoples and other times.

5. A Note on Translation

Translation is not an exact science. (Given its failure to achieve any sort of objectivity, who would call it a "science" at all?) It is a constant and complicated struggle to find the right balance between remaining faithful to the original text, to the author's original intentions, and to the anticipated demands of a future readership, all the while attempting to render them into compelling English prose. Translating *philosophical* texts adds an extra layer of complexity, as the translator must always keep his or her eye on philosophy's historical horizon. In this way, translating philosophical texts turns into a multifaceted dialogue with the original author *and* future readers of philosophy. As such, translators (and editors) are charged with employing the principle of charity *and* the principle of significance: not only must they present the original in the best light, but they must also do so with the firm belief that the author is saying something significant, something that future readers will or should care about. Sometimes this requires bending or manipulating the original into English, and sometimes it means even doing some violence to the original. A case in point is the debate between Caso and Lombardo Toledano, which was originally an unedited transcription of a public debate. In this case, we, the editors, took it upon ourselves both to edit *and* to translate the original. So, although we neither put words in the speakers' mouths nor subtracted anything important from what was said, in an effort to bring coherence and structure to the exchange, and while aiming to make both sides of the debate as compelling as possible, all the while considering our future readers, we were forced to take a few more liberties than usual. In a word, if we have learned anything from translating and from editing translations, it is that the effort to be as literal as possible while retaining the aim, spirit, and content of the original makes translating as *creative* an endeavor as any other art.

Often there is simply no direct translation of a Spanish word or phrase in English, in which case it is better not to ask *how does one say this in English?* but rather, *what would an English speaker say here?* Obvious examples are idioms. There is no direct translation, for example, of *genio y figura hasta la sepultura,* but it is clear that the speaker is trying to convey something close to what we mean when we say that "a leopard cannot change its spots." Sometimes the issue is not that there is no direct translation, but that there is more than one, such as the Spanish *espíritu, enseñanza, conciencia, sentimientos, cátedra, pueblo,* all of which are especially problematic in philosophy. Take *espíritu.* As with the German *Geist* or the French *esprit,* it can be translated as "mind" or "spirit," with important philosophical implications either way, depending on the context. In response to the challenge of translating this kind of word—*pueblo* is another good example, as it can be translated as "town," "people," or "nation"—we have chosen readability over consistency. Thus we have allowed ourselves and encouraged our translators to translate *espíritu* as either "mind" or "spirit," depending on the context and what reads or sounds more natural in English.

A particularly challenging word is *hombre,* which can be translated as "man," "person," or "human being." Where it refers to human beings, we considered using a gender-neutral abstract noun, like "persons" or "human beings" or the clunkier "men and women" with the corresponding "his or her." The problem, however, is that although *we* are more critical of using "man" to speak of human beings, this is not true of the authors represented here. And so to translate *hombre* into more inclusive pronouns is to grant the authors and texts a form of considerateness that we do not have reason to believe was intended. Doing so also raises certain philosophical confusions. For instance, although *hombre* can be interpreted as "person" or "human being," it would be a mistake to use them interchangeably, since the question might be what it takes for a human being to count as a person. So again, for the sake of not cluttering the prose with the clunky "his or her" or attributing to our authors more considerateness than they deserve, we have mostly preserved the gender-neutral use of "man." But, as our goal is readability and not consistency, we have encouraged our translators to use "person" or "human being" where it does not cause any confusion.

There was also a question about what to do with Spanish translations of works that are originally in Greek, French, Latin, or English—especially when our translators had reason to believe that the Spanish translation is flawed or incomplete. Rather than translate the original directly into English, which may be an improvement on the author's own translation, we encouraged our translators to translate the author's Spanish translation into English (making our translation twice removed from the original). Our reason is that for the sake of capturing the philosophical dialogue in its historical context, we thought it better to represent how Spanish readers would have encountered the original in Spanish. We wanted the text to remain as a contemporaneous reader would have found it, warts and all.

One final lesson we learned from such an ambitious project is that translating is a "team sport," as Amy Oliver, one our translators, put it. Not only could we not have produced this anthology in a reasonable amount of time without the collaboration of our several translators, but all the translations included here are the result of multiple people engaged in dialogue in one form or another about meaning, sentence structure, context, and so on. Throughout it all, we have all been part of an international community of translators and interpreters tasked with giving voice to a philosophical tradition that would continue to be unavailable in the United States if not for these dialogues and exchanges. However, although the credit for the realization of this work goes to this, our new community, we, the editors, take full responsibility for any faults that our translations or our interpretation may contain.

CHAPTER 1

Gabino Barreda and Contemporary Ideas (September 12, 1910)

José Vasconcelos

Translated by Robert Eli Sanchez, Jr., and Cecilia Beristáin

José Vasconcelos Calderón was born in Oaxaca, Oaxaca, in 1881 and died in Mexico City in 1959. He grew up in Piedras Negras, Coahuila, and attended school in Eagle Pass, Texas. He graduated with a law degree in Mexico City before joining the Ateneo de la juventud and beginning his life as a philosopher and public figure. Vasconcelos (unsuccessfully) ran for president of Mexico in 1929 and is best known for his work as a public educator. He was named rector of the National University in 1920 and then secretary of public education, a post he held for four years (1921–1924) and through which he famously promoted national culture and the ideals of the Mexican Revolution. Though Vasconcelos would eventually produce a systematic philosophy, which he termed "aesthetic monism" as early as 1916, he is better known in English for his writings on Mexican and Latin American history and identity, including The Cosmic Race (1925), The Harris Foundation Lecture Series titled Aspects of Mexican Civilization (1926), and A Mexican Ulysses (1935).

Rather than look at Gabino Barreda's work in social science, which has already been much discussed and eulogized, I will endeavor to remember him as a great philosopher, paying what he may have thought of as the kindest type of tribute—a tribute that consists in showing which of his teachings have had sufficient procreative value to guide us on a path toward a better view of the world and our own being.

A doctrine that creates only sectarians and dogmatists kills spontaneity and cancels alternatives [*anula otras vidas*]. It is a glorious thing when a teacher revives hopes more than he inspires fervent adoration. And I bet that if teachers could witness the generations that succeed them, they would be much prouder of those who carry their doctrines beyond their original limits, or of those who renounce them if something else excites them more. Because, in the end, what teachers love is the mysterious ideal, and work is better when it bears diverse and youthful fruit, instead of wasting its virtue in repetition.

For this reason, I offer our contemporary ideas in the name of Barreda, who understood his time, and I do so respectfully [*filial*] and with devotion.

One might say that the force that sustains what is noble in the universe endures alternatives, and outdoing itself at times, it expends so much virtue, elaborates prodigious idealities so magnificently, that it is overcome by fatigue, it temporarily relaxes, and the spirit, without the impulse to produce, obstructs the creation of novelties, and sadly resigns itself to repeating and commenting on the inexhaustible abundance of what came before. Periods of critique, in which wise spirits determine the worth of the preceding generation, conserve what is valuable and defend it against oblivion. However, they do so fully discouraged by sterility.

The excitement of living in the same time, in the same environment in which the inexhaustibly protean ideal is revealed and formed in the minds of our contemporaries, energizes and dignifies our lives. By contrast, the repetition of an old thought makes us uncertain, troubles us, and makes us nostalgic, because it does not matter how wonderful the expressions of a bottomless ministry may be, humanity periodically feels the need to ask again, to listen to themselves, to interpret for themselves all the manifestations, all the revelations, of renewed life, of life enriched by the past—the owner of a limitless country [*campo*] that widens still more with each new vision and each new virtue.

We are so lucky, the men of our generation, to live in a time when, far from wasting our time talking about the past, intellectuals are deepening the fecund ministry on their own initiative. They increase novelty, which must be the form of our expression, and which, in this way, carries out the ideal, gives shape to the soul, and explains the external world—a world that, despite a certain apparent decay, is dominated by a feeling of confidence common to those exalted periods in which pains are forgotten and doubts dispelled, periods dominated by moments of clarity and a prophetic message that announces the coming enunciation of creeds that guide generations.

But so much is said and thought with disconcerting vagueness—the modern ideal is doubted so much—that it is not enough simply to announce the arrival of the new ideal. It needs to be conveyed to the incredulous, shown to those who ignore it, and shaped into the formula in which it will crystalize. Are we sure that we have surpassed what came before? Do we really belong to a glorious epoch in which values are reconceived? Or is it only the vigor of youth that makes us love our present and which makes it seem more fertile than the past?

Let us reflect dispassionately, consult one another, purify the meaning of words, and think without the help of rhetoric—only with ideas. Let us do this in such a way that we do not get caught up on the sound or texture of language, but rather use it as a channel of transmission within whose banks thought flows and is revealed to souls, in such a way that, for the sake of mental precision, the word and writing possess a neutral rhythm with which the movement of the idea passes and is transmitted undistorted, as images (the representation of objects) change as they pass through diaphanous air and then through the eye, without our noticing that the visual organ is working.

In order to specify the contemporary state of intellectual life, we should give an account of its origins in the recent past, where we will surely find the germ of what we think today and where we will find, on the basis of a fair comparison, how much we have advanced or at least how much we have changed.

For this reason, and for some time to come, I will have recourse to Gabino Barreda, recalling that he introduced to us the foundations of a system of thinking distinct from that which prevailed in the centuries that the Spaniards and Catholicism dominated. By introducing them to the free thought of Europe, Barreda brought entire generations up to speed, not only so that they might assimilate European culture, but also so that they, with an education that teaches solid discipline, might develop their own speculative and moral potential. If what he taught can be criticized for being incomplete, in the most charitable sense of the word, the good of his method bore fruit, despite forgivable excesses in students convinced of the doctrines of slightly deficient teachers. Name a creator of a great system who, sensing the infinitude of the ideal, upon reflecting on his finished work, doesn't think that perhaps it would be better to start over, that many mysterious insights [*visiones*] still remain without expression and without memory. By contrast, he who does not produce a brilliant way of conceptualizing the world hides easily behind a conception that he believes is definitive and that he in good faith tries to impose on others.

In order to rescue [*salvar*] the tremendous responsibility of propagating systems that perhaps omit fundamental concepts, one of the greatest and most sincere teachers, the tragic Zarathustra, announced his immortal words that have become the pedagogical creed of the philosopher today: "My friends, he who obsequiously obeys a doctrine is unworthy of my teaching; I am a liberator of hearts; my reason cannot be your reason: learn from me the flight of the eagle."

Nietzsche, moreover, the apostle of greatness, was not translated from German, and in Mexico religious fanaticism was substituted with another doctrine more fitting of the time and which signified progress: the scientific fanaticism of positivism.

Let us quickly review the theories of positivism concerning the four great problems that, according to Hoffding, every comprehensive philosophy should be occupied with: the problem of knowledge, cosmology, values, and the psychological problem of the relation between mind and body.

Phenomena are produced, according to the indubitable testimony of the senses, in a determinate order. Chance and disorder are appearances that deceive because we attribute the whims of our imagination to nature, as well as our ignorance of the necessary causes of phenomena. And, proceeding by basic analogy, we explain chance and order by comparing them to human action, that is, anthropomorphically. Thus the movement of a body, the flow of a river, have to be the work of a god, a man more powerful than the rest, one capable of grasping a lake in his arms and letting it spill over a plain between the banks of a river. We only imagine our own attitudes as they are reflected in the universe. This is the poetic or theological stage of the mind. But positivism did not consider that the poetic sense is a form of interpretation that does not correspond only to a determinate period of history,[1] but rather to the nature of human understanding itself, which frequently uses analogy in its investigations to greater effect than any other kind of reasoning, and which is especially essential to art, a transformative power that refines and exalts representation.

The modern critique has also restored the right to reason by analogy in the domain of pure science, not only in inferences from particular to particular, but also in the solutions to the difficult problems of human understanding [*la solución de los difíciles problemas de la conciencia*], which are tested and clarified by means of intuitive analogies that expose certain kinds of identity among diverse objects.

Poincaré says, "In the domain of pure science, in mathematics and physics, in order to simplify a law of experience, one needs to generalize. But a fact of experience can be understood in an infinite number of ways and it is necessary to choose among the thousand possibilities presented by our investigation, and we can only make this choice by analogy. The mathematical mind, which teaches us to scorn *overly* objective appearances, gives us true, profound analogies which the eyes don't see and reason only guesses at, in order to be able to notice others that are deeper and more hidden. But in order to produce these analogies [*estas adivinaciones*], it is necessary to cultivate analysis without immediately worrying about utility. It is necessary that the mathematician work as an artist." The poetic sense, which Comte called theological—as is shown in the preceding quote— continues to provide very useful resources in the most constructive and basic development of civilization.

---

[1] [Nineteenth-century positivists, including Gabino Barreda, spoke of three progressive stages of intellectual and historical development: the poetic or theological, the metaphysical, and the positive. In his famous "Oración Cívica" of 1867, Barreda applied this tripartite division to Mexican history, interpreting the success of Benito Juárez and the Reform as confirming that Mexico had entered into the positive stage of its history.—Trans.]

For this reason, the advent of the so-called metaphysical stage is not a form of progress, but the use of a different method in which the universe is explained by abstract ideas, through principles and conflicting powers. The metaphysical system reduces these oppositions and the machinery of principles [engranajes de los principios] to a single unity, but does so not by taking into account all of the phenomena, nor by explaining the contradictions of its own postulates.

In the positive stage, the senses (the observation of facts and their constant correlations) provide the only fixed laws of truth. It is true that through observation alone we will not arrive at solutions to the problems that bother us most, but we should content ourselves with this science, the only one that is possible and true. The outside world [lo exterior] in flux exercises its influence on the human mind and impresses upon it the necessities, patterns, and laws of change. What happens in the human mind [en nuestro interior] is a correspondence, immediate or distant, among external phenomena that have shaped our consciousness. Kant, reflecting on this thesis, had already observed that an organism receives the objective fact, an immediate perception, through the intervention of reasoning; moreover, reason itself, before any experience, bounds perception within its forms in such a way that they could not emerge from the indefinite sum of experience.

From the cosmological point of view, the world appears to the positivist as phenomena that unfold in a process that moves from the particular to the general, from the simple to the complex. In this movement, phenomena are grouped into irreducible classes, the various sciences, which are connected subjectively by relating the particular and the general. The reason we go from the particular to the general, and not the other way around, is that the founder of positivism believed that the potential results of going from the general to the particular led to forbidden [vedados] problems that he believed we would never be able to resolve, and whose unknowability Spencer believed could not be penetrated.

Concerning morality, Gabino Barreda borrowed three fundamental ideas from the system of Comte, his teacher: solidarity, a virtue that derives from the instinct to be sociable and which allows for collective life in which civilization develops; altruism, a social inclination to work for whatever benefit there is for us in our working for the benefit of others; and as a reward for the highest services, the immortality of living in the memory of future generations.

The most fruitful of these notions is that which recommends solidarity among men. Advocating for solidarity in Mexico, Barreda fulfilled a need at a crucial time. Altruism is an old virtue, limited to its social consequences: sacrifice is not for God to reward but is to be made use of by the individual and society (the benefit does not extend beyond one's own life or the lives of others, but is a benefit in life [un beneficio positivo]).

The immortality of living in the memory of future generations, a reward for the noblest actions, is regulated by the religion of humanity, destined for the cult of memory and gratitude; but there are those who do not value the memory of their actions, who do not desire gratitude, and for whom the religion of humanity, conformist and modest, offers little encouragement and no hope.[2]

Concerning what is referred to as the problem of psychology, it is enough to recall that positivism believed in a radical subordination of the psychological to the biological, of the mental to the organic. Free will is explained as conditioned by its antecedents, a form of fatalism, just as the fall of bodies is governed by the law of attraction, which is mysterious only in appearance because we do not know the multiple causes of desire, the motives that operate in what today is called the subconscious.

In short, such were the ideas with which Barreda rebuilt the national mind, orienting it definitively in the direction of modern thought. These lessons not only enabled Mexican civilization to make practical economic and industrial advances, training generations in the application of useful scientific knowledge, but they also bequeathed to us an irreplaceable mental discipline as we try to orient the hopes for our destiny and our historical progress [el progreso de los acontecimientos].

Thanks to this illustrative and sincere education, we have been able to avoid internal feedback that might have brought us old concepts that no longer have real power to uplift us. And this is how, even if Barreda and positivism did not give us everything we longed for, they did keep us from going backward on the road of improvement. And without suspecting it (their own postulates cut them off from the domain of speculation), we were forced to explore other potentialities of our being, which were closed off to them in their scientistic turn inward [su ensimismamiento cientificista], but which were available and fruitful to others during their time, and even richer today in unlimited possibilities.

However, there is an abyss between the ideas of yesterday and those of today. What is that modern element—in what does it consist—that makes us feel like we are different men, even though not even a half century has passed since the propagation of those lessons? How, if barely yesterday Spencer was our official philosopher, do we find ourselves at such a great distance from the systematizer of evolutionary theory?

I believe that our generation has the right to affirm that it owes almost all of its progress to itself. It is not in the classroom where we have been able to cultivate

---

[2] ["Religion of humanity" refers to a secular religion established by Auguste Comte. According to Tony Davies, Comte's religion was "a complete system of belief and ritual, with liturgy and sacraments, priesthood and pontiff, all organized around the public veneration of Humanity." In Humanism, The New Critical Idiom (Stirling, UK: Routledge, 1997), 28–29.—Trans.]

what is the noblest in our spirit. It is not in the classroom, where the morality of positivism is taught, that we receive radiant inspiration, the murmur of deep music, the voice of mystery, that fills the contemporary feeling with renewed and abundant vitality. The new general feeling has brought with it our own despair, the quiet pain of contemplating life without nobility or hope. When we abandoned society to take refuge in meditation—an ironic teacher, which we found by chance in the windows of the bookstore—it was made our ally, it gave voice to our pain and energy to our protest. Since then, our disdain was well reasoned and made us noble. Certainly we encountered abysses, dark powers that devour us and take back what is theirs, but despite that, its doctrine had the power to save us. Because who does not desire to live, even if it is only to contemplate the spectacle of the will denying itself? Who does not desire the "eternity of the moment" in which the teacher leaves free will in a desert where there is no end to applying oneself and gazes at himself—powerful and without object?

"The world is my will and my representation." This statement contains the germ of the entire modern age. For a long time, philosophy had been occupied almost exclusively with representation; thereafter, the philosopher also considered *the thing in itself*, with universal information, with the help of religion, literature, art, and the experience of life. At the same time, German music, the other nerve of the modern feeling, achieved in the work of Wagner a meaning that represented, not pure ideas in Platonic harmony, but the clamor of that which is incessantly becoming in the apparent uniformity of things; potential being in life, preoccupied by a choice of formulas in which to express itself, adopting, as if it were rehearsing, the momentary life of sound.

The anti-intellectualism of Schopenhauer and the music of Wagner, two expressions of the unintelligible, are the fountains of wealth that exhibit the modern spirit and its wise liberty, and that stand very far from romanticism or any other anti-intellectualism developed before.

The solution to the problem of knowledge, which cannot be solved within the bounds of reason, should be sought using other faculties; here the anti-intellectualist's and the pragmatist's criteria become relevant.

Representation understands the world of experience and the world of ideas. It always depends on the image or memory. The thing in itself, which ideas cannot penetrate, is action, something analogous to movement, a tendency, a desire to be. But one has to think of how all tendency goes somewhere and that, achieving that aim, it can undertake another or stop there. If it remains stationary, it ceases to be will, because it ceases to want to be. If it continuously keeps moving in pursuit of new aims, the result will be that the will is an endless movement. But the movement is only explained in relation to stability; to imagine movement, it is necessary to suppose an immovable point. All movement is made in relation to a point of reference less mobile. If the point of reference also moves, it will outline some kind of curve in relation to another point also less mobile, and this is how we will arrive successively at an absolutely fixed point, which is a theoretical and mechanical necessity. Thus the idea of movement implied in the concept of will is not simple, but contains its correlative: stability. By contrast, this last concept has the character of being fundamental, both positively and negatively, because rest is understood as the absolute absence of the variation of a being and also as a perennial nothing.

Aside from time, changing and transitory, in which a moving object follows an indefinite trajectory, there is a moment of expectation, a moment of *what will come, what awaits* at the end of a short or infinite amount of time: the arrival of the moving object, a definite instance in which the movement ends, never to begin again, and so that the path of the obligatory pull toward the center is never reproduced, and the power of movement is liberated, being transformed into total diffusion.

The thing in itself, therefore, is not a movement, nor a future, because these notions belong to what cannot be completed [*lo incompleto*] in the struggle of progress. The thing in itself is not an act or desire, *it is a being*, but to fathom it, all analogies are suspicious since they all consider the thing in itself as a representation, which, as we have said, is different from being. Does this mean that we will fall prey to the vagueness of an intuitive [*subjetiva*] mystic whose non-transferable results can never serve as a standard for men? Is it not preferable instead to search the universe for some potential that is irreducible to the laws of representation? Is there something contradictory about the laws of phenomena, a contradiction that reveals another order of possibilities? The laws of phenomena are the theoretical equivalent of energy in the organic world, or of adaptation in the biological, the equivalent of every striving toward an end. If an act seems not to have any end, or to be subject to determinism, if it is free and un-teleological [*atélico*], that is, disinterested, will this not be the work of the spirit?

The cosmological concept of the universe has also endured profound changes since Gabino Barreda founded the Preparatory School. Lavoisier's principle of the conservation of mass, and of the conservation of energy, justified a certain belief in the immutability of the natural laws. However, Carnot had already spelled out his celebrated principle that cannot be reconciled with the hypothesis of the conservation of energy and of the theoretical absolute reversibility of every dynamic variation. For example, a moving object that travels a trajectory can, with the same amount of energy, complete the opposite trajectory, but Carnot observed that there are things that are not governed by this reversibility. Heat can be transmitted from a warm body to a cold body, but it is impossible to immediately make the cold body warm again through the original states of temperature. In all mechanical phenomena, heat is produced, but heat by itself, spent heat that does not proceed from a chemical or electrical source, is incapable of producing [mechanical] work. These kinds of observation led Carnot to consider that there are two things that differ in quality: an energy that is totally (or almost totally) reversible and useful for vital and mechanical phenomena, capable of producing work, on the one hand, and calorific energy, which is inferior and irreversible, and which dissolves the heterogeneous into a homogeneity that it cannot possibly escape. Experience and calculation suggest that this form of superior energy (the motor and the useful) tends to disappear, to dissipate into the other. The total quantity of energy is conserved, but the quality of energy of the superior form is slightly decreased such that, as Clausius says, "entropy (deterioration) of the Universe is always increasing." Energy does not return to the forms in which it can be used as motor potential, but contrary to the Spencerien formula of the movement from the homogeneous to the heterogeneous, the heterogeneous is constantly impoverished for the benefit of the homogeneous.

With more reserve but with the same enthusiasm, the great English chemist Lord Kelvin Thompson stated that "in the universe mechanical energy tends to dissipate." "The planet was inhospitable for human life in an era far from ours, and in the future, in an era equally far away, it will be inhospitable for human life again, unless something that is *impossible under the rule of the laws of the material world* changes." This is the sense in which the principle of conservation of energy should be considered essentially modified, and this is why nobody can legitimately say that in nature nothing is lost, because if there is something uniform that remains equal, the quality that is useful in life, the phenomenal sense that interests us is dissipated and fades away. We cannot expect anything definite of matter. It is, by contrast, perishable. Those who dream of the perpetual renewal of worlds in the universe, and those who believe in the eternal return of phenomena, are mistaken because nothing returns to its original state, but rather, in each moment, the most important aspect of energy is lost in silence, in inert stillness.

And out of a duty both to be sincere and to appreciate the value of the principles in which we necessarily find our most significant concepts, I will add a few words about the experimental objection that the principle of degradation of energy has already encountered: Brownian movement. A drop of water observed on a slide under a microscope shows in its interior, in perpetual motion, a multitude of extremely tenuous particles; detritus of mineral and organic matter are agitated in every way without ever coming to rest. This movement is perfectly distinguishable from the movement of microscopic living organisms that exist in a drop of water. The smaller the particle, the faster the movement. This is explained by the fact that molecules, despite their appearance of being at rest, are perpetually moving, and a particle of matter, barely the size of a molecule, moves at the molecular level. The larger the particle, the more it resists molecular movement, which proves, even more clearly, that the movement of particles in suspension is owed to the reciprocal repulsion and attraction of molecules. The experimental evidence of this continuous movement seems to demonstrate the law of the conservation of energy and to refute Carnot's principle. This explanation of a still imperfect experience is enough reason to doubt the law of degradation of energy, but not enough to endorse the principle of conservation again, which is disproven by more evident and numerous experiences. This is to say that scientific principles are subject to correction, that they are merely hypotheses on the basis of the results of experience, and that they depend on experience.

As Bergson says, matter is a movement of falling; life is a reaction opposed to a downward movement. Life is an impulse that becomes detached from the rule of material laws. The acts of life are like the chlorophyllic function and the reflexes of the nervous system, which store the energy of the sun and slow down the dissipation of strength.

The vital impulse, which is contrary to the law of the degradation of energy, cannot be material. It is by definition immaterial. Life, then, is a stream of perpetual growth, a creation that strives without end. But one might object: does that contrary function—life—not draw its own energy from the same energy that will eventually degrade? Is it not of the same nature as that energy? Exactly when is the difference in the nature of the chlorophyllic function, or in the function of the nervous system, introduced? Are these functions not just a change in direction of energy spent—a simple reversal that will be impossible when the superior energy of the universe has been exhausted, when the cooling of the sun renders impossible the chlorophyllic transformation and cellular irritability? Therefore, to establish the principle of life, it is necessary to look, not for a phenomenon of energy, which we have already seen is perishable; nor for an intellectual phenomenon, which is not explained without its correlative, the object of thought, which is, according to Bergson, a simple adaptation of an organism to its environment; but rather for a fact that does not depend on anything that inevitably degrades [fatalidades], because only that fact will respond to the intuitive yearning that asks for resoluteness, a certainty, an absolute. The creative act, in which only the unintended, spontaneously oriented result of impulse can be seen, does not bring about this fact. Perhaps the disinterested act can bring it about, because it can be produced only by violating all material laws: the disinterested act is the only miracle in the cosmos.

The deep concept, the Dionysian concept of the flow of infinite potential, gets to the heart of our lives; it makes them powerful and leads them toward endless immensities; it transforms mystery into a treasure where we always find new potential, new hope, new thrills; and it leads us to value personal originality in the highest degree, to look deep inside and mold ourselves according to the most profound and persistent tendency that reflection reveals to us. In that depth—like the voice itself of that being which, in music, takes the most disturbing form—Ibsen's *be thyself* was born, that desire not to be the reflection of another life or the actions of another, but a desire to know what true *birth* means within the multiplicity and richness of the world. This desire implied the necessity of being sincere in order to know when we really have achieved the personal note, the singular, that which will never sound the same in existence because, after uniting with the concert of the universe and being enriched by later creations, it will continue to be modified, while the evolution of things that aim toward desire, the formless, and directionless [*la atelesis*] is completed.

To be honest with ourselves, the honest acceptance of the facts, has thus become crucially important in our contemporary ethical lives. These virile qualities and faith in indefinite improvement are the dominant features of the modern moral ideal; and, rooted in this attitude of struggle and confidence, the growing certainty of an ideal in which the spirit triumphs emerges in us. But we don't want to give into the vagaries of personal intuition; we need facts that demonstrate the legitimacy of our hopes. It is criminal to offer meaningless words when men hope for effective gifts, the substance of the ideal. That's why it is necessary to ground our hope for a better life on facts. Why, if the flow of life is capable of producing all the phenomena of which we are aware, is the ideal power incapable of the slightest manifestation? If we briefly think about the actions of men, we see that just as material phenomena obey a strict law of the economy of effort, the corresponding law in the biological order is egoism along with its extension: altruism and charity in the name of God that rewards our actions. Every—absolutely every—intention and effort tend toward an increase in the well-being and power of the individual. But in this circular law in which everything starts at the center and goes to the periphery to return to the center, in this inescapably centripetal [*fatalmente centrípeto*] movement, there is an exception: the sincerely disinterested act, done not for love or piety; the heroic act without purpose, spread endlessly.

The ideal demands an absolute foundation, the *noumenon*, a word that itself has been assigned every meaning, all significations, that asks for a voice and expression. Kant could not define it, but could sense its very real presence. About it he had to be silent. Schopenhauer went deeper and found an intuition of what was not phenomenal: the will. What is the structure of that intuition? It is such that, given its very nature, does not satisfy us. It is preparatory, a necessary means to achieve something else. What does being desire in its most private depths? Power? But what will it do with power? Being desires to persist. And nothing answers to this fundamental desire in the phenomenal world. But is the spirit also governed by the law of inevitable unfolding [*de desenvolvimiento fatal*]? Is there something that cannot be reduced to determinism and decay [*el perecer*]? When one thinks as if without ideas, outside every norm, in a kind of drifting that is sufficient unto itself, does time pass and can the phenomenon change the state of mind once it has already been produced? When one perceives without the feeling of pleasure or pain, without emotion in which a free essence is affirmed, is the law of biology there reached? When one works absolutely disinterestedly, does one not underestimate the natural laws? Does not the mysterious speak here? The modern illusion of divinity has to be founded on the reality and meaning of absolute disinterest; but is this a process in formation that needs to be crystallized in the future?

Be this as it may, our age lives as if the universe were governed by laws that are distinct from those that govern the phenomenal world. And men, upon reflecting, find in themselves, in their own consciousness, an outbreak of that indestructible potential, a consciousness that is capable of abnegation and which is thereby more powerful than anything else in the universe, that stands upright against the laws of destruction with a creative rebellion of a world that persists. The generous act within the stinginess of the universe is the strangest contradiction among facts, but it has not been sufficiently reflected on.

Each cosmological hypothesis gives rise to a new metaphysics. We have already reviewed the concept of life that Bergson refers to as a new form of the law of energy. The spirit, upon changing the mental aspect of the external, modifies its relative position, aims at a relation of harmony, and continues its mysterious and silent life. In this way, according to the new psychology of Bergson, "our body is an element of action that is interposed between the spirit and matter, serving both as an intermediary. Perceiving consists in separating those objects over which my body can exercise action. The faculty of choosing which perception among a multiplicity of images best serves us is the effect of a *discernment* that the spirit announces. The operation of selecting, helped by memory, constructs the present, enriching it with memory, and freeing it from the law of necessity. Passing from direct perception to memory, we definitively abandon the material for the spirit."

Memory is not a weakened perception that is reproduced by association, as positivism teaches: "it is an operation through which we are suddenly placed in the past; through memory, the past progresses to the present; memory is a potential that actualizes the past when sensation in the present gives it vitality. The spirit takes from the material perceptions and returns them in the form of movement onto which it has stamped its liberty."

As you can see, the new psychology does not hesitate to affirm freedom as the basis of spirit. But this concept of transition is beyond the scope of metaphysics. Freedom must exert itself, show its inclination, say where it will take us. When one is free, one is more interested in knowing the extent of one's potential. The freedom that gradually separates us from the dominion of the laws of phenomena will increasingly take us further, to an antithetical order, to the total absence of purpose—freedom will turn into *disinterest*.

We have spoken of spirit and this requires explanation. Independent minds have been habituated to listen with suspicion to these and other words that science is believed to have eradicated. Notwithstanding the worldwide authority of Bergson, will our philosophy be taken as an illusion of theoreticians, without a basis in reality, without consequence, ignoring the facts, the late fruit of absurdities that positivism believed it had killed? Are we the legitimate children of a truly scientific tradition, or hapless children who dream, having given up hope of finding the truth? These doubts, as always, force us to reflect on the criteria of method.

It has to be that what confuses people who are not very reflective is that each one of the millions of human beings who populate the planet has the apparent right to live out his [or her] own convictions and consider true his [or her] own explanations and fantasies about the universe, its aim, the purpose of men and things. I confess that I become uncertain and sad if I consider the range of theories—necessarily false, necessarily narrow-minded—that are propagated and prosper because of the absolute freedom of thought—

This raises a seemingly disconcerting question: Which thinker among so many is right? Or, to put it in more mundane terms, is the universe as I understand it, as it is understood by my neighbor whom I have perhaps asked, as it is understood by the civil servant of my town, or as someone who doesn't understand anything says it is? Disconcerting because it could happen that the question becomes complete nonsense.

Such a difficult question for whoever is convinced—as every sincere thinker perhaps always is—that the absolute concept of the world has not been discovered. But in every era there is a certain set of facts, of experiences, reasons, that intuition, at least philosophical intuition, does not have the right to ignore. We will find out if the thinker is extravagant, mistaken, a false prophet, or if he belongs to the serious development of philosophy and looks at the world as one should, according to recent philosophical advances—and whether, with his more or less personal intuition, the relations that distinguish his system or his genius adhere to those standards of human knowledge that have always enabled one to distinguish philosophy from sophistry, fruitful intuition from puerile "enlightenment." Science, logic, and traditional moral philosophy are the instruments used to verify and purify philosophical synthesis.

The fundamental intuition of a philosophical system should never conflict with scientific laws as they are understood in the era in which the system is produced, unless the system gives the modification or transformation of those laws a new sense, without forgetting that an important change in the significance of natural laws can only be upheld by a scientific experience. Generally, the postulates and assertions of a philosophical system are not only supported by the science of the time in which they are produced, but they also help science advance in accordance with its own rational spirit. In order to determine which science is real, it is enough to stick to the facts and the positive use [*servicios positivos*] that men derive from their affirmations and hypotheses.

Second, the synthesis should not violate the formal laws of logic, indispensable rules of thought, so long as our biological constitution is what is and has been thus far. Rationality [*la inteligencia*] will serve as a guide and necessary instrument used to verify what is true.

Finally, the moral consequences of the system are at once a realization of vague intuition and proof of its vitality.

These three standards, which are not limitations but which guide the way of intuitive reflection, will lead the philosopher to discover truth.

Whichever system, whichever theory does not demonstrate the value of these criteria, should be rejected as a deception that obscures the true light from the eyes of men.

In the name of these ultimate criteria we accept the new French philosophy, worthy of a position next to the greatest speculations to date.

After a quick review, we reject American pragmatism, which has no antecedent, for the following reason. It is in large part the fruit of an arbitrary use of empiricism, whose criticisms are interesting, but which unfortunately have been prostituted by authors who bring it close to occultism and spiritism and so many other absurdities that, although they have centuries of (spurious and fragmented) tradition to rely on, have not helped civilization at all. They have not produced any material progress, helping science to advance in theory or practice; or any intellectual progress, introducing elevated and coherent ideas; or any noble or exemplary moral principles, of which they are slavish scribes of precepts developed by philosophies and religions.

Only philosophy has a tradition of discriminating thought [*pensamiento selecto*]. Only philosophical thought, which simultaneously considers the three problems—those concerning sensibility, the intellect, and morality—has been able to survive without significant interruption, throughout the centuries, constantly renewing itself in the form of ever fruitful schools and systems, in the form of novel directives, in the form of unparalleled deeds and virtues, and also with very important applications, rich in practical consequences for the sake of advancing the science of nature and life.

Anyone who does not think it through might think that, in the moral realm, the serious rival of philosophy is religion. But it should be observed that religious intuition, when it is clear and at its best, is tantamount to philosophical intuition, and if it later becomes less pure, that is because faith tries to extend itself beyond its legitimate limits. Faith wants to deduce the world from itself instead of modifying itself and progressing, conforming to the experiences of the world. There is no doubt that the praiseworthy desire to conserve a fundamental intuition intact justifies the rigidity of dogma up to a point, but it also has to take account of the possible novelty of what has still not been revealed. Having fewer theologians who besmirch faith, more visionaries who spread it, and more saints who demonstrate it would make religion a perennial source of adoration and beatitude.

With the prudence that the standards previously studied recommend, we have tried to greet the new ideas. The positivism of Comte and Spencer could never contain our aspirations. Today, because we do not agree with the data of science by itself, which is lifeless and unreasonable, it seems that we have found relief and that life has been expanded. The desire to renew, which fills us, has already begun to empty its indeterminate potential in limitless space, where everything seems possible. The world that a well-intentioned but narrow philosophy wanted to close is now open, thinkers! We are ready to embrace every great innovation; but let us habituate ourselves to be exacting for the sake of the seriousness of the ideal.

Upon proclaiming that we are free, we urgently need to take precautions against the hallucinations and perversions of speculation. We have all known the feeling of the absolute certainty of truth, some moment in our lives, a moment of clarity that can return, that can produce itself again, perhaps very suddenly—right now—or while thinking in the next moment. But life also frequently completely absorbs us, keeps us blind and oblivious. We are provoked and oppressed by the idea that always surrounds us like an atmosphere, that we do not understand, that we are unaware of; and we continue hesitantly like soap bubbles that float in the air, empty and uncertain, until the pressure pops them and enlarges them in their ethereal universality.

But blind or enlightened, let us not lack the strength to overcome our stumbling blocks. Stand up straight, man of the ideal! Lift up your heart like a lake that overflows with pure water. Drown your violent egoism in the most powerful disinterest. A lofty disregard—a firm indifference, fear—will kill the desire for enjoyment. And when you are no longer bound by your desire and ambition, your love and happiness, you will be unconquerable. You will achieve a radiance of serene grandeur above the things that come and go—without direction.

The great systems are open-ended and mysterious, always unfinished, because even the most rigorous among them, from a dialectical point of view, ends in an elusive state of mind, and is therefore subject to endless reflection. This silence might be considered a failure, but why is there so much fear of this accident? Is the lengthening of life, the postponement of our triumph, the blow that defeats us, but which cannot kill the momentum, are these forms of failure? When the objective is not achieved, strength, if it endures, preserves the potential that will make it try over and over again. Thus each defeat enriches a determined struggle. Others will try what we did not achieve, and our desire will be revived. To imagine that others will repeat our deeds in the remote future is a way of anticipating immortality. By contrast, success is sterile and mediocre; it lives in the moment and dies with it; it does not generate hope or virtues. Whatever the fault of flying so high, it preserves vitality at the root, which recommends braving such heights. The broken spine is a symbol of the commitment to anticipate another tomorrow when one might return to fight. A work without a conclusion beckons future generations; it leads us to think that the unfinished work will be completed by distant data watched over by destiny. And in the strange pain of expectation, a glimmer of the future, rapid and tragic, that which we lack, the elusive and faraway, shows itself. We can sense the uselessness of our individuality and we sacrifice it for a desire for what will come, with the felling of catastrophe that accompanies all forms of grandeur.

CHAPTER 2

Discourse at the Inauguration of the National University (September 22, 1910)

Justo Sierra

Translated by Robert Eli Sanchez, Jr.

Justo Sierra Méndez was born in Campeche, Campeche, Mexico in 1848 and died in Madrid, Spain, in 1912. In addition to teaching history for many years at the National Preparatory School, he served in various political and public posts, including as justice of the Supreme Court, as minister of public education (under Porfirio Díaz), and as director of the Mexican Academy of Letters. He is considered the founder of Mexico's National University (Universidad Nacional Autónoma de México). Historian, educator, poet, essayist, literary critic, and politician, Sierra wrote widely and was very prolific. The Political Evolution of the Mexican People (Evolución política del pueblo mexicano) remains one of his most widely read works of Mexican history.

President of the Republic, Ladies, and Gentlemen:

Two prominent authors who admired turning strength into law are the author of *The German Empire* and the author of *The Strenuous Life.*[1] The first conceived of strength as an instrument of domination, the superior agent of what Nietzsche calls the will to power. The second advocated for strength as an agent of civilization, that is, of justice. Together they are mainly responsible for having instilled in the spirit of all peoples capable of looking toward the future the profound desire and tenacious aim of transforming all of their activities—mental, as light is transformed; emotional, as heat is transformed; and physical, as motion is transformed—into a single energy, a kind of moral electricity that is precisely

[1] [Sierra is referring, respectively, to *The History of the German Empire* by W. H. Dawson and to *The Strenuous Life: Essays and Addresses* by Theodore Roosevelt—Trans.]

what integrates man, what converts him into a value, what causes him to enter as a conscious molecule into the distinct evolutions that determine the sense of human evolution in the torrent of eternal becoming. . . .

This resolve to be strong, through which select groups in antiquity achieved magnificent results, and which is now entering into the field of what entire nations have achieved, demonstrates that the basis of the entire problem—be it social or political, taking these terms in their broadest sense—is pedagogical, a problem of education.

Because to be strong, let us be clear, is to condense one's entire development—physical, intellectual, ethical, and aesthetic—into the formation of character. It is clear that the essential element of the character is in the will. To encourage it to evolve tirelessly, by means of physical, intellectual, and moral development, from childhood to adulthood, is the sovereign purpose of primary school, of the "school" par excellence. The character is formed when that mysterious magnetism, analogous to what is called "true north" [brújula hacia el polo], a moral compass [el magnetismo del bien], has been impressed upon the will. To cultivate wills in order to harvest egoists would be the bankruptcy of pedagogy. It is necessary to magnetize characters with love; it is necessary to saturate man with the spirit of sacrifice to make him feel the immense value of social life, to convert him into a moral being, in all of the serene beauty of the expression. To sail always along the course of this ideal, aiming to achieve it day by day, minute by minute—this is the divine mission of the teacher.

The University, you will tell me, cannot be an "educator" in the full sense of the word. The University simply produces knowledge; it is an "intellectualizer" [es una intellectualizadora]; its only function is to shape intellects. But in response I might add that it would be unfortunate if the groups of Mexicans already initiated into human culture, scaling a gigantic pyramid with the hope of being able to see the stars better, and of being seen by everyone below, as our Toltec ancestors did, ended by creating an altar around which a learned caste gathered, increasingly removed from its earthly function, increasingly removed from the people who support them, increasingly indifferent to the pulsations of the turbid, heterogeneous social reality, barely aware of where they draw their lifeblood, and on top of whose highest peak their minds shine like a lamp radiating in the solitude of space!

I'll say it again: this would be a misfortune, as psycho-sociologists of the highest rank have already said. No, it is inconceivable in our time that an organism created by a society that aspires to take an increasingly active part in the human concert should feel detached from the bond that joins it to the mother's womb, in order to become part of an imaginary country of souls without a nation. No, the University is not a person destined never to turn its eyes away from the telescope or microscope, even if the nation is falling apart all around it. No, the Fall of Constantinople will not catch the people of the University by surprise, discussing the nature of the Light of Tabor.

I imagine it like this: a group of students of all ages adding up to a single age, the age of full intellectual proficiency, forming a real personality through solidarity and a consciousness of mission, which, drawing from every source of culture, wherever it springs forth, provided the spring is pure and diaphanous, sets out to acquire the means of nationalizing science and Mexicanizing knowledge. Turn the telescope toward our sky, a collection of prodigious asterisms, in whose blackness, made of mystery and the infinite, the Septentrion, eternally inscribing the Arctic furrow around the virginal pole star, and the sidereal diamonds that fix the Southern Cross in the firmament shine brightly at same time. Turn the microscope toward the germs that swarm invisibly in the retort of the organic world, which, in the constant cycle of their transformations, turn all existence into a means through which to carry out their evolutions, that ensconce themselves in our fauna, in our flora, in the atmosphere in which we are immersed, in the course of water that flows above ground, in the flow of blood that circulates through our veins, and that conspire, as skillfully as if they were conscious beings, to decompose all life and extract from death new forms of life.

Life will probably be exhausted on our planet before science can complete its observation of the many phenomena that distinguish us and characterize life [*de cuantos fenómenos nos particularizaran y la particularizasen a ella*]. Our subsoil, which in so many ways justifies the epithet "new" that has been given to our country; the peculiar composition of our territory, made of a gigantic horseshoe of mountain ranges that, having emerged from the ocean in the middle of the torrid zone, transforms it into a temperate zone, leads it to the frigid zone, rises to seek the crown of snow in its volcanoes in the middle of a polar climate, and there, in those altitudes, the internal arc of the horseshoe tapers off in a ramp of plateaus that die off toward the north. These particularities present us with the fact, perhaps unique in ethnic life on earth, of large groups of humans organizing themselves and persistently continuing to exist and evolve, and of constructing large societies and a nation resolved to live at an altitude at which, in similar regions on earth, human society has either not succeeded in growing, has not succeeded in establishing itself, or has languished unable to form self-conscious and developing nations.

And what is of special interest is that, on account of those conditions, not only do social—and, therefore, economic, demographic, and historical—phenomena here have forms *sui generis*, but so do other phenomena that are produced more ostensibly within the inescapable uniformity of the natural laws. Physical, chemical, and biological phenomena here obey particularities so intimately related to the meteorological and barological conditions of our location [*habitáculo*] that it can be said that they constitute, within the vast empire of knowledge, not an autonomic province—because all of nature falls within the sovereign domain of science—but one that is distinct and characteristic.

And if from nature we pass to man, who, certainly, is an atom, but an atom that not only mirrors the universe, but ponders it, how many peculiarities we will encounter! Did a single race dwell here? Do the (morphological, not structural) differences among the languages spoken here indicate distinct origins relating to a diversity (of form and appearance, though not of psychology) of the inhabitants of these regions? If our continent is not the center of creation, whence the first strain of these groups? Is there, perhaps, an underlying unity in this human species that runs from one pole to the other? These men who constructed incredible monuments amidst cities—apparently conceived by the single brain of a giant and brought into existence by several generations of the conquered or by slaves of religious passion, servants of the idea of pride and domination, but convinced that they were serving a god—also erected spiritual monuments in their cosmogonies and theogonies that were much greater than their physical monuments. Their spiritual monuments, with their motley peaks similar to those of the *teocalis*, touched the eternal problems, those in the presence of which man is no more than man, in all climates and all races—that is, a question in the night [*una interrogación ante la noche*]. Who were these men, where did they come from, where at the bottom of this indigenous sea are their living relics—above whose depths a level of superstition and servitude has passed since prehistoric times, but which reveals to us, every once in a while, its formidable latent energy in personalities charged with the spiritual electricity of character and intelligence?

Then there is the history of the Contact between these aboriginal cultures that seem strange to us and the most energetic representatives of Christian culture; and, as an effect of the contact that began here 400 years ago and which is still not consummated, the extinction of a culture that developed here in so many forms; and the persistence of the indigenous soul, coupled but not identical to or fused with the Spanish soul, not even in the new race, in the genuine Mexican family, born, as has been said, of the first kiss of Hernán Cortés and Malintzin; and the necessity of finding in a common education the shape of that supreme unification of the nation—and all this studied through its consequences, in view of the series of phenomena that determines our social condition. What a profusion of topics for our intellectual laborers, and how much wealth for human knowledge can be extracted from these gold mines, still hidden, of revelations that cover every branch of learning of which man is both subject and object.

By carrying out this vast work of culture and by attracting all the energies of the Republic that are fit for scientific exertion, the institution of the University will merit the epithet "national" that the legislator has given it. It is up to the University to demonstrate that our personality has indestructible roots in our nature and our history; that, sharing some elements with other American peoples, our ways are such that they constitute a perfectly distinct entity among the others, and that Tacitus's *tantum sui simile gentem* can be rightfully applied to the Mexican people.[2]

So that this work is not only Mexican but also human, we should not waste a single day of the century in which it is to be carried out, nor can the University forget, lest it burn all the oil of its lamp, that it will be necessary to live in close communion with the march of general culture—that its methods, research, its conclusions, cannot acquire permanent value if they are not tested against the touchstone of the scientific research carried out in our age, mainly in universities. Science advances, projecting its light ahead, its method, like an immaculate theory of truths in search of *the* truth. We must and want to take our place in that divine procession of torches.

The educational activity of the University will thus accrue from its scientific activity, bringing together select groups of the Mexican intelligentsia and intensely cultivating in them the pure love of truth, stamina in their daily work in the pursuit of it, and the conviction that the interests of science and the interests of the nation must be combined in the soul of every Mexican student. This activity will create types of character destined to crown, to put the seal on, the great work of popular education for which school and family, the great school that teaches by example, beautifully pave the way when they work together. Emerson, quoted by the eminent president of Columbia University, says:

> Culture consists in suggesting to man, in the name of certain higher principles, the idea that in him there is a series of affinities that serve to curb the violence of master notes that are discordant in their scale, affinities that are of help to us against ourselves. Culture reestablishes the equilibrium, puts man in his place among his equals and his superiors, reanimates in him the exquisite feelings of sympathy, and warns him in time of the danger of solitude and of antipathetic impulses.

And this suggestion about which the great North American moralist speaks, this suggestion of higher principles, of reasonable ideas turned into altruistic feelings, is the work of all men who have a voice in history, who have earned a decisive vote in the moral problems that trouble society. It is the work of these men who, without knowing it, from their grave or from their desk, their workshop, their camp or their altar, are the true social educators: Victor Hugo, Juárez,

---

[2] [This line by Tacitus, "a people similar only to itself," is from his *Germania* and was used as part of Nazi propaganda. See Allan Lund's *Germanenideologie im Nationalsozialismus: Zur Rezeption der 'Germania' des Tacitus im "Dritten Reich."*—Trans.]

Abraham Lincoln, Léon Gambetta, Garibaldi, Kossuth, Gladstone, Leo XIII, Emilio Castelar, Sarmiento, Bjoernson, Karl Marx, to speak only of those who were alive but yesterday, have a greater influence and suggest more to democracies in formation today than all the world's moral treatises.

This widespread education, penetrating by example and word, that for a period of time saturates the atmosphere of national life with powerful ideas [*ideas-fuerzas*]—it is now the University's turn to concentrate it, systematize it, and disseminate it through action. It should strive to produce fruitful incarnations of those higher principles Emerson speaks of. It should carry out the enormous task of receiving within the school doors—within which the teacher has succeeded in instilling moral and physical habits that orient our instincts toward the good—the child who will turn his instincts into the constant auxiliaries of his reason as he passes through the decisive stage of youth, and who will acquire mental habits that lead him toward the truth, who will acquire aesthetic habits that make him worthy of the exclamation of Agrippa d'Aubigné:

Oh! Celestial Beauty,
Fair daughter of heaven, torch of eternity!

When the youth becomes a man, the University needs to send him off to struggle for his living in a higher social sphere or to lift him to the lofty heights of scientific research, but either way, without ever letting him forget that all contemplation must be a preamble for action, that it is not lawful for a University person to think only of his own interests, and that even if it is possible to forget spirit and matter inside the doors of the laboratory, as Claude Bernard said, we will not be able, morally, to forget either humanity or the nation.

The University, then, will have sufficient power to coordinate the guiding principles of national character, which it will always hold high before the nascent consciousness of the Mexican people, so that it can project its rays in every darkness, the beacon of the ideal, of an ideal of health, truth, goodness and beauty. That is the torch of life of which the Latin poet speaks and which generations, in their course, pass on to one another. [. . .]

The University born today, then, can have nothing in common with its predecessor, the Royal and Pontifical University of Mexico. Both have arisen from the desire of the representatives of the State to entrust men of great learning with the mission of utilizing national resources for scientific education and research—because men of great learning constitute an organ better suited for these functions, because the State knows of no other function more important, and because it does not believe it is better able to fulfill them. The founders of the former University said, "The truth is defined; teach it"; we say to people of the University today, "The truth is in the process of being defined; seek it." They said, "You are a select group charged with inculcating a religious and political ideal, summarized in the following words: 'God and the King.'" We say, "You are a group perpetually being selected from the people, and you have been tasked with achieving a social and political ideal that can be summarized thus: 'democracy and liberty.'"

To succeed more quickly—not in realizing its ends, because the history of human thought proves that they are never realized, even if every day they are in the process of being realized, but in mastering the means of realizing them—the legislator wanted to minimize the reach of the University in order to strengthen it. However, for the same reason, we have not created the University so that it has no involvement with primary education—the most fundamental and most essentially national [form of education]. But that involvement was limited to providing detailed information from the most authoritative source. It could do no more because of an agreement between the people and government stated in our laws, which reserves for the government [authority over] everything concerning primary education. This agreement is indisputable, and we Mexicans consider it indisputable. It belongs to the political order. The agreement states that, deeply committed to the inescapable duty to transform the Mexican population into a people, a democracy, we consider ourselves obliged to use, directly and constantly, the most important means of achieving this end: the primary school. All other means are subsidiary. There is not a single means which signifies peace and progress that is not educative, because not one of them does not increase the coefficient of cohesion in peoples, promote the love of work, and facilitate the march of the school. But the school, which suggests habits, which converts external into internal discipline, which unifies the language, raising a national language above the dust of all the languages of indigenous origin, thus creating the primordial element of the soul of the nation—this school, which systematically prepares the child to become a citizen, initiating him in the religion of the homeland and the cult of civic duty, this school is an integral part of the State, constitutes one of its prime obligations, and must be considered a public service. The school is the State itself, projected into the future.

This is the first reason for our system, and this is the reason for keeping normal schools outside the sphere of the University, despite the fact that we are aware of the tendency today of replacing normal school training with pedagogical training in the University. I do not know what the results would be elsewhere but here we denounce such a system as disastrous in the present stage in the development of our schools.

The University is responsible for national education in its higher, more idealistic pursuits. It is the peak from which the fountain flows, clear as the crystal of the Horatian spring, which descends to water the plants germinating in the national soil, and which raises the soul of the people to its height. At the same time, all that forms the concrete and utilitarian disciplines tied to the changing necessities that the life of the State partly depends on—such as commercial and industrial studies, fields for future universities—is included as part of our pedagogical plan currently, in close dependence on the State. As is everything economic that, with persistence, it is necessary to protect, since the tenuousness of the environment in which the State evolves demands the temporary creation of artificial means that favor the evolution of that which we take to be indispensable to national culture—I am referring to instruction in aesthetics.

This, then, is how the new University will organize its selection of the elements that the primary school sends to secondary school. But here the University will make them its own, will refine them in tough crucibles from which it will ultimately extract the gold that, formed into medallions and engraved with the national coat of arms, it will put into circulation. This secondary education is organized, here as in almost all of the Republic, in a two-part series of programs that succeed each other, the one preparing the other, both logically and chronologically, both in science and literature. Such a system is preferred to simultaneous programs because our experience and the composition of our Mexican spirit seem to credit it with more didactic value. Undoubtedly it is at odds with the current interdependence of the sciences, but its relation with the history of science and with the laws of psychology, which are based in the passing from the more to the less complex, is undeniable.

Upon this scientific "series" that informs the curriculum of our secondary education—"the series of abstract sciences," as Auguste Comte named them—is erected the higher professional studies, paid for by the State and supported with as much splendor as it can muster—not because it believes that its mission is to provide free education to those who reach that third or fourth grade of selection, but because it judges it necessary for the benefit of everyone that there be good lawyers, doctors, engineers, and architects. It believes that social peace, public health, and social decorum and wealth, which satisfy our basic needs, require it. Upon these professional careers, we have founded the School of Higher Studies. There, the student's education is concluded; there, instruction is divided into *many* areas of learning; there, there will be an ever-widening distribution of key ingredients [*elementos de trabajo*]; there, we will gather together, to the best of our ability, the princes of the sciences and of the humanities, because we wish that those who are the best prepared by our system of national education can listen to the most renowned voices in the world of learning, those voices that come from the highest and travel the farthest, not only those voices that stir ephemeral emotions but those that initiate, encourage, reveal, and create. One day those voices will be heard in our school. They will spread the love of science, a divine love, for its serenity and purity, which produces ideals as earthly love produces human beings [*como el amor terrestre funda humanidades*].

Our ambition is that in that School, which is the highest rung in the University edifice, established there to discover in knowledge the most expansive horizons, the most open-minded, such as those that can only be contemplated from the loftiest heights on the planet—our ambition would be that in that School students are taught to think and research by thinking and researching, and that the substance of their research does not crystalize deep within, but that those ideas become a dynamism perennially translatable into teaching and action. Only then can ideas be called powerful. We should never like to see ideas reserved for ivory towers or a contemplative life or in raptures in search for artistic expression. That might exist elsewhere and perhaps it is good that it does. But not here, not here.

For some time, an imploring figure has been wandering about in the *templa serena* of our official education system—philosophy. Nothing is more respectable or more beautiful. Since the mysterious doors of the Oriental sanctuaries were opened centuries ago, philosophy has served as a guide to human thought, which is sometimes blind. With human thought, it stopped to rest on the highest steps of the Parthenon, which it would never have liked to leave. Philosophy almost lost thought in the tumult of the barbarous ages, and, joining with it and guiding it once again, it remained in the doors of the University of Paris, the *alma mater* of thinking humanity in the Middle Ages. That imploring figure is philosophy, a tragic figure that leads to Oedipus, who sees through the eyes of his daughter the only thing worth seeing in this world, that which does not come to an end, the eternal.

How we have been called cruel, and perhaps stupid, for keeping the gates closed to the ideal of Antigone! The truth is that in the curriculum of positivist education, the scientific series constitutes a fundamental philosophy. The higher studies [*el cielo*] that begin with mathematics and conclude with psychology, moral philosophy, philosophy, logic, and sociology, are a philosophical education; they are an explanation of the universe. But, even if we could not give philosophy its marble throne in our programs, we—who had traditions to respect but none to extend or follow—could show how the universe works as far as science could project its floodlights, but we could not go any further. Nor could we fit into our catalogue of subjects the splendid hypotheses that try to explain, not the how of the universe, but the why. [It is not the case, however,] that we have adopted positivism as a philosophical creed. To correct the view that we have, one need only compare the series of abstract sciences that we have adopted to that proposed by the great thinker who founded [positivism]. No, a secular spirit reins in our schools. Here, due to the peculiar circumstances of our history and institutions, the State could impose any creed without betraying its duty. It leaves everyone in the absolute freedom to profess whatever moves them, be it reason or faith. Metaphysical speculation that answers to an invincible yearning of the spirit, and that constitutes a kind of religion in the intellectual order, cannot be the stuff of science. Metaphysics is the supreme synthesis that hovers above science and frequently loses contact with it. It remains the responsibility of a talented individual, sometimes of a genius, but always of a self-conscious individual. There is nothing like that kind of intellectual training to elevate the soul, to better satisfy the spirit, even though, as often happens, it leads to tragic disappointment.

There are, however, works of coordination, attempts to summarize knowledge, that do have their entire basis in science, and one department in the School of Advanced Studies classifies it under the title of philosophy. There we will open courses in the history of philosophy, beginning with the history of modern doctrines and new systems, or renovated systems, from the appearance of positivism to today, to the days of Bergson and William James. And we will leave open, completely free, the fields of negative or positive metaphysics, pluralism as well as monism, so that we are made to think and feel while pursuing the pure vision of those eternal ideas that forever appear and reappear in the course of intellectual life—a God distinct from the universe, a God immanent in the universe, a universe without God.

What would we have achieved if, upon realizing this dream we completed, with a Mexican star, an asterism that did not shine in our sky? No, the new man, whom the dedication to science turns into a young neophyte who has the lifeblood of his soil and the blood of his people in his veins, cannot forget to whom he is indebted and to whom he belongs. The *sursum corda* that issues from his lips to the foot of the altar should be directed to those who have loved with him, to those who have suffered with him. Let him hold up before them, as a promise of liberty and redemption, the immaculate host of truth. We do not want in the temple erected today an Athena without eyes for humanity, and without a heart for the people, within her contours of white marble. We want the best Mexicans to come here with incessant theories to worship the Athena Promachos and the science that defends the homeland.

CHAPTER 3

Existence as Economy and as Charity

AN ESSAY ON THE ESSENCE OF CHRISTIANITY (1916)

Antonio Caso

Translated by Alexander V. Stehn and Jose G. Rodriguez, Jr.

Antonio Caso Andrade was born in Mexico City in 1883 and died in the capital in 1946. Like several other members of the Ateneo de la juventud, *he studied at the National Preparatory School and then studied law at the School of Jurisprudence, where he later became professor of sociology in 1909 (while also teaching philosophy at the National Preparatory School). After Justo Sierra founded the National University in 1910, Caso became a professor of philosophy in, and would eventually direct, the School of Higher Studies, which would later become the Faculty of Philosophy and Letters. In addition to being a charismatic professor who inspired an entire generation of philosophers in Mexico, he also served in administrative roles, as rector of the National University (1920–1923) and as a founding member of the now prestigious College of Mexico (Colegio de México, founded in 1942). Among his many publications on a wide variety of themes, the following are especially relevant to the question of Mexican identity and philosophy:* Discursos a la nación mexicana *(Discourses on a Mexican Nation, 1922),* El problema de México y la ideología nacional *(The Problem of Mexican and National Ideology, 1924),* La persona humana y el estado totalitario *(The Human Person and the Totalitarian State, 1941).*

Struggle for life.
   —Darwin

All bodies, the firmament, the stars, the earth and its kingdoms, are not worth the least of minds. For mind knows all of these, and itself, and bodies know nothing.

All bodies together, and all minds together, and all their productions, are not worth the least movement of charity. . . .
   —Pascal

To my disinterested friends: Don Julio Corredor Latorre, Consul General
of the Republic of Columbia in Mexico, and Doña Clotilde Quijano de
Corredor Latorre.

Preface

A short time ago, the author of this brief essay was invited to give a series of lectures at the Mexican Popular University, a free institution of education founded
by the Athenaeum of Mexico for the diffusion of culture. The author thought
of offering his audience a synthesis of Christianity gathered from the moral
biography of some great Christians. Such a synthesis would have to be—to use
Carlyle's beautiful expression now consecrated by use, a *worship of heroes and
the heroic in history*[1]—dedicated to the most important event in the evolution of
humanity: the development of evangelical ideas and feelings over time.

In summary form, here are the great representative figures of Christian evolution to bear in mind, along with a rough indication of their symbolism:

Saint John the Baptist is *the precursor*, the seer idealized by the beautiful evangelical legend, interpreted in the contemporary art of Gustave Flaubert, Oscar Wilde,
and in the music of Strauss. Situated between the Old and the New Testament,
John the Baptist appears as Israel's last prophet and the world's first Christian. He
is a fierce heroic figure who possesses the majestic solitude of the desert.

Saint Paul is *the apostle*, the practical author of Christianity (someone has
spoken of *Paulism*) as a universal and not simply Jewish phenomenon. The
apostle common to Catholicism and Protestantism, Paul is the eternal symbol
of religious conversion, of the *twice-born* that William James discusses in his philosophy of religion.

Saint Augustine is *the father of the Church*. He represents this incalculable
event: the alliance of the humanities and classical culture with divine inspiration, opposing the skeptics of his time with the victorious Cartesian argument that gave birth to modern philosophy. Catholicism, Protestantism, and
Cartesianism: he intuits or paves the way for all of them. He is one of humanity's
most richly gifted minds [*los espíritus*].

Charlemagne, *the emperor of the flowery beard* (according to the *Song of Roland*)
and immortal soldier of the Church, confirms the feudal Catholic regime on
Christmas Eve in the year 800 by creating the temporal power of the popes. He is
the medieval king par excellence, the leader of the barbarian West, Christian and
Roman, the main character of the chivalrous epic.

---

[1] [Scottish philosopher and essayist Thomas Carlyle (1795–1881). Caso's remark refers to *On
Heroes, Hero-Worship, and The Heroic in History* (1841).—Trans.]

Gregory VII is *the pope,* a monk who dons the crown and brings to Europe's throne the austere virtues of the cloister and the incorruptible zeal of Christ's true vicar. He represents, as Guizot says, the theocratic and monastic Church.

Saint Francis of Assisi is *the mystic,* sweet and generous, of the Beatitudes; the hero of feeling and simple charitable action; Christianizer not only of humanity, but also of nature as a whole; the favored son of Jesus Christ. He is the symbol of expansive, contagious, boundless Christian joy.

When the Renaissance seems to resurrect paganism as victorious despite the triumph of civilization, Luther, the intrepid disciple of Saint Paul and Saint Augustine, opposes the Renaissance with the Reformation, opposes what seemed to be the apotheosis of the classical world with the apotheosis of the Christian idea, intimately united with the spirit of free inquiry characteristic of modern times. And what the rebellious German friar represents outside of the Catholic Communion, Saint Teresa represents inside the bosom of the Church with the most genuinely orthodox piety. She is the simultaneously brilliant and submissive Christian woman, the tireless reformer (of the traditional Catholic type), and founder of the *universal society of spirits and hearts.* Teresa is *the saint* by antonomasia.

Pascal and Tolstoy are history's latest great Christians. Pascal is the personifica-tion of literary, scientific, and philosophical genius, who sacrifices intellectual vanity to the ineffable good of grace. He is the enlightened one who, while capable of the most profound rationality, is subsequently convinced that any rationality that does not lead to Jesus Christ is nothing compared to action, nothing compared to the feeling of humanity. Nietzsche gave him the highest praise by calling him *the most instructive victim of Christianity.*

Tolstoy launches the Christian anathema against people in power, against social and political institutions, against blood-stained patriotism and militarism:

> The relation between the men who command and those who obey forms the essence of the concept of power. Without the exaltation of oneself and the humiliation of others, without hypocrisy and deceit, without prisons, fortresses, executions, and murders, no power could come into existence or be maintained.[2]

[2] [Russian writer and religious theorist Leo Tolstoy (1828–1910). The quote is from Tolstoy's *The Kingdom of God Is Within You* (1894). The first sentence appears to be a paraphrase, but the second is a quotation.—Trans.]

Tolstoy is an exemplar of this other Christian heroism, anarchism, that considers ordering and obeying to be equally vile.

This is, synthetically, Christianity in the history of humanity: the Precursor, the Apostle, the Father of the Church, the Medieval Emperor, the Pope, the Mystic, the Reformer, the Saint, the Jansenist, the Anarchist—and along with them, holiest of all, the glorious and innumerable legion of martyrs.

Once this plan of labor was defined, the projected lectures were developed over the course of roughly three months. And from dealing with what history has to say about the example and doctrine of the great Christians, my final plan was born: an interpretation of the essence of Christianity. This humble interpretation, in the eyes of the author, does not in any way contradict the philosophical and scientific conclusions of our time. It is offered to the reader in what follows with the title *Existence as Economy and as Charity*.

Existence as Economy and as Charity

To be is to struggle, to live is to conquer, according to Le Dantec. It is interesting to recognize that nothing has been investigated that was empirical [*positivo*] and congruent with respect to life and its manifestations, except when it was conceived as struggle. Without consenting to the synthetic expression of the French biologist, without subscribing to his philosophical thesis of universal struggle, or in other words, without *speaking his language*, it is nevertheless necessary to admit that, if not all being, then at least the living being is defined by the idea of struggle. To struggle and to live are synonymous. Life, in its economy, is a triumph over the environment, over the enemy, or over the fellow man, who, by the similarity of his necessities and organization, is the enemy by another name.

Since Darwin, the economy of nature has been the supreme principle of biology. We know that Malthus's celebrated economic theory, founded on the disproportion between the food supply and population growth, inspired Darwin's thesis of natural selection.

The economist's thesis is too narrow for the super-organic world. Like all of the other theses of classical political economy, it has not been proven by history. In contrast, Darwin's theory is still the common axis of biological discussion today, the scientific theory or law that unites (like a bridge, as [John] Stuart Mill would say) and coordinates the diverse chapters of the study of living beings.

There is nothing obscure, nothing mythical, in Darwin's explanation. Some living beings prosper and develop their species through time, while others die. As J. M. Baldwin interprets Darwin:

Life is a *natural selection*, a selection without external intervention, that occurs with no more reason than the simple fact that some naturally survive while others die.[3]

The number of possible individuals far exceeds the actual individuals that in fact live on the earth's surface in a given moment. The germs that represent the potential of the beings endowed with life are immense in number when compared to the individuals that actually develop, especially in comparison to those that reach the age of reproduction.

Spinoza said that *everything tends to persist in its being*. According to Haeckel, the biological form of this tendency to preserve oneself, the drive that makes struggle necessary and provides its features, is that of individual preservation (the nutritive drive) or species-preservation (the reproductive drive).[4] "The mechanism of the universe maintains itself through hunger and love," as Schiller sang.[5]

Thus, by virtue of egoism, which relies on an excess of forces to engender new kindred beings, species are established and die out. A chemical reaction produces a strictly synthetic compound from the elements that comprise it; the reaction expends itself completely in synthesis. Primitive plants and animals divide themselves to engender new beings once they reach maturity and have accumulated energy by nourishing themselves, which is to say, by adapting. Higher order animals engender their offspring by means of sexual reproduction due to functions of greater complexity. Struggle, adaptation, and heredity sustain the immense assembly of living beings. *Maximum gain with minimum effort*: such is the universal economy or the universal as economy. Adaptation—nutrition and heredity-reproduction, that is, hunger—is life's sole motive of action. (So-called "love"—appetite—is reduced to this elemental necessity, to sex and offspring.)

The effect of egoism over time is incalculable. In a limited, but very true sense, one could say that whatever is not egoist is stupid in the face of reason informed by scientific data. When formulating his celebrated doctrine, Malthus did not think that he was indirectly formulating a universal aspect of existence. Thanks to Darwin, political economy has become the economy of the entire world.

Egoist or economic activity is so real that it even explains some seemingly unrelated activities, and it gains in certainty and extension when they are

---

[3] *Le Darwinisme dans les sciences morales*, p. 5. [Trans. note: Guillaume Léonce Duprat's 1911 French translation of James Mark Baldwin, *Darwin and the Humanities* (Baltimore, MD: Review Publishing, 1909).]

[4] *Historia de la creación natural*, p. 156 of C. Litrán's Spanish translation. [Cristóbal Litrán's 1905 Spanish translation of Ernst Haeckel, *Natürliche Schöpfungsgeschichte* (1868), translated into English as *The History of Creation*, 2 vols. (New York: D. Appleton, 1876).—Trans.]

[5] [German poet and philosopher Friedrich Schiller (1759–1805). The line is from the poem "Die Weltweisen," which is typically translated as "The Philosophers."—Trans.]

explained. Human industry is the very definition of man's intelligence. According to Bergson, we should say *homo faber* instead of *homo sapiens*.[6] Intelligence, an *elegant solution* to the problem of life (as the great French thinker says), is the faculty of creating tools, instruments of action. And science, which at first glance is a disinterested knowledge, has as its objective:

> [t]o order sense data, to investigate *with all possible economy of thought* the relations of dependence that exist between sensations, and to realize a structure so uniform that intellectual fatigue can be avoided. Scientific knowledge implies the description, that is, the mental imitation of a fact, *and this description should be able to replace experience and economize it.*[7]

This is *Science*, or rather, *the sciences* (in the plural without capital letters).

Science is the same biological interest, subtler and more human, but no less real. The sciences are arrangements of abstract concepts that enable us to think and speak comfortably. The ideal of the sciences is to reduce themselves to Science (with a capital S), to a single discipline. And the ideal of this single Science is to reduce itself to a single truth. If there is an economic ideal, this is it: an intellectual egoism so refined and subtle that its devotees erect a *monistic philosophical doctrine* and decorate it with epithets of disinterest and enthusiasm. This is egoism and egoism alone.

Just as we previously saw political economy converted into universal economy, we now demonstrate that its principle of maximum gain achieved with minimum effort is converted into a systematic epistemology. According to pragmatism, scientific truth is summed up in *what is advantageous for our thinking*, as William James says.[8] Intelligence, industry, sciences, and logic are biological forms on a Malthusian base. The only things that are neither biology nor Malthusianism are the beautiful and the good.

But before going any further, we should pause to consider the mystery of a purely biological activity that seems disinterested: play.

---

[6] [French philosopher Henri Bergson (1859–1941). He discusses *homo faber* (Latin for "man the maker") in contrast to *homo sapiens* ("man the wise") in *Creative Evolution* (1907).—Trans.]

[7] E. Mach, *La connaissance et l'erreur*, p. 3. Avant-propos. [Caso's quote is from Marcel Dufour's introduction to his 1908 French translation of Mach's *Erkenntnis und Irrtum* (1905). The following English translation is available: Ernst Mach, *Knowledge and Error: Sketches on the Psychology of Enquiry*, translated by T. J. McCormack and P. Fouldes (Dordrecht, The Netherlands: D. Reidel, 1976).—Trans.]

[8] [US philosopher and psychologist William James (1842–1910). Caso paraphrases the conception of truth found in *Pragmatism: A New Name for Some Old Ways of Thinking* (1907).—Trans.]

Spencer, who was always a deficient and fussy philosopher with respect to art and beauty, once read "in a German author whose name escapes my memory" (perhaps in Schiller) the hypothesis of art referred back to play.[9] And with this memory, Spencer elaborated a doctrine of aesthetic feelings that makes play the basis of art in the final chapter of his *Principles of Psychology*, as well as in some minor essays.

The only animals that play are those higher animals capable of accumulating more energy than their individual economy requires. Play appears to be a squandering of what one has in surplus. But if art, like play, proceeds from the dynamic surplus accumulated in life, then both activities would be nothing more in this respect than equipping oneself for the future, since artistic disinterest is not a mode of immediate struggle. And if it just so happens that all play, which seems to be carried out without an egoist impulse, is, at bottom, of the economic type,[10] then play is *always an imitation of struggle*. In other words, play is something that mediately, if not immediately, serves interested ends.

The animal that plays, that imitates or simulates struggle with unreal adversaries, unconsciously practices struggling with real adversaries. To play is to serve the economy of life without knowing it and without deciding to do so deliberately. Life, if any remains, is spent on life. Life has no disinterest, only egoism, and that which could be given is spent or consumed in the same habitual forms of consuming and spending. All animal energy is employed in the singular ends of life, just like a machine that does not have raw material at its disposal for production ridiculously repeats for us the movements that would result in a product were the material present, as long as the force that makes it move is not extinguished.

Moreover, the higher animal, as opposed to the machine that destroys itself gradually by moving, strengthens itself for action by means of movements without a straightforward aim. Play is a beautiful paradox that might be indicated by saying that animals only know how to struggle. If they do not have anyone to struggle against, they comically imitate struggle and thus expend their surplus force. The economy of nature, upset in outward appearance, gives itself the most brilliant confirmation, the most complete satisfaction, in the facts that appear to negate it. As Goethe says on an extraordinary page of *Werther*:

> Oh! It is neither the great and infrequent catastrophes of the world, nor the floods and earthquakes that annihilate our cities that move me. What gnaws at my heart is the devouring force that lies concealed in all

---

[9] See *Principles of Psychology*, The Aesthetic Feelings.
[10] I owe this idea of assimilating play to struggle to my brother, Alfonso Caso.

of nature, a force that has produced nothing that does not destroy itself and everything near it.

In this way I advance on my insecure path with anxiety. Surrounded by heaven, earth, and its active powers, I see nothing more than a monster eternally occupied by chewing and swallowing.[11]

The economy of nature governs the world of life and its fruits completely, like an empire. Purely biological life, industry, science, play: all of these are the diverse expression, more or less complex, of the simple mechanical axiom of the path of least resistance. Everything is summarized in this fundamental equation of the universe as economy:

$$\text{Life} = \text{Minimum Effort} \times \text{Maximum Gain}$$

Nevertheless, in play this important fact has already appeared: there exist living beings—higher animals—that have a surplus of energies that life does not individually claim in each being. In spite of this, *because no principle of disinterested action exists in the animal*, we have just seen how the vital surplus is employed in the imitation or comic parody of the struggle that drills the player and trains him for later conflicts with real enemies rather than imaginary ones.

Life, the energy of egoism that is spent resolving the complex problem of hunger, consumes itself if it does not encounter a force from a divergent order. Life alone, in surplus or excess, is finally economized as a real ability formed in exercises of movement that appear useless.

Bergson and James have observed how vital energy has a *surplus* that engenders fertility and abundance:

Reality, as James sees it, is abundant, superabundant. I think that the American philosopher would have established the same relation between this reality and the one that philosophers reconstruct as between the daily life that we live and the life that actors represent for us on stage at night. In the theater every actor says only what is necessary to say and does nothing except what is necessary to do. But in life we say a multitude of useless things.... Things neither begin nor

---

[11] [German novelist, poet, scientist, and philosopher Johann Wolfgang Goethe (1749–1832). Caso quotes from his most famous work, *The Sorrows of Young Werther* (1774). Most of the novel is presented as letters written by Werther to his friend Wilhelm. The letter quoted is dated August 18.—Trans.]

end. There are neither completely satisfactory endings nor absolutely decisive acts.... Such is human life and such is reality according to James.[12]

This excess of living demonstrated in play can serve as a vital condition of other diverse ends of animal life, but only the *surplus* accumulated in man makes them achievable. The animal and the child play. Man makes works of art and carries out charitable acts. If there were no vital surplus, if man were not a privileged higher mammal, the *biological condition* of the aesthetic and moral order would be lacking. However, as we will see and thoroughly corroborate later, this does not mean that the good and the beautiful are equivalents or transformations of vital force. Higher animals, in being animals, spend their energy strictly on themselves; but the *surplus* of human energy makes man into a possible instrument of disinterested action and heroism.

No one among the wise has said such profound things concerning the economy of life and aesthetic disinterest as Schopenhauer. His pessimistic conception did not impede his genius from locating the very essence of the work of art. On the contrary, it was the reason that his philosophical speculations ascertained that in beauty there is a renunciation of the economic or animal ends of existence.

Ribot and other critics dismiss the aesthetics of *The World as Will and as Representation* as containing little originality. Croce scarcely does justice to the great philosopher [*al gran filósofo telematista*] in the historical part of the book titled *The Aesthetic as Science of Expression and General Linguistics*. In contrast, we believe that nothing has been written in this philosophical discipline that equals in force and truth what the great German philosopher teaches concerning the nature of the work of art and the feeling of the sublime. Bergson himself, in some of his most admirable pages on the sense and value of art, is a Schopenhauerian who freely interprets the work of the German master:

As a general rule, knowledge is always occupied in serving the will. Knowledge was born for this service and, in a sense, it has emerged from the will like the head from the body. In animals, this servitude can never be suppressed. In man, it may be suspended as an exception, as we will see in more detail in what follows....

Vulgar man, that wholesale product which nature manufactures by the thousands each day, is, as we have said, not capable, or at least not consistently capable, of completely disinterested apperception, which ultimately constitutes true contemplation. He can only direct his attention to things insofar as they have some relation to his will, however

[12] *Le Pragmatisme*, Introduction. [Bergson wrote the introduction, "Truth and Reality," to E. Le Brun's 1911 French translation of William James's *Pragmatism.*—Trans.]

indirect the relation may be. And from this point of view, which never demands more than the knowledge of relations, the abstract notion of the thing is sufficient and even preferable in the majority of cases. Vulgar man does not linger over the pure intuition, does not fix his gaze on an object for long, but instead hastily seeks the concept under which he may bring everything presented to him, like the lazy man seeks a chair, and then it is no longer his concern.

How could we more eloquently enrich the utilitarian, economic, egoist, and, in sum, biological essence of the concept? What else are the abstract ideas, the genera and species of logicians, the syntheses of abstract ideas that, when economized in a more abstract and general sense, constitute the sciences? In what form could we better declare that intelligence is an industry, an economy that obeys the imperative of the least effort and the most gain?

Schopenhauer adds:

> Thus vulgar man immediately ceases to contemplate whatever presents itself to him: an artistic creation, a beautiful work of nature, or any aspect of eminent importance from the scenes of life. Lingering over nothing, he seeks his path through life, or, at most, that which could be his path some-day, and gathers topographical information in the widest sense of the word. As for the contemplation of life itself, he does not waste his time on it.[13]

It has been sufficiently clarified that art is an opposition to material life, *an idealism or immaterialism*, a clear attitude that *renounces possessing in order to consecrate oneself to contemplating.* The more one renounces, the more completely one achieves an artistic spirit, to the point that if one were disinterested in all senses, one would become the supreme artist. As Bergson says,

> If the detachment were complete, if the soul were no longer clinging to action by any of its perceptions, it would be an artistic soul such as the world has never seen. This artist would stand out in all of the arts at the same time, or rather, would meld them all into one. This artist's soul would perceive all things in their original purity: the forms, colors, and sounds of the material world as well as the subtlest movements of interior life.[14]

---

[13] *The World as Will and as Representation*, Volume II of the Spanish translation, p. 33. [Caso's previous block quote from Schopenhauer is from the same volume.—Trans.]

[14] *Le rire. Quel est l'objet de l'art?* [Henri Bergson, *Laughter: An Essay on the Meaning of the Comic*, translated by Cloudesley Brereton and Fred Rothwell (New York: MacMillan, 1914). From the section "What is the Object of Art?"—Trans.]

Art is an *innate disinterest* that life does not explain; art demands enormous effort and its results are useless. Works of art *do not serve* the economy of existence.

The essence of genius consists in a superior aptitude for contemplation. Genius is nothing other than the most complete objectivity or the objective direction of the spirit in opposition to the subjective direction aimed at one's own person, toward the will. Genius thus consists in the faculty of maintaining oneself in pure intuition, of being entirely absorbed in it, and of separating knowledge from the will it was originally put in place to serve.[15]

If the aristocratic tone of the German philosopher is suppressed and one remembers that the *spiritual virginity* that Bergson speaks of is the genuine *treasure of the poor*, the inheritance of the cultured and the uncultured, of ancients and moderns; if one thinks about the fact that, from the cave-dweller to the contemporary European, art has been associated with humanity throughout history and prehistory; if one remembers that—whether as creator or as imitator, as actor or as admirer, as artist or as public, great or small, strong or weak—man has never completely been the *vulgar man* that Schopenhauer speaks of as totally imprisoned in his subjectivity, in his absolute animality; if one bears all of these limitations in mind, then one would have to admit and endorse Schopenhauer's affirmation of aesthetic truth.

The individuals of the human species are not divided into beasts and superhumans, into vulgar men and heroes. One could truthfully say that the vulgar man only exists in the minds of vulgar men. There is an immense gradation between the modest and the great, but each person is the master of lifting his head above his body (like the Apollo Belvedere that Schopenhauer discusses) in order to employ spirit in aesthetic contemplation, instead of inclining it toward the earth in the enduring search for sustenance (like the animals do). Artistic intuition is more evenly distributed than contemporary *aestheticism* believes it to be.

Economy of effort cannot explain this *innate disinterest* or artistic individuality, whether modest or brilliant. When compared to the biological imperative of minimum effort, art appears to be a shocking waste, a violent and mysterious antithesis.

It has been observed that ideas, whose sole mission is to explain things, are also employed to negate or hide them. Mind [*el espíritu*]—more loving of its abstract principles, of its symbols that are comfortable for intelligence—then prefers not achieving its objective to abandoning its attitude.

---

[15] *The World as Will*, Volume II, p. 30. [While remaining faithful to Schopenhauer's overall meaning, Caso has rearranged the text and rewritten it slightly to mend his own omissions.—Trans.]

The laws of adaptation, heredity, and struggle, which together produce *natural selection*, serve as an economic explanation of many aspects of existence, but they do not explain all of them. Nevertheless, intelligence persists in its monistic tendency, in its line of least effort, and, far from confessing its inability to explain disinterested activity by economic principles, tends to refer all experience to only one of its forms, to a single aspect of being, without remembering that reality does not exist in order to be explained by science. Rather, science exists to interpret, with the fewest possible imperfections, multiform and diverse reality.

Just as play is the biological antecedent to art, aesthetic contemplation or intuition engenders that kind of artistic feeling called the feeling of the sublime, which appears to be the closest aesthetic antecedent (not the cause) of moral activity. The sublime has been explained by Schopenhauer as a struggle between will and contemplation, between the desire to live seriously threatened by a great antagonistic force and the disinterested intuition of the object. The will is in danger, and in spite of this, it persists in contemplation. This state of consciousness is the sublime.

One notes, of course, its ethical character, its moral sense. The struggle in the sublime is between life, which wants to preserve itself above all else, and intuition, which occurs as a result of the *innate disinterest* that Bergson discusses. It is the conflict between subjective utilitarianism and innate idealism, the clash of two forms of existence that plays out on the stage of human consciousness. There is always a profound grandeur in the life of artists and poor geniuses, in a difficult or tragic life that sacrifices animal pleasure to disinterested contemplation. Humanity recognizes such lives as its most noble, most human exemplars, and perpetually honors them. They are sublime beings.

But the smallest act of charity is of an incomparably greater sublimity. For the artist sacrifices the economy of life to the objectivity of innate intuition, whereas the good man sacrifices egoism to come to the aid of the neighbor, to prevent his pain, and such a sacrifice is free. That is why Pascal said:

> All bodies, the firmament, the stars, the earth and its kingdoms, are not worth the least of minds [*los espíritus*], because the mind [*el espíritu*] knows all of this and knows itself but bodies do not. All bodies together, all minds together, and all of their productions are not worth the least movement of charity.[16]

[16] [This fragment from Pascal's *Pensées* is also Caso's epigraph. Here, Caso gives his own translation (or at least, we have been unable to find a published Spanish translation that matches exactly). Caso translates Pascal's French *esprit* straightforwardly in Spanish as *espíritu*, which we in turn translate as "mind" to reflect typical scholarly discussions of Pascal's three metaphysical levels or epistemological orders: body, mind, and heart (or charity). See, for example, Graeme Hunter, *Pascal the*

In sum, *the table of human values is this: the more one sacrifices and the more difficult it is to sacrifice merely animal life to disinterested ends—from aesthetic contemplation and ordinary good actions up to the point of heroic action—the nobler one is.*

God is this spirit of sacrificing what is one's own, this sublime inspiration, this higher and more energetic life, this being-possessed, this enthusiasm (understood in its purest etymological sense), which manifests itself by carrying out acts of charity.

Disinterest, charity, and sacrifice are irreducible to the economy of nature. As Schopenhauer says, if the world were only will, the fact that the will negates itself in sacrifice would be inexplicable. The world is the will of egoism and the *good will*, which is, moreover, irreducible to and in conflict with the will of egoism. This experientially proves that there is another order and another life, together with the order and life that govern with the iron fist of Darwin's savage imperative: the *struggle for life.* The equation of the good could thus be formulated:

$$\text{Sacrifice} = \text{Maximum Effort} \times \text{Minimum Gain}$$

The good is not an imperative, a law of reason, as Kant thought, but rather an enthusiasm. The good never commands; it inspires. It does not impose or come from the outside; it sprouts from within intimate consciousness, from the feeling that has its roots in the profundities of spiritual existence. The good is like music that captivates and charms—easy, spontaneous, intimate—the most intimate part of the soul. It is the coercion of neither pure reason nor external life. It is neither deduced, nor inferred, nor admitted; *it is created.* The good is freedom, personality, divinity. It is, to sum up with the expression of an illustrious Mexican thinker, "the supernatural that feels like the most natural thing in the world."[17]

The three classical virtues of Christianity are in obvious agreement. Charity is neither demonstrated nor deduced. It is the fundamental religious and moral experience. It consists in going out of oneself, in giving oneself to others, in offering oneself, in making oneself available and lavishing oneself without fear of exhaustion. This is, in essence, the Christian.

Philosopher: An Introduction (Toronto: University of Toronto Press, 2013), 159–169. Our decision to translate *espíritu* as "mind" in this particular passage (as opposed to most other places in the text, where we translate it as "spirit") also aims to foreground a philosophical problem of interpretation: Caso's discussion of divergent "orders" of existence does not seem to line up in any straightforward way with Pascal's, in spite of the fact that the epigraph from Pascal frames Caso's entire essay. It seems that for Caso, *espíritu* animates all three of Pascal's orders insofar as a person's spirit moves his or her body, mind, and heart. In contrast, Pascal believes that charity is a work of the heart rather than of the mind [*esprit*]. In short, Pascal believes that mind [*esprit*] is not responsible for charity, whereas Caso believes that spirit [*espíritu*] is responsible for charity, which leads us to believe that they are using the same word in their own respective languages differently.—Trans.]

[17] [The unnamed "illustrious Mexican thinker" is Justo Sierra (1848–1912).—Trans.]

For this one has to be strong, personal, *to be oneself*, as Ibsen would say.[18] The weak one cannot be Christian, except to the extent that one's aim in being strong is to offer oneself as a center of charitable activity.

In the universe as economy, each living being is a point of centripetal action. In the universe as charity, each moral being is a point of centrifugal action.

Nietzsche's "overman" [*Übermensch*], conceived in all of his magnitude of sacrifice, in all of his desire to elevate life, has what the Christian has of nobility. The overman's *longing for the other shore* is Christianity implausibly tied to a particular biological end, *not to a kind of contentment but rather to more power*, which is a vile economic interest of wild ferocious beasts.

The weak one who does not want to be generous, who as a victim of sloth is not even *himself*, cannot be heroic; and Christianity, like art, has heroic inspirations. Just as aesthetic errors (deficient or ineffective works) do not count in the history of the arts, moral vacillations (compromises with egoism) do not count for anything in the moral biography of a Christian.

Whoever lacks a charitable will does not live according to the doctrine of Christ. How could such a person live according to Christ's teaching, if Jesus was always action, never laziness; always heroism, never making deals or compromising with evil?

The illustrious Spanish thinker Diego Ruiz has properly explained how Christian humility, far from being an attribute of the weak, is a quality of the charitable, the strong, the heroic:

> I see clearly that there is no middle ground between these two primary movements called *pride* and *humility*, but I conceive of such a state, in which pride, as it is purified, is completely transformed in *work*. Consequently, the individual does not exist except for this work, *of which he is the son*, as one says precisely in Hebrew.
>
> This is how I interpret that essentially Christian virtue of humility, which is brought together in Christ with the repeated confession of being the son of the father and of having descended in order to save us.
>
> Each time a man goes out of himself and puts all of his pride into *work*, up to the point that he can feel and call himself the son of his work, I say that this man is Christian. I do not currently recognize a better explanation of the virtue of humility.[19]

---

[18] [Norwegian playwright and poet Henrik Ibsen (1828–1906). Caso is presumably referring to this line from his play, *Peer Gynt*: "To be oneself is to slay oneself."—Trans.]

[19] [The quoted passage is from *Jesus as Will: Dialectic of Christian Belief* (1906).—Trans.]

Humility is the other face of Christian charity and heroism. How could someone who is only conscious of himself to the extent that he collaborates in the work of the good fail to be humble? How will he who gives to others to the point of annihilation have pride? What would be the purpose of having pride? What would he be proud of? If he were proud, his feeling that he was keeping something for himself would be a sign that something spiritual had remained inactive, slothful, inert. He would not have been Christian to the extent that he failed to dedicate himself to liberating action.

Like struggle, charity is *a fact*. It is not demonstrated, it is practiced, *it is made*, like life. It is another way of life. You will never have the intuition of an order that is opposed to biological life, you will not understand existence in its profound richness, you will mutilate it beyond remedy, if you are not charitable.[20] Fundamental intuitions must be lived. He who does not sacrifice himself does not understand the whole world, nor is it possible to explain it to him, just as it is impossible to explain what sound is to a deaf person, or what light is to a person blind since birth. There is neither sight for the blind, nor hearing for the deaf, and neither morality nor religion for egoists. That is why you see egoists denying them. But just as the deaf person does not disprove the existence of music and the blind person does not disprove the existence of painting, the evil person does not disprove the existence of charity, the incomparable work of art. In order to comprehend existence as economy and as charity, as disinterest and as sacrifice, it is necessary to have all the facts and to consider man in his integrity as neither angel nor beast.

Faith is the confirmation that—alongside the world ruled by the natural law of life—there is a world ruled by the supernatural law of love.[21] The good is a contradiction in the face of life. For the believer, life is a pain that must be relieved, a pain that is essential to relieve. *Life always wants and the good always gives.* Believing in God is a direct consequence of doing good. If you are not charitable, you will not be believers.

"Only faith saves," says the Reformer. This is not true. Faith is impossible without charity, as light is impossible without the sun, as the corollary is impossible without the axiom. Because the corollary is in a way the axiom, but the axiom exists by itself; and the sun is in a way light, but the sun is the source and light its gleam—although

---

[20] [Each of the four verbs that appear in this sentence are written in the second-person plural, which has not appeared previously. This grammatical person, the formal but nonetheless personal addressee of Caso's message on charity, crescendos up through the subsequent presentation of the Beatitudes.—Trans.]

[21] [Up until this point in the text, Caso has been using "charity" [*la caridad*], but here he uses the more general term "love" [*el amor*] for the first time, suggesting in a broader way that the supernatural work of God and humans redeems, revolutionizes, or otherwise transforms the economic order of the world.—Trans.]

one could truly say that it all amounts to the same thing because faith is immediate, the concomitant of charity. Good works, when they are reflected in the consciousness of he who practices them, are faith itself:

> And if I have the gift of prophesy, and understand all mysteries, and all knowledge, and if I have all faith, so as to be able to move mountains, but do not have charity, I am nothing.
>
> And if I divide up all of my estate to give food to the poor; *and if I give my body over to be burned, but do not have charity, it is of no use.*[22]

Like charity, which is the crown of virtue, hope, the wisdom [*sagesse* in French] of the Christian is the most philosophical and thoughtful of all the virtues, much greater than Socratic wisdom. The astronomer believes in the return of celestial bodies for only one reason—because they have previously returned—and he hopes that they will consistently return in the same way. The believer believes in the perennial nature of the good—that the good will always return—for the same reason: because good actions were committed previously, are committed today, and will be committed tomorrow and forever.

There is no disorder in the world, only *diverse orders*, as Bergson would say. Sacrifice would be a disorder of life, which is pure economy. Life would be a disorder of charity. But the fact is that, to the postulate of the uniformity of nature, the postulate of the uniformity of charity should be added. Hope is an induction like the inductions of the sciences: the world and its laws on the one side, providence and its action on the other. He who hopes knows that today, tomorrow, and always men will sacrifice themselves to prevent the suffering of their neighbors; knows that men will always commit good actions; knows that spirits will always spend lavishly outside of themselves, that all moral value will be conserved indefinitely on God's diamond table. How could he not have this hope, if *he himself* is conscious of his capacity to do good insofar as he realizes it? "Charity," says Saint Paul, "never ends, even though prophecies will end, tongues will cease, and sciences will disappear."[23] And Chrysostom comments in his beautiful homily *De perfecta caritate*: "It is not words alone, but deeds, that teach charity."

There is, therefore, a single law of the moral world: love. Not the profoundly interested biological love that is, in short, hunger (economy of the species if not of the individual). Not love of what is near, but rather of the neighbor, *of the distant*, as Nietzsche would say. Not love of the flesh for pleasure, not love of the other sex nor love of family. Strictly speaking, there are no precepts of love, as

---

[22] 1 Corinthians 13:2–3.
[23] 1 Corinthians 13:8.

Stirner teaches. One loves because love is supernatural, because man is supernatural. This is the sense in which Jesus spoke: "Who is my mother, and who are my brothers?" And stretching out his hand toward his disciples, he said: "Here are my mother, and my brothers. . . . Because everyone who does the will of my father, who is in heaven, is my brother, and sister, and mother."[24]

According to Tolstoy's interpretation, enthusiasm, love, projection beyond oneself, and Christian charity must be pure; they must be free from all violence and all bargaining with life. There is nothing more undilutedly Christian than these paragraphs:

> That which men who do not understand existence call love consists in the predominance of certain conditions of personal well-being over any others. If the man who does not understand life says that he loves his wife, his children, his friends, he is only saying that the presence of his wife, his children, or his friends in his life improves his personal well-being.
>
> True love is the renunciation of personal well-being. It consists in a state of benevolence toward all men, such as that which is typical of children but only appears in adults through self-abnegation.
>
> What living man does not know—even if he has only felt it once during his earliest childhood—what man has not experienced this feeling of emotion, when one wants to love everything: neighbor, father, mother, brothers, evil men, dog, horse, grass? When one wants everything to go well, for everyone to be happy; even more, when one would like to find oneself in the situation of making everyone in the world happy; when one would like to sacrifice oneself, to hand over one's own life so that all would be well, overflowing with happiness? Precisely this, and this alone, is what constitutes the love that comprises human life.

Such is the Franciscan feeling of existence; such is the Saint of Assisi, the Christianizer of not only humanity but of all nature, the archetype of the contagious happiness of the Christian. In this way, the supernatural order falls upon the biological and inundates it with divine force.

> "Do not resist evil" signifies: never resist the evildoer. In other words, never do violence to another, that is, never carry out an act that contradicts love. Christian love does not prohibit the struggle against evil, but rather *the violent struggle* against evil.[25]

[24] Matthew 12:48–50.

[25] See *Anarchism According to Its Most Illustrious Representatives* by P. Eltzbacher, the entry marked "Tolstoy." [Caso is drawing upon a Spanish translation of Pablo Eltzbacher's German original, which

Tolstoy's doctrine is the systematic enunciation of the final verses of the fifth chapter of the *Gospel according to Saint Matthew*:

> You have heard that it was said to the ancients: eye for eye; tooth for tooth. But I say to you: *do not resist evil:* when facing anyone who strikes you on your right cheek, turn to him the other as well.
>
> You have heard that it was said: you shall love your neighbor, and abhor your enemy.
>
> Now I say to you: love your enemies, bless those who curse you, do good to those who abhor you, and pray for those who slander you and persecute you.
>
> In order that you may be sons of our father in heaven, who makes his sun rise on the evil and the good, and sends rain on the just and the unjust.
>
> For if you love those who love you, what reward will you have? Do not the tax collectors also do the same?
>
> And if you greet only your brothers, what more will you do? Do not the tax collectors also do this?
>
> Be, then, perfect, as your father in heaven is perfect.

Be perfect, that is to say, be active, charitable.[26] "Perfect" signifies the completion of action, accomplished, realized. It signifies everything *in actu*, nothing *in potentia*. God, according to Aristotle and Saint Thomas Aquinas, is *pure act*.

Be like God, the verse teaches. Be *pure act*, perfect in the accomplishment of your ends, within your limited perfection. Do not hold on to something virtual. Live in your works. Throw yourselves into constant charitable action, like our father in heaven who is perfect and *still works*, according to Jesus. This interpretation is deduced from the same expression of Matthew: "Be, then, perfect . . . ," as if to say, be lovers with no strings attached, without limit, without measure. Realize yourselves as abnegation.

consists largely of extended quotations from Tolstoy. The lines selected by Caso come from an 1884 work by Tolstoy that has been published in English under at least three different titles: *What I Believe; My Religion;* and *My Faith*. Eltzbacher's article is also Caso's source for the previous block quotation from Tolstoy's *On Life*.—Trans.]

[26] [Caso's imperative, "Be perfect," is addressed to all of his readers in the plural. It grammatically mirrors the quoted verses from Matthew, where all verbs also appear in the second-person plural, with some even repeating the subject—*vosotros* (the plural form of "you," i.e., "you all"), which is already contained in the verb endings—for emphasis. The full effect is lost in translation because standard English uses "you" for the second-person singular and plural interchangeably, and English verb endings do not communicate their subjects as clearly.

Reader:[27] what is said here is only philosophy, and philosophy is an interest of knowledge. Charity is action. Go and commit acts of charity. Then, more than sage, you will be saint. Philosophy is impossible without charity, but charity is perfectly possible without philosophy because philosophy is an idea, a thought, and charity is an experience, an action. Your century is egoist and perverse. Nevertheless, love the men of your century who seem no longer to know how to love, who only work by hunger and greed. He who commits a good act knows that the supernatural exists. He who does not do it will never know. All the philosophies of the men of science are worth nothing compared to the disinterested action of one good man.

[27] [Here and throughout his final paragraph, Caso calls each individual reader to a life of charity by using the second-person singular, which is a less formal and more intimate form of address. Caso's essay as a whole thus enacts an extended movement from the impersonal third-person world of existence as economy to the intimate second-person world of existence as charity, all subtly performed by shifts in verbal grammar. The beginning of Caso's essay is dominated by third-person impersonal verbs, which describe an economic world populated by egoistic creatures that are nevertheless devoid of personality. The middle of Caso's essay transitions away from this "vulgar" and impersonal consumer of the world to the artist, in whose soul the world still appears impersonally but now as beautiful in its own right, apart from any question of economic usefulness. The third and final part of the essay addresses readers in an increasingly personal way, with Caso moving from the second-person plural to the second-person singular in the final paragraph.—Trans.]

CHAPTER 4

Neither Irrationalism nor Rationalism but Critical Philosophy (1928)

José Romano Muñoz
Translated by Carlos Alberto Sánchez

José Romano Muñoz was born in Villa de Cos, Zacatecas, in 1890 and died in Mexico City in 1967. He studied under Antonio Caso and belonged, along with Samuel Ramos, to the philosophical generation known as the "Comtemporáneos," which began to promote the historicism and existentialism of José Ortega y Gasset. In addition to being a professor of philosophy at the National University from 1918 until his retirement in 1965, he served as director of Higher Education and Scientific Investigations in the Office of Public Education, as president of the Mexican Academy of Education, and he represented Mexico in UNESCO. Among his major works are El secreto del bien y del mal (The Secret of Good and Evil, 1938) and Hacia una filosofía existencial (Towards an Existential Philosophy, 1953).

An article published in a previous issue of this journal by my friend Samuel Ramos on certain philosophical matters has had the privilege of awakening a bit of interest in these kinds of question, something rare since Mexican culture, as is well known, is oriented more toward literature than it is toward philosophy.[1] The article in question is clearly written with the aim of striking a fatal blow to intuition as a method of knowledge. Its purpose is excellent, but, to tell the truth,

---

[1] [Ramos's article, to which Romano refers to throughout this essay, examined and criticized the philosophy of Antonio Caso and was published in 1927 in volumes I and II of the journal *Ulises*. Ramos's article is reprinted under the title of "*Hipótesis*" in *Obras completas*. Tomo I. *Prólogo de Francisco Larroyo*. México: Universidad Nacional Autónoma de México, 1985. pp. 73–74.—Trans.]

I do not think my dear friend succeeds at all. The blow is not as fatal as it may initially seem to people little versed in these matters. What we have here is a very valuable opinion that, frankly, is not decisive, something that has motivated me to write the following lines.

I belong to a group of thinkers who believe that a philosophical attitude is a temperamental thing. "The history of philosophy," as William James puts it, "considered in its greatest texts, is nothing but the clash of diverse human temperaments." In my opinion, there are two types of well-defined philosophical temperaments:

(a) the *rationalist temperament*, which includes two subtypes: the *empirical*, which enjoys sticking to facts (e.g., gnosiological Thomism[2]) and interpretations in a somewhat narrow manner, that is, within the marked horizons of natural science—all materialism, positivism, and naïve naturalism have their origins in this peculiar tendency; and the *intellectual*, a temperament inclined to critical observation, grand generalizations, conceptual evaluations, the structure of knowledge (this group includes idealists, realists, critics, phenomenologists, etc.);

(b) the *sentimental temperament*, which likewise includes a bifurcation of types: the *mystic*, whose sense of the numinous, of the cosmic, of the absolute, gives his thought a romantic, or better yet, a religious orientation; and the *intuitionist*, whose idiosyncrasy inclines him to subordinate the good of knowledge or the good of life, preferring instead to interpret reality through a certain kind of immediate, irrational evidence that relies on historical orientation, on artistic vision and superior instinct. The evidence of intuitionism is thought to be clear and insightful.

We can see how these classifications can help us to clarify sufficiently a few misunderstandings and thus save us from unnecessary commentaries. But personalities are not artifacts in a museum that easily fit into the rigid framework of a classification—much less when we are talking about personalities with as much complexity and richness as those that preoccupy me here. Thus, in the sense in which we can speak of a "style," of a "tone," of a peculiar "texture" of consciousness, Samuel Ramos is clearly of the *intellectual* temperament and, because of that, is a harsh critic of intuition.

It is not my purpose in what follows to engage in an exegesis, much less an apology, of Bergsonian philosophy, since Bergson, together with Spengler, Frobenius, Freud, Yung, Coué, Le Bon, Lenin, Mussolini, Wells, and Bernard Shaw, is one of those personalities that has powerfully communicated to this

---

[2] [*"El santotomasismo gnoseológico"* refers to the epistemological tradition derived from the theology of St. Thomas Aquinas.—Trans.]

generation the vital impulse of an actively historical character (as Count Hermann Keyserling puts it). No, my goal is to point out that intuition, understood as an epistemological method, is not negligible and, moreover, to affirm emphatically that Ramos's assertion, arrived at from a shallow and superficial study and restricted by the space available in a journal article, namely, that "the doctrine of metaphysical intuition must be strongly repudiated because its positive content is nil" is, frankly, one thought too many.

Moreover, the proponents of intuitionism do not possess such misology, such hatred toward reason. There is antipathy—again, this is a matter of temperament—there is distrust toward the purely speculative results of reason. See how, for instance, August Messer, an inscrutable "man of reason," expresses himself as a conspicuous representative of contemporary critical realism: "But, must we accept [the results of reason] simply because we are 'men of reason'? We may still discover through our philosophizing that the hidden development of human spiritual life depends not so much on what is theoretical and philosophical, but rather on a *sentimental estimation of objective values* and of a free and persistent will in the service of the realization of such values or ideals. What philosopher, if he values the rational unfolding of our cultural life could desire that men be merely philosophers?" Moreover, Count Keyserling writes, "the exclusive emphasis on [rational] intellectualism indirectly contributes to the speed in which man arrives at the conclusion that [rational] intellectualism does not close off the totality of life *but rather excludes what is most important*, because what remains excluded from consciousness will demonstrate its real character in more sinister ways, via the irrational and irresistible action of the unconscious."

Afterward, reason, which is incapable of exhausting the spiritual content of life, cannot choose itself as supreme arbiter of the total estimation of values which, as Ramos puts it, "is the main function of philosophical cognition."

Ramos goes on to say, "We admit, in sum, intuition as an instrument for the collection of facts about which reason must [necessarily] declare its final judgment." Anyone can see what this means, namely, that once those facts that intuition has collected in a manner that "by its mystery inspires distrust" are placed in the light of reason, it will subject them to the infallible mechanism of its categories, imposing upon them its royal seal and launching them into circulation as minted ideological coin of legal tender. And should reason be proud of this? Is it not clear that the primal matter—the substance of cognition—is given by intuition, and that the role of reason is merely instrumental, technical, of an industrial type for the manufacture of articles sold at wholesale, that its role is to give intuited facts the character of valid truth, that is, a truth good for all mankind?

Philosophy has as much vitality, as much humanity, as it has brilliance and as it has individual perspicuity [*clarividencia*]. For this purpose I present a concept that can provide a clue to many other things: *the genius*. The essence of the genius lies in clear-sightedness [*clarividencia*], in intuition. "The genius," we read in Ramos, "surpasses mere talent with the power to engender as an idea what nature has engendered as a physical thing; *as such, he does not know, he divines.*" Well, divining, inventing, intuiting—therein lies the true task of the philosopher.

The philosopher is charged with making intelligible—or what is the same, rational—a worldview to those of us who are still unable to sufficiently open the eyes of the spirit, just as the engineer is charged with building bridges for the benefit of those who are born blind to mathematics. Being illogical, a-systematic, contradictory, irrational, Nietzsche is a *philosopher*, as opposed to, for example, Spencer, who is so rational, so logical, so consequential, but—oh!—so ignorant of philosophy, that is, so ignorant of wisdom.

Invention and *criticism*—here we have the two necessary and irreplaceable ingredients for a philosophical interpretation of reality. After summaries, after the rich and productive apprehension in the deepest chasm of the real, then we have the labor of classification, of selection, of purification. The philosophical genius invents, intuits, and discovers new truths or horizons; the philosophical technician purifies, decants, makes a task of limitations and critical refinements. Both clearly complement each other, but they do not exclude each other. To make philosophy a purely critical task would be to condemn it to an irremediable infertility.

Hence, it is one thing to philosophize [*filosofar*] and another to do philosophy [*hacer filosofía*], just as it is one thing to organically cultivate the earth for sugarcane and another to seize it mechanically in the sugar mill. It will be objected that just as civilization would be impossible without the industrial manipulation of raw materials, culture would likewise be impossible without this kind of socialization (i.e., the economic production and distribution of the fruits of knowledge).

Very well, then. Intuition and reason, collaborating together in the process of purifying [*decantación*] human cultural values—in science, morality, art, religion—that is the best case scenario [*miel sobre hojuelas*]. But attributing a renegade function to intuition, just like that, and without due process, while this is permissible as a political procedure, it is not as a legal maneuver in the civil war of ideas.

"The sole function of philosophy," writes Ramos, "is to formulate judgments of value through which it attributes essential categories to intuited givenness." From the point of view of pure reason, to reach the essential, the intimate, the simple, the irreducible of a thing, does not require any judgment of value; it requires a simple analytical process of dissection. Reasoning is a different kind of operation than valuing, and if the purpose of philosophy is rational knowledge, then valorization is disqualified as the proper function of philosophy. To value is not to measure, or compare, or purify; it is to esteem, and to esteem is to glance at the non-real properties that reside in things and that make of those things something estimable, valuable.

Moreover, if what is essential is synonymous with what is real, pure reason is incapacitated by nature itself, which limits its function to reach essences, that is, that which is real in things. "Essences," Husserl affirms, "that is, the real content of objects are neither general nor individual; they are ultimate facts that are neither susceptible to proof nor in need of it; they can only be presented or brought to evidence." For pure reason, what is essential is what is ideologically simple or irreducible in things. This is why the great labor of reason is the definition, that is, the rational apprehension of what is essential, what is real. But between conceptual and real reality there is an abyss, an abyss that only intuition can bridge.

Intuition is the conformity of intelligence with instinct. Instinct is the wisdom of life applied to the organic realization of its own designs; that is why, without knowledge, the insect executes acts of a consummate wisdom. Instinct is, then, the clear-sightedness [clarividencia] of life itself, but working through an agent who is blind, unconscious, and unintelligent. Intelligence, on the other hand, as clarity and awareness, lacks wisdom. Intelligence is able, but not wise. Life, then, fully considered, turned over onto itself through intelligence, that is, instinct turned intelligent, reflected onto the vital content of phenomena, constitutes the desideratum as a source of cognition, since it now comes to fill the abyss that stretched between the subject that thinks and the subject that lives.

This means that the real philosophical method, the method belonging solely to philosophy, as has already been declared by Antonio Caso in his "Philosophical Problems," is that which, taking advantage of intuited facts, submits them to a conscious critical examination that will delimit, clarify, and fix the truth contained in intuition; or better yet, that which, utilizing the facts of intelligence, is capable of overcoming its own merely conceptual content through the rectifying process of intuition.

I believe that a less literal, more generous, interpretation of Bergson will bring about a better estimation of his method and his philosophical thought. Particularly in psychology, he has made truly significant contributions. He has proposed the objectivity of memory as the foundation of psychology, perhaps dealing a mortal blow to psycho-physiology. He has broken, moreover, with the traditional idea of the temporal category so as to reveal it for what it is, as pure duration (durée reelle). He has undone the Gordian knot in his chapter on "Freedom," defending it not as a problem, but as a primary fact of the spirit, a revelation of transcendent importance for ethics and general metaphysics. Within cosmology, he has established the basis for an intuitive synthesis of the vital process in nature that allows combination, integrating the scientific theory of evolution with the cosmological thesis of becoming, not in the mechanistic sense nor as finalism, but in the sense of a "creative evolution."

Finally, in aesthetics (i.e., in his "Laughter"), Bergson delivers a valuable essay on the value of the comic on objective grounds, which gives us insight into the possibilities of his method when applied to art in general. As such, if a method of investigation is to be judged based on its results, we can well see that intuition cannot be so severely condemned as something negligible because it is useless or fruitless.

For his part, Spengler has intuited historical content as a cultural process in which "cultures" have the significance of real spiritual organisms under the control of biological rhythms . . . [referring to] a morphological law through which it is possible to predict the future. At the same time, he has brilliantly established that nature's supreme law is causality and that what corresponds to it in history is the *either–or*, [that is,] "the necessity of life, felt as an internal *direction*, but not considered by the intellect as an *end*." And we must concede that, whether or not we agree with his naturalist conception of the world (since, as Messer writes, "to consider the spiritual development as a natural process is to be ignorant of its essence"), Spengler is formidable, a true mountain, an authentic success in the world of culture. There lies, without going too far off base, sufficient material for Keyserling later to develop, and free from Spengler's pessimism, his admirable philosophical interpretation of history in *The World That Is Born*, a book in which, on my view, one can find the key and the method for an irreproachable vision of history as a process of cultural values.

Two more important points by way of conclusion. The first point, which Ramos announces in a subtitle, is that "intuition is not a gnoseological theory." Obviously. Neither is reason. Of no cognitive method can one affirm that. A method can have as a philosophical foundation a theory of knowledge (a gnoseological doctrine), but we must not confuse one with the other. As such, then, this new charge against intuition is not valid.

Finally, the penultimate epigraph is subtitled, "Return to Reason," which is intelligently suggestive and tendentious (anyone can see that it reveals a cordial hatred toward intuition), from which the idea that "irrationalism" is synonymous with philosophical barbarism, if not with "educated idiocy," implicitly appears to emerge. And—for goodness sake!—it is quite something to decide to apply such a stringent qualifier to such solid and level heads as those of Spengler and Bergson!

Further on in the article, one is assured that "[irrationalism] is only a small step from a deep hatred toward civilization." I truly believe that this consequence is disproportionate in relation with the premise [that suggests a] "hatred toward reason," which is, if anything, unproven. In effect, whoever has read Spengler will have a hard time concluding that it is due to a hate of reason that he affirms that we live in a historical moment of decadence. On the contrary, with the help of reason, he examines the available evidence to arrive logically at his conclusion.

This is an opposite thesis to that unfortunate thesis of Lathrop Stoddard in "Rebellion against Civilization." In any case, this hatred toward civilization—the cause, according to Stoddard, of the contemporary worldwide revolution—is conceivable in the subhuman [*infrahombre*], but not in the most conspicuous representatives of our culture.

However, in philosophy, as in everything else, style imposes itself and we must remember that Bergson has gone out of style. At the same time, I believe that the moment has come to renovate philosophical thought in Mexico with the new and productive orientations in Germanic cultural science (day by day Germany appears to revive the spirit of the "good ol' days" of Kant and Hegel), as well as with the very rich Italian philosophical archive of the postwar era— which is not well known among us—while not forgetting the contributions of North and South America.

I believe that my friend Samuel Ramos has decided to cut ties with intu-itionism because he believes, perhaps rightly so, that among us (lazy and apathetic as we are) intuition, so successfully defended and promoted by the great Antonio Caso, is a species of neurotoxin [*tósigo enervante*] that has the effect of rendering us useless in the task of cultural construction, since intuition, ultimately, lacks a solid intellectual ground. I do believe that he is more than justified in thinking so. It is a danger already alluded to by the eminent José Ortega y Gasset in his "Letter to a Young Argentinian Who Studies Philosophy" when he says, "You [and your culture] are more *sensible* than you are *precise*, and if this stays as it is, you will continue to depend on Europe in the intellectual realm—the only one that matters. This because, in being sensible, any rich or elegant idea that is produced in Europe will move your sensuous receptors, whether you want it to or not. But in trying to react to the received idea—to judge it, refute it, value it, or oppose it—you will find within yourselves that imprecision, that vagueness. Let us call it by its name: you will find a lack of a clear, firm, and secure criterion that can only be obtained through rigorous disciplines."

CHAPTER 5

Twenty Years of Education in Mexico (1941)

Samuel Ramos

Translated by Robert Eli Sanchez, Jr.

Samuel Ramos Magaña was born in Zitácuaro, Michoacán, in 1897 and died in Mexico City in 1959. He studied at what is today known as University of Michoacán de San Nicolás de Hidalgo, which is considered the oldest institution of higher education in the Americas. Although he began to study philosophy in Morelia, Michoacán, under a well-known positivist, José Torres Orozco, it wasn't until he attended the lectures of Antonio Caso at the School of Higher Studies in Mexico City that he decided to pursue a career in philosophy. (He briefly studied to be a medical doctor.) In 1927, Ramos began to criticize the philosophy of Caso in the journal Ulysses *and sought what he considered to be a more rational approach to philosophy. In 1940, six years after he published his most influential book,* Profile of Man and Culture in Mexico *(1934), he began to teach aesthetics and the history of Mexican philosophy at the Faculty of Philosophy and Letters (Ffyl), where he would earn his Ph.D. in 1944. He was director of the Ffyl from 1945 to 1952, and became a member of the National College (Colegio Nacional), a prestigious Mexican honorary academy. He is best known for his work on the philosophy of Mexican culture, which he attempted to universalize into a new kind of humanism in* Toward a New Humanism *(Hacia un nuevo humanismo, published in 1940). For a later work on aesthetics, see* Philosophy of an Artistic Life *(filosofía de la vida artística, published in 1950).*

Vasconcelos and the Revolution in Education

Here I will consider the problems of education in Mexico, offering a critical examination of the various systems that have followed the education reform of Vasconcelos.[1,2] My aim is to shed some light on a subject that has become

[1] This brief history of education was published as a series of articles in the magazine *Hoy* in 1939.

[2] [In 1920, José Vasconcelos briefly served as the rector of the National University before being named secretary of public education by Alvaro Obregón in 1921. For a brief autobiographical

confused in recent years. Education is a problem of national interest that should not be subordinated to the passions of party politics because it involves the destiny of millions of human beings who await adequate preparation to confront life in the future. A country's dominant system of education cannot be chosen freely according to personal ideas and tastes, as if man could easily be shaped by any form of culture. A nation like ours, which, for a variety of reasons, has acquired a certain personality, is only receptive to a particular culture, one that responds to the peculiar demands of its character and the environment in which it exists. As long as educators are not familiar with the Mexican character, so that they might adapt their teaching to it, their work will be a blind effort that puts the fate of those under their care in danger.

During the colonial period and the early years of the Republic, the Church was almost exclusively in charge of education in our country. Only after 1857 did the State take charge of this function of culture. The idea that the State has an obligation to educate the people was adopted by the Encyclopedists before the French Revolution, and was then enshrined as law in the constitutions of democratic countries. After the Reform, the Mexican State's education policy was that of secularism, that is, it was neutral with regard to religious instruction. In fact, Mexico's administrations, including that of Porfirio Diaz, were relatively unconcerned with popular education and preferred to attend to higher education, which was available only to a privileged minority. Notwithstanding the exceptional gifts of a secretary of education like Don Justo Sierra, who surely must have understood the needs of the country, educational initiatives were limited to the capital of the Republic. During the Carranza administration, it was believed that public education should remain the responsibility of municipalities, following the United States, so the Department of Public Education was eliminated. This was the state of affairs in Mexico when José Vasconcelos was named head of national education.

Destiny brought a philosopher—as Vasconcelos himself has said—to the great task of educating a nation. Magnanimously, he knew how to fulfill the responsibility that fell upon his shoulders. The project which began at that time represents a major event in the nation's history, and Vasconcelos became, on account of his brilliant vision, one of America's great national educators, along with Sarmiento and Andrés Bello. To be sure, in his work, man and work became one, as in artistic creation. This is the only way to explain the love, strength, and enthusiasm with which Vasconcelos worked and which he imparted on those he supervised. He managed to interest everyone in the problems of education

account of his education reform, see José Vasconcelos, *A Mexican Ulysses: An Autobiography*, trans. W. Rex Crawford (Bloomington: Indiana University Press, 1963).—Trans.]

and in discussing them publicly, which at that time lent intellectual life a tone of vitality. Because even when Vasconcelos's proposal was focused primarily on instruction, he continued to endorse and defend philosophy, literature, and art. The renaissance in Mexican painting will forever be associated with his name.[3]

Vasconcelos's personality united a realism [*sentido de realidad*] with an idealism that sometimes soared to mystical heights. But his mysticism was not contemplative; it was dynamic, with the drive of a powerful will, which was overwhelming, like a force of nature. He was a man possessed by a demonic spirit, one that inspired fear in those who surrounded him. When he was mad, there was a blaze in his eyes, and his words were fire, like those of the biblical prophet. After a violent explosion, his countenance would become serene, leaving a mysterious light in his eyes, the indefinable expression of a visionary. First in the University, and later in the Ministry of Public Education, he would work feverishly, at a fast pace, to organize and occasionally initiate new activities, all thought through by Vasconcelos, down to the smallest detail.

It was necessary to restore the Ministry of Public Education, eliminated by Carranza, since without this apparatus no state-sponsored education initiative is possible. This is how Vasconcelos expresses the situation in his book *From Robinson to Odysseus*, a work in which he retrospectively develops his definition of and blueprint for education:

> Every nation needs a central and well-funded agency to make possible
> a wide-ranging education reform that is capable of influencing public
> life. And it is the job of this agency, generally called the Ministry of
> Education, to show us the general direction of educational policy and
> methods. This agency is also responsible for assuring the cohesion of
> what is taught in the distinct faculties and schools. It is not a question
> of knowing whether the actual performance of a Ministry of Education
> is desirable or not; the possibility of substituting it does not exist today.
> Independently of whether the State is qualified to educate, it must be
> recognized that only the State provides or can provide the funds neces-
> sary for meaningful change in education.

From the beginning, Vasconcelos's project could be interpreted as a social movement to destroy the idea that school is for the privileged, to make education a

---

[3] [One of the many movements to emerge from Vasconcelos's tenure as secretary was Mexican muralism, much better known perhaps than the education reform that stimulated and supported it. As Vasconcelos was a proponent of informal education, he commissioned Mexico's great artists— most notably Diego Rivera, José Clemente Orozco, and David Alfaro Siqueiros—to visually represent Mexican history and identity, particularly what they took to be the ideals of the Revolution of 1910, in public spaces. Their frescoes were not without political controversy.—Trans.]

benefit for everyone, regardless of social class. His strategy for education was essentially popular, leaning toward the education of the masses. For a moment he even had to neglect higher education, the University itself, for the benefit of elementary school, primary education. It was necessary to provide primary education throughout the entire country, to send teachers to the most remote villages, which had never had a school.[4] The federalization of education provided the indispensable legal means to give the government jurisdiction everywhere in the country where the influence of local agents of education did not reach. The success of this movement, which was a response to a national need, is demonstrated by the fact that, since then, the sphere of federal educational initiatives has had to increase continually. Vasconcelos began where he had to, at the very bottom: combating illiteracy. He then continued with primary schools, which not only needed to be multiplied, but whose guidelines and methods also had to be modified. Perhaps the methods and systems that were used were not the most adequate or the most efficient to achieve its aims, according to the opinion of specialists. But there is no doubt that the aim that inspired reform emerged from a profound understanding of the needs of the Mexican people. In my judgment, Vasconcelos was the first to understand this very simple truth (so simple that nobody had seen it): that what most urgently has to be taught to the Mexican people is how to live. Because although it seems that knowing how to live is a question of instinct, what is certain is that all peoples require long and painful experience to learn the science of life. There we find our people, who know how to *endure* life, which is not the same as knowing how to *live*, but rather, knowing how to die, which is the negation of all wisdom.

We must distinguish the intention of Vasconcelos's project from its realization. His education proposal is surely the wisest, the most just, the most Mexican of all the proposals one can think of. He created the school for small-scale industry, the technical school aimed at training technical specialists and qualified workers in tune with the demands of Mexico's industrial development. He also created the school for agriculture in order to pull the peasant farmer out of his primitive methods of cultivation. The rural school also represents Vasconcelos's outreach effort to educate. Inspired by the example of the great Spanish missionaries who brought European culture to America, he also promoted what he called the "missionary teacher," in order to bring education to those regions in the country farthest from all of civilization.

Vasconcelos could not forget one of the most important roles of schooling: aesthetic education. He convinced an entire people to sing their own songs, which they previously had scorned. Mexican music and popular art are now

---

[4] [Between 1920 and 1924, as many as 1,000 rural schools and 2,000 libraries were established.—Trans.]

valued and in fashion thanks to Vasconcelos. He protected and promoted them by all the means at his disposal. That is why his project is genuinely Mexican—national. But, at the same time, his ideal was set on widening the narrow limits of nationalism. He explained it this way: "Motivated by an eagerness to lend education the ideal that it lacked, I made another desperate attempt. It consisted in widening the nationalist program, grounding it in [our] language and blood." Returning to the Spanish tradition, he tried to revive the relationship with all other Spanish-speaking countries and to make Hispano-Americanism a greater kind of patriotism.

A project of national education of this magnitude is not something that can be realized overnight, but through many years of continuous labor. If many of Vasconcelos's ideas failed or could not be brought to fruition, that is only because of the short time he had in which to realize them.

What is regrettable is that he did not remain firmly in charge of the Ministry of Education, looking after his project, allowing it more time to mature, and correcting it as was necessary. The interruption of the project by the labor of subsequent regimes, often destructive, was the reason that Vasconcelos's vision was not completely realized. However, it can be argued, as we will see, that everything good [in education reform] that has been done since is an extension of Vasconcelian ideas, and that the Secretariat retains in its general features the structure that Vasconcelos gave it. The only difference is that when he was at the head of national education, one could feel that it was inspired by a strong spiritual impulse, that there was an intelligence—a wise director—throughout. [. . .]

The Phantom of Socialist Education

"Socialist education" was inherited by the present regime from *Callismo*.[5] The aim was originally to establish in Mexico an "ideological" dictatorship, sanctioned by law and according to the political orientation of the State, without taking into account the fact that this contradicted the spirit of the Constitution [of 1917]. This aim was realized without consulting the leading experts, specialists in education, and without knowledge of the actual problems with the country's education. It was education reform forged in the fire of demagoguery and in which, consequently, sectarian passion intervened more than reflective intelligence. Its authors were, for the most part, ignorant in matters of education,

---

[5] By "present," I am referring to the government of [Lázaro] Cárdenas. [By *Callismo*, Ramos is referring to the long rule of Plutarco Elías Calles, who was president of Mexico during 1924–1928, but whose social and political influence between 1928–1934 bordered on that of a dictator. The period of Calles's influence and the various reforms that he spearheaded is known as *el maximato*.—Trans.]

blinded by a phrase whose significance they did not believe they needed to ascertain before converting it into law.[6]

The reform was begun hastily, a rash movement that did not want to listen to any enlightened or prudent opinion. It was believed that a revolution in public consciousness was in the making, without realizing that such revolutions cannot be ordered by decree, least of all in Mexico, where one of history's successful achievements has been to convince the working classes of the sovereignty of consciousness and freedom of thought. They can deny the Mexican people many liberties, but freedom of thought is a right that cannot be taken away.

Once the reform designated in Article 3 became a reality, those in charge of putting it into practice, that is, the teachers, did not understand what about it made it "socialist." They would ask the more educated among them, those better informed, but nobody knew what it meant; they had never heard anyone explain such a thing. Authorities on education set out to investigate it, but to no avail, because they did not know what it meant either. A number of teachers believed they could settle their doubts by reading the essential works of socialist literature, but after doing so, they were met with more disappointment, because it contained nothing of what they were looking for. So what went wrong? What happened was that a name was given to something that, in reality, did not exist. "Socialist education" was nothing but a phantom, though they were very careful not to call it that. The law is the law and must be obeyed.

The law suggests various aims of socialist education, the first of which is to combat religious fanaticism. In Mexico, such a Jacobin attitude represents the substance of the old Liberal and Positivist schools, now re-baptized under the name of "socialism." But one of the most important goals of socialist education, its fundamental ideological basis, is the following: to give pupils "a rational and exact conception of the universe." But I wonder if such an aim is not perhaps the intention of all schooling that is not denominational, even though the current state of human knowledge cannot achieve that ideal. The previous phrase—[a rational and exact conception of the universe]—either is a puerility, or it bears witness to a total lack of awareness of the possibilities of human reason. What

[6] [In 1933, the National Revolutionary Party (*Partido Nacional Revolucionario* or PNR), later named the Institutional Revolutionary Party (*Partido Revolucionario Institucional* or PRI) nominated Lázaro Cárdenas as their presidential candidate. As part of its platform, the PNR intended to teach socialist doctrine in primary education, complete with a socialist curriculum, as well as enforce Article 3 of the 1917 Constitution, which states that public education recognized by the State will be secular, democratic, national, and free. On October 11, 1934, just before Cárdenas was elected president of Mexico, Congress approved the following amendment of Article 3: "Education provided by the State will be socialist and, in addition to removing all religious doctrine, will combat fanaticism and prejudice, for the sake of which the school will organize its instruction and activities in such a way that builds in the youth a rational and exact concept of the universe and social life."—Trans.]

scientific or philosophical doctrine is capable of offering that conception of the universe? The law, then, asks of the Mexican school what no law in the world would dare to ask: to teach the absolute truth. Here the authors of the law reveal a complete lack of intellectual maturity; the phrase sounds like that of a student who believes that with a manifesto she can change the face of the world or reform the universe.

What is absolute truth? "Dialectical materialism" perhaps? But dialectical materialism is not a scientific doctrine. It is a philosophical interpretation that rests on very controversial metaphysical presuppositions—for example, that physical matter possesses a rational principle. Aside from its naiveté, an echo of positivism can be found in the preceding phrase. Perhaps what the authors of the law wanted to say—but did not so as not to make their thought sound pedantic—was that the "socialist school" should teach a *scientific* conception of the universe. But in that case what would be the difference between a socialist and a positivist school? Is the socialist school the only one that until now has tried to provide a scientific education? If this is supposed to be the novelty of the socialist school, then it forces us to take a step back to the times of Juárez and Porfirio Díaz, and a school that takes us backward is a reactionary school!

But the phrase "socialist education" not only suggests a doctrine, but also, more than anything, a method—a new system of instruction that encompasses every aspect and level without restriction. So, what does "socialist education" mean for mathematics, for the physical and natural sciences, for the teaching of the manifold branches of culture? Does science not have an objective value that is the same for all schools and all systems of education? I do not think a school that is based in the "rational and exact knowledge of the universe" can be thought of any other way. If one accepts Marx's dogma concerning a "bourgeois culture," we are left with nothing, because even Marxism and socialism itself are the fruit of the modern European bourgeois spirit. That is why a "socialist education" that rejects everything about bourgeois culture must end up empty-handed. This has been the case in Mexico.

I have just demonstrated how the words "socialist education" do not refer to anything. It is not that I am an enemy of socialist education: it is not possible to be the enemy of something that does not exist. What I am an enemy of is mystification and deception. Besides all political sectarianism, there is a national interest bound up in this issue; put at risk is the destiny of a generation, which cannot be sacrificed for the sake of an experiment in education. If someone thinks that I am wrong, they may teach me what "socialist education" is. And let them not tell me that it is the system or systems of education instituted in Soviet Russia, because on this point the Russians have not invented a new system. They have simply established an educational dictatorship that keeps the youth ignorant of any beliefs that the Communist Party considers heresy, that could cause students to stray from its fundamental political directives. This system is not new; it was invented by the Catholic Church in the Middle Ages and is still practiced in its schools and seminaries. It is the system of all dictatorships. It is the system of Hitler's Germany, of Mussolini's Italy, and also of Franco's Spain.

Mexican schools have followed two paths after the reform of Article 3. Faced with the impossibility of meeting demands that cannot be fulfilled by anything, they have considered the law a dead letter, and have continued employing traditional systems. That is why all the fuss that has been stirring around "socialist education" is unsubstantiated. In reality, after a brief lapse of demagoguery, once the passions have settled a bit, schools return to the same path as always and continue on as if there had never been education reform. Some schools, perhaps the minority, in which one finds persons who have no other way of standing out than making displays of radicalism, while also facing the impossibility of realizing "socialist education," eliminate everything having to do with education and substitute it with the political propaganda of an unparalleled extremism. The most harmful ambiguity that the reform has produced in the deepest recesses of the teacher's mind is the confusion of propaganda with education—the teacher with the leader. I do not think "socialist education" is the name for teaching only socialism. The name for that is "socialist propaganda by means of school." In short, there is no, there can be no, "socialist education." The only thing that can be—and this is something very different—is "socialist politics in education." But this cannot be written into law, just as the government's general political orientation cannot, because it is something that essentially changes, and the law should remain free to respond to the movements of social reality.

Today, for instance, the law is an obstacle to correcting all the errors of reforming education for the sake of national culture. If I were asked what is a socialist policy in education, I would not find a better answer than to refer the reader to Vasconcelos's great reform in education, which, given its aim of bringing education to the popular masses and giving them the knowledge necessary for their development, deserves the name "socialist." I am not saying that Vasconcelos's program is perfect; one would also have to take into account the additions and adjustments of other ministers who understood the problems of popular education, such as Sáenz, and much later, Bassols. Nor am I saying that an intelligent socialist policy would be enough to solve all the problems of education in Mexico. True education reform, that which gets to the bottom of the problems of national culture, has yet to be achieved. It would be that reform which, on the basis of a profound understanding of the Mexican spirit, tried to correct its vices and develop its virtues, aiming toward the creation of a new type of human, superior to the existing one. The system of education sought would be that which would yield to the Mexican race its greatest fruits. Such education could not be purely intellectual [espiritual], but neither could it be purely material; neither oriented only toward technology, nor only toward spiritual culture. Rather, it would be oriented toward the formation of men, in the complete sense of the word. Now is moment to overcome partial points of view and to fuse them in an all-embracing synthesis.

Notwithstanding its recent futility, education reform has the value of a symptom that denounces the deep social and spiritual crisis that has plagued the contemporary world. Many standards and values have lost their validity; the structure of society itself is affected down to its very foundation. Nobody knows exactly what's going to happen tomorrow and, meanwhile, men march on disoriented, without reliable standards of existence, groping around as if in a dark forest, *che la diritta via era smarrita*.[7] The feeling of confusion and misdirection was manifest in the Mexican consciousness, which anxiously searches for the common thread to escape the chaos. The movements of reform in education represent nothing other than the frustrated attempts to overcome its crisis. But as there has only been reform in name only, and things continue as before, the problems that constitute the origin of this crisis remain. The only thing for sure in such movements is the concern and need for reform. Until now, we have waved our arms about desperately, castaways in search of salvation. But it is better not to latch onto an empty solution [*no asirse de un clavo ardiendo*]. What makes the situation especially critical is that the values of the future have yet to be discovered, and that we should create the standards ourselves.

In Mexico, Marxism has represented the easiest and most comfortable solution. It has come to fill an intellectual vacuum with its ready-made formulas that are taken for the definitive truth and which give the illusion that every problem is resolved. This path of least resistance is, of course, the most attractive to lazy thinking, which has slept peacefully stretched out above Marxism, without a trouble or worry in the world. But life itself interrupts that dream with its harsh realities. Each day that passes reveals the inefficiencies of formulas, the inaccuracy of predictions. Life experience teaches that it is necessary to think about real problems directly and resolve them according to their own demands. Education reform is a great lesson that shows precisely what the results are of solving a problem a priori, on the basis of ideological prejudice, without being familiar with the facts and empirical necessities.

Of one thing I am convinced: we will not make it through our crisis with imported doctrines, with ready-made formulas. There is a difficult, but inevitable, task ahead of us: that of creating our own standards and doctrines. We have to commit ourselves tirelessly to this work, without worrying about whether we are called "revolutionaries" or "reactionaries," since, in the end, those names are

[7] [This is a reference to the first few lines of Dante's *Divine Comedy*: "Midway upon the journey of life/I found myself within a dark forest, / For the straightforward path had been lost."—Trans.]

misleading labels, mere political fictions. The important thing is to think about the nation's problems objectively, not on the basis of our interests or personal passions. As long as we live plagiarizing and imitating the foreigner, we are lost. A nation's destiny depends on nothing other than itself, on the potential of its own mind and well-practiced and disciplined will. At this point we should not try to solve our problems with culture and education blindly, because it would be unforgivable to repeat the same mistakes. We will prove our intellectual maturity by honestly recognizing our failures and converting them into standards of what we should not do. On that the salvation of Mexico depends.

CHAPTER 6

The History of Philosophy
in Mexico (1943)

Samuel Ramos

Translated by Robert Eli Sanchez, Jr.

Prologue

During the year of 1941, the author of this book wanted to establish a course in the history of philosophy in Mexico at the Faculty of Philosophy in the University of Mexico. The project was made possible under the auspices of the College of Mexico, though there were few students at the time because the majority of them were suspicious of the topic.[1] They did not believe that there was an abundant philosophical past in our country that merited its own history. In 1942, during the winter session at the Faculty of Philosophy, the author was able, in a short time, to develop a course in the history of philosophy in Mexico, which was received with much interest. The material now included in this book is the result of that pedagogical project.

I have wanted to write a history of philosophy in Mexico for a long time, to look for a tradition that could lend a sense of nationality to the recent philosophical movement that has been growing and deepening in our country. Philosophy in Mexico was practiced before the founding of the Pontifical University in 1553, and has continued to be studied in our colleges and universities ever since. This fact alone suggests that philosophy has been thoroughly absorbed by Mexican culture, as would any activity that has continued for four centuries almost without interruption. It has always seemed to me that one of the ways of doing Mexican philosophy is to reflect on our own philosophical reality, the reality of Mexican philosophers and their ideas, to find out if there

---

[1] [Here Ramos is referring to the *Universidad Nacional Autónoma de México* (UNAM), located in Mexico City and founded in 1910, as well as the *Colegio de México*, also located in Mexico City and founded in 1940.—Trans.]

are dominant features that characterize a national mind. For the realization of that project, I had been interested in the idea that a general history of our philosophical past could only be established after undertaking a series of individual studies of epochs and particular philosophers. Of course only a collective effort can carry out this task, but not without first awakening an interest in this kind of study, little appreciated in our philosophical environment. I was soon convinced that a hypothetical history of philosophy was not enough to activate the desire to undertake such individual studies and that it was necessary to follow the opposite path. So I thought that a general panorama of the history of philosophy in Mexico, however imperfect it might be, would be the best impetus for research on this topic, and that it was precisely its deficiencies that are indispensable to proposing the concrete issues that demand deeper study. [. . .]

It is only natural that the interest in philosophy in Mexico, like everywhere, has had its highs and lows, which indicate shifts in the internal tensions of intellectual forces, driven by different historical pressures. Philosophical activity in our country, it should be noted, has not been confined to academic forms of development, even though it has had to begin there. The myth that the Hispanic race and its American branch have not been endowed with rational thought is an unjust exaggeration that needs to be corrected. Our history proves that ideas have shaped reality, even if not as decisively as other human factors. At any rate, there is a backdrop of philosophical ideas, more or less visible, in the great social and political events of Mexican history that reveals a concern for adjusting life to certain intellectual norms. Nobody can deny the existence of philosophy in our culture, and that's why it is not futile to make philosophy in Mexico the object of its own history.

But then one has to look for philosophical ideas not only in the works of specialists, written for the most part by professors of philosophy, but also among the ideas of humanists, scientists, politicians, educators, moralists, and so on. What has to be investigated in those philosophical ideas is not the originality of innovative thought, since our history derives from the currents of European ideas, but [the originality of] the peculiar form in which these ideas have been reflected in our intellectual life. The truly important thing in our philosophical history is to demonstrate which ideas or doctrines have contributed to the development of the character of our being and of our national culture, and how they have done so: which philosophical ideas have been assimilated, becoming vital elements in our Mexican existence. Thus, for example, this book shows how the introduction of Cartesian rationalism, a culture of science, and the philosophy of the Enlightenment awakened our sense of national identity. The entire development of our national character in the last century was directed at these three intellectual movements. Ideally, perhaps, the Mexican history of philosophy consists not in the mere exposition of doctrines, as occurs in the European history [of philosophy], but rather in producing, at the same time, a kind of sociology of philosophical knowledge. The historical essay before you ... belongs to the inevitable stage in which the facts of our historical evolution need to be collected and organized. Even with the help of a few specific texts, no doubt well known to historians and Mexican philosophers, it has still been an arduous task for the author to ascertain the true historical situation in the evolution of our national life. So if the author can make a contribution, it is not in the exposition of philosophical ideas, still much in need of work, but in the reconstruction of a historical framework in which those ideas acquire a significance they do not have in isolation.

The search for philosophical significance in writings that do not belong, strictly speaking, to the particular domain of philosophy—such as myth, religion, science, art, education, and so on—is an approach that is fully justified by the fact that when those activities are born in the profound spiritual necessity of society, they imply a conception of life and world, even if it is not explicitly formulated. I refer the reader who is interested in the development of this thesis to William Dilthey's outstanding essay, "The Essence of Philosophy."

Benito Díaz de Gamarra

The person who eminently embodied philosophical reform in the second half of the eighteenth century is Benito Díaz de Gamarra, a man who completed his historic mission deliberately and consciously. Juan Benito Díaz de Gamarra was born in Zamora, Michoacán, in 1745. He was a brilliant student at the great College of San Ildefonso in Mexico City. He entered the Oratory in 1764. He traveled throughout Europe and earned his doctorate at the University of Pisa. Pope Clemente XIII named him Protonotary Apostolic. He was a member of the Academy of Bologna. Throughout his travels, he learned of modern philosophy and became a fervent advocate for it. He fought tirelessly to spread it throughout New Spain until his death, which occurred late in old age in 1783. [. . .]

Gamarra, inspired by Descartes, discovered and resolutely affirmed the autonomy of reason, opposed to the principle of authority and Scholastic dogmatism.[2] "Philosophy," he says, "is knowledge of the true, the good, and the honest, obtained only by the light of reason and by exercising reason." In this definition of Cartesian flavor, the declaration of the principles of rationalism in

---

[2] In this exposition we are following the study of Antonio Caso, already cited. [Here Ramos is referring to Antonio Caso's *Benito Díaz de Gamarra*, published in the *Revista de Literatura Mexicana*, No. 2, 1940, pp. 197–213.—Trans.]

Mexico was stamped. For Gamarra, logic was an instrument for the acquisition of truth. In logic, where Aristotle and the Scholastics had made the most lasting mark, it was difficult for Gamarra to prove more innovative. That is why Antonio Caso says that his Cartesianism is entwined with Scholasticism. If, on the one hand, he admits the Cartesian distinction between "clear and distinct" ideas, he still follows the Scholastics concerning the theory of judgments and the syllogism, and he barely treats of induction. [. . .]

Gamarra was fully aware of the value of his mission and would say so without the least bit of modesty: "The glory of having been the first of our compatriots to dare to combat the ancient method, giving us a philosophy that suits the tastes of nations more cultured than Europe, cannot be denied to this sage. It is left to our youth to figure out how to take advantage of the very useful doctrines that this philosophy contains, tastefully selected from the best that has been written by modern philosophers." (This is a note that appears in *Errors of Human Understanding*. It has to be taken into account that this book was published for the first time under a pseudonym, and Gamarra voices this opinion through the mouth of a phony author.) In Caso's opinion, Gamarra was

> a clear and lucid mind full of knowledge, but not original or coherent in equal measure. Two of the most valuable attributes of truly superior minds do not appear on the famous pages of *Elementa Recentioris Philosophiae*. To be broad-minded is not enough. The autonomous thinker needs to be broad-minded, coherent, *and original*. But only the best minds are capable of exhibiting such admirable qualities to the same degree. All the same, the works of Díaz de Gamarra constitute an important chapter in the history of ideas in Mexico.

We may reconsider Caso's harsh judgment if one takes into account other important reasons that are worth mentioning. I think that the philosophical works of American thinkers can be assessed from two very different points of reference. First, they can be judged under the universal scale of values that applies to all thinkers on the abstract plane of philosophy, according to whether or not they have discovered a new idea or doctrine that is added to the general repertoire of knowledge. From this point of view, it is clear that there is not in the entire history of our thought a single philosopher who can be considered original or creative. To this day, we cannot boast of having contributed a great philosophical view to universal culture. But that does not detract from the fact that we have had philosophers throughout our history, since in order to be a philosopher it is enough to think deeply and sincerely about the great philosophical questions. Philosophy is a particular function of the spirit that reaches its full potential in itself, even if it only reproduces the thought process that in the great philosophers led to the creation of new ideas. Gamarra is not an imitator of modern philosophers; he is a mind that has assimilated the content of their philosophy, on his own, after examining and selecting what seemed true in the light of his rational consciousness.

There is another criterion for evaluating Hispanic-American philosophical production, which is to ascertain whether a work, more than being original in the strict sense of the term, has been assimilated to our American existence and influences the organization of our culture. It seems to me that the most eminent value that a philosophical work can have for us lies in its effectiveness in somehow awakening an awareness of our own being, in helping us to define the formation of our character. Philosophy for us Hispano-Americans is not worthwhile only as a conception of the world and human life, but as an instrument to locate our world, life, and position in the more general picture of human understanding. We want to see that world discovered by European philosophy, but with American eyes, and we want to determine our own destiny in relation to that world. Since historically we found ourselves with a ready-made philosophy, we are forced to begin, as a method of study, with the whole and descend from there to the parts. The *Errors of Human Understanding* is the first Mexican step in the effort to apply philosophy to the interpretation and service of our circumstance. It is the first attempt, still very imperfect, of seeing certain facts of Mexican society and morality with the critical eye of a philosopher.

Díaz de Gamarra was, without doubt, a pure "intellectual." He did not use his critical intelligence to examine the value of the prevailing political system, which he complied with and approved of. The regime of Carlos III under which he lived deserved his most favorable judgments. But without a deliberate aim and unconsciously, Gamarra's philosophical reform collaborated in secret with the interests and will of the new Mexican race. Mexicans were not well acquainted with themselves; they did not realize how they differed from the Spanish, in part because they were not educated to think freely; their concept of life was the result of a set of dogmas imposed upon them by the Church and State. The rationalism taught by Gamarra for the first time, upon establishing the sovereignty of reason, awoke Mexicans from their dogmatic slumber, liberated their thought, so that they could then apply themselves to the project of knowing their country and elucidating their national character. Nicolás Rangel justly considers Gamarra one of the "ideological precursors" of our independence, even though the philosopher never concerned himself with politics.

The point is that Mexicans would never have realized that they had certain human rights, they would never have understood the vices of Spain and its colonial regime, or understood the value of the new political conceptions that arrived from France and the Saxon countries, if Gamarra had not taught that, above all, the only legitimate authority is reason, and that reason, therefore, can be exercised freely. Rationalism prepared Mexicans to understand the political doctrines of the Encyclopedists. In the sixteenth and seventeenth centuries, the intellectual future of New Spain was in the hands of the Spanish; in the eighteenth century, thanks to Gamarra, that future passed to the hands of the Mexicans. The philosophical and scientific production of Gamarra, together with the entire generation of Alzate,[3] constitutes without any doubt the first autochthonous intellectual movement in this region of America. It is not arbitrary to say, then, that rationalism in philosophy and science was, in that moment, in tune with the most intimate Mexican will, and was the first freedom won on the path to the Revolution of Independence. Opposed to this was the aging Scholasticism that represented one of the oppressive systems of Spain in Mexico.

New Directions for Philosophy

THE INFLUENCE OF ORTEGA Y GASSET

An intellectual generation that began to act publicly between 1925 and 1930 was uncomfortable with the philosophical romanticism of Caso and Vasconcelos. After a critical examination of their doctrines, they found anti-intellectualism groundless, but they also did not want to return to classical rationalism. Amidst this perplexity, the books of José Ortega y Gasset began to arrive in Mexico, and in the first of them, the *Meditations on Quixote*, they found the solution to their problem in the doctrine of *vital reason*. Additionally, because of the Revolution, there had been a spiritual change that, beginning around 1915, had become clearer in the minds of the people and could be defined in these terms: Mexico had been discovered. It was a nationalist movement that spread little by little throughout Mexican culture—in the poetry of Ramón López Velarde, in the paintings of Diego Rivera, in the novels of Mariano Azuela. Vasconcelos himself, from the Ministry of Education, had spoken of forming a national culture and promoted all efforts in that direction. Meanwhile, philosophy did not seem to fit into this ideal portrait of nationalism because she always pretended to look at things from the point of view of man in general, rebelling against the concrete commitments of space and time, that is to say, of history. Ortega y Gasset again offered a solution to the problem by demonstrating the historicity of philosophy in his *The Modern Theme*. Uniting these ideas with others that had been expressed in the *Meditations on Quixote*, that Mexican generation found the epistemological justification of a national philosophy.

---

[3] [José Antonio Alzate (1737–1799) was a contemporary of Gamarra and was well known for his criticisms of Aristotle.—Trans.]

Ortega said, "When will we open ourselves to the belief that the ultimate Being in the world is not matter, nor soul, nor anything determinate, but a perspective. God is perspective and hierarchy: Satan's sin was an error of perspective." "Cosmic reality is such that it can only be seen under a determinate perspective. Perspective is one of the constituents of reality. Far from being a distortion of reality, it is how reality is organized. A reality that, seen from any point of view, is always the same, is an absurd concept." "From different points of view, two men look at the same landscape. However, what they see is not the same. To both, a different situation presents a different landscape. What for one person is in the foreground with all of its details illuminated, for another person remains in the background, obscure and blurry." "Moreover, as some things are placed behind others, partially or entirely hidden, each person perceives parts of the landscape that the other does not. Would it make sense for each person to say that the other's perception is false? Obviously not: one is as real as the other. Nor would it make sense if, comparing the two landscapes, each dismissed the other as illusory. For this would imply that there exists a third authentic landscape which is not subject to the same limitations of the other two. However, this archetypical landscape does not exist and could not exist." (*The Modern Theme*) "This way of thinking leads to a radical reform of philosophy and, what is more important, of our idea of the cosmos."

"Every life is a point of view of the universe. Strictly speaking, what one sees cannot be seen by another. Every individual—a person, a people, an epoch—is an irreplaceable organ for discovering truth." For these reasons, with indisputable evidence, Ortega defends his right to develop his own philosophy from his personal point of view and under the perspective of Spain. Ortega said, "I am myself and my circumstance and if I do not save my circumstance I do not save myself." "My natural exit toward the universe goes through the gates of the Guadarrama and the Ontígola country. This region of my surrounding reality forms the other half of my self: only through it can I become whole and wholly myself. Biological science has recently begun to study the living organism as a unity made up of body and its local environment. . . ." "Preparing the eyes to look at the world map, we should return to Guadarrama. Perhaps we will not find anything profound there. But we will be confident that the defect and sterility comes from our point of view. Manzanares also has a *logos*: this modest river, this liquid irony that licks the foundations of our city, undoubtedly has among its few drops of water one drop of spirituality."

THE PHILOSOPHY OF MEXICAN CULTURE

In Ortega's "I am myself and my circumstances and if I do not save my circumstances I do not save myself," the intellectual generation between 1925 and 1930 found a standard that applies to Mexico, whose reality and problems were completely unknown to philosophy. Philosophical reflection could very well help to define the Mexican circumstance, to determine what is or could be its culture, taking into account the features of our own history and how they have shaped the peculiar physiognomy of the Mexican man. With that objective in mind, the author published a book titled *El Perfil del Hombre y la Cultura en México* in 1934, in which an attempt was made for the first time to explore philosophically the historical past of Mexico, in order to explain and clarify the specific characteristics of its present life, which might constitute a kind of "characterology" of the Mexican and his [or her] culture. The author considered this preliminary investigation indispensable for grounding the ideals of a future Mexico in empirical data. He ended that book by affirming that the most urgent work in Mexican culture is the full realization of man—the full integration of his character as Mexican. In other words, Mexican culture today should be, first of all, *humanistic*. In order to develop the concept of *humanism* philosophically—a concept that had remained underdeveloped—the author published a book titled *Toward a New Humanism* in 1940.

In my previous book I had already pointed out that one of the most likely dangers that awaits modern man is the mechanization of civilization. In my last book [*Toward a New Humanism*] I wanted to amplify this idea in order to explain the crisis of human values. If Mexico is not yet a completely industrialized country, it is on its way to becoming one, and it is necessary to understand how to avoid the monstrosities that arise from fetishizing the machine [*maquinismo*], which has distorted man's highest potential in other countries. The philosophical theses of the book looked for a substitute for romanticism, which, with its vagueness, can contribute to its disorientation in a country that lacks norms for organizing its life. I tried first to define with some clarity the concept of man and then to show how culture depends on objective norms. The book offers a philosophical anthropology and a theory of knowledge, values, morality, freedom, and subjectivity. And its conclusions are, according to the author, the best suited to improve and organize our spiritual culture. The book ends by developing an idea that, philosophical speaking, would overcome the classic antithesis between materialism and spiritualism.

The Present Situation of Philosophy in Mexico

Since Antonio Caso began teaching philosophy at the University of Mexico in 1911, interest in studying philosophy has continued to grow. Spain, whose intellectual influence came to a halt a century ago, recovered its prestige when the books of Ortega y Gasset began to arrive and when he founded the *Revista de Occidente* in 1922. Through the publication of the *Revista de Occidente*, Mexican scholars were put in contact with contemporary German thought, and their interest in reading the work of its great philosophers was awakened. Ortega's thought had the virtue of unifying the Spanish-speaking mind and encouraging it to develop the discipline of philosophy. The initiative of Caso, amplified and complemented by that of Ortega, has served to mold the mind of a group that has devoted itself to philosophy. Many members of this group have pursued philosophy as a true vocation and have become professors at both the high school and university level. Each one of our scholars has tried, on his own, to stay current with contemporary philosophy.

The center of philosophy in Mexico is the Faculty of Philosophy and Letters, in which its current director, Eduardo García Máynez, has tried to concentrate the overall activity at the *Center for Philosophical Studies*.[4] The Center publishes a "Bibliographic Bulletin" and has reproduced some editions of the philosophical classics. The Faculty's journal, *Filosofía y Letras*, also founded by García Máynez, regularly publishes the philosophical works of Mexican professors.

Since 1938, a group of Spanish professors (José Gaos, Joaquín Xirau, Juan Roura-Parella, Luis Recaséns Siches, and Eduardo Nicol) have contributed to the intellectual life of Mexico, and their work has stimulated and enriched our philosophical activity. All the Mexican philosophers who have been cited in this book, as well as the Spaniards just named, have taught in the Faculty of Philosophy.

Caso's influence has been fruitful over the years. He has educated several generations and has inspired many a student to pursue philosophy as a vocation. Thanks to his tireless effort, the philosophical landscape has radically changed in Mexico. Today philosophy is not a rare or eccentric occupation among other more accepted forms of culture, as it was some twenty years ago. It is a normal activity. We have entered into "philosophical normalcy," to borrow Francisco Romero's happy expression. This means that among us, philosophy is naturalized [*tiene su carta de naturalización*], and its cultivation does not depend only on scholarly demands. Outside the walls of academia, a general interest in philosophy has been awakened in all cultural media. Books about philosophy can count on an increasing number of readers. A multitude of articles about philosophical themes are appearing in specialized and non-specialized journals. Philosophical production grows every day. Today those who dedicate themselves to the requirements of philosophy are not isolated but can count on an atmosphere of attention and interest in their work. And this transformation has occurred not only in our country. Today we can speak of a philosophical renaissance in all of

---

[4] [*The Center for Philosophical Studies*, founded by García Máynez in 1940, was the precursor to the *Instituto de Investigaciones Filosóficas* at UNAM (Institute of Philosophical Research), which continues to be the leading philosophical institution in Mexico.—Trans.]

Hispanic America, with Mexico and Argentina at the head of this renaissance. The efforts of personalities like that of Caso have promoted the development of philosophy in certain American countries: for example, Alejandro Korn and now Francisco Romero in Argentina; Vaz y Ferreira in Uruguay and Deustúa in Peru; Enrique José Varona in Cuba, who is now dead.

In Mexico, philosophy has developed to the point that it cannot ignore any philosophy produced in Europe. But as soon as we have familiarized ourselves with the totality of European philosophy, we face the challenge of incorporating and assimilating it into our national mind. One might say that one issue that dominates our philosophical world is this: the problem of beginning to produce our own philosophy. The present European war has made this issue more acute and urgent. If the current catastrophe does not destroy European civilization, it is very probable that its creative activities, specifically its intellectual production, will suffer a collapse for a long time. During these times, only America can save the continuation of that cultural production. It is a responsibility that recent events have hurled upon our shoulders.

CHAPTER 7

The University Debate
Between Antonio Caso and
Vicente Lombardo Toledano (1933)

Translated by Carlos Alberto Sánchez (Caso) and
Robert Eli Sanchez, Jr. (Lombardo Toledano)

Vicente Lombardo Toledano was born in Teziutlán, Puebla, in 1894 and died in Mexico City in 1968. He was Mexico's foremost Marxist intellectual, labor leader, and champion of Mexico's working class. Toledano studied law at the National University of Mexico, where he taught law and philosophy until 1933. In 1936 Toledano founded the Universidad Obrera de Mexico, a university structured on Marxist social principles whose mission was to awaken the Mexican proletariat to a consciousness of class and class struggle. He was its rector until the 1960s. Toledano is still considered one of Mexico's most distinguished public intellectuals. Among his most important writings are Ethics: System and Method for Moral Instruction in Elementary and Professional Schools *(Ética. Sistema y método para la enseñanza de la moral en las escuelas elementales y profesionales, 1932),* Philosophical Currents in Mexican Life *(Las corrientes filosóficas en la vida de México, 1963),* Summa *(1964), and* Materialism vs. Idealism: The Polemic between Caso and Lombardo *(Materialismo versus idealismo. Polémica Caso-Lombardo, 1975).*

The socialist proposal: *The courses that constitute the curriculum for the bachelor's degree will obey the principle of essential identity in regard to the different phenomena of the Universe and will culminate with the teaching of philosophy based on nature.*

History will be taught as the evolution of social institutions, giving preference to economics as the key factor in modern societies; ethics, as a valorization of life that points to, as the norm for collective conduct, the constant effort directed toward the arrival of a classless society, based on equal economic and cultural possibilities for all.

I. Argument against the Proposal: Doctor Antonio Caso

This conference considers an idea that I am pleased to discuss, although it is not my idea, and as such, and with all humility and respect, I oppose it.

I believe that the University is a cultural community; that is, that its essence is the following: to be a community and to be a cultural community. In all of human society there is society considered *latu sensu* ["in a general sense"], society considered *stricto sensu* ["in the strict sense"], and *communities*. Society considered *latu sensu* encompasses society considered *stricto sensu* and all other social communities. The essence of community is this: to subordinate the interests of the individual to the interests of the group. That is its essence. There can be no community if this subordination of the individual interest by the general interest does not take place. Let us take any community whatsoever, say a political party. Can we imagine a political party in which those that comprise it do not subordinate their individual interest to the interest of the party? What frequently happens in the history of political parties is that a certain individual member, dissatisfied with the general thesis that constitutes the party, goes on to form a new party. Or, consider what has happened in religious communities. A religious community exists in itself as unified, integrated, perfect; but time passes and, as with the Greeks, some Catholics adopted a different position; then the Church divided itself and now we have a community of Greek Catholics and a community of Roman Catholics. And what happens later with the position of the esteemed authors of the Reformation, with Luther, Calvin, with Zwingli, is that they did not agree with the general postulates of the community of the "Roman Church," so they founded the "Protestant Church." The same thing happens in social life; but the essence of the community is the subordination of individual interests to the interests of the community. For me, the University is a community, a thesis that I believe no one will deny since in the University, alumni, professors, teachers, directors, and so on, all submit to the institutional objectives, and we take as our guide the action of the cultural community to which we belong.

Before going further, we ask, *what is culture?* Culture, in a word, is the creation of values, including economic value, aesthetic value, intellectual value (which is called truth), and religious value (which is called holiness). All human societies continuously create and produce values (especially, economic, esthetic, logical, religious); that is, culture itself is the production of values. Humanity has always been elaborating on these values. Thus, I suggest that the University of Mexico is a cultural community.[1] But, aren't there many types of cultural communities? There is the religious cultural community, the political cultural community, and

---

[1] [Caso and Lombardo are referring to the *Universidad Nacional Autónoma de México* (UNAM), the National University in Mexico City.—Trans.]

so on. What kind of community is the University? In order to clarify this, we must see how it produces its values. Ultimately, I will characterize the University in the following way: The University of Mexico is a cultural community of research and teaching.

Thus, the University has two purposes: the first, and its most important purpose, is teaching; the second is research. José Ortega y Gasset has clearly seen this and argues that the general purpose of universities is to teach, or to transmit knowledge through teaching; but, what is it that is taught? What is taught is science, which through its teaching is produced. There is also the implicit objective of the university, which is investigation. Again, the University of Mexico is a cultural community that teaches and investigates. This last attribute means that it must never officially endorse any philosophical ideology or creed, artistic or scientific. The reason that it should not promote any specific ideology is obvious: because it is a community that investigates. Suppose that today we swear allegiance to an ideology. It might be the case that tomorrow, in our work as investigators, this ideology has no merit. Hence, as the essence of the University is investigation, we cannot take a definitive position on an ideology a priori.

If a man elevates a particular social system to the category of philosophical-social creed or ideology, he will expose himself to a tomorrow in which that ideology is declared without merit, and having declared it without merit, he would have compromised the essence of the institution. I am an advocate of orienting the University toward the resolution of social problems; but I am not comfortable with aligning the University along the lines provided by contemporary socialist theories, such as the socialist theory of collectivism, as the University's educational ideology. To those who promote such as an ideology, or who promote the collectivist system, I would say: as a cultural institution, the essential duty of the University of Mexico is to help the proletariat classes in our country as they work toward self-realization, and it must do this within the limits of justice, but without imposing any prescribed economic theory, since theories are transitory by nature, and the good of men is an eternal value that communities and individuals need to pursue by whatever rational means possible.

That is, I believe that if this place of learning shuts its ears and its heart and its intelligence to the good of all, then this place of learning will turn into a tomb. Of course, outside the classroom Mexico will continue to produce its culture because people must live, and if Mexico cannot live culturally or intellectually within the walls of the University, then it will live outside those walls; and then, before the people the University will be a *joke* [*ludibrio*], and since the people are strength and supreme intelligence, the cultural community will suffer the discredit as a result of its negative or merely apathetic attitude toward the conditions of humanity and justice. Thus, I advocate an *orientation* toward the social good, but not an orientation bound to a determinate socialist system.

Today, among the Mexican socialist parties we have some who are collectivists and others who are communists. Why should we proclaim one ideology over the other? Under what circumstances will we say that one socialist system is better than the other? This is dangerous. But this is what is happening today. What about tomorrow? What will the popular ideology be then? And since we are an institution of teaching and research, or investigation, we will only teach that which we investigate, and if we investigate and discover that our ideology is deficient, then it shows that we must not limit ourselves to any philosophical ideology. What we know is that the philosophy of collectivism is a form of historical materialism, and we know this thesis to be false. However, the proponents of collectivism accept historical materialism, and to prove their thesis they argue the following: We are going to wait a little longer because not everyone agrees with the essential identity of the phenomena in the universe, as Montaigne would say; but if the essential identity of the phenomena in the universe is the object of discussion, are we going to challenge the University by forcing it to teach the identity of the phenomena in the universe?

Some will say that we go wrong when we proceed in this way because philosophy cannot base itself only on nature; philosophy also bases itself on culture. A philosophy that bases itself only on nature is called naturalism, which has been out of vogue for quite a while. We cannot teach naturalism in the classroom, and we cannot because culture always reclaims its mission. Philosophy has two spheres: the natural world and the cultural world. A philosophy that bases itself only on the natural world is incompetent; a philosophy that bases itself only on the cultural world is also incompetent, although to a lesser extent. Ultimately, while philosophy must base itself on nature, it must be allowed to flourish in society or culture. Moreover, to base philosophy strictly on nature is contrary to the objectives of the proponents of a socialist education, since what is sought is a *natural* justification of society, but this is not possible, since in *nature* only the strong survive and the weak perish. We are reminded of Spinoza, who says, and I paraphrase, "the limits of each person's abilities extend no further than his willpower." So, if we propose naturalism where oppression exists, what we are saying is that if the oppressed can defend himself, then he will and ought to survive, but if he cannot defend himself, then we are fine with him being hanged by the neck since he is weaker than the rest. This is naturalism.

But culture, as opposed to nature, is a completely different thing. In culture, allowing the weakest members of society to be hanged by the neck because they are weaker is nefarious. Philosophy in such cases opposes itself to that kind of naturalism, teaching that justice is superior to nature. What about the thesis (noted earlier) that "history will be taught as the evolution of social institutions"? Well, history cannot be taught as the evolution of social institutions because history is more than that; there is the history of social institutions and then there is the history of everything else. We can certainly teach the history of social institutions, but we must also teach the history that includes Julius Caesar, even if Julius Caesar is not an institution.

Social institutions are part of history. Whoever teaches about social institutions teaches an aspect of history. History encompasses the history of institutions and many other things that are not social institutions. Moreover, history is essentially knowledge of individual deeds, and consequently there is no history if knowledge of those deeds is missing; the work of social institutions is only part of universal history. One must add that aspect of historical knowledge that is not contained in the expression "history will be taught as the evolution of social institutions. . . . " Proponents of collectivist socialist education have attempted to exclude the teaching of history in general, so that only the history of social institutions is taught. This is absurd.

Proponents also promote a teaching of history "as a valorization of life that would refer as a norm for individual conduct the constant effort directed toward the advent of a classless society, based on equal economic and cultural possibilities for all." But that is not all that ethics is about. Ethics deals with that and many other problems. But proponents seem fascinated with one idea, one creed or ideology, and promote it while necessarily suppressing other branches of knowledge, including ethics and philosophy itself, giving us naturalism in place of philosophical knowledge. They give us a history of social institutions in place of history and a very skewed conception of ethics in place of ethics itself.

Ultimately, we can conceive of the task of the University in the following terms: first, as an institution without ideology, but with an orientation, and its orientation must realize its primary objectives by helping the proletariat classes in our country fully realize themselves without having to accept the collectivist ideology. Second, the University of Mexico will allow professors the freedom to teach in those areas in which they have competence and experience, and will not require them to subscribe to the same thesis as everyone else. This is an important argument against the proposed thesis, since a professor with the freedom of investigation and teaching will always offer critical points of view. This is what happens in the great universities on the planet.

To conclude, here is my position: first, the University of Mexico is a cultural community of teaching and investigation; as such, it must never officially promote, as morality requires, any particular philosophical, social, artistic, or scientific creed or ideology. Second, each member of the faculty must be able to express freely his personal philosophical, scientific, artistic, social, or religious opinions, without any constraints other than those established by law. Third, as a cultural institution, the University of Mexico will have an essential duty to help the nation's working class in their work of self-realization, within the postulates of justice, but without promoting any particular economic theory, since theories are transitory in essence and the good of mankind is an eternal value that the community of individuals must always seek to achieve by any means necessary. Fourth, the University must endeavor to discuss and analyze, through its professors and students, the problems that occupy the general public, and each individual will be personally responsible for his or her own opinions. Finally, and as proof of the absolute loosening of the criteria for membership in this cultural community, and especially as it relates to sectarianism, I will say: each student can enroll in the academic subject of his or her choosing. Every student will study under the direction of a professor of his or her choosing, but among those that lend their services to the teaching of the subject.

This is what I offer as an argument against the proposal you are currently considering. . . . I understand that an individual, firmly convinced by his social or political ideology, will want to promote the propaganda of a sociopolitical ideology, and I respect him, because as far as I am concerned, that is where the beauty of thought resides: in thinking in a certain way and acting in accordance with that thinking, not in thinking in one way and acting in a radically distinct way. However, I beg of you to think about the danger that resides in having the University declare its allegiance to a particular ideology. I say this because the essence of the University is investigation, and the essence of the University is teaching and learning, and, just as science is never finished, and is not laid out in an eternal perspective, neither will the University, which will likewise constantly seek truths that it did not have before. No man has the right to impose a dogma. I insist, we must give the University an orientation of humanity and justice.

I would like to thank the person who promotes the view that I am criticizing today for being here, Vicente Lombardo Toledano.

II. Argument for the Proposal: Doctor Vicente Lombardo Toledano

The question before this Congress today is surely the most serious, the most difficult to resolve, and, at the same time, the most significant, not only for Mexican culture but also for its historical destiny. For this reason, we should be thankful for the circumstances that made the meeting of this Assembly possible, since these basic questions of national interest have not been discussed seriously or deeply.

So, it is with the profound affection that I have always had for my teacher, Antonio Caso, it is with all the respect and esteem that I have for him, that I am going to respond to the reasons you have heard in opposition to the Second Commission of the Congress.[2]

[2] [Here Lombardo Toledano is referring to the second meeting of the *Congreso de Universitario Mexicanos* (Congress of Members of the University), which he was president of and which

Professor Caso[3] defined the University as a cultural community and claimed that the essence of the community is to subordinate individual to collective interest, a principle that applies to the three kinds of community he distinguishes. And culture, he says, is the creation of value—economic, ethical, intellectual, or logical, and the religious value of holiness. So Caso concludes that the University is a cultural institution, a cultural community. But, now, which of the cultural communities, of the cultural values, are embodied in the University? Economic, aesthetic, logical, or religious? Caso says that the culture of the University can be reduced to two fundamental activities: investigation and teaching. What is taught, Caso again asks? Science is taught. And what does science investigate? The truth. Is the truth already established? No, it is in the process of formation. Therefore, to teach is not only to transmit knowledge but, at the same time, to acquire new knowledge and correct previous beliefs. So, Caso says that if the University is a cultural community, it cannot advocate [*preconizar*] any thesis, because to do so is contrary to the aims and task of scientific investigation, which is a part of the mission of the University. Caso claims, then, that no creed of any kind can be advocated, since he who investigates knows that the creed of today is not the creed of tomorrow; he runs the risk of not being able to innovate or the risk of endorsing a creed that, from a scientific point of view, is not proven.

For these reasons, Caso does not agree with the creed of collectivist socialism, which he believes lies behind the Second Commission's proposition to the Assembly. Besides, there are many socialist creeds and the proposition only refers to one of them, and Caso asks, by what right can we assert a thesis that might be refuted tomorrow? Caso says also that the essence of historical materialism is false. We cannot accept the essential identity of the phenomena of the Universe, as the Commission does, because a philosophy based on nature is just naturalism. By contrast, the correct view is one that bases philosophy in nature *and* culture. Thus Caso claims that the Commission's thesis is contradictory, since, insofar as it endorses naturalism, à la Spinoza, the only valid law of life would be that of the strongest, but the aim of culture is to correct this materialist thesis.

Therefore, Caso continues, history cannot be understood as a process of economic facts or events. History is more than the evolution of social institutions; it is the evolution of institutions *and* individuals. So, one only studies

recommended five theses of national reform of education, the third of which Caso and Lombardo Toledano are here debating. See our Introduction.—Trans.]

[3] [As part of his show of respect, Lombardo Toledano refers to Antonio Caso as *el maestro Caso* throughout his response. Here we have left out *el maestro* (the teacher) because "the teacher Caso" or simply "the teacher" is too awkward in English.—Trans.]

history by studying both institutions and individuals through time. That is why Caso also believes that the ethics the Commission proposes is partial. It only covers one aspect of the spirit and so does not offer a philosophical vision of life. This is yet another reason Caso thinks the University cannot have a creed, though it should have an orientation. That is why he thinks that the only constraint of academic freedom should be that prescribed by the law. A professor who is partial to a doctrine not shared by his students is preferable to one who only delivers our thesis because the first does a service to culture, while the second does not do a service to anyone. Like the Peripatetic schools, Caso reminds us, it is better that the University presents all sides of an argument so that culture is learned a posteriori. There can be culture a priori. And, finally, Caso says that so long as the Constitution of the Republic survives, the University will not be able to adopt a creed, especially not one that endorses a political thesis. He concludes: orientation, yes; dogma, no. The true and the good are eternal. We cannot advocate what is good in a particular set of circumstances. The good for humans is permanent. And since investigation should proceed along these lines, the highest cultural institution in Mexico should not adopt a definitive attitude. Science [the truth] is not already established. All dogma eventually runs its course. Thus Caso concludes his objection.

I will now respond to Caso's arguments. We agree that the essence of every community is the subordination of individual interests to those of the group. We also agree that culture is the creation of values. But we do not agree—or at least I do not—that all cultural values have the same value. We do not agree with Caso that aesthetic value is similar to economic value. Within the cultural valorization of life, there are ranges, hierarchies, degrees, and relations of order. And I also believe that culture is not the same throughout time, because it is not an end. Let me outline what is perhaps the difference of opinion between Caso and us.

According to Caso, culture is an end. But we, or at least I, believe that culture is simply an instrument for man and therefore not an end in itself. And because I believe that culture in itself and for itself does not exist, I also believe that humanity in the abstract, the good in the abstract, does not exist, because no value in the abstract exists. I do not believe in entelechies. I do not believe in abstract values, let alone abstract *historical* values. Culture is the product of various factors, of different circumstances of historical evolution—nothing else. Each historical regime has its own culture. Why? Because that is precisely what culture is: valuation, the expression of collective judgments, communal opinions about life, through the community, and for the sake of a determinate community and its ends. I will not cite examples, but in our own country, we can draw from the experience of centuries. We can recall here what the main epochs of our historical evolution were, and we will see, by looking at them all, that each regime has a particular way of understanding culture, because culture is an instrument and not an end, a means of action for collective life.

The first great stage of historical evolution in Mexico was the Viceroyalty, which was characterized by the Catholic Church as both a spiritual and temporal institution. What culture corresponds to that stage? That of dogmatic instruction, which believed that truth is not the fruit of investigation but of divine revelation, an ideological position in the service of the Church, understood as both a spiritual and political institution. The second major stage is the Reform, which saw the secularization of the property of the Church, the separation of Church and State, free inquiry, investigation of the truth, the critique of already established truths, the censure of all dogma, the foundation of the National Preparatory School, which made science the backbone of its curriculum. Why was this the focus? Because it was trying to form a State based on individualism and for the benefit of the individual. Now, a historical regime that takes the individual as the base and object of its institutions naturally supports an individualist pedagogy. That is why the development of positivism and a "Barredian" curriculum was the doctrine of the day; that is why they were offered as institutions of public service, consecrated for the sake of maintaining a set of political institutions that, I repeat, placed the physical individual, the physical person, as its object and base. That is why, for many years, moral philosophy was tied to biology: the triumph of the fittest, even though in truth they also spoke to us of altruism or ego-altruism. The third major stage of history in Mexico—whose profile has not yet been defined because we are still living in it—is the stage of the Revolution.

Of course everyone preoccupied with the problems of culture today rejects the dogmatic thesis of the Viceroyalty, as well as the idea that individuals are the basis of social institutions. It is true that this state of mind or attitude has not yet crystallized into political and economic regimes that, in turn, support a new pedagogy, a new philosophy, a new way of understanding education to be established in national institutions and colleges of higher learning. But this attitude, which is unanimous, palpitates across our landscape. It is the majority view. Therefore, if we understand culture as a means, if we accept that not all values are equal, if we believe that in the modern age, more than any other, social problems can only be understood taking economic phenomena as the axis or base of a solution, then to be consistent with our scientific attitude, we will have to admit that all other cultural values are intimately tied to economic value. And we do not accept this as an "article of faith," but as a consequence of historical observation. We do not have the time here to discuss the fundamentality of economic value. But its objective reality is so clear that it can only be denied on account of religious conviction.

These are the reasons we do not agree with the Caso's explanations. We believe that the University is a cultural institution of learning and investigation, which is precisely why we believe that it is in teaching that the University has the obligation to provide orientation. There is no incompatibility in defending a theory today and changing it for another tomorrow because, in reality, fellow delegates, when has that not been the case? When has there been a historical regime without a corresponding social theory? When has there been a system of education without a corresponding social theory? Never, I would say. That is why I cannot conceive of a professor who does not present his own opinion to his students. Consequently, there is also no historical regime that does not manifest a scientific, philosophical, or pedagogical theory, whatever it may be. In the last century it was genuinely believed that education was neutral concerning social or human problems. But, in reality, there was no neutrality. We were serving, consciously or unconsciously, explicitly or implicitly, a regime that had prevailed in our country for a long time. And this is not just true of our country but of all countries.

The nineteenth century, which created the capitalist regime, is a historical stage in the evolution of all peoples, a stage that gave rise to a capitalist pedagogy. There was no neutrality. Academic freedom only served to orient the student toward a political end along the lines of the bourgeois State. That is the reality. The State is not neutral concerning the struggles of workers, but, through its agencies, has served only one class, the capitalist class. And the instruction of the official schools has been nothing other than a vehicle for preserving the regime that has prevailed in the minds of men. There was no academic freedom. It has always been like this; it has always happened in the same way.

I ask, fellow delegates, something of great importance: should the *University* teach? Yes, of course. And what should it teach? Should it teach everything that is known? We see what has happened in every country that, like Mexico, is transitioning between past and future regimes. Because of academic freedom, students hear all opinions from their professors, which naturally include contrary or contradictory opinions. We believe that upon entering high school [*bachillerato*], a student who is uneducated and barely beginning his pursuit of culture is sufficiently able to distinguish black from white, gray from white, black from gray.[4] We are not just talking about putting students in a position to choose.

---

[4] [The system of education in Mexico is slightly different from the United States. Although *bachillerato* can be translated as "bachelor's degree," as we translated it here it refers to high school or *preparatoria* (preparatory school). However, the preparatory school can be shorter than four years and is typically associated with a University. For example, the famous *Escuela Nacional Preparatoria* (National Preparatory School), founded by Gabino Barreda and referred to later in this discussion, was a two-year program at the time of the debate (it is now three years) and belonged to the *Universidad Nacional Autónoma de México* (UNAM). And there are other networks of high schools that belong to different universities, public and private. The idea is that the preparatory school is

We are not just talking about the freedom of scientific investigation. We are talking about providing them with a framework, and it is not possible to give them a framework without knowing what it consists in. So, what is it to teach? It is not a simple transmission of knowledge; even in the case of transmission, opinion sneaks in. In the transmission of knowledge, which can seem mechanical, a judgment is already made, there is already orientation. It is not possible to teach without transmitting a framework, and it is not possible to have a framework without knowing which it will be.

What happens is that students, given their natural intelligence and age, imitate [*son simuladores de*] all the various positions, within the diverse frameworks of the professors, but without an opinion of their own. That is why, for many years, the University has sent imitators out into the world who are able to practice a profession but nothing else. Why are they not capable of anything more? Because the University did not orient them, because it did not give them direction, because the only political and social principle of professionalism is to generate wealth, to amass a fortune, to triumph at all costs, to be successful. The words "success" and "triumph," that incentive which has so damaged us, especially recently, is one of the fundamental causes of the moral bankruptcy that this country suffers from, because its educated men are also imitators in life, men who are only driven by personal success.

That is the attitude and contemporary product of the University today, and we do not want this situation to prevail, fellow delegates. It is necessary that undergraduate education, including the Preparatory School, orient its students. And that—which is more urgent now than ever—does not contradict the aims of scientific investigation. If tomorrow it is discovered in our research institutes that matter is not the same as energy, then we will have to revise our opinion and say: yesterday we thought this principle was right and today we understand that it is not. To state an opinion, endorse a creed, or have a framework does not entail keeping it for all of eternity. This is precisely how we differ from religious dogma.

What we desire is freedom of thought, not in accordance with the past, but in accordance with the present and future. Human freedom, then, has limits, and the main limit of academic freedom is not to say what cannot be supported from a scientific point of view. We want what is to come, or at least what is current, not the stuff of yesterday. There is no contradiction or incongruity, then, in letting students hear all theories in the Faculty of Philosophy and Letters[5]—the

supposed to provide students with the basic knowledge they need to succeed at the University, where in the past they would earn their master's degree, not their bachelor's. Thus, the debate between Caso and Lombardo Toledano is about the curriculum of both the *preparatoria* and the University, since part of the question is how to help students *transition* from one to the other.—Trans.]

5 [*La Facultad de filosofía y letras* at UNAM is more than a Faculty or department, as the name suggests. Instead, it is closer to a college within the National University, and one of particular importance for students of Mexican philosophy.—Trans.]

Institute that embodies the spirit of the University, the School where culture reaches its summit—because when students arrive at the Faculty, they will already have their own framework, since the basis of culture was already given to them. What difference does it make if an undergraduate who is already oriented hears every political and scientific theory? Nor does it matter if another student who is also oriented works in the biology lab and discovers tomorrow, with his own eyes and scientific instruments, that his belief of yesterday is wrong today. So much the better. That just means that the march of culture is aligned with the time, and that the truth will be incrementally better and purer. What is important is to know the truth of today, and we do not advocate for anything closed or hermetic, because if it is right that there are many nuances in socialist doctrine, it is also right that all types of socialism, without exception, agree with this fundamental fact: there is an injustice in the world, and it springs from the wrong form of production and the unequal distribution of material wealth. The only way of ending this crisis, of ending this historical drama, is to socialize what today belongs to a small and privileged minority, to make the assets of a very few serve the community.

I will imitate Caso's manner of presenting ideas and say: "We should remind institutions and their leaders that the essence of community is subordinating the interests of the individual to those of the community, and so long as capital is in the hands of the few, there can be no happiness for everyone on earth." By saying this, we are not affiliating ourselves with any political party, or even with a specific doctrine. We are not speaking on behalf of socialists or collectivists. We are simply saying, proclaiming, this undeniable fact: herein lies the tragedy, and the only way to end it is to remove the bases that sustain it, socializing what should belong to all, putting in the hands of the many what today is in the hands of a few. This is not to support any specific doctrine, but to support a scientific thesis and, at the same time, a moral thesis. The day it is pointed out to us that the historical tragedy in which we live is resolved, then we will say: No, gentlemen, the solution to the current economic crisis does not depend on socializing the instruments and means of economic production, but on something else. But until that day and that something else, and since success at opposing unbridled individualism consists today in socializing property, we have to do our part to make sure property is socialized. How? Through what means? Through the only means possible within the University: in the domain of science, orienting the classroom toward a human end: to serve the country, to explore its territory, to understand its population, to examine its institutions, to work toward the formation of government programs from an impersonal point of view, to try, in short, to truly serve the community without necessarily advocating any determinate, contingent theory that takes a side in the political fights of today, in Mexico or any other country. It is for the sake of ending this tragedy, and doing so by examining it within the historical regime that characterizes us, that we affirm our position.

Should philosophy be based on both nature and culture? About this we agree. The only thing we do not agree on is the meaning Caso gives to the term *nature*. We are not endorsing *naturalism*. What we want is that the progress of science, the current state of scientific culture around the globe, is taken into account, since physics, chemistry, and biology have made great discoveries for the benefit of human culture. Today, as never before, we are grounding philosophy in nature. We are drawing connections in the world, in the eagerness for the synthesis of, for intimate communion between, the individual and the world. Between man and nature is where we have found the unshakeable base of our eagerness to continue seeking the truth. As culture is not an independent entity of men, but a service to them, basing philosophy on nature is basing it in culture. Because there is no philosophy without man, and as man himself is the fundamental element of thought, by linking man with the world we are basing culture in nature, and, at the same time, philosophy in culture. We cannot refute this because there is no philosophy that is not based in human thought.

We also disagree with Caso about history. Individual knowledge, while certainly interesting, is nothing more than the result of the knowledge of historical and social institutions. Caso says that Julius Caesar is not a social institution, but he is a social institution, more so than any other man has been. Exceptional men are the product of social institutions. That is why we do not teach history as a biography of heroes. And it is precisely because in Mexico, we learned history as a biography of heroes and not the history of social institutions that we do not know the history of Mexico. We also disagree with Caso about ethics. It is true that ethics should require the knowledge of opinions about human culture through time. But during the course of history one has to say what his opinion is. It would be inexcusable for a professor of moral philosophy to explain every opinion about human conduct from Socrates on, but not say what human conduct should be. He would not be a professor of philosophy or moral philosophy. We have to state opinions, not individually, but together as professors, colleges, across undergraduate education, because if a professor is Christian and another is Catholic, and yet another is a socialist or Hindu, the students of the Preparatory school will not know how to conduct themselves in life.

It is undeniable that we are increasing human culture in the Preparatory school. We have to say how one ought to live and that the search of present-day values is realized in the centers where they are carried out—in laboratories and research institutes. But we are not going to open a biology laboratory or one for political science or economics to justify the bourgeois regime or to say whether the socialist regime endorsed by this or that party is the most acceptable. That would be anti-philosophical and anti-scientific. The scientist or scholar is a man who works objectively, with generally incomplete information. He is always doubting what his eyes put before him. He does not know what the results will be or what he is going to discover, but he is always eager to find something new. By contrast, how is the adolescent who has barely reached puberty when he arrives at Preparatory School going to discuss the various opinions if he does not know what they are? He has to receive instruction; he has to be oriented, and that is precisely what ethics consists in: an assessment of life—precise, concrete, affirmative. So, academic freedom, yes; but a freedom to opine in accordance with the reality in which we live and in accordance with future truth.

What we do not want is anarchy, or that this lamentable confusion that currently afflicts us continues to prevail. On the whole we are not endorsing any specific party or social doctrine. When Caso advocates for orientation, he is basically confirming our attitude. An orientation is exactly what we want. But to achieve this, we have to say what life is, what truth is, and how to transform social institutions. Caso embroils himself in contradiction when he says that the University should help and exalt the proletariat class. I ask: How? Is he only saying to us that life today is bad and life tomorrow should be better? To a certain point, that is fine, but it is useless. The important thing is to say how and to say it concretely. To say to the proletariats, "Your situation is very bad and the intellectuals are here to the help," will not make them feel any better. In reality we cannot help them with the things they know better than we do. What we need is to say to them that the University, an institution charged with a historical mission, can help them in a concrete way, clear and definite. And we believe that the concrete action is to try to realize the socialization of all the instruments and all the means of economic production. That is how we are helping the proletariat, in clear and distinct terms, using the means that are within our reach, with science and culture as we understand them.

Fellow delegates: I do not want to try your patience any further, but I believe it is necessary to insist that we are not here to issue propaganda in defense of a creed, since propaganda is for the street. Moreover, we believe that the University is not waging a social revolution. I wish it could, but that is impossible. It cannot. Not only does it not know how, but it simply cannot. Social revolution is waged by the masses. But we, who want to serve the masses, simply have to cooperate so that the truths that are accepted today and that we consider acceptable are transmitted in such a way that they instill a sense of responsibility in every undergraduate, in every graduate, of the University of Mexico and any of the institutions that represent it throughout the country. Now, if the University does not adopt a definite attitude concerning the tragedies it faces, as Caso says, the people will be done with the University and we will find ourselves in the worst kind of mess. The University cannot be a fortress whose inhabitants retreat to the back, who forever remain there, to become the laughing stock of the masses.

When a regime changes, education needs to be changed. Why have we always needed to be in the historical past? Why can't we at least be in the historical present? Let's hope to be the historical future. That is what we want: at least to belong to our epoch.

III. Caso's Response to Lombardo Toledano

I have listened to the objections to my thesis, which have only strengthened my resolve and have served to highlight the position to which I object. That position states that the University must have a creed or an ideology, a declaration of doctrine. I object. I will always insist that the University, as a moral entity, cannot sponsor any thesis or creed or ideology. This is the conception of University in its essential form. I cannot advocate for this decision. I have used the word "advocate" [*preconizar*] because the University, as I had the honor of telling you earlier, is a center of investigation and learning, and whoever is investigating cannot say with certainty that he has investigated everything; or, whoever is teaching cannot say with certainty that he teaches everything about the ideology that he supports. So if we were to say that the University of Mexico has an ideology, a purpose, and that this purpose was that all teaching is done so as to fulfill this or that scientific, religious, or philosophical thesis—if men are honest with themselves they would have to pronounce loudly: it is not possible that we realize our function within those postulates that you have imposed upon us!

Lombardo Toledano was just telling us: we want the academy to remain free! But I cannot see how it can remain free if we are obligated to teach a set curriculum. What will that freedom consist in? If, as a member of a community, I support a certain thesis, and if the essence of community is, as those who argue against me proclaim, the teaching of subordination to the constitutive principles of community, then what kind of freedom can one have in the academy? What we have here is the proposal of a thesis that is composed of four minor theses: (1) economic, (2) social, (3) historical, and (4) philosophical. But I am not convinced by any of these theses, nor the larger one of which they are a part.

Allow me to give you my reasons as to why I am not convinced by any of the theses, which run counter to what I believe the mission of the University to be, namely, to bring about the realization of the human good. Take, for instance, the *philosophical* thesis: I do not agree that "the teachings that will form part of the curriculum for the high school diploma [must] obey the principle of essential identity of the universe's diverse phenomena." Nor do I agree with the second part of that thesis, which states that education "will culminate with the teaching of philosophy based on nature." Philosophy cannot base itself solely on nature. How can I teach within the limits of that thesis? Moreover, what about my own beliefs, wherein my entire spiritual constitution and whatever I have learned or contributed to knowledge has served to negate precisely the thesis of essential identity?[6]

We cannot base philosophy in the realm of nature or natural science. Take physics: physics is associated with mathematics, with chemistry, with the natural sciences, and its discoveries profoundly affect those fields. Thus, the mathematician will say that the problems that physics proposes to him cannot be solved if he does not modify his investigative methods, and so new mathematical methods are proposed to solve the problems in physics, and so on, and this is the way of science. Physicists today ask, "What is matter?" And they answer, "wave particles." On this view, matter is made up of waves, matter does not have individual existence; hence, there is no matter. What exists in the world is a cosmic electrical state of affairs that refers only to the phenomena of nature, *not to the phenomena of culture*. That is, it is believed that it is impossible to resolve social and moral questions with elements from physical science; it is believed that the postulates of the social sciences are essentially different from those of the physical sciences.

Naturalism, supported by physical investigation, supports the work of the chemist; then the physicist splits the atom and finds within it the solar system, that incredibly complex system, with a proton at the center and surrounded by electrons. But what have we gained from this discovery in our efforts to untangle the problem of ethics? Ethics cannot found itself on physics because it is preoccupied with totally different problems, and whoever does not admit this great truth does not belong to his historical moment. He is an individual stuck in the past century. It is impossible, absolutely impossible, to ground ethics, to ground justice, to ground economics in physical knowledge. And so I repeat here, I cannot teach the essential identity of the diverse phenomena in the universe, nor can I found my moral doctrine on the science of those phenomena, because *I simply cannot do so*. The history of moral thought teaches me that it is impossible to ground ethics in physical theories. The materialist school, which promotes historical materialism, and which I oppose, believes this to be the case.

There is only one realm in which laws of nature do not operate absolutely— the human realm. As such, the human realm cannot base itself on the postulates of physical science. That is, the human realm is an ideal, and this ideal is eternal, and an eternal ideal cannot be based on the contingencies of the laboratories, nor can it be at the mercy of the findings of chemistry, because it is a different realm, because, as Pascal said, man is the only creature that can say "no" to life. I can resist nature when it demands that I live: if you take me to the gallows, I will gladly die saying, "Blessed be Jesus." This is another way of saying that the

---

[6] [See Caso's *Existence as Economy and as Charity*, included in this anthology.—Trans.]

science of morals cannot be based on physics nor on physical nature, since it is not possible to create moral values on top of material foundations.

Moreover, since I have famously said that I believe in God, I will put my objections in the following way: the Cross is sufficiently strong to carry me and the destiny of humanity; thus I will always oppose the materialist thesis, especially when, through the efforts of intelligent men, historical materialism is forced upon theory and upon my *alma mater*, the National University of Mexico, by way of forcing the teaching of philosophy based on nature. On this point, the response of Lombardo Toledano was not as effective as it might have been, as he was not as forthright as he could have been regarding his understanding of the materialist thesis.

You will thus allow me, my esteemed student (I called you "esteemed" because I recognize you as such), that I do not agree with you, but I am also of the mind that I cannot agree with anyone who does not satisfy the demands of my frame of mind or the values of my intelligence. Moreover, I strongly reject that teaching philosophy must be based on nature—again, because we must base philosophy on two things: one that we call culture, the other nature. Nature is not culture, and culture is not nature. Philosophy is a luminous guide, the light through which accompanied the Platos and the Aristotles in antiquity, as well as the masters of our own time, Husserl and Bergson, who are the greatest philosophers today, and who affirm that it is impossible to base philosophy on considerations of nature. *Naturalism* cannot be the foundation of human thought because it does not respect the autonomy of the individual. Neither does it respect culture. But culture is what is properly human, and what is properly human is something else, not nature but what stands over nature, the supernatural. Culture is supernatural and so is the individual, who as the work of Creation, is also the work of the will and the ideal.

Unfortunately, no one has yet demonstrated how history will be "taught as the evolution of social institutions, giving preference to the economic fact as the main factor in modern society; and ethics, as the valorization of the life. . . ." If I did not agree with this definition of philosophy as *naturalism*, neither do I agree with this definition of ethics. I repeat: history is universal history, not the history of institutions, of politics, of the economy, or of a particular people.

But is it even possible to refer to history as the history of social institutions? Whoever believes that history can be reduced to the history of institutions commits a very common error by taking the part for the whole. Who denies the history of institutions? Who would dare say that institutions do not have a history? The same people who reduce history to the history of institutions. What about the genius and the hero? Proponents of socialist education and collectivism are fascinated by the social; they are hypnotized by socialism, by collectivism, by the "isms" of the masses. No. History can never be conceived only as the history of institutions. History is also the history of exceptional individuals. Can you imagine what history would be like if it were only the history of the institutions? It would be the history of the ant farm, the history of the beehive, the history of animal colonies; that is, the history of collectives. But men have souls within them and there are individuals and a history of geniuses. Humanity distinguishes itself through that series of exceptional individuals who mark history, who carry that luminous torch that passes from hand to hand, illuminating all mankind. Man's essential ability is to oppose himself to the mob, to reject it if possible, to confront it with its errors if he finds it following a false idea.

IV. Lombardo Toledano's Response to Caso

All Caso did in his second response is state his ideological position and his philosophical-religious doctrine. He says, "I cannot accept a philosophy that supports the identity of the phenomena of the Universe; consequently, I cannot accept a philosophy based on nature. It is a mistaken thesis because today physics, the center of scientific investigation, which extends to mathematics, chemistry, and biology, has invalidated many of the scientific concepts we accepted as valid, but that is all it has done. There is an abyss between the natural and human world that cannot be filled and never will be. Science cannot bridge them because man is not entirely the product of nature; he is and he acts above nature." That is why, Caso insists, "the postulates of moral science cannot be based on nature. What progress have we made after four centuries? Have the aims of ethics, laws, or economics progressed? Can we say that laws and economics can be based on physics, biology, and mathematics? Historical materialism says so, but it does not recognize that the human order cannot be founded on the natural order. Between nature and the supernatural, there is an abyss and no possible essence common to them, because the ideal is given a priori and we know that nature is given a posteriori." Thus Caso concludes, consistent with his thesis.

But Caso's thesis, I claim, is at bottom no more than a spiritualist philosophy, whose only aim is to justify granting priority to religious value over the other human values. That is why I am opposed to his thesis—not because it is not respectable, or because the era to which it belonged was not luminous, but because today we do not accept religious feeling as an explanation of the human process. Who would not agree that there is a deep difference between the natural and supernatural world? Anyone who thinks there isn't does not base his assertion on investigation and endorses a simplistic attitude, one of four hundred years ago. We do not live in the time of Saint Thomas or in the time of Aristotle, but in a period in which culture [not the belief in the supernatural] is man's compass.

Ten years ago, philosophers who subscribed to neo-spiritualism spoke of the contingency of the natural laws as they pass from one order to another. Bergson and Boutroux said that there is not one but multiple orders. But we know that is wrong, and Boutroux would no longer defend it because it has been completely disproven by the progress of science. Ten years ago, it was said that mathematics, the most general of the sciences, was only occupied with quantity—that it begins where matter ends. Mechanics, with studying the notion of force; physics, with matter and the transformation of bodies; chemistry, with the essence of matter—which suggests that there is no essential identity between physical and chemical phenomena, that they belong to two different worlds, different orders of the cosmos. Similarly, there is yet another abyss and contingency as we move from the biological to the psychological, and yet another between the psychological and sociological. So Boutroux said that there is not one but many orders, and yet, by contrast, to justify the religious, it is said that there is only one single, supreme order [the supernatural].

If we know today that it is not possible to understand the movements of the heart without calculus, or to manage an important public institution without the infinitesimal calculus; if it has been proven that mathematics is not concerned with what does not move and that everything that exists moves; if we know that the orders of the world are different, why state that we live in the supernatural world and not the natural? It is not possible to declare in 1933 that the religious is the only a priori ideal. Why is it impossible today? Because all other human ideals are, without exception, a posteriori, and the only thing that distinguishes the religious is that it is based on the view that the truth is already established, once and for all. However, we—who do not believe that religion is what moves the world forward, who do not think the truth is already established—must claim emphatically that every ideal is the fruit of human evolution. Consequently, we believe that history is the history of institutions and not of individuals. Exceptional men no doubt matter, but we cannot imagine how Jesus would be received in the twentieth century. Can we conceive of a Newton twelve centuries before Christ? Or an Edison in the fourteenth century, or Marx in the tenth century? We cannot because peoples of different eras have to create new structures or visions of life on top of the obstacles that they themselves encountered in the past. Thus it is communities that produce exceptional men. No one is ahead of their time. Nothing is more powerful than a people, and that is why I cannot accept that history is principally the history of individuals, or that, as Caso says, man's supreme duty is to face the crowd, to push against it, or even to abandon it if necessary. No. This is not to say that we think the masses possess a higher culture, but we know that the masses must never succumb [to the individual]. Show me just one example of the masses not building what they need, just one, but there are not any. And when those "superior" men "of exception" want to face and oppose the crowd, they inevitably succumb to the drive of the masses. That is the historical truth.

I will now conclude. This is not a question of personal opinion. This is an issue of great significance for culture and the future of Mexico, as I said in my first defense. Fellow delegates, remember your knowledge of history and you will recall that when Don Gabino Barreda founded this educational establishment, when he established the National Preparatory School, the entire country was shaken at its foundations. Then Mexican society, the middle class, and the so-called aristocracy above all, campaigned ruthlessly against Barreda, against the teachers who followed him, against Juárez, against everyone who was for cultural reform. The reformers were mocked and threatened and those who enrolled in the Preparatory School were warned that they would be excommunicated for all of eternity. Barreda, then, and the men of his century, of his era, set a new course for national culture. We should not forget these things, since we are also in a position to set a new course for national culture, of not having to live in the chaos we find ourselves in, in this atmosphere of individualism disguised as romanticism and religious feeling, which is the main axis of our conduct. Fellow delegates, I would rather—and I say this with all sincerity—that the University hand itself over to the clergy because a Catholic school is preferable to a bourgeois school grounded in individualism, romanticism, without any definite orientation, and it is preferable because to lack orientation is chaos.

By contrast, the Catholic man always knows where he is going, and when intelligent and sincere, he is respectable. But we cannot respect the individual who goes through life without orientation, with the title of "university graduate," clinging to the coattails of just any professional politician [*a pegarse a los faldones de cualquier político profesional*]. We would like to see Mexico saved by the masses, not by personal interest, and the only way the masses will save Mexico is for the University to correct, scientifically and as far as it can, the unjust regime that characterizes our era. These are not empty phrases or rhetorical devices. Unfortunately, there are many who go hungry—not just spiritually but materially. And we do not want to continue discussing eternal values when there is palpable misery, blatant poverty, unkempt beggars, masses who are in need of a clear and concrete solution! Will the University continue discussing every idea, every principle, only to offer the student nothing more than hesitation and doubt? No. The University should not educate through and for doubt, but through affirmation.

CHAPTER 8

Two Ideas of Philosophy (1940)

Francisco Larroyo and José Gaos

Translated by Aurelia Valero Pie and Robert Eli Sanchez, Jr.

Francisco Luna Arroyo, later known as Francisco Larroyo, was born in Jerez, Zacatecas, in 1908 and died in Mexico City in 1981. After earning a teacher's credential, he studied philosophy at the National University, where he met Antonio Caso. During 1931–1933 he studied in Germany and embraced Neo-Kantianism according to the Baden School. Back in Mexico, he founded, along with Guillermo Héctor Rodríguez, the Circle of Friends of Critical Philosophy (Círculo de amigos de la filosofía crítica), and devoted himself to educational and pedagogical issues. Although most of his written work consists of student manuals, some of his books were highly influential and have been reprinted in as many as twenty different venues. Such is the case of his General History of Pedagogy *(Historia general de la pedagogía, 1944) and, to a slightly lesser extent, his* Science of Education *(La ciencia de la educación, 1949).*

José Gaos was born in Gijón, Spain, in 1900 and died in Mexico City in 1969. He studied philosophy at the Universidad Central in Madrid, where he became a close disciple of José Ortega y Gasset and a frequent contributor to Revista de Occidente, *a cultural and scientific journal founded by Ortega y Gasset in 1923, which was very influential in the Spanish-speaking world. Gaos actively supported the Second Spanish Republic and, besides various diplomatic and cultural missions, he was named rector of the Universidad Central during the Spanish Civil War. His refusal to return to Spain during Franco's regime made him a symbol of the Spanish Republican Exile, a "transterrado," a term Gaos coined to refer to his own experience as a Spanish exile in Mexico, and which was later popularized and extended to all Spanish exiles. He is remembered for having introduced existentialism in Mexico and for having translated Heidegger's* Being and Time *into Spanish, which was also the first translation into a Western language. Considered the most important professor of philosophy in Mexico in the mid-twentieth century, he fostered the study of Mexican philosophy and was the main supporter of Leopoldo Zea and the Hiperión group. Among his main books are* On Philosophy *(De la Filosofía, 1965) and* On Man *(Del Hombre, 1970).*

Article I: Larroyo

Some decades ago, the profound German philosopher Emil Lask (1875–1915) undertook the difficult task of writing a book about the logic of philosophy. With characteristic insight, he advocated for a higher, more fundamental knowledge than the one provided by "everyday logic," which, as is well known, constitutes the initial part of philosophy itself (along with [formal] logic, ethics, aesthetics, metaphysics, etc., which are usually counted among the constituent parts of philosophy). In sum, he was trying to surpass the limits of philosophical investigation, to create a new science directed at founding the basic laws and cognitive principles of philosophy itself. Soon after, Lask's essay was a focal point of discussion among professional circles in Europe, on both sides of the Pyrenees.

Now, in an interesting series of lectures, Professor Dr. José Gaos revisits those problems posed by Lask. His aim, however, is certainly more comprehensive. He not only hopes to develop a logic of philosophy; with an intellectual extremism motivating him, he tries to define the nature of metaphilosophy. In light of those problems that awaken new interest, it is worth remembering old truths. So, what is the point of talking about metaphilosophy?[1]

I. PHILOSOPHY: ITS PRIMACY

Philosophy has always served as first and ultimate knowledge; its subject matter consists in that unified set of principles that cannot be derived from any other kind of human knowledge. Within this basic sphere of knowledge par excellence, the philosopher has always investigated the nature of truth, beauty, the good, God, the universe.[2] "Philosophy," then, refers to "underivable and original knowledge." What could be more primary than the problem of truth? Nothing, since in order to decide the validity of some belief, it would first be necessary to determine its truth or falsity (this is the inalienable problem of logic considered as philosophy's first science). Therefore, the attempt to enter into an area of research higher than philosophy inexorably leads to a vicious circle. But perhaps someone might say with Professor Gaos that "for twenty-five centuries,

---

[1] [The subtitle of this selection is *La filosofía de la filosofía* which might be translated into English as "the philosophy of philosophy." One reason to translate the title this way is to emphasize that Larroyo and Gaos are debating whether it makes sense to speak of higher-order philosophical reflections. However, we have chosen to translate all instances of *la filosofía de la filosofía* as "metaphilosophy," since what they are ultimately debating is whether metaphilosophy ought to be introduced as a new, independent discipline, within or above philosophy, or whether it is simply a different name for the very old question concerning the definition or essence of philosophy.—Trans.]

[2] With great authority, philosophers at the end of the nineteenth century referred to this group of principles with the name "values." Philosophy, then, is the science of values.

philosophy has been discussing all things to some extent, including philosophy itself. Thus, one speaks of the philosophy of nature, the philosophy of history, the philosophy of religion or the philosophy of culture, when philosophy considers nature, history, religion or culture. And if this is how we refer to this kind of investigation, what, then, should we call the philosophy of itself, if not the metaphilosophy [*filosofía de la filosofía*]?" From this point of view, metaphilosophy, according to Professor Gaos, has to clarify first and foremost what philosophy is (i.e., its essence). For instance, he has even asserted, unacceptably, that, among other things, philosophy is a "personal confession." But is such a use of those terms logically justified? Does the specialist who begins his research by defining, let us say, the exclusive domain of physics, that is, by defining the object of study of his discipline, develop a meta-physics [*física de la física*]? Is it not more modest and logical to say that with that problem the first question of his scientific reflection is raised? It cannot be the case that anyone who simply asks what the essence of physics is [*que es pura y simplemente la física*] is doing meta-physics.

Now, since metaphilosophy can only be understood as the philosophical reflection on philosophy, this first problem (establishing what philosophy is) makes no sense, something that Professor Gaos does not take into account in his lecture, as he is trying to make clear the rigorous concept of *philosophy*. Besides, whoever grants a second-order reflection on philosophy cannot argue against the existence of a third-order reflection above the already elevated knowledge of metaphilosophy, that is, a metaphilosophy of metaphilosophy, and so on ad infinitum, which is a total absurdity.[3]

II. HISTORY OF PHILOSOPHY: ITS UNIVERSALITY

Assuming that there is such a thing as metaphilosophy, Professor Gaos adds: "metaphilosophy is as old as philosophy itself, because it is the nature of philosophy to advocate for itself, to speak about itself. However, in this lecture series, I am not going to expound on metaphilosophy from its origins but will limit myself to metaphilosophy today, to what it says and cannot but say about itself at present."

The foregoing words seem to indicate clearly how and to what extent it is possible to speak about metaphilosophy—of course, only from the perspective of history. Granted, Professor Gaos does not aim to provide an overview of metaphilosophy; he does not want to talk about it going back as far as its origins. He limits himself to current research in metaphilosophy.

---

[3] Compare to Kant's transcendental illusions.

To make headway in such a specific task, it would not be out of place to bring up the classic concept of the "history" of philosophy—to recall, at the very least, its universal object of study. To be sure, no one will deny that this discipline (the history of philosophy) deals with the old problem—since Hegel, with the objectivity of science [con cientificidad]—of describing the origin and development of philosophy. Professor Gaos, then, speaks, with every right of what philosophy has meant to each of its distinguished representatives, including what such philosophers may have thought at one point about their own doctrines. For instance, in that brilliant system, Hegel finds a harmonious synthesis, so to speak, of the entire future of philosophy. But this account, which can be extended to apply to the great thinkers today—every idea that is conceived already belongs to the past—is, and continues to be, the history of philosophy. Thus an account of what the main heroes of philosophy have believed is the essence of philosophy constitutes the first chapter of the history of philosophy when, for example, this branch of knowledge is written as a history of philosophical problems, as it is the case in the already classic text by W. Windelband.[4] Would Professor Gaos prefer to call the history of the problem treating the conception of philosophy—the description of the various ideas philosophers have maintained about philosophy—metaphilosophy? By all lights, it seems unjustified to refer to such an essential theme of philosophy using this title.

III. THE PSYCHOLOGY OF THE PHILOSOPHER: ITS ASSUMPTIONS

In his dramatic lecture, however, Professor Gaos did not address so much the conception of philosophy defended today, but something very different. He analyzed in full detail the personal and subjective events that overtake the philosopher who surrenders to his calling, that is, to philosophy. He points out, in an original and otherwise commendable manner, that the true philosopher always gives into the feeling of arrogance—not a relative and passing arrogance, but a satanic, diabolical arrogance, an arrogance that aims to surpass God. It would not be difficult to object to Professor Gaos's thesis about the philosopher's psychology using rich historical evidence. Let us recall, at random, Socrates' strange knowledge of what he does not know, Plato's subsuming eros under agape, the contemplative life of Thomas Aquinas, Descartes' pledge to go on a pilgrimage to Loreto after his brilliant discovery, Bacon's de nobis ipsis silemus [of ourselves we remain silent], a line that Kant still deemed worthy enough to use as an epigraph to his Critique of Pure Reason.

---

[4] Wilhelm Windelband, Treatise on the History of Philosophy.

We can call this kind of reflection on the subjective attitude of the philosopher "the philosopher's psychology," since it endeavors to describe and explain the psyche of the person who commits himself to the tasks of philosophy. And, in truth, such elucidations were to a great extent the *leitmotif* of Professor Gaos's lectures. Already in the first lecture one can see the point of his meditation:

What metaphilosophy says today, to sum up in advance, is this: he who is called to philosophy, he who is touched one youthful day by the philosophical vocation, he who enters the order, that is, who lets philosophy become the most important part of his life, in his own life, in his own being, in himself, arrives, has arrived at modern times, at the present day, to a moment of being disappointed in himself, in his life, in his own being. In this drama, what is he who is disappointed by philosophy to do? He will start to reflect on his disappointment, that is, continue to philosophize; he will not abandon philosophy, but persist in this new situation. In this revelation and the description of it, why does the philosopher persist and tell us about it? We will discuss this in the following lecture.

My series of lectures—which I titled "metaphilosophy"—offers the history, the story, and also the confession of this vocation, of this profession, of this disappointment, of this persistence, in chronological order, which is the nature of things. My series of lectures consists of confessions, for reasons that we will see in the last lecture, because we will not be able to see them before. To talk about philosophy is always to talk about oneself. Now, to talk about oneself in public is all but impossible without wearing certain protective masks. Even a private confession to receive the holy sacrament would be much more difficult than it already is if one did not resort to certain techniques or means of what might be called "depersonalization." For example, the person who examines himself and then confesses in response to set questions is not so-and-so, but a "sinner." It is clear that a confession can take a different course after one confesses one's sins as a result of the guidance of the spiritual director chosen by the penitent. Imagine the public confession, then, which is impossible without resorting to certain expository devices, such as irony or "humor," speaking in general terms, myth, story, or fable, even lying! Who would dare to undress in public without at least posing or standing beneath a favorable light, except for a zoologically minded nudist. That is why I will speak in general terms, but allow me to warn you not to be fooled by general terms. I am mainly talking about myself, but not just about myself or only about myself, because to speak about oneself is always to speak to some extent about everyone else. Even the most peculiar of men have much in common with their fellow human beings. And I am a common man, not a peculiar man, so I share quite a lot with everyone else. [...] The nature of what we all share is something I will come back to in the last lecture, but it is roughly this: that is why this is not only a confession, but a history or story of what has happened to, for example, my generation, a little bit about what has happened to contemporary man. And to the extent that my generation and contemporary man are a part of man in general, I am going to present a history of something that has happened to man in general, and therefore, something that has happened to you, perhaps without you knowing it.

The history or story of the personal experiences of Professor Gaos, no matter how similar or different it is from those of his generation, is no less an empirical analysis of his consciousness, miles away from the philosophical method of transcendental reflection. Now, I do not believe that the conception of philosophy can be revealed by a psychological description, nor that such a description deserves the name of "metaphilosophy." Rather, I am of the opinion that to describe the psychology of the philosopher, just like that of the artist or that of the believer, it is necessary to possess the concepts of philosophy, art, or religion in advance. What criteria can we use to affirm that the *philosopher* exhibits these or those feelings, if we do not decide in advance what philosophy is in selecting exactly whom to examine? It could, mistakenly, be stated that it is the philosopher who is carried away by these or those subjective experiences, when in fact one is referring to the [psychological] attitude of the rhetorician or that of the politician. Because besides the subjective experience, there is also the object of knowledge that consciousness refers to or to which it is specifically directed, case by case, as Kant (1724–1804) has shown. From that point of view, for instance, we arrive at an account that is diametrically opposed to that of Professor Gaos. So, on the supposition that philosophy is a theoretical reflection on the values of culture, I am inclined to believe that the philosopher is far from arrogant, but someone whose attitude toward acquiring knowledge [*en actitud cognoscitiva*] is truly humbled by the non-empirical laws of the sacred and the good, the beautiful and the true.

No, the description of psychology is not the ideal way to discover fundamental concepts. Psychology is not the first but the last of the sciences that has to do with [the values of] human culture—a statement that does not in any way deny the value of such an important discipline. Before the psychology of science, morality, art, and religion, it is necessary to discuss logic, ethics, aesthetics, and the philosophy of religion. Psychology in general, and the psychology of the philosopher in particular, presupposes the results of philosophy itself.

Nevertheless, it might be objected that Professor Gaos's analysis is not psychological, but phenomenological. But it is unclear how this can be if Husserl's philosophical phenomenology, understood as "transcendental reflection," leads to the firm Neo-Kantian belief that philosophy should "rise to the ranks of rigorous science," while Doctor Gaos endorses the thought—unacceptable to us— that the essence of philosophy, besides being diabolical, is that it is "a personal confession."

IV. CONCLUDING REMARKS

1. Since *philosophy is, by definition, fundamental* and insuperable knowledge, the expression "metaphilosophy" is at bottom a contradiction in terms. "Philosophy is the self-knowledge of the Absolute Spirit" (Hegel).
2. The description of the philosophical ideas of all the great thinkers (even of those today) is an inalienable problem of the history of philosophy. The history of philosophy as a history of philosophical problems should first describe what philosophers have believed about the nature of philosophy itself (what W. Windelband calls the "name and concept of philosophy").
3. The method of psychology is not capable of discovering the fundamental truths of philosophy. Only by means of transcendental (phenomenological) reflection can genuine philosophy rise to the ranks of rigorous science (Husserl).[5]

Response: Gaos's First Letter to Larroyo

To My Distinguished Colleague and Friend:

I have received your review of my lectures. I truly appreciate it. For someone to take an interest in one's work, even if to disagree, is to bestow a great honor.

Some observations have occurred to me after reading your review, which I should communicate in return, particularly in reference to the following points: (1) my influences in general and, in particular, Lask's logic of philosophy; (2) the concept of metaphilosophy itself and the infinite regress and contradiction in terms it entails, and the concept of metaphysics that you compare it to; (3) the interpretation of metaphilosophy as history of philosophy, or more precisely, as history of the concept of philosophy; (4) the evidence against interpreting philosophy as arrogance [*soberbia*] and, particularly, using the example of the philosophy of values as a counterexample of this interpretation; and (5) the psychological or phenomenological character of metaphilosophy and

---

[5] Compare, especially, to Husserl's "Cartesian Meditations" (French translation available).

the difficulties with the concept of "personal confession" from a phenomenological point of view. Here, then, are my observations in the order of these points.

(1) My main influence is not Lask but Dilthey. I took the expression "metaphilosophy" from volume VIII of his *Collected Works*. Please refer to *The Essence of Philosophy*.

The *logic of philosophy* does not seem to bother you as much as *metaphilosophy* does. However, the logic of philosophy is, like all logic, a part of metaphilosophy.

(2) Metaphilosophy is not second-order philosophy, that is, higher than it, as you interpret it and from which you infer certain consequences and difficulties, including an infinite regress and contradiction in terms. Metaphilosophy is a part of philosophy, that part that reflects on itself, that is, on its reflections—in the broad sense of the term—and on the reflections on its other objects (i.e., values, as you say). Philosophy consists of two parts: reflections on values and reflections on those reflections. These two parts, the second included, exist in every philosophy *as a matter of fact*. Metaphilosophy is the be-all and end-all [*cifra y compendio*] of everything designated by "philosophy." Plato's discussions of rhetoric, politics, sophistry, and so on, the first two chapters of Aristotle's *Metaphysics*, most of the *Discourse on Method*, all of *The Critique of Pure Reason*, the *Phenomenology of Spirit*, the *Discourse on the Positive Spirit*, and so on, are metaphilosophy. Book XII of Aristotle's *Metaphysics*, the *Meditations*, the *Lectures on the Philosophy of History*, and so on, constitute a philosophy of nature, a philosophy of man, a philosophy of God, and a philosophy of history. To me, Dilthey's concept and expression "metaphilosophy" is the only correct concept, the only precise expression, to refer to that part [of philosophy], and is therefore preferable to any other concept or expression, which is inexact for reasons I will now consider.

It might be that infinite regresses in human, historical matters, seem absurd to us simply as an artifact of traditional, ahistorical, Greek ideology. But if infinite regresses—the infinitude of superimpositions, of reflections, of higher-order reflections on consciousness [*de la conciencia de la conciencia*]—were thought of from a modern point of view, they would be considered part of the course and progress of history. Of course, as a matter of fact and strictly speaking, given the finitude of man and history, one will not arrive at the infinite. In any case, the concept should be explored before rejecting it.

The physics of physics is not metaphysics, but the philosophy of physics. The first chapter of a treatise on arithmetic, grammar, geography, history, and physics is not arithmetic, grammar, geography, history, or physics. To define arithmetic is not to do arithmetic, and so on. To define arithmetic is to do the logic of arithmetic, the theory of the science of arithmetic, the philosophy of arithmetic. Every scientist possesses the beginnings of the philosophy of his respective science. Philosophy arises in every science, to enlarge or deepen it, because, as a result of specifying and distinguishing, it has been the intellectual fountainhead [*matriz*] of scientific thought.

There is only one exception: the first chapter of treatises on philosophy. To define philosophy is to do philosophy—metaphilosophy, naturally! It is to do the logic of philosophy, the theory of the science of philosophy, supposing that philosophy is a science. In sum, it is to do metaphilosophy, as must be repeated one more time. If you care so much for the primacy of philosophy, which is what makes philosophy exceptional, I hope you will not care any less for the exceptionality of philosophy. "Metaphilosophy" is a particularly eloquent way of naming the reflexiveness essential to philosophy in its exceptional primacy. Philosophy is primary because of its reflexiveness. Metaphilosophy is first philosophy or the foundation of philosophy by which philosophy distinguishes itself, more or less consciously, from what is not philosophy. Reflexiveness and primacy are certainly extraordinary characteristics—philosophy is more astonishing—but they are not more contradictory than those qualities that constitute man's *double* nature.

(3) To reflect on philosophy is increasingly to do the History of Philosophy. The reason is that philosophy is a historical reality [*realidad histórica*]; it is something that unfolds historically, something that has or is history. But the History of Philosophy must be done philosophically—as Hegel teaches and Windelband repeats, to name just two philosophers you consider authorities—that is, it *is* philosophy. In the History of Philosophy, history and philosophy coincide; the History of Philosophy and metaphilosophy coincide. How they coincide is a subject as interesting as it is difficult to study. It is the one I have undertaken.

History cannot be done except from the present, *in* the present. Those who philosophize can be distinguished from one another based on whether they are aware or unaware that they can only think of the past from the point of view of their own present thought.

The history of the concept of philosophy is the history of metaphilosophy, which has a history, as all philosophy does. And [the history of metaphilosophy] is also metaphilosophy, for the reasons mentioned in the previous observation. This is precisely what the [history of metaphilosophy] is about: to define the nature and understand the structure of what that first chapter of treatises on philosophy and the History of Philosophy is supposed to be.

(4) The historical evidence against the idea that arrogance is the essence of philosophy is evidence of the arrogance that the "weak" philosopher conceals behind a mask, for I have not characterized the philosopher only by his arrogance but also by his "weakness." To disguise arrogance as humility is a sophistication not at all uncommon to human passion or strange to the connoisseur. The challenge is not to adduce appearances, but to penetrate into the reality behind them, of which the subjects themselves are more or less conscious.

To reflect theoretically on the values of culture—one of which is God, as you say yourself—can be seen and even felt as an instance of humility, but my thesis is that, with respect to God, the only humble relationship is the personal and religious. The theoretical relationship with God, insofar as it is not religious, is arrogance. The Kantian and Neo-Kantian concept of the legislating subject does not resemble the humble person with regard to the non-empirical laws of what is sacred and good, of the beautiful and the true.

(5) Metaphilosophy includes a psychology of the philosopher. But this psychology, like all psychology, can only be done using concepts that are the object of phenomenology. Thus, the phenomenological description of arrogance is indispensable to the psychology of the philosopher insofar as he is arrogant. But there is also a phenomenology of philosophy and of the philosopher. This phenomenology, like all phenomenology, can only be done on the basis of cases and empirical examples, even if there is only one case, or an imaginary or fictitious case, a lesson very well expressed by Husserl.

Besides, phenomenology has developed from Husserl to Heidegger in a way that is increasingly attentive to the circumstantiality of human phenomena, as Ortega has taught since his *Meditations on Quixote*. Husserl considers mental phenomena in the same abstract way that general psychology used to. It is now widely accepted, not only by philosophers, but also by psychologists (empirical psychology, characterology), that human phenomena are concrete and should be described and narrated, historicized, in its concretion, which is its only authenticity.

Defining philosophy as personal confession is not incompatible with the phenomenology of philosophy. The phenomenology of philosophy might demonstrate definitively that the essence of philosophy is personal confession. The concept of "personal confession" might be—it is—an essential concept. Therefore, it can be an object of phenomenology, just as any other analogous concept: "personal confession" has an *eidos*. And this *eidos* can be described, has to be described, on the basis of a particular, empirical case, one that is, one that by the very nature of things has to be a *personal* case.

In short, Husserl, who defines and practices philosophy as phenomenology, was satisfied by this definition without offering an explicit and rigorous phenomenology of philosophy—an omission or inconsistency that is not uncommon or strange in the history of philosophy. (Sometimes philosophers leave the task of defining their own philosophy—the essence of one's philosophy being the least evident to the one who practices it—to their followers or to the future of philosophy. That is how the history of philosophy unfolds historically.) Had Husserl tried to [do a phenomenology of philosophy] he might have concluded that philosophy as a human activity is a personal confession.

And if philosophy is essentially a personal confession, it is clear that it cannot be practiced, it is not really practiced, as anything else, even if one believes that it can be done otherwise.

In any event, consider the following questions:

1. Have philosophers reflected on the nature of philosophy or not? If they have, is this reflection philosophy or not?

   If you agree that it is philosophy, that a reflection on philosophy is philosophy too, is this not the same as saying that [this reflection] is "metaphilosophy"?

   If you say instead that it is plain philosophy, what name would you use to refer to this philosophical reflection on the nature of philosophy in order to distinguish it from those philosophical "reflections" on the nature of anything other than philosophy?

2. Is the task of defining philosophy, philosophy or not?

   If it is philosophy, that is, if it is *part* of philosophy, what would you call it to distinguish it (within and as a part of philosophy) from its other parts, such as the philosophy of nature, the philosophy of history, and so on?

3. Is the History of Philosophy, philosophy or not?

   If you agree that it is, that the History of Philosophy is philosophy as well, is this not the same as saying that it is "metaphilosophy"?

4. Is psychology philosophy or not?[6]

   If you agree that it is, is the psychology of the philosopher, philosophy or not?

   If you agree that it is, that the psychology of the philosopher is philosophy too, is this not the same as saying that it is a metaphilosophical examination of philosophers?

   If you say instead that it is plain philosophy [not metaphilosophy], what would you call it in order to distinguish it from those philosophical reflections on anything other than the philosopher's psychology?

5. Is the phenomenology of philosophy and of the philosopher, philosophy or not?

   If you agree that it is, that the phenomenology of philosophy and of the philosopher is philosophy too, is this not the same as saying that it is a metaphilosophical examination of philosophy and the philosopher?

---

[6] [In the late 1930s in Mexico, psychology was still an area of philosophy in the university curriculum.—Trans.]

If you say instead that it is plain philosophy [not metaphilosophy], what would you call it in order to distinguish it from those philosophical—phenomenological—reflections on anything other than philosophy and the philosopher?

But the lessons of the History of Philosophy lead me to consider the possibility, the probability even, that I am wrong and you are right. Beneath the logic of truth, truth is an ethical concept very close to the Scholastic concept of *invincible ignorance* and the Christian concept of a *clear conscience*: to make every effort to find the truth and to be true to oneself and to others. This is one of the many subjects that I did not cover in my lectures, though I do discuss them in class.

I hope that, and I will be very pleased if, you consider these observations as I have considered your review: as a dialogue—a dialogue as unphilosophical as possible, that is, not driven by the will to impose [one's ideas on another], but inspired by a *historical* drive to understand one another empathetically. Allow me to remind you of what I pointed out in one of my lectures about [the relation between] *theory* and *history*.

Yours truly,
José Gaos

Disputatio de Nomine

Article II: Larroyo

All too often it is said, not without reason, that progress in philosophy, as in any other science, primarily consists in identifying hidden problems, in the discovery of new areas of research. The greatest systems of philosophy are timeless, not so much because of the concrete solutions they provide, but because of their style of questioning, their mastery of raising questions about the essence and value of the universe.

Hence my great interest in theoretically calling into question, in methodically assessing, Professor Gaos's suggesting the possibility of metaphilosophy, and his aim—put briefly—of highlighting an area of research that to a certain extent has not been emphasized in the great classics of philosophy. My question was the following: Is there a unique field of study untouched by any of the already existing branches of philosophy that *deserves* to be called metaphilosophy? Besides the traditional problems about the essence of philosophy, about truth and falsity, about the beautiful and the ugly, about right or wrong, about the sacred or profane, and so on, has metaphilosophy the right to exist? Professor Gaos insists, in the first part of his reply, on the possibility of such an autonomous discipline; but later, as the reader will notice in my detailed response to his letter, he is arguing for a relatively new name for old, traditional objects of knowledge. Strictly speaking, he throws himself into a *disputatio de nomine* [argument concerning a name].

I. NEITHER LASK NOR GAOS

In truth,[7] it was never my aim to identify Professor Gaos's philosophical antecedents. The only purpose of referring to Lask was to show that other thinkers have possessed the dramatic desire to somehow go further than the first science par excellence, philosophy, although never with such a flattering view of their own success. To me, Lask's logic of philosophy continues to be unjustified, like any *metaphilosophy*. It was precisely what I affirmed in my first article with the following words: " 'Philosophy,' then, refers to 'underivable and original knowledge.' What could be more primary than the problem of truth? Nothing, since in order to decide the validity of some belief, it would first be necessary to determine its truth or falsity (this is the inalienable problem of logic considered as philosophy's first science). Therefore, the attempt to enter into an area of research higher than philosophy inexorably leads to a vicious circle."

II. METAPHILOSOPHY AS PART OF PHILOSOPHY

Professor Gaos states that metaphilosophy is not a discipline superimposed on philosophy proper; it is, so to speak, a chapter of philosophy. He points out: "In all of philosophy there are two parts: reflections on values (what is good, what is beautiful, what is sacred, etc.), and reflections on those reflections. These two parts, the second included, exist in every philosophy *as a matter of fact.*" It is only because I did not interpret metaphilosophy in this way that I was led to a contradiction in terms and an infinite regress.

Let us carefully consider this statement as clearly as possible in order to exhibit its "senselessness." To do so, I will once again emphasize that the primary purpose of philosophy is to ascertain the values of culture and its essential laws.

It is also evident that, in such an exalted task, philosophers continuously devote their most costly intellectual energy; they develop a kind of mental skill oriented at obtaining this essence and sense of values. Borrowing from the Greek, let us use *logos* to refer to the values and their universal principles, to

---

[7] The numbering of the parts of this article corresponds to the numbering of Professor Gaos's letter.

the non-empirical content of philosophical meditation. And let us use *psyche* to refer to the subjective, relatively changing, activity of the philosopher's mental life.

There is no doubt that philosophy *stricto sensu* is, like any other science, that set of trans-subjective truths (the concepts and laws of values) that philosophers have discovered in the course of time. Further, it is something radically different from the mental process that in each case thinkers achieve in the process of obtaining those universal laws. *It is appropriate to distinguish, then, two perfectly different aspects or dimensions of philosophical thought: the content of reflection (philosophy, stricto sensu) and the changing psychological activity of the philosopher (the subjective act of philosophizing).*

Let us now consider to what extent these [two] dimensions can be the objects of a repeated reflection. Naturally, we will begin with the psychological aspect. In this aspect it does make sense to speak about a reflection on a reflection *ad infinitum*. I am able to recall—to relive—mental states that I experienced yesterday in the same spot, and tomorrow [I will be able to recall] the series of mental experiences that crossed my mind today, and so on without limit. Surely, the memory of a memory is a psychological fact that does not involve any contradiction.

By contrast, in the other aspect concerning the content of philosophical reflection, this kind of reflection on a reflection is not possible. The theory of science teaches that all knowledge, including the philosophical, presupposes a point of view in order to exist (in order to be obtained). Concerning a fact of culture, for example, it is possible to achieve historical, psychological, or philosophical "knowledge" [*un saber*], depending on the point of view from which it is considered. Looking at a sculpture by Rodin, one might formulate a historical judgment; or one might analyze the subjective experience of those who take pleasure in the master's work and, *eo ipso*, remain in psychological reflection; or, finally, one might rise to the height of philosophical interpretation and make an effort to define, for example, the essence of the beautiful. Now, the result of each one of these *considerations* cannot be the object of the *same consideration*. It would be completely absurd to submit the notion of beauty obtained from the aesthetic-philosophical interpretation of the French master's creation to the same aesthetic interpretation while inquiring, once again, into the essence of the beautiful. It is another thing to inquire, based on the notion just acquired, into more knowledge, perhaps the relations between beauty and other values. But, needless to say, in this case the notion of beauty is judged from a different point of view. It is no longer a reflection on a reflection, in the strict sense of the term.

However, such conceptual precision is sometimes clouded by a misuse of words. When one speaks easily about the history of history, for example, one never has in mind the idea of a historical description of the same cultural event; one is clearly referring to the history of the science of history (a different and possible object of consideration in its own right). The history of the history of a single historical fact is, like it or not, an absurdity. The same is true of supposed metaphilosophy, *mutatis mutandi*. Suppose one comes across the following definition: "philosophy is the science of values, including the value of its essence," as Dilthey says from the place he occupies in the intellectual world. I ask: would it make sense to apply the same consideration again to the definition just discovered? Obviously not. It is possible, of course, taking the definition obtained as a starting point, to gradually address other problems about philosophy, such as the question concerning the parts of philosophy, or concerning the relation between philosophy and the rest of the sciences or culture as a whole, and so on. But, for clear reasons, neither Plato, Aristotle, Descartes, Kant, Hegel, nor Comte—just to mention the names of the great heroes of philosophical thought that Professor Gaos refers to—have called it metaphilosophy. On the other hand, the fact that philosophy (historically) has not mired itself in self-reflexive considerations, has not fallen into an infinite regress, is not to say that its future does not harbor within it an infinite task in the same way science in general does.

In fact, Plato had already placed the critical concept of the "limit of the unlimited" (*apeiron orizein*) at the center of his philosophy, as the Marburg School has astutely noted, even though Professor Gaos has announced in public the death of this Neo-Kantian school. An infinite regress, understood as a logical mistake, that is, as the endless and senseless regress in search for a firm point of departure, is one thing; infinite progress, constantly in search of new and deeper truths, is another thing and very different. It was Rickert, another Neo-Kantian, who, while glossing H. Cohen, has accurately coined the interesting expression of the "open system" of philosophy.

To say that the first chapter of every particular science (the problem of defining arithmetic, physics, etc.) is a topic of logic is a grave error that had already been refuted long before Doctor Gaos declared, with full sincerity, that critical idealism was breathing its last breath. Logic is not obliged to create science; its task does not consist in determining its general problems or the special topics of a particular investigation. Nobody can take seriously this kind of speculative logic. Logic, like all branches of philosophy, reflects on a fact of culture (*factum culturae*). Its specific area of culture is science as it already exists. And only on the basis of science is logic able to ascertain its fundamental truths through the transcendental method. Otherwise, as must constantly be repeated, "philosophy would breathe in a vacuum."

The same is true regarding the essence of philosophy (its definition). This problem is, and will continue to be, the first chapter of philosophy as science. Professor Gaos's use of "metaphilosophy" derives from the confusion between subjective *philosophizing* and objective *philosophy*. The mental (psychological) reflection on the essence of philosophy is not philosophy in itself, as no subjective event can be. Philosophy as the unity of non-empirical principles is not a temporal phenomenon of any kind. To overlook this distinction would mean to fall into psychologism, to reduce *logos* to *psyche*.

III. A PHILOSOPHICAL HISTORICISM

More than anyone else, it was Hegel who taught professional philosophers to ponder the importance of the philosophical past. The greatest systems are not relics that the philosopher should exhume every so often to pay tribute to them on their anniversary. There is something timeless about them, something so alive that is, so to speak, the flesh and blood of eternal philosophy. No brilliant thought fades: the central ideas of the systems of Plato, Aristotle, Descartes, Kant, Hegel are a perennial part of philosophy, that is, principles and presuppositions of the infinite task of philosophical investigation.

But it does not follow, as Doctor Gaos contends, that philosophy is history understood as a temporal succession of events. It could be said that philosophy rests on history, but it is not history. Indeed, neither the methods nor the results of philosophy are identified with their history, just as mathematics, physics, chemistry, and so on, are far from being one and the same thing as their respective histories. In this way, as the history of philosophy achieves its purpose, to faithfully review the origin and evolution of philosophical thought, it is the task of philosophy, as the science of essences (the science of laws) to formulate interdependent truths—a priori or independently of all temporal experience. The *desideratum* of the history of philosophy as a descriptive science of singular facts is grounded in finding the internal and incremental unity of the future of philosophy, as is the case with all historical research of culture, ideographic science. By contrast, philosophy is the nomothetic science par excellence. In other words, given the *factum* of culture, it is possible to practice, among other things, two forms of conceptualization: the eidetic-philosophical and the historico-factical. To subsume the first under and in the service of the second is to overestimate the genetic-descriptive—the historical—to the detriment of philosophy. It is to fall once again into philosophical historicism: *history* swallows the *eidos*.

Hence, Professor Gaos's attempt to underpin the possibility of a metaphilosophy by identifying philosophy as first science and history seems to me, by all lights, a failure.

IV. THE ARROGANCE OF HUMILITY

To inquire, from a psychological point of view, whether the philosopher gives into the feeling of arrogance can ultimately only be done by the method of introspection (self-examination). That is why I was justified in bringing up, in my first article, the testimony of the great figures of the history of philosophy who contradict this particular assertion.

But Professor Gaos interprets the confessions of Aquinas and Descartes, Kant and Bacon, among others, as masks behind which weak philosophers conceal their arrogance. For him, such an attitude is perhaps a refinement of arrogance, which makes it appear as humility.

And he concludes: "The challenge is not to adduce appearances, but to penetrate into the reality behind them, of which the subjects themselves are more or less conscious." By saying this, he dismisses, without proof, the confessions of those extraordinary thinkers. That is why I think that, until he produces the relevant psychological evidence, we should defer to the testimony of such great philosophers.

The examples of this issue that he offers immediately after, concerning the problem of God, are also ungrounded. Regarding the Kantian and Neo-Kantian concept of a legislating subject as the supposed paradigm of arrogance, a clear distinction needs to be made. The legislating subject is not the philosopher: it is the cultural consciousness whose law the investigator tries to describe. It is, as Kant would say himself, the *factum* of reflection. The philosophical mind only describes the essential lawfulness of the culture that makes it possible.

Moreover, even in the moral sphere, the legislating subject usually aspires to the purest virtue, justice, in which he recognizes and admires the equal dignity of every rational subject before the moral law, and feels infinitely small before the total realization of culture (God)—none of which is anything like the feeling of arrogance, but rather its opposite. Only the concept of the "arrogance of humility" could distort this obvious point.

V. PHILOSOPHY AS PERSONAL CONFESSION

I agree with Professor Gaos that phenomenology has evolved from Husserl to Heidegger, passing through Ortega's perspectivism. How can anyone say otherwise? What is more: aside from some of his students, the better known philosophers after Husserl (Scheler, Heidegger, etc.) have offered such widely different interpretations of the phenomenological method that their only common denominator is the name "phenomenology." In the winter of 1932, Husserl himself warned that his system had been misunderstood. The attempt to revive metaphysics as a science of, and through, the phenomenological method is one that the Professor of Freiburg had expressly declared nonsense. Phenomenology is to him a science of essences of and through the given phenomena.

I also agree with Professor Gaos that personal confession has an essence that can be described phenomenologically. But though phenomenology can define the essence of personal confession, it does not in any way follow that philosophy is characterized by that essence. As long as Professor Gaos does not produce evidence that philosophy is not an eidetic science (universal) that investigates the essence and laws of values, he has no right to define first science [philosophy] in the terms of philosophical romanticism.

OVERVIEW

The previous discussion reiterated the initial point about the impossibility of a metaphilosophy as a discipline about or as one of the classical problems of philosophical investigation. In what follows, Professor Gaos's last attempt to salvage at least the name "metaphilosophy"—and, in my opinion, its evident inappropriateness—will be revealed.

Gaos:

> 1. Have philosophers reflected on the nature of philosophy or not? If they have, is this reflection philosophy or not?
>
> If you agree that it is philosophy, that a reflection on philosophy is philosophy too, is this not the same as saying that [this reflection] is "metaphilosophy"?
>
> If you say instead that it is plain philosophy, what name would you use to refer to this philosophical reflection on the nature of philosophy in order to distinguish it from those philosophical "reflections" on the nature of anything other than philosophy?

Response: To be extremely clear in this reply, let us suppose that one accepts this idea of philosophy as a "pure science of values," which Professor Gaos has not refuted. It is evident that new judgements (knowledge) can be formulated about such an idea; with justification, one can reflect on it from different points of view. It is accurate to say, for example, that philosophy studies a diversity of values and, therefore, that it consists in a variety of disciplines; that philosophy distinguishes itself from rhetoric, art, religion, the special sciences through particular central characteristics, and so on. Now, the results of these philosophical reflections have, within philosophy (broken up into chapters), precise and strict titles. They are the names, respectively, for the problem of classifying philosophy, for the relations between philosophy and other regions of culture, and so on. Does Doctor Gaos prefer the title "metaphilosophy," which is ambiguous, over this clearly more precise nomenclature? *Quaestio de nomine.*

Gaos:

2. Is the task of defining philosophy, philosophy or not?

If it is philosophy, that is, if it is *part* of philosophy, what would you call it to distinguish it (within and as a part of philosophy) from its other parts, such as the philosophy of nature, the philosophy of history, and so on?

Response: Professor Gaos naturally recognizes that there is a problem of defining philosophy. But he supposes there is something in the solution, apart from describing or discovering the essence of philosophy, that deserves the name "metaphilosophy." Phantasm! The pure, ideal content of this reflection on the essence of philosophy is the defining characteristic of philosophy (its essence). The other aspects of the concrete act of philosophizing (psychological phenomena, the expression of thought, etc.) are not philosophy *stricto sensu*. But Professor Gaos does not want to simply call it "the problem of the essence or definition of philosophy"—as Dilthey, among others, does—but "metaphilosophy," alongside the philosophy of nature, the philosophy of history, and so on. *Quaestio de nomine.*

Gaos:

3. Is the History of Philosophy, philosophy or not?

If you agree that it is, that the History of Philosophy is philosophy as well, is this not the same as saying that it is "metaphilosophy"?

Response: Philosophy, like all science, has a history from which it is distinguished by its method and cognitive aim, as was proven earlier. However, given his historicism, Doctor Gaos considers the history of philosophy a part of philosophy and goes even further, calling its incorporation "philosophy." *Quaestio de nomine.*

Gaos:

4. Is psychology philosophy or not?

If you agree that it is, is the psychology of the philosopher, philosophy or not?

If you agree that it is, that the psychology of the philosopher is philosophy too, is this not the same as saying that it is a metaphilosophical examination of philosophers?

If you say instead that it is plain philosophy [not metaphilosophy], what would you call it in order to distinguish it from those philosophical reflections on anything other than the philosopher's psychology?

Response: The psychology of the philosopher, that is, the description and explanation of his concrete and subjective (temporal) phenomena, is one thing. The psychology of philosophy—an utterly absurd concept—is quite another thing. Indeed, there cannot be a psychology of philosophy because philosophy is, strictly speaking, a unity of non-empirical principles; and essences do not have a *psyche* and, *eo ipso*, they do not have a psychology. Therefore, allowing that psychology is a part of philosophy (not fundamental but the most derivative) it would still be wrong to speak of this part (psychology) as metaphilosophy. There is only the psychology of the person who philosophizes. However, Doctor Gaos wants to give the psychology of the philosopher the title of "metaphilosophy." *Quaestio de nomine.*

Gaos:

5. Is the phenomenology of philosophy and of the philosopher, philosophy or not?

If you agree that it is, that the phenomenology of philosophy and of the philosopher is philosophy too, is this not the same as saying that it is a metaphilosophical examination of philosophy and the philosopher?

If you say instead that it is plain philosophy [not metaphilosophy], what would you call it in order to distinguish it from those philosophical—phenomenological—reflections on anything other than philosophy and the philosopher?

Response: I accept Husserl's terminology. Phenomenology is a discipline of unbiased investigation. When it is applied to philosophy, Husserl calls it "phenomenological philosophy." Does Professor Gaos recall the title of the book *Ideas Pertaining to a Pure Phenomenology and a Phenomenological Philosophy*? Does the name used by the founder of the method not seem to Professor Gaos more specific and accurate? Why, then, give it the additional title of "metaphilosophy"? *Quaestio de nomine.*

In short, the name "metaphilosophy" from the pen of Doctor Gaos does not refer to a single specific problem of philosophy. Each one of his conclusions reveals his effort to find new names for old problems, which in my opinion were accurately named centuries ago. In any case, one must applaud that eagerness for nonconformity of the rector of the Central University of Madrid—a symptom of a fine philosophical mind.

Response: Gaos's Second Letter to Larroyo

To My Distinguished Colleague and Friend:

I beg your pardon for taking so long to reply to your letter of January 25, when you sent me your new article "*Disputatio de nomine.*" I could not read it properly when I received it, as other activities contributed to me forgetting about it. Until today.

Carefully considered, and despite its length, it can be reduced to the following points:

I. The thesis about the impossibility, the "nonsense," of metaphilosophy.

One must distinguish *psyche* and *logos, history* and *eidos*. Not to distinguish them would be to fall into psychologism or historicism, which has already been refuted. "There is no doubt" that philosophy *stricto sensu* is *logos* or *eidos*, not a temporal phenomenon of any kind, "an idea of philosophy which Professor Gaos has not refuted." *Psyche* is subjective philosophizing; *history*, the History of Philosophy. *Psyche* in fact reflects on itself, the *psyche* of *psyche*. It does not make sense to speak of *logos* reflecting on itself, the *logos* of *logos*, nor does the history of history make sense. Since philosophy = *logos*, and a *logos* of *logos* makes no sense, metaphilosophy does not make sense either. There is a question about the definition of philosophy, to which philosophy traditionally refers as such, and which we now propose to call "metaphilosophy": *quaestio de nomine*.

II. Objections to three particular points about my supposed metaphilosophy, in order of their importance.

1. Philosophy, "personal confession," has an *eidos* that can be the object of phenomenology. We grant that "personal confession" has an *eidos* and the possibility that it is the object of phenomenology. We deny that it has been proven that "personal confession" is the *eidos* of philosophy.

2. (A) A general thesis. Philosophy is arrogance even in those cases of "declared" humility. We deny that arrogance has been proved in those cases.

(B) A particular case: the conception of a "transcendental" subject is the conception of an arrogant subject. We reply: the conception of a transcendental subject cannot be the conception of an arrogant subject.

3. You (first article): if defining philosophy were metaphilosophy, then defining arithmetic would be a meta-arithmetic. Me (first letter): The definition of arithmetic is not meta-arithmetic, but the logic of arithmetic, the philosophy of arithmetic. You (second article): to say that the definition of arithmetic is the logic of arithmetic is to say that logic creates the object of arithmetic and of this science, a "grave error already refuted."

These points, then, suggest to me the following observations:

1. A question of name is usually more than a mere question of name. It is usually a question about the thing itself. To give something some name or other is usually to express a conception and even pick out different things. It seems to me that this is what the following observations reveal.

Even admitting your conception of philosophy—the precise and exclusive equation "philosophy = *logos* or *eidos*"—I insist on the fact that there is room to speak meaningfully of metaphilosophy. I will forego the question of the impossibility (as you say) or the possibility (as I contend) of a *logos* of *logos*. There is a passage in your article in which you define philosophy according to your own conception of it: philosophy is the determination of values. Now, to define, on one hand, and to determine, on the other, are ontologically and logically distinct operations. If philosophy is a determination of values, such a definition of philosophy is not in itself a determination of values, it is not philosophy: the definition of philosophy would not be philosophy. In order to be philosophy—as it seems to be and as it should be considered—it is necessary to broaden the given definition with another element, besides the determination of values, which would be capable of including the definition of philosophy. In my opinion, that other element would be metaphilosophy. But in truth the meaning of these observations makes one suspect, at the very least, that the conception of philosophy as the determination of values is in fact insufficient. It makes one doubt at least the correctness and the exhaustiveness of the equation "philosophy = *logos* or *eidos*." This equation leaves out of *philosophy*, in the strict sense, subjective philosophizing. Are the words "philosophy" and "philosophizing," "strict sense" and "subjective," enough to settle whether this problem is philosophical or not? This observation leads to the following considerations.

One decisive thing about your article is that it allows us to point out rigorously and clearly what distinguishes our views. It is not a disagreement about a name; it is the entire conception of philosophy to which each of us adheres. In my opinion, instead of distinguishing *psyche* and *logos, history* and *eidos*, one should say "*logos* and *eidos* within *anthropos* = *history*." Not to distinguish *psyche* and *logos, history* and *eidos* is to be ignorant of the path traveled by philosophy from 1896 to our own time, from the time Husserl presented his critique of psychologism on the basis of a positivist conception of the psyche as psychological "facts" of man (as a species and as reality)—this was the thesis of my doctoral dissertation *Husserl's Critique of Psychologism* (1928)—to the time in which we no longer think of "humanism" and "historicism" as "psychologism" or "empiricism," even though it is a reality—"transcendental" *reality*, not "transcendental" *ideality*—to which this ideality can and should be reduced without any trace of "psychologism" or "empiricism." Consequently, philosophy *stricto sensu* and *solo sensu* is not your *logos* and *eidos* (strictly speaking it is, but your mistake is too obvious to be dangerous), but a human activity and, as such, temporal and historical. The history of history makes sense as that reality of the past in the present, which as such is both present and past and which generates an *infinite progress* in reality precisely through an *infinite regress* in consciousness. It is the same continuity, both real and conscious, of history. No history is possible without fundamental ideas, but the history of philosophy is not possible without a conception of philosophy, which turns the history of philosophy into genuine philosophical discipline—into philosophy—not a merely historical one. I entertained the idea of philosophy as *logos* or *eidos* just to go on with our dialogue, not because I embrace it. I did not reject it because it did not occur to me to rewrite the history of philosophy of the last decades. What separates us, then, is our basic conception of philosophy and, at bottom, a conception of *logos* or *eidos*, on one hand, and of *man*, on the other. And consequently I believe, as Fichte says, "What kind of philosophy one chooses depends on what kind of man one is," dear Larroyo, *haud de nomine, sed de homine disputatio*.

II. 1. If you mean to say that I have not produced any evidence in favor of the claim that philosophy is personal confession, then I regret expressing myself so poorly in my lectures, for I believed that I did produce some evidence, throughout all the lectures, but particularly and explicitly in the last one. If what you mean to say is that I did not produce enough evidence, I might agree with that. But I hope you will grant that six lectures for a non-specialized audience is not a substitute for a philosophical treatise.

II. 2. (A) If you mean to say that I have not produced any evidence in favor of the claim that philosophy = personal confession, I can only repeat what I have just stated. The interpretation of the *archikotate sophia* of Aristotle, on one hand, and the phenomenological description of arrogance, on the other, seem to me sufficiently demonstrative not to be dismissed without a refutation as detailed as the examples themselves—*more scholastico*, as you like to say. If what you mean to say is that I have not offered a similar interpretation of other philosophers, that is a fact. But allow me to inform you that it is a fact particular to these lectures and letters, not to my private work or my overall activity as a teacher and lecturer.

II. 2. (B) The concept of a "transcendental" subject cannot be the concept *of* an arrogant subject in the objective sense of the genitive: *the "transcendental" subject* cannot *be* an arrogant subject. The concept of a "transcendental" subject is the conception *of* an arrogant subject in the *subjective* sense of the genitive: the "transcendental" subject is *conceived* of by an *arrogant subject*. Concerning the evidence for this statement, I refer to what was said at the end of the previous paragraph.

3. To say that defining arithmetic is to do the logic of arithmetic does not seem to me to say that logic creates the object of arithmetic and of this science.

It is simply to say that logic tries to define ontologically the object defined ontically by arithmetic, and to study the science of arithmetic as it is in fact constituted from a logical point of view.

Yours truly,
José Gaos

The Pre-Kantian Logic of Doctor Gaos

Article III: Larroyo

The discussion concerning the possibility of metaphilosophy—a central topic in
our philosophical conversation—has revealed, so to speak, some relatively interesting arguments. After discussing in great detail whether so-called metaphilosophy encompasses the problem of the philosopher's psychology, or that of
the relation between philosophy and other areas of culture—problems that for
me were properly named long ago—Doctor Gaos seems to be hiding behind
the possible meaning of the question, the basic question par excellence, of the
essence of philosophy, that is, of its definition.

In what follows, however, I will show that he has chosen the worst topic in
philosophy in his effort to successfully defend his new discipline. Moreover, this
time his central argument leads to a conceptual confusion whose origin can only
be explained by that speculative (pre-Kantian) logic which, when it was being
developed, did not look for its principles inside the structure of the sciences
already available, but legislated them, unaware of concrete investigations and
their corresponding theoretical failures.

I. DEFINING EVERY SCIENCE: A PROBLEM

It is clear that the exposition of every science begins with the unavoidable task of
defining the boundaries of its field of study, of pointing out its subject matter, the
object of its research. The same is true of philosophy itself. Now, if this is its *first*
problem, I am convinced that—logically speaking—it does not constitute the
final results of philosophical clarification. For example, whether being a nomothetic science of values is the correct definition of philosophy does not depend
on the final conception of beauty, the good, in short, on the essence and laws
of values. And this is because, to define philosophy, like any other science, is to
determine the problem that is to be solved by the never-ending labor of research.
It could be said that to define a science in terms of its results is an *aporia* or
insoluble scientific question. Therefore, to declare that philosophy is the science of

values is only to establish the direction that will orientate philosophical research, its task, or problem.

How, then, can the task of defining philosophy be metaphilosophy? For that to be the case, it should not be the first question, but the last, as I have said throughout: only then can one speak of a *logos* of *logos* which Doctor Gaos defends with exemplary tenacity. In other words, the problem and solution are related terms that constitute an indivisible unity in the labor of the sciences. Therefore, when one defines philosophy as a theory of values (axiology), the definition itself is not excluded from philosophical reflection. Only a traditional logic like constructivism that does not tie aporia and judgement together can provide Doctor Gaos with arguments, regardless of the modern tone with which his attractive words resound.

I agree with him, therefore, that we are discussing two different conceptions of philosophy. I also agree with Fichte, who says that "what kind of philosophy one subscribes to depends on what kind of man one is," not as an expression of a relativism implied in defining philosophy as personal confession, but as the capacity to raise—oh, Fichte!—to the Idea of the Absolute Self. In this, Heraclitus's maxim *hen to sofon mounon* continues to be true,[8] my admirable Doctor Gaos.

As to whether historicism is the true philosophy, I cannot agree, even though it means being out of philosophical fashion. The enduring nature [*reviviscencia*] of the historical (Doctor Gaos's "the reality of the past in the present") has all the traits of phenomenon or fact.

"Transcendental reality" is a kind of contradiction in terms—an example of which is the phrase "dialectical materialism,"—if by "reality" we mean the spatio-temporal, or the temporal, and if by "transcendental" we mean the a priori condition of the possibility of every fact, that is, something non-temporal (ideal).

Concerning the particular, it might be objected that we should change the meaning of these terms in order to conform to the neo-Romantic philosophy of our times. But why don't the countless philosophers who try to restore metaphysics, the epigones of the twentieth century, coin new terms to avoid failing to stall philosophical progress and causing confusion in philosophical terminology?

II. A VERY TWENTIETH-CENTURY PSYCHOLOGISM

1. I do not deny that Doctor Gaos has produced enough evidence for the view that philosophy is personal confession; I only claim that such a thought is

---

[8] [Larroyo is referring to fragment 32 of Heraclitus, which reads: *hen to sophon mounon legesthai ouk ethelei kai ethelei Zenos onoma*, and which translates "The wise is one only. It is unwilling and willing to be called by the name of Zeus."—Trans.]

incompatible with the idea of philosophy as an eidetic science of cultural values, something very different according to the interpretation of the transcendental method already mentioned.

2. On the other hand, to insist, drawing upon the latest phenomenological method (not Husserl's), that *arrogance* (Gaos: "philosophy as arrogance") is also an essential part of philosophy, is psychologism. The argumentation is clear and of the classic variety. Is arrogance not a psychological phenomenon and, as such, an object of psychological study? To draw upon such a psychological principle to manipulate philosophical problems—is this not pure psychologism? However, until now it had not occurred to anyone to define philosophy, among other things, in this diabolical tone.[9]

III. AN ORIGINAL BUT FALSE DOCTRINE OF DEFINITION

But if one considers his argumentation carefully, this whole sequence of errors has its roots in the false notion of definition to which Doctor Gaos appeals. He writes: "To say that the definition of arithmetic is the logic of arithmetic does not seem to me to say that logic creates the object of arithmetic and of this science. It is simply to say that logic tries to define ontologically the object defined ontically by arithmetic, and to study the science of arithmetic as it is in fact constituted from a logical point of view."

For Doctor Gaos, then, there are two definitions of arithmetic (as well as with any science, *mutatis mutandis*): the ontic definition and the ontological definition. Here is a definition: "arithmetic is the part of mathematics that deals with determinate quantities and their relations." Is it an ontic or ontological definition? What distinguishes the first from the second?

And if traditionally there are two types of definitions, what do we mean by a general definition?

Does this distinction not remind Doctor Gaos, who is indisputably a modern philosopher, of the famous, classic argument of the "third" man? More to the point, is there perhaps some (true) definition that is not logical, that is, a definition untouched by the principles and laws of *logos*? Do mathematicians offer a-logical definitions?

No, Doctor Gaos, all definitions are necessarily ontological, since "science is science insofar it proceeds logically." A science that is anti-logical or even just

---

[9] [Gaos defined the philosopher as a rational being who tried to intellectualize everything, including God. The philosopher could therefore be compared to Satan, the fallen angel, who tried to make sense of God and question Him. However, since the philosopher cannot make sense of everything, he is in the end only a "poor devil" (*pobre diablo*).—Trans.]

a-logical is simply inconceivable. The validity of every new piece of knowledge is determined, first and foremost, by the absence of contradiction, that is, according to the fundamental law of logic. It would not be an exaggeration to claim that the great investigator in any particular science is always someone who possesses a superior logical insight. This is not to say, thanks to the division of labor in the sciences, that the scientist himself is aware of his own assumptions [*su proceder*], of what does not hinder but promotes scientific progress.

The fact that logic reflects on the particular sciences, that logic is, in this sense, the self-consciousness of knowledge, does not imply anything circular in its foundations, as might be supposed. Logic does not make up the various ways of being of *logos*; it discovers them in its always unfinished and particular investigations. But *logos* itself is one thing, which is not exclusive to any particular science, but common to all of them. The concrete results of the particular sciences, expressed in definitions, axioms, principles, and so on, is something else. Logic does not start with the results of the sciences as its premises; it penetrates those results until their logical dimension emerges and in that way the autonomous laws of logic are formulated. It does not define any particular science; it provides them with their defining traits in general. It is not interested in the results of special sciences as propositions of this or that discipline, but insofar as they deliver the *logos*. In other words, through the results of particular research, it arrives at the logical aspect of thought, which is, precisely, the core of every demonstrated truth [*saber*].[10]

---

[10] Francisco Larroyo, *The Logic of Science*, p. 121.

CHAPTER 9

My Two Cents

"AMERICAN" PHILOSOPHY? (1942)

José Gaos

Translated by Robert Eli Sanchez, Jr. and Aurelia Valero Pie

Throughout the year that just ended, there has been a debate in Spanish-speaking countries in America concerning the creation of a philosophy peculiar to them. They aspire to have a Mexican, Argentinian, or American philosophy, in the same way there is a French, German, or European philosophy. The Old continent is seen as moribund and in this New and shiny continent, one feels called to capture and continue European culture—a feeling that might make the mistake of being hasty, Cartesian. Bloodletting can be a healthy response to a dangerous excess of vitality. America is now deemed mature enough for such a historical mission. It is a topic that reproduces, not exactly but in good measure, some concerns that were held in Spain for some time. Since the first decades of this century, Spain has also wanted to introduce once and for all a particular philosophy that would one day be *Spanish* in the sense that philosophies are French or German, Italian or English. There was an awareness that Spanish philosophy in this sense did not truly exist. A question about this matter is overtly at the center of the originary and most original goals of Ortega y Gasset's project. The important and decisive thing about this project is that it started out as a program to "save" Spanish "circumstances" bit by bit, and this program has been the basis of all of Ortega's work from 1914, the beginning of the First World War, until today in the middle of the second global war. Saving the Spanish circumstance piece by piece is how philosophy achieves the great salvation of the Spanish circumstance because "I am myself and my circumstance, and if I do not save my circumstance, I do not save myself."[1]

---

[1] [Gaos switches from the plural *salvaciones* to the singular *salvación*, suggesting that the progress of philosophy is incremental, and that the great Salvation would only be achieved by minor salvations or acts of salvation.—Trans.]

The same preoccupations turned us into disciples of Ortega, that is, we devoted ourselves to philosophy and working our way through philosophy in Spain and for a Spanish philosophy, drawing on and reflecting on the work of our teacher. This historical background of the topic being debated in these [American] countries throughout the year that just ended leads me to offer "my two cents," with the hope that in "unofficially [*oficiosamente*] taking part in the conversation of others"—which is how the Spanish Academy explains the phrase [*cuarto a espadas*[2]]—"the inappropriateness and affectations of whoever meddles in someone else's business" does not prevail over "the diligence and care in the business of friendship," which are both accepted definitions of "officiousness" [*oficiosidad*] in the dictionary, not always a helpful explanatory or defining device.

There is still not, or not yet, Spanish philosophy, or, more generally, a Spanish-language philosophy, in the sense that there are French and English philosophies, or the philosophies of those languages. There is not yet an American philosophy that can be contrasted with European philosophy. But there is a desire, a vehement desire, that there be one. That there is a desire is the first point to reflect on. Is it justified? Correct? First, and generally speaking, is philosophy, doing philosophy, having philosophy, having philosophers, being a philosopher, desirable such that having a Spanish-language or American philosophy might also be desirable? This question is surprising because there is a long and illustrious tradition, ultimately triumphant throughout history to the present day, that highly values philosophy, even as the height of all perfect and complete culture. The fact that philosophers themselves are primarily responsible for this assessment has not caused suspicion that it might be partial or unfounded. . . . But the truth seems to be that philosophy is not necessary for individual or collective human life; it is certainly not necessary for the simplest human life, but neither is it necessary for the highest, the most supreme, human life. The great princes, *caudillos*, and statesmen, the great heroes, the great saints, the great artists, the great men of science themselves, are not great philosophers. The most illustrious or most influential peoples or cultures in all human history have not had, or have not really had, a sufficiently substantive or sufficiently original philosophy: Egypt, Chaldea, Persia, Judea, Rome, Spain, the Slavic nations. . . . A whole era in history, the positivist era, values science at the expense of, or in opposition to, philosophy, and this evaluation is still far from completely extinct. The value of science over philosophy is still somewhat prominent in America, although not as much in Spanish as it is in English.

Even Athens tried, exiled, condemned to death, or at the very least reduced to private activity and embittered the first and greatest philosophers who appeared

[2] [The title of Gaos's essay is "Cuarto a espadas," a phrase that roughly translates into "my two cents," but which has both a negative and a positive connotation in Spanish, as Gaos explains here.]

in Athens or nearby: Anaxagoras, Protagoras, Socrates, Plato, Aristotle. And there seems to be reason to believe that the mistrust of philosophers, the hostility against them, was not unique to an uncultured and unreasonable people. Calicles' speech in Plato's *Gorgias* shows that in the upper and influential classes of the city there was a very different estimation of the philosopher from the traditional views of the philosophers themselves. Perhaps it should also be taken into account here that even in cultures and for peoples that do have a philosophy, philosophy did not always (from the beginning) play a regular role in the life of a culture or people; it is more of a burst of intense but ephemeral blooming, spread apart by great intervals, kind of like an abnormal and sensual spasm. In Greece, philosophy began two or three centuries after Homer, which is to say, it was not exactly an original phenomenon. It flourished for three or four hundred years unrivaled by any other development in all of Antiquity. From the time Justinian closed the School of Athens—the event, more symbolic than real, that signals the end of ancient philosophy—five centuries passed until the beginning of the uninterrupted course of Christian Scholasticism, which lasted for another five hundred years. Then modern philosophy achieved, at the end of the seventeenth century and the turn of the nineteenth, unprecedented advances in metaphysics unlike anything since the height of Greek philosophy; in both cases the developments were concentrated into a few decades, the peak of two or three generations.

It must be remembered that what is desired is not simply philosophy, general philosophy, but a Spanish-language philosophy or, more precisely, an American philosophy. If all that was desired was philosophy in general, at one's disposal are all the philosophies of other languages or all Eurasian philosophies (ancient, modern, and future); for, in the future, if one wishes for general philosophy, not a specifically Spanish-language philosophy or American philosophy, we could leave the task of providing philosophy to Spanish-speakers or Americans to well-seasoned Eurasian philosophers who speak other languages. But what is desired is rightly not to continue translating or importing philosophy from overseas, but to produce original work in situ. One might ask again: is the desire for more specificity justified, correct? Why shouldn't Spanish-speakers or Americans be satisfied with, for example, English-language, European, or Asian philosophy? Of all people, the Latin-speaking philosophers of Antiquity and the Middle Ages felt compelled to adopt Greek philosophy. Cartesians and positivists, Kantians, Hegelians, or Krausians in countries other than France and Germany, or even in continents other than Europe, felt compelled, and still do, to adopt philosophies in foreign languages and from foreign countries. Neo-Scholastics all over the world feel compelled to adopt the philosophy of Western medieval Europe. And, finally, it is not clear that Descartes or Comte, Kant or Hegel wanted to do French or German philosophy, or anything other than universal and eternal philosophy, not to mention Plato and Aristotle, who could not have wanted a Greek philosophy for the simple reason that world and history were for them much smaller. The desire, then—the deliberate, explicit wish—to do and have an original philosophy specific to one's own language and territory, more or less broadly construed, seems to be an unjustified novelty, at least one not justified by history. In the first place, it is possible that what is desired by or for some peoples or cultures might not be desired by or for others. So the first thing that should be carefully considered with regard to Spanish-language or American philosophy is, in short, whether having a philosophy, doing philosophy, possessing philosophy, being a philosopher, is really something so desirable as it seems or is believed to be, both in general and particularly in Spanish-speaking or American countries.

But let us assume that having a philosophy is as desirable as it seems or is believed to be by and for all peoples and cultures. The question, then, is the following: how is this desire satisfied? Philosophy in general, not to speak of an original philosophy, one peculiar to a language or part of the world, is it not necessarily a spontaneous fruit? Is it possible to produce it intentionally? It is well known that those who left for the Thirty Year's War did not know they were headed to a thirty-year war. Could Thales of Miletus have aimed for universal philosophy, or even toward Greek philosophy, or Descartes toward at least French philosophy, since he could not have aimed for modern philosophy? Let us imagine that absolutely every Spanish-speaker or every American shares the interest in creating a philosophy of our language or this continent, and that these millions of human beings begin to think, long for, and say in earnest, "Alas, we do not have a philosophy! We want a philosophy! We must create a Spanish-language philosophy! Let us create American philosophy!" Such determination would be as vast, dense, superb, and noisy as the jungles of this New World and it would rise to the heavens of propitious gods. Would it do any good to create a Spanish-language or American philosophy, if philosophy were the product of certain talents given to some but denied to other human groups that speak different languages and inhabit different parts of the globe, and it turned out that Americans and Spanish-speakers belonged to the second group? But a desire that stops seeking its own fulfillment on the basis of such considerations is overly rational. The idea that completely original innovations in the future are impossible is a philosophical idea about history that is not exactly set in stone.

Given the desire to have an original philosophy, the only consistent thing to do is to make an effort to produce philosophy, to philosophize, to succeed in doing anything in one's power to achieve the desired result, to decidedly and courageously take the risk of ultimately wasting one's time. . . . Here's why: it could be the case that philosophy cannot satisfy a desire for philosophy unless that desire is already philosophical, a desire injected into philosophizing. A desire for philosophy might be a desire to *continue* philosophizing, an activity in which one is already engaged. It could be that the desire is not deliberately to start philosophizing, but that the desire only emerges from philosophizing, from being a philosopher. In this case, we could ask: is the desire for a Spanish-language or American philosophy already philosophical? Is it already injected into philosophizing? Are Spanish-speakers or Americans already philosophizing? Are these questions themselves already philosophical?

In any case, what one should start doing or find oneself doing is philosophy, pure and simple. It has already been suggested that philosophy is not Greek, French, or German because Greek, French, or German philosophers intended it to be so, or that philosophy is European because European philosophers intended it to be so, but because Greeks, the French, Germans, or Europeans did philosophy in general. Philosophy acquires a nationality or "continentality," *sit venia verbo*, when authors, perhaps even despite themselves, do nothing more than philosophy *sin más*, but do so authentically. If Spaniards, Mexicans, or Argentinians produce enough philosophy, there will be Spanish, Mexican, Argentinian, American philosophy. Is this tautological? Perhaps so, by necessity. . . . Is philosophy original in itself, by its nature? Is philosophy (when it is authentic) essentially original? [*¿Filosofía (si auténtica) = original?*] *The challenge, then, is not to do* Spanish or American *philosophy*, the challenge is for *Spaniards or Americans to produce* philosophy.

What should concern us is not, ultimately, what is Spanish or American, but what is philosophical about Spanish or American philosophy. How is philosophy done? Or, more precisely, how does one do philosophy? That is the question. Now, there is no difference between "doing philosophy" or "philosophizing," and "philosophy." Accordingly, there is no difference between the questions, "How does one do philosophy?" or "How is philosophy done?" and "What is philosophy?" The challenge before us can thus also be formulated in this last question. But formulated this way, or simply reduced to the previous questions, [the relation between philosophy *sin más* and nationality] seems less tautological than it appears, and certainly too difficult to settle in this article. Perhaps this article will make the interested reader aware of what is truly involved in the question of creating philosophy peculiar to these countries. And if the interested reader has a solution to this question, if he knows what philosophy is, then he will know *eo ipso* what needs to be done or what he needs to continue doing. For my part, I hope to have an opportunity to pick up where this ending leaves off.

CHAPTER 10

Philosophy as Commitment (1952)

Leopoldo Zea

Translated by Amy A. Oliver

Leopoldo Zea Aguilar was born in Mexico City in 1912 and died there almost a century later in 2004, at the age of 92. His was a long and productive life to which dozens of books and hundreds of articles attest. Zea's intellectual adventures were many, but outstanding among them were his investigations into nineteenth-century positivism in Mexico, his arguments for the possibility of an authentic and genuine Latin American philosophy, his existentialist-inspired analysis of the Mexican character (of which the text included here is a representative example), and his preoccupations with colonialism, marginality, and social justice. A common concern underlying Zea's philosophical production focuses on the nature and role of philosophy in concrete human communities, together with the responsibility that philosophers assume in those communities by virtue of being philosophers. A number of Zea's works have been translated into English: "Concerning an American Philosophy" (1948), Positivism in Mexico (1974), The Latin American Mind (1975), and The Role of the Americas in History (1991). The last of these was edited and introduced by Amy Oliver, who translated the essay that follows.

"Wherever a man has taken a position that he believes to be best, or has been placed by his commander, there he must, I think, remain and face danger, without a thought for death or anything else, rather than disgrace. It would have been a dreadful way to behave, men of Athens, if, at Potidea, Amphipolis and Delium, I had, at the risk of death, like anyone else, remained at my post where those you had elected to command had ordered me, and then, when the god ordered me, as I thought and believed, to live the life of a philosopher, to examine myself and others, I had abandoned my post for fear of death or anything else."[1] In Socrates, therefore, we encounter the first and clearest example of philosophy

[1] Plato, *Apology*, 28 E. [The translator followed this edition: *Plato Complete Works*, John M. Cooper, ed. (Indianapolis, IN: Hackett, 1997).—Trans.]

as commitment. However, let us not think of "commitment" as some philosophers do, as those offended by the term when applied to the field of philosophy, though they find it acceptable for other, less meritorious, but more useful fields. Commitment in philosophy does not refer to a pact or to an obligation contracted in exchange for certain political, social, or economic favors, but to the inevitable commitment that everyone, philosopher or not, has to their circumstances, reality, or world. In this sense, every person is a committed agent, that is, inserted, *thrown*, or placed in a world in which one must act and for which one must be responsible. Commitment is a sentence and not a comfortable agreement that one freely enters into when it is convenient in light of certain interests. The only liberty that fits within this mode of being *sentenced* is that of one's attitude: shame or shamelessness, courage or cowardice, responsibility or irresponsibility. Commitment is assumed freely, that is, consciously or through continued presence within certain contexts.

Everyone, anyone, any of us, from the very moment we become conscious of our existence, we also become conscious of our committed being. We find ourselves committed, or *sentenced* to living in a physical and cultural world not of our making. We are committed, *thrown* into a world that from a physical point of view can be rich or poor, sufficient or insufficient, but always indifferent to what we need as human beings. We are committed to a cultural world created by others, by our fellow humans, a world with their religion, laws, customs, politics, economy, art, and many other forms of human expression, but a world in the making of which we have not participated, a world about which no one has been consulted, a world that never has to attend to our needs, desires, and dreams, yet nonetheless, a world that we have to accept as our own. We are committed in the company of our fellow humans, obliged to answer for our deeds, but also to witness their deeds. Faced with this commitment or these commitments, we do not have more liberty than that of our attitude. Yet this is already more than enough. It is this liberty that commits us in a fitting way. We are committed by existing, but it is by freely *assuming* these commitments that we become committed. Our freedom is expressed in the *form* in which we assume the inevitable commitment to our circumstances. It is this form that individualizes us, that distinguishes us among humankind. As we assume a certain form of commitment, we also assume our responsibility as individuals. No one escapes from this responsibility, not even those who deny their individuality, believing that by doing so they can shirk their responsibility. They will have to be just as responsible for this denial.

We have to be responsible for our attitudes because through them we not only commit to our own existence, but also commit to the existence of others. Just as others commit to us with their attitudes, we similarly commit to our fellow humans. In each of our attitudes we gamble with our existence; we also gamble with the existence of others. In turn, in gambling with their existence, they gamble with ours. Our responsibility follows. We have to be responsible for others, and for ourselves in a never-ending chain, as long as humanity exists. Historical consciousness is freely taking responsibility for the past in the present, at the same time as committing to be responsible for the future. We have to take responsibility for a past not of our making: yet at the same time, with our attitude, whatever it might be, we commit and take responsibility for a future that must be made by us. In this way, we are responsible for others in the presence of others. This is, in short, the essence of commitment. It is to this I refer when I speak of philosophy as commitment.

Philosophy as human work could not avoid this human commitment. Quite the contrary, if there is a human form that best captures commitment, it is philosophy. The philosopher is the person most conscious of his or her committed *situation*. Thus, the philosopher tries to take responsibility as if he or she were to embody all of humanity. In the name of all mortals, conceived of as the Human Race, Humanity, Culture, Nation, or Class, the philosopher adopts an attitude, attempting to respond on his or her behalf for eternity. In each philosophy, one tries to *respond*, to give a response, to every problem, to every possible human situation. In philosophy, the philosopher is committed to humanity in the presence of humanity. In the name of all that is human, the philosopher assumes responsibility for the past, the present, and all possible futures.

Socrates, upon dying, takes responsibility for the injustice of the Polis, Greek society, faced with the justice that every Polis should embody. Plato takes responsibility for the most esteemed ideals of Greek culture, of whose destruction he is a witness, to save them for eternity. Aristotle assumes responsibility in his philosophy for commitments not yet realized by Greek philosophy, of which his is the grandest synthesis. The Bishop of Hippo, Saint Augustine, assumes responsibility in his philosophy for the whole human race, condemned by original sin, by saving it in the City of God. Thomas Aquinas assumes responsibility as a Christian for pagan philosophy and other ways of life and conceptions of the world that are very different from Christian ways. Kant takes responsibility for the errors of dogmatism and skepticism in order to find a metaphysics that satisfies the most precious yearnings of the human race. Then Hegel, in a sweeping gesture, takes on the past of all Humanity, all of history, of which his lead will be the greatest synthesis, the embodiment of the Objective Spirit. Then we have philosophers who make a determinate class of people into the expression of all humanity, and who only think about the future of that class, never to a past that does not belong to them. These include Descartes, who only assumes responsibility for the future of the so-called new man, a member of the bourgeoisie, or Marx, who attends only to the future of a new class, the proletariat. There have been many others leading up to our own day, and to Jean-Paul Sartre, who, unlike his compatriot Descartes, assumes responsibility for the bourgeoisie's past, including its errors, with the hope, it would seem, of managing to save for the future the positive values of the bourgeoisie.

In this "being in the world," in being knowingly committed, one can adopt various attitudes, which in broad outline can be reduced to two. One is the tacit acceptance of this commitment. The other is postponement or deferment of the acceptance of responsibility, or pretending to take it on provisionally. Ancient philosophy expresses the first, and modern philosophy the second. Two human types emerge in these philosophies. On the one hand, there is one who recognizes and clearly accepts one's relationship to community, one's firm commitment to it. On the other hand, there is one for whom community is only an instrument for one's own ends, in service to one's individuality. The first conceives one's relationship with community as a *condemnation*, which cannot be postponed, and is an unavoidable commitment. The second sees the relationship as a *contract*, through which the individual accepts certain commitments in exchange for certain advantages. For the first, social hierarchy is already determined; for the second, individual effort can establish it. In one society, the gods or chiefs determine positions for which each individual must be responsible; in the other, the individual's free will allows one to choose positions and commitments.

In the philosophy of Socrates, the first attitude is clear. Plato's teacher is more than an ascetic, as some histories of philosophy portray him. He is more than a servant of truth for truth's sake, as some who aspire to be ascetics would say. Socrates is a symbol of a way of life, a symbol of a world whose crisis Plato witnessed. In the symbol of Socrates, Plato saved the essence of this world. The philosophy of Socrates is the philosophy of a world in which community is thought of as an inevitable commitment. "You must either persuade it or obey its orders, and endure in silence whatever it instructs you to endure, whether blows or bonds, and if it leads you into war to be wounded or killed, you must obey. To do so is right, and one must not give way or retreat or leave one's post, but both in war and in courts and everywhere else, one must obey the commands of one's city and country, or persuade it as to the nature of justice."[2]

The individual owes everything to the community. It is the community that has brought us into the world, nourished us, educated us, informed us of our benefits, and given us rights. Acceptance of all of these goods commits us to our community. Commitment rests not only on benefits received, but also on setbacks that may arise. Someone who lives in a community, by definition, is committed to it. No one requires an individual to live in a particular community. "Whoever of you remains, when he sees how we conduct our trials and manage the city in other ways, has in fact come to an agreement with us to obey our instructions. We say that the one who disobeys does wrong in three ways,

[2] Plato, *Crito*, 51 B, C.

first because in us he disobeys his parents, those who also brought him up, and because, in spite of his agreement, he neither obeys us nor, if we do something wrong, does he try to persuade us to do better."[3]

Thus, from birth individuals are committed to their community. Upon living in it, upon interacting with it, one cannot help but take on this commitment, the assumption of which one must attend to when called to account. Socrates pays with his life as a result of this commitment. In my case, he writes, the laws of my community would have more right to mistreat me by "reminding me that I am one of the citizens who has most intimately assumed such *commitment*. Socrates, we have convincing proofs that the city and we were congenial to you. You would not have dwelt here most consistently of all the Athenians if the city had not been exceedingly pleasing to you. You have never left the city, even to see a festival, nor for any other reason except military service; you have never gone to stay in any other city, as people do; you have had no desire to know another city or other laws; we and our city satisfied you."[4]

Moreover, the philosopher has not only tacitly committed to living in the Athenian community, but he has also committed to his philosophy. In the name of this philosophy, assuming the responsibility that it implies, he has abandoned living before giving up philosophy. For this reason, in order to justify accepting his sentence and refusing to follow the advice of his friends who ask him to flee, he listens to the laws that continue to tell him:

> So decisively did you choose us and agree to be a citizen under us. Also, you have had children in this city, thus showing that it was congenial to you. Then at your trial you could have assessed your penalty at exile if you wished, and you are now attempting to do against the city's wishes what you could then have done with her consent. Then you prided yourself that you did not resent death, but you chose, as you said, death in preference to exile. Now, however, those words do not make you ashamed, and you pay no heed to us, the laws, as you plan to destroy us, and you act like the meanest type of slave by trying to run away, contrary to your commitments and your agreement to live as a citizen under us. First, then, answer us on this very point, whether we speak the truth when we say that you agreed, not only in words but by your deeds, to live in accordance with us.[5]

What could I say to this, Socrates wonders. Do we not recognize that they are right?

[3] Ibid., 51 E, 52 A.
[4] Ibid., 52 B.
[5] Ibid., 52 D.

By dying, Socrates has done nothing other than assume responsibility for his philosophy, accepting the commitment it involves. For him, philosophizing is not about pure zeal, or knowledge for knowledge's sake, but a commitment that one has to the community. Philosophizing is not simply doing philosophy, but serving one's community, which needs its philosophy as much as it needs policy from lawmakers, strategy from military thinkers, and the art of making shoes from shoemakers. Socrates taught the youth of Athens that each person has a specific place in the community, to which he or she must be faithful. All citizens have a mission with which they have been entrusted by the authorities of the city. Within the community there are no high or low functions because all are equally worthy if they are faithfully executed. Some people have governance as their function, others lawmaking, others defense of the city, others singing its praises, and others feeding and clothing the members of the community. Socrates also has his: doing philosophy; that is, seeking the truth. However, he does not seek pure and abstract truth, but the truth of each person, the truth of each citizen, the being of each one of them, that for which each was made, their function, their role, and their place in the community. As his function, Socrates has to subject to examination each of his fellow citizens, to find out if they know the art they presume to practice, and to make them aware of their roles. He wants them to find and know themselves. Socrates wants to be the gadfly of his community, its moral conscience. This is his vocation, his calling, and that which gives meaning to his existence. The gods have condemned him to do philosophy, as in other times the leaders of the community had condemned him to stay in a particular place during the war, and like now, they condemn him to suffer the justice of the community. "For by the dog, I think these sinews and bones could long ago have been in Megara or among the Boeotians, taken there by my belief as to the best course, if I had not thought it more right and honorable to endure whatever penalty the city ordered rather than escape and run away."[6]

In this way, by his acts, Socrates takes responsibility for all the commitments acquired in his life. He also takes responsibility for others, for his community, and for his sentence. It is not the Greek community that has condemned him to death. Rather, he has been sentenced by his own existence, by his works, deeds, and attitudes. He is the only one responsible for his death, as he was for his life. The community has done nothing other than require him to carry out a commitment he has made.

Many centuries later, a Frenchman, René Descartes, seated next to a stove to ward off the frigid European winter, entertains a thought: "There is usually not much perfection in works composed of several parts and produced by various

[6] Plato, *Phaedo*, 99.

different craftsmen as there is in the works of one man."[7] For example, there were those old cities, during the construction of which many hands and many minds intervened. Usually these cities were poorly built with alleys and back streets, which formed uneven terrain, difficult to negotiate. One could compare these with even plazas built on the level, designed to an engineer's fancy. "You will understand how difficult it is to make something perfect by working only on what others have produced," added Descartes. What is said about cities can also be said about laws, customs, morality, and even religion, but the cautious Frenchman would not have dared to say this with so much clarity. From here he would deduce a terrible conclusion for his era:

> So, too, I reflected that we were all children before being men and had to be governed for some time by our appetites and our teachers, which were often opposed to each other and neither of which, perhaps, always gave us the best advice; hence I thought it virtually impossible that our judgements should be as unclouded and firm as they would have been if we had had the full use of our reason from the moment of our birth, and if we had always been guided by it alone.[8]

With these thoughts, with these few words, Descartes was proposing nothing less than tossing overboard all of history, the entire past, the whole world in which he found himself, a world he did not create and in which he was unwilling to take any responsibility whatsoever. In this way, the philosopher was precisely expressing the ideal of the new man with whom he had arisen: the so-called modern man, the bourgeois. This person, who emerges in a Christian, feudal, and medieval community, refuses to recognize this community as his own. Its laws, customs, morality, religion, art, and politics have nothing to do with what he wants to accomplish. None of this is his doing. No one has consulted him about this. Why, then, should he be expected to take responsibility for a world that is not his? The only responsibility he is willing to take is that of his future, a responsibility that becomes clear with the idea of Progress.

Suddenly, in one fell swoop, he wants to break with the past. The modern man wants to destroy whatever he finds in order to start something totally new, for which he will bear sole responsibility. He does not want to accept any commitment. However, reality intrudes. Despite his wishes, yearnings, and dreams, he, along with all people, is also a committed being. A world not of his making,

---

[7] Descartes, *Discourse on Method*, II. [The translator followed this edition: *Descartes, Selected Philosophical Writings*, John Cottingham, trans. (Cambridge: Cambridge University Press, 1988).—Trans.]

[8] Ibid., II.

but into which he has been inserted, is there. Owing to all his efforts, he intends somehow to escape this commitment that appears unavoidable. What to do? How can he resolve this conflict between what is and how he would like the world to be? Descartes finds the answer in his philosophy:

> Now, before starting to rebuild your house, it is not enough simply to pull it down, to make provision for materials and architects (or else train yourself in architecture), and to have carefully drawn up the plans; you must also provide yourself with some other place where you can live comfortably while building is in progress. Likewise, lest I should remain indecisive in my actions while reason obliged me to be so in my judgements, and in order to live as happily as I could during this time, I formed for myself a provisional moral code. . . .[9]

In this way, the new man, the bourgeois, takes responsibility for his past and for the world in which he finds himself, but only in a provisional way. To live, it is necessary to live well with others, and it is toward this inevitable coexistence that he provisionally takes on what the community has established: religion, laws, customs, and opinions. This is only provisional, however, subject to everything changing, piece by piece. "But like a man who walks alone in the dark, I resolved to proceed very slowly, and to use such circumspection in all things, that even if I made but little progress I should at least be sure not to fall."[10]

Thus, Descartes embodies the kind of person who only accepts commitments required by coexistence, commitments to which others subject us because there is no recourse, because this is what is needed to live. However, in solitude, when he is completely alone, because this man does not trust others, he will find step by step, slowly but surely, a way to make it possible to escape such commitments. He will oppose *essential* coexistence with *formal* coexistence. He will establish laws, rules of conduct, and manners that serve to establish boundaries against the intrusions of others. In each of these laws or rules, the commitments the individual is willing to make are clearly expressed, and nothing more. Anything that is not clearly established is up to his discretion. In this space he will not have to answer to anyone. Formalism absolves him of having to answer to anyone. Once his commitments are clearly delineated, his freedom is fully guaranteed. He moves from living with others in community to living with others in society. The person ceases to be a being with *obligations* and is transformed into a being with *rights*. With the rise of the bourgeoisie, he knows all the rights that protect him. The *contract* is the expression of this formal commitment, which frees him

[9] Ibid., III.
[10] Ibid., II.

from the responsibility to which he was subjected as a member of a community. Thus, faced with a nagging reality that expects him to take responsibility, he builds a defensive fence of empty, pure, and ideal forms. These are the panaceas with which he thinks he can stop being hemmed in by reality, history, and the commitments he acquires with his acts and the acts of others. In his empty, uncorrupted world, our bourgeois thinks he has attained maximum freedom, with no commitments save for legal ones.

Nonetheless, reality is there, it is alive, and it has all the strength only it can have. Owing to all the legalities, it is necessary to live with and take on commitments that involve more than legalities. Descartes wrote, "I thought it would be most useful for me to be guided by those with whom I should have to live." Our bourgeois came to accept his commitments to others, at least provisionally, out of utility or social convenience. This man hoped eventually to be able to convert those commitments to the ideal status of legality. However, while in the process of attempting to make legalities of these commitments, he took them on *as if they were* his own. While developing his ideal morality, he adopted the morality of others *as if* it were his own, *as if* he believed in it, though he only adopted it out of social convenience. The French philosopher writes, "My second maxim was to be as firm and decisive in my actions as I could, and to follow even the most doubtful opinions, once I had adopted them, with no less constancy than if they had been quite certain . . . in this way, even if one does not go exactly where one wishes, he will at least end up in a place where he is likely to be better off." He added, "By following this maxim I could free myself from all the regret and remorse which usually trouble the consciences of those weak and faltering spirits who allow themselves to set out on some supposedly good course of action which later, in their inconstancy, they judge to be bad."[11] Bad faith is thus firmly established within this morality.

In Mexico, some who aspire to be theoreticians of a possible Mexican bourgeoisie support this double morality with bad faith. On the one hand, there is pure, ideal, and formal morality. This is a legal morality that is freely established by a supposed person who self-legislates and assumes legally established commitments. On the other hand, there is unlegislated morality of pure action that is wide open. It is timely and daily. This is the morality of the world of material commitments to which a philosopher is bound by virtue of being a person. This is lived morality, in contrast to the morality of "thou shalts" in which it is necessary to apply criteria such as comfort and usefulness to behaving "as if," as Descartes expressed it. In the latter morality, everything is permitted because nothing is prohibited in the world of pure legality. In other words, this is the morality of irresponsibility.

[11] Ibid., III.

However, because of all the efforts of the bourgeoisie to commit themselves only formally, a series of concrete actions commits them materially. Marxism is one of the first philosophies to become aware of these commitments. The established formal legal framework is nothing other than a mask, which conceals a series of concrete interests that benefit only one class. The entire ideal world is just the superstructure of a real and concrete world. Marx wrote, "It is not the consciousness of men that determines reality; on the contrary, social reality is what determines their consciousness." The bourgeoisie, in spite of everything, find themselves committed after all. Step by step, act by act, the bourgeoisie has been committing "the others," the other classes. These commitments lead to other commitments. Marx continues, "Evolving from the means of production that these relationships used to be, they become obstacles to the means. Thus, an era of social revolution is ushered in."[12]

The same philosophers of the bourgeoisie become aware of this fact. They become aware of the commitments their class has acquired. Historicism, sociology of knowledge, and existentialism make these commitments clear. What Mannheim calls the "process of unmasking" begins. Individuals can no longer elude their responsibility. Subterfuges are worthless. Every subterfuge that an individual used to avoid responsibility has been subjected to a keen analysis, after which it becomes unmasked and in need of explanation. Not even Marxist social determinism works. Philosophy of the bourgeoisie, still faithful to its idea of freedom, is forced to take responsibility. Only a responsible individual is free. Social determinism is accepted rather than refuted, but this acceptance is already an act of freedom. The existentialist idea of situated freedom arose. Concrete situations are inescapable. Every person is committed in a particular concrete situation. Faced with this, one nonetheless is free to adopt an attitude of conformity or non-conformity, responsibility or irresponsibility. A particular inescapable situation can be confronted consciously or unconsciously. One can live in such a situation *as if* nothing had changed; that is, one can live in bad faith or accept a situation for what it is, with all the responsibility that this implies.

Taking responsibility is what contemporary philosophy asks of the bourgeoisie, of the bourgeois person. Avoiding commitments is no longer possible. Whether or not the bourgeoisie accepts commitments, it has to answer to them. Again, the living community, now more powerful, holds this class accountable for attending to a multitude of concrete circumstances to which others have committed themselves. The bourgeoisie, which refused to attend to a past it did not consider its own, now must attend to a past that is its own work. The existentialism of the French philosopher Jean-Paul Sartre is a contemporary philosophy that addresses this call to accountability. In the name of the bourgeoisie, a bourgeoisie

[12] Karl Marx, *A Contribution to the Critique of Political Economy*, "Prologue."

in decline, this philosophy takes responsibility for all the commitments the bourgeoisie has acquired in making their history. It is a philosophy that attempts, in the name of the bourgeoisie, to attend to all the mistakes, deceptions, falsehoods, and vileness hidden beneath a mask of empty, abstract forms. It attempts to react to a world that has witnessed the still irresponsible bourgeois mind becoming offended and frightened, or to the bourgeois who think they are something other than bourgeois. For such minds it is preferable to change nothing, touch nothing, discover or reveal nothing. It is better to leave things as they are, *as if* they were other. If not, they ask, what becomes of morality? What about the enterprising and heroic spirit? What about values? This is to say, what will become of the bourgeoisie? What will happen to the beautiful moral artifact the bourgeoisie built?

Nevertheless, what Jean-Paul Sartre attempted was to bring about something similar to what another philosopher did many centuries ago: Plato. Like Sartre, he found himself in a *situation* of crisis. It also fell to him to see the end of a way of life; it fell to him to bear witness to the end of a social class to which he belonged, the Greek aristocracy. In his works he also reveals the mistakes, deceptions, falsehoods, and vileness of his world. In the face of these, his purest, most authentic ideas and his truest values arise. We associate these ideas and values with Greek culture, despite the world of mistakes the Greek world also was. In Sartre, the same keen desire becomes apparent: like Plato, he wants to save the most authentic ideas of his class and its truest values. Among these, one value in particular forms the crux of bourgeois history and the pivot of Sartre's philosophy: freedom. This is the freedom the bourgeoisie never knew how to interpret. This is not absolute freedom, the freedom to allow people to do things, but situated, committed freedom.

It is no longer possible to maintain the idea of freedom in a full and absolute sense, which would be irresponsible. Responsible freedom is aware of its limits, but always aware. Faced with an incomprehensible situation with no possibility of action for the bourgeoisie, Sartre believes the idea of responsibility is the salvation of the concept of freedom. Where there is no responsibility, there cannot be freedom. If it is not possible for the bourgeoisie to be responsible for others, at least it must be responsible for itself. If the bourgeoisie cannot choose something other than its own destruction, at least it is left with the path of freely and consciously choosing its destruction. Conscious of its destruction, it can attend to all the commitments it *freely* acquired in its history. As a class, in the presence of the community that has condemned it to be destroyed, it can take responsibility for this destruction. Sartre, through his philosophy, wishes to be the responsible conscience.

All we can do is reveal its unfortunate conscience in our mirrors, or advance the decomposition of its principles a little more. We have the thankless task of reproaching its failings when they become curses. As bourgeois people ourselves, we are familiar with bourgeois anguish, and we have had our souls ripped apart. However, since an unfortunate conscience characteristically wishes to get out of its unfortunate state, we cannot stay calmly in the womb of our class, and since it is not possible to exit with a push, giving ourselves airs of parasitic aristocracy, it will be necessary for us to be its gravediggers, and even run the risk of entombing ourselves in it.[13]

The bourgeoisie as a class is thus viewed as condemned to destruction. However, its best members can save themselves from this destruction. That is, its responsible members recognize their responsibility as members of a disappearing class and as participants in a situation that is no longer theirs. Sartre wrote, "We were born into the bourgeoisie, and this class has taught us the value of its conquests: political freedom, freedom of expression, *habeas corpus*, etc. We continue to be bourgeois in our culture, our way of life, and our present-day public. But at the same time our historical situation induces us to join the proletariat to build a society without classes." So these individuals, the best in their class for their capacity to be responsible, do not yet have a mission as a class, but only as private individuals. Their job, wrote Sartre, is "to take sides against all injustices, wherever they may come from." This does not mean they expect to end the injustices, but only that they will take responsibility by condemning them when faced with them. Sartre continues, "If they tell us that we have become self-important and that we are puerile to expect that we can change the world, we will respond that we have no illusions, but that nonetheless it's worthwhile to say certain things even if only to save face with our children."

When Plato was unable to save the ways of the society of his era, as expressed in the Greek *Polis*, he proposed saving the best of its members, the abstemious. That is, those who knew how to control themselves before learning how to govern others. With the best members of that society in crisis, he attempted to save the most valuable parts of his culture to incorporate these parts into Universal Culture. Such appears also to be the aim of Sartre's philosophical work: save the best people, the responsible ones, and with them the most valuable aspects of their culture to incorporate them into Universal Culture as well. But let us allow the philosopher to be the one to tell us which is the person who should be saved: "The whole person, totally committed and totally free," is the person we conceived. "Nonetheless, it is this free person who needs *rescuing*, increasing his or her possibilities for choice. In some situations, there is only one alternative, one whose end is death. However, it is necessary to work in such a way that the

---

[13] Jean-Paul Sartre, *Situations*, II.

person can in all circumstances choose to live.[14] We wonder how this *rescue* is going to be achieved. Like Plato, will Sartre found an Academy, a community of chosen people? We do not know, nor do we know what the results of this effort will be; for now, the only positive is his *consciousness* of the terrible commitment he must take on.

But what should we, the Americans, or more specifically, we, the Latin Americans, take on? For what situation must we be responsible? What commitments must our philosophy responsibly make? After all, if we are to be faithful to what we have laid out here, we have to affirm that our *situation* is not that of Jean-Paul Sartre. Our *situation* is not that of the European bourgeoisie. Our philosophy, if it is to be responsible, does not have to make the same commitments that contemporary European philosophy does. However, this does not mean we should disregard as part of our own the situation that falls to us as humans and for that very reason is universal. From this point of view, existentialism makes clear many aspects of the human condition, which for this same reason are also ours. Necessarily, it is starting with these aspects that we sustain a responsible philosophy, a philosophy that is conscious of its situation. Furthermore, well aware of our situation, we also know that we belong to a great community in which nations, peoples, or societies are none other than individuals and, as such, are responsible or irresponsible. It is also for this reason that we want a philosophy that makes itself aware of the *position* that falls to Latin American peoples within this community, to take responsibility for it.

But before taking such responsibility, we must begin taking certain responsibilities that fall upon us as a people. Before making ourselves responsible for the world's commitments, we must be responsible for our own concrete situations. We must be conscious of our situation to make ourselves responsible for it. This is what we have tried to avoid until now, perhaps because of an inferiority complex or because we are irresponsible.[15] Whatever the reason, it is necessary that we also come to know it. In evading knowledge of our concrete situation, we also avoid our responsibility. Who, then, is going to hold us responsible for our commitments, and for actions that we have managed to take? Whether we wanted to or not, we have created a history, although this may not be the history we would like to have made. Whether we wanted to or not, we have formed a concrete world, our Latin American world, though ours may not be comparable to those worlds along the lines of which we might have wanted to model ours. Taking circumstances into account and, as such, realities in which we find

[14] Ibid.

[15] [The notion of a possible Mexican inferiority complex was developed by Samuel Ramos in his classic, self-critical diagnosis of national character, *El perfil del hombre y la cultura en México* (Profile of Man and Culture in Mexico), published in 1934.—Trans.]

ourselves committed, we must attend to the commitments because they have come to commit others. No one can attend to these commitments but us.

The not wanting to become aware of our *situation* explains in part why we have been unable to have our own philosophy, as other great peoples of the world have. What would our philosophy attend to? What kind of person or what kind of culture would it *rescue*? In the face of what situation would philosophy develop? About what would our philosophers philosophize? It is possible to answer that philosophy is universal and that the philosopher may only commit to the universal and the eternal. Answering this way is not to answer at all. Committing ourselves to the universal and the eternal, without making a single concrete commitment, does not commit us to anything. This is merely a subterfuge, a convenient way to avoid responsibilities. We can comfortably speak of the universality of the good, values, knowledge, and so on, without such words requiring us to make any commitment at all. We will not be considered philosophy professors teaching those who aspire to be philosophy professors. Philosophy professors never commit themselves to what they are teaching, or at least they think they do not. They view themselves as only being responsible for the authors of the philosophies taught.

Then what is our situation and, consequently, what should the position of our philosophy be? How should we do philosophy? After all, our situation is unlike that of many peoples in the world. More concretely, ours is not the situation of the European bourgeoisie, though many of its cultural ways may be ours, including the philosophy we teach in our professorships and the basis it gives us for doing philosophy. Here it is necessary to add that our issues, if we are to have any, must necessarily be those that sustain this philosophy in terms of referring to specific problems in their concrete situation. Other issues are those that refer to our concrete situation or to that larger situation that is our human condition. The concrete situation, for example, of Sartre's existentialism is not necessarily our situation. As a representative of a class and a culture, Sartre finds a situation incomprehensible, with no other exit than responsible recognition of his own aim. We Latin Americans have yet to find ourselves in such a situation. We remain peoples whose responsibility within the universal community is unwritten. Sartre found himself in a situation in which the intellectual lacks an active role in society. He had no other path than to join the masses, not as an individual, the ranks of the oppressors, or the ranks of the oppressed. However, these no longer need him because by organizing they have ceased to be oppressed, moving from the defensive to the offensive against their oppressors. He writes on other occasions, "circumstances allowed one to position oneself in favor of the oppressed against the oppressor and to help the oppressed become aware of themselves." But today, "the oppressed class, organized as a party and stuck in a rigid ideology, becomes a closed society with which others cannot communicate without intermediaries." He adds, "since our historical perspective is war, as it threatens us into choosing between the Anglo-Saxon block and the Soviet block, and we decline to do either, we fall outside history and are speaking in the desert."[16]

It is fitting for Latin Americans to ask themselves, "Can we describe our situation in the same terms?" No. Though in general the world situation is also ours, we nevertheless possess a situation that is our own and that, consequently, makes our position at least minimally different. In our countries we cannot claim that all the oppressed are organized. Nor can we claim that they are all aware of their situation. For example, we still have the indigenous problem, which involves a primitive kind of exploitation compared with that of the bourgeoisie over the proletariat. Alongside imperialist and local bourgeois exploitation, in many Latin American countries we still have the same kind of exploitation that the Conquest imposed on our peoples four centuries ago. Alongside the great captains of the enterprise of world imperialism and the minor ones of our colonial bourgeoisie, we encountered our typical dictators: caudillos, caciques, and "strongmen." Here, our intellectuals, as such, have much to do if they want to consider themselves responsible. Yet their voice will not be a voice in the desert.

Furthermore, there exists another set of circumstances that proves to us the diversity of the *situation* of our peoples. The bourgeoisie grew and became strong through industrial development and the conquest of markets where it could obtain low-cost raw materials and sell its products for maximum profit. Industry and colonialism were the bases of its greatness. However, because of an unavoidable historical dialectic, at the same time as the bourgeoisie grew, the forces that threatened to defeat it were growing in its innards. The development of industry was accompanied by the development of the class that would combat it, the proletariat. This is the class that is thought possibly to achieve a new kind of community. However, colonialism remains at the other extreme, within which Latin American peoples occupy a special place.

Thus, we find ourselves in two kinds of struggle. One, which we could call *vertical*, develops in all the industrialized countries, including ours: class struggle. The other kind, which we could call *horizontal*, develops with more or less force among colonial peoples and imperialist countries. This struggle is typical in Latin America. This is no longer class struggle, even though the Latin American proletariat may take a great interest in it. Together with this are other forces that debate other problems, such as those rooted in the Conquest. Latin American peoples are also heirs to a Western tradition within which they belong to a culture that was vanquished when it opposed the powerful force of the ascending bourgeoisie. Our peoples have tried in vain to break with the tradition that fell

[16] Jean-Paul Sartre, *Situations*, II.

to them, uprooting themselves from a legacy that they considered negative. The entire nineteenth century was a futile effort to establish in Latin America a bourgeoisie similar to the great European and American models. Internal hereditary forces frustrated this effort at the same time as the bourgeoisie, in its imperialist version, exercised care so that no such change would happen.

Thus, in Latin America we have only a pseudo-bourgeoisie in the service of the great bourgeoisie. We do not have a bourgeoisie, strictly speaking, just as we lack defined classes. A set of typical Latin American problems is interwoven with a series of international problems, setting up a competition between one and the other. Our *situation*, in other words, is simply ambiguous. Perhaps the distinctions highlighted herein are unimportant details within the evolution of universal history. I do not believe such a thing, however. These details are important for showing our own situation and the commitments that fall to us within history. Somehow we act, and by acting we commit ourselves and we commit others.

Thus far, in order to speak of our *situation*, we have only engaged in denial— that is, we have only talked of what we are not. What, then, is our *situation* from the point of view of who we are? What is our *being*? I have here a task for our philosophy. From the answers we may give to these questions, our long-sought philosophy will have to surface. Some young friends of ours have committed themselves to carrying out various tasks whose aim is to find and define our *being*.[17] If we achieve this, we will also know our proper *place* in the community of peoples. Knowing this will enable us to freely take on their responsibility. Doing so, we will be able to repeat the words of Socrates with which we began this essay. It is necessary that we hold ourselves to this: "Wherever a man has taken a position that he believes to be best, or has been placed by his commander, there he must, I think, remain and face danger, without a thought for death or anything else, rather than disgrace."

---

[17] [Here Zea refers to a group of young professors and students at UNAM who formed the Hiperión group, a philosophical circle that met in the late 1940s and early 1950s. Zea led the group, which included philosophers Emilio Uranga, Jorge Portilla, Luis Villoro, Ricardo Guerra, Joaquín Sánchez Macgrégor, Salvador Reyes Nevares, and Fausto Vega y Gómez.—Trans.]

CHAPTER 11

Solitude and Communion (1948)

Luis Villoro
Translated by Minerva Ahumada

Luis Villoro Toranzo was born in 1922 in Barcelona, Spain, and died in Mexico City in 2014. His mother was Mexican, his father Spanish. He began his teaching career at UNAM in 1948. With Zea, Portilla, and Uranga, Villoro formed part of the famed Hiperión group during 1948–1952. He is widely credited with popularizing analytic philosophy after the 1960s, thus bringing an end to the emphasis on the philosophy of culture that had preoccupied Mexican philosophers for the first half of the twentieth century. Villoro was also a political activist, and in the last decade of his life was a staunch supporter and defender of the Zapatista uprising in southwestern Mexico. Among his most outstanding earlier works are The Ideological Process of the Revolution for Independence *(El proceso ideologico de la revolucion de independencia, 1953), and* Philosophical Pages *(Paginas filosoficas, 1962). Only a few of his works have been translated into English, including* Belief, Personal, and Propositional Knowledge *(1998) and* Sahagún, or, The Limits of the Discovery of the Other *(1989).*

Rarely has there been so much discussion about the need for a new sense of community as there is now. And that is because we have seldom experienced such a piercing awareness of our solitude. Contemporary man is, above all, a solitary being; he singularly reflects the era's feeling of solitude. Ours is a vacillating civilization, suspended over the agony of our world, the agony of the bourgeoisie, and the announcement of another world that will not be ours. It is an insecure civilization that delivers a clear awareness of an original abandonment. But this awareness does not come out of the blue—it is nothing else but the final result of a slow and continuous process.

Let us follow, then, in an abbreviated way, the imperceptible evolution of our contemporary solitary consciousness [*conciencia solitaria*].

Christianity proposes a first step on a path of progressive detachment from nature and the gradual abstraction into one's own being. With this step, one begins to reject an affective [*afectiva*][1] unification with the cosmos, a sympathetic participation in it, which was one of the characteristics of paganism. Before the zoomorphic conception of the Greeks, Judaism de-animates nature in order to place the human spirit radically on top of it. Jehovah, God the creator, legislates and rules the cosmos without ever being confused by it. The divine force, which the Greeks never saw as totally alienated from the world, now acts infinitely removed from its creation. Nature is no longer that universal mother whose lap offered all beings an opportunity to communicate. God is outside the universe, and mankind's spirit—in God's image—independently dominates his own body. Nature and flesh are relegated to an inferior rank. All affective unification of men with nature tends to be perceived or stigmatized as pagan. Man knows himself as a being apart from the world; his nature is the sad vestige of a fallen world, a remnant of his original sin. Man would be wrong if he aimed to knit a close relationship with nature, as this would mean that he is forgetting that he is not a citizen of this world and that his promised land is a different one. We must go through our time on earth detached from it, with our gaze aimed at a different path. Humanity, while dominating nature spiritually, also acts toward it, seeking an initial and purifying detachment. However, nature preserves a certain status due to its participation in the spirit. God is not only creator; He is also the kind-hearted father of all natural beings. All creatures are united through a universal bond of paternity. On the other hand, nature represents a table of contents, a manifestation full of its own meaning pointing toward the Creator; it is a path toward the divine, a mirror of the Lord. His beauty still overflows onto nature, and nature is as kind as its Creator. And maybe one of the biggest glories of Christianity is the reconciliation of the individual person with the feeling of community with nature, embodied in the monumental figure of Saint Francis of Assisi.

The modern world gives birth to a new understanding of the relation between man and nature. The organic [*organológica*] conception of the world disappears entirely so as to make room for a mechanistic one. The universe reveals itself to the eyes of the new physics as a combination of phenomena determined perfectly by precise laws. The celestial bodies that are regulated like parts of a gigantic clock, the Cartesian animal-machine, and the hypothesis of a *Mathesis universalis* that would determine every occurrence in a precise way are all manifestations of this new spirit. Of the four traditional causes, only the efficient—a sign of determinism—continues its reign. Endowed with a new way of knowing, the knowing of dominion, modern man begins to dream about possessing nature, enslaving it to his whims. All indications toward

---

[1] [The use of *afectiva* here, which the translator has rendered into English as "affective," refers to emotion or mood, as it is used in the phenomenology of Scheler and Merleau-Ponty. –Editors]

sympathy, toward affective communication with the world, are considered childish illusions or clumsy anthropomorphisms. The spontaneous connection between man and nature seems to have been broken at its core. Nature does not speak to us on its own; it will only have value if it can respond to our scientific hypotheses. Nature's meaning disappears as soon as it is determined by our universalizing laws; whatever escapes them does not retain our interest. Thus, nature will speak if it uses our language; on its own, it is a silent flow of ice, it makes no sounds, can no longer be the supreme sign that reveals the path toward God. It has been definitively reduced to a simple object of domination, not only of a spiritual sort, as it was during medieval Christianity, but also of material domination, thanks to the recent advances of technology. The natural world is there—lifeless, passive; it is a city waiting to be pillaged, a shapeless mass that awaits to be granted intelligibility by man.

The rejection of all affective unification with the cosmos leads us to the devaluation of those feelings of love toward man himself. Scheler has discovered that affective unification works as the base of every act of sympathetic participation. When affective unification is devalued to the point where it is considered a farce or an illusion, all impulses of human connection seem thwarted at their base. There is one last form of sympathetic participation that can survive this shift: the love of Humanity in the abstract, an ideal being, a distant goal that can regulate my actions, the final objective of progress. Thus begins, with modern man, the slow process of withdrawal into oneself [*ensimismamiento*] that will culminate with the height of the bourgeoisie period.

As long as an object is something that can be handled or dominated, it presents itself to us as an entity "to have"—a possession. This entity is something separate from us, which, due to our distance, we can handle through technology or use as an object in our possession. In tearing himself from nature in order to dominate it, the bourgeoisie begins to see all beings as entities that can be possessed and dominated. As long as things are perceived as basic tools for individual possession, this domination can be direct, or the domination can take place in an indirect way, such as "administration" or management. It is not surprising that the principles of private property and free enterprise are the grounding principles of bourgeoisie economy. The typical contemporary man, a creation of the most enterprising class in history, seems possessed by a mentality directed to the utilization of his possessions. His life revolves around continually taking inventory of his diminished or lavished belongings. The bourgeois is the man who has everything: he has a family, has material possessions, has dignity and values and—above everything—he has his rights, his sacred rights, intangible because they are . . . "private property." He has a right to life, to health, to enjoy private property, and a right to be respected by others; he even has the right to a quiet death and a noble burial. But, above all, he has the supreme right to have his rights protected, to have no one threaten his possessions.

If he judges everything in terms of "having," contemporary man will also judge his neighbor as a species of living thing capable of being possessed. Among different kinds of people there will be established a simple external relation of possessors, a relation always of division, of separation between the participants beholden to a common limit. The contract expresses this relation: there is no participation of people in contracts, but a separation of rights. Between an object of possession and its owner we will not find agreed-upon terms of sympathetic participation, just as there are no such terms between master and slave. Neither will sympathetic participation exist between two owners who suspiciously separate their possessions. Once the possibilities of participation with the other have been weakened and undermined in the aforementioned ways, modern man sees no alternative but to withdraw into himself.

It is no coincidence that idealism corresponded to this kind of man as his philosophical expression. Nature can only be dominated by a universal subject that can impose his own laws. The Transcendental "I," the subject of idealism, valid for all mankind, legislator of nature, grants nature regularity and form. Man, when considered as a universal subject and a technological potentiality, appears as the only source of order and organization in the world. Through the Transcendental "I," experience will become detached from its concrete empirical existence and will be elevated to the realm of the objective and universal. In that realm, the separation between subject and object seems irreducible. The whole world appears before me, objectified, regulated in accordance with my own laws. In the Transcendental "I," nature, as an independent reality with its own meaning, becomes thoroughly rejected; nature is only that which the subject of knowledge creates when he imposes his own laws. The problem, however, is that the personal subject himself, as a concrete being, finds himself placed outside the sphere of objective knowledge. The subject of scientific knowledge is, necessarily, impersonal. He is everyone at once and no one in particular; he is an anonymous and universal subject. Before the Transcendental "I," the individual subject, the man of flesh and bone, turns out to be a mere lab specimen. He turns into an object that can also be dominated by technology, that can be measured in every which way by science. In the realm of objective knowledge, the self and the other are seen merely as objects among objects. The impersonal subject of science explains us perfectly in accordance with general specifications, be they economic or psychological. Ultimately, the only subject capable of personal communication, that is, concrete existences, remains outside the realm of objective science.

The subject of idealism is a universal subject. As such, it does not know the individual "you" or "I." Before the "I," the world, the Not-"I," the universal subject appears as the strange, the inevitably separate, that in whose existence the "I" can neither dwell nor participate. But just as it cuts itself off from the subject due to its way of being, the Not-"I" appears centered on the "I," like the satellite in the planet's orbit. The things-in-themselves, the ones that form the Not-"I," are passive, lifeless, devoid of reason. They have as much significance as I decide to give them. They depend on me; only from me do they receive an order, intelligibility, and meaning. They themselves are mere cold, empty masses. Expressionless in and of themselves, every time they want to say something, they reflect me, like mirrors in which I find my own image. Thus, I find myself enclosed in a circle of silent objects aimed, ceaselessly, at me. In the fabric of phenomena, which lacks continuity, I can only imprint my own signs. At first glance, it thus appears impossible for me to cross that enclosure, since all reality always reveals itself as phenomena before my consciousness and, as such, only through my consciousness does it acquire meaning. The fabric envelops me on all sides, nothing can appear before me that is not a part of it, that is not an object before me or does not acquire meaning through me; nothing can appear before me without a meaning bestowed on it by me. That is why the things in themselves glue themselves, viscously, around me, because they depend on me; they receive nourishment from me, as if they were huge dead parasites. Hence, as the last step in the process of my separation from the world, I finally become aware of the prison I have created for myself.

At the heart of that enclosure, concrete existence turns against itself. Absorbed in the universal "I," the individual subject, the man of flesh and bone, understands himself as something entirely foreign. Enclosed by the walls of objectivity, he feels alien in this world. Unable to escape the tightly knit fabric of phenomena in which it has enclosed itself, without shelter in the impersonal subject that objectifies it, existence, for the first time, becomes aware of its radical abandonment. Confronted by Hegel's Absolute Spirit, Kierkegaard, the Danish pastor, experiences the excruciating pain of his absolute solitude. At the same, and due to this fundamental experience, existence reveals itself to Kierkegaard in its authenticity. Kierkegaard recognizes that it is only when I know myself in solitude that I experience my originality, my irreducible singularity, the infinite distance that separates my existence from the way of being of any other reality. When the feeling of my solitude reaches its extreme acuteness, everything appears to flee, everything becomes alien, false, indifferent. Thrown into a strange world, I know myself as unique, the exception, the unnamable.

Suddenly, anxiety presents itself as consciousness of my freedom. Sartre has seen, admirably, the originary relation between my feeling of alienation toward the world and my consciousness of freedom. He points out that I distance myself from being *in itself,* from things both silent and without reason. Through this movement, I establish these things as entities in themselves, which are other than me; they are that which I am not. I isolate myself from objects in a cocoon of nothingness. They are what I am not and what I cannot be; *nothing* separates us, there is nothingness between them and me. The existent finds itself in a world that is not its own: the phenomenal and objectified world. But, in experiencing its strangeness, the existent feels itself capable of detaching itself from the world through its own impulse, it knows itself totally free. It is due to this negation of what it is not that the existent grounds its freedom. Thus, freedom and solitude find themselves in mutual company. In knowing my solitude, I know myself free. The abandoned existent must ground its acts on itself. Freedom hovers over things, it is detached from them. It does not allow itself to be caught by them, because if it did, freedom would become alien to itself, enslaved to others, and it would lose its meaning as freedom. Freedom reveals itself both as my total abandonment, and, at the same time, as my total self-sufficiency. I am enough to maintain my actions; if I were not, I would be a prisoner of things and become lost in them. If my freedom were not enough to ground my actions, if I needed a cause to ground my decisions, there would be no more freedom. By elevating itself from any motive, by affirming itself in its own sufficiency, freedom rejects any other grounds than itself. This is why, behind every fundamentally free act, we see an evanescent silhouette forming: hubris. Beyond the awareness of the complete self-sufficiency of my act, there is always a trace of satanic pride.

But there is something worse than arrogance. I think that if Adam sinned, it was because in an instant he looked deep within himself and discovered himself terribly alone. His sin was born in solitude, as every sin of mankind is born in solitude. It is not because solitude determines sin, but because solitude always precedes sin . . . I am before the abyss. I could fall at any moment, and vertigo takes over my being. But not because the depth will swallow me, but because, in a moment of decision, I can throw myself in willingly. And before that thought of that act, nothing or no one can help me. No one will be able to stop me at the edge of the precipice, nothing will be capable of forcing me to jump. I am alone before my actions. I am on my own, in solitude, I must chose between falling and holding on. This is the source of my angst. Not even my own past can offer me shelter. The decision that I may have made a second ago, I must renew now, and again in the seconds that follow. My previous decisions have no bearing over my present ones, because no previous act can restrict my freedom. Even if I had kept myself at the edge of the abyss a thousand times, it does not mean that I will succeed next time. I might have made the same decision hundreds of times, but now I know that all of them are impotent, they are not enough. With or without my past decisions, I can still throw myself into the abyss. I am still, before myself, alone in each one of my acts. And this is the how of my existence, always up in the air, supporting itself, abandoned by others, alone before its own past.

Yet it is not only before sin that my action stands alone; this is also the case when it comes to salvation. Abraham walks alone toward Mount Moriah. He is on his way to fulfill the sacrifice, and even his heart is speechless. There are no words, as no one can understand him: not even Isaac, his beloved son, could read what was in Abraham's sprit. That is because Abraham's act does not obey universal reason or precise motives. His act is not compelled by specific motivations that are easily discernible; it is absurd, just as his faith is absurd. He does not follow universal laws, which would most likely condemn his act; his law is solitary, unique. That is why his act is well beyond the ethical; that is how action establishes the individual over the universal. Abraham acted according to his faith, even when all reasons and motives were pushing him to act differently. He disobeyed reason, because his faith was beyond reason. He chose to act this way through his absolute freedom; sustained by himself, in angst and solitude, he threw himself into salvation. It was in solitude that Adam sinned. It was in solitude that Abraham kept his promise. That is because we are alone beyond repair, whether we choose salvation or damnation.

Thus solitude reveals itself to me in a two-sided way. The side that looks at existence reveals my freedom; the one that looks at things-in-themselves reveals the tightly woven fabric of phenomena that imprisons me. I am condemned to die between a rock and a hard place.

But it is here, when we seem to grasp our total abandonment, that something shows us a decisive signal and, from our utmost solitude, begins to take hold of us. It appears that the proper condition of extreme situations is instability. Incapable of remaining in an unstable situation for too long, a small change is all that is needed in order to transform one situation into another: the coin flips and presents, then, its other face, and the game of existence continues. Only someone who reaches the limit of a situation will be able to fully comprehend its opposite. It is possible to know the existence of air by pondering it, but we would most fully comprehend its existence if we were gasping for air for a second, as if immersed in a vacuum chamber. The vacuum and our asphyxiation will best signal its antipode: air. Thus, it is only as we are going through the most extreme solitude that we start to feel the fascinating presence of an evanescent and strange company.

Scheler has created a curious character in whose face we seem to discover a certain family resemblance. Imagine—Scheler tells us—a Robinson from birth, a man who never met similar men and who could not use any experience to infer the existence of others like him. Well, then, our desolate Robinson would begin to feel a strange yet persistent uneasiness that would, little by little, grow into a stifling obsession. It would be a peculiar way of feeling "dissatisfied," mutilated or deformed, aware that something is missing. At that point our man would think along these lines: "I know there are communities and that I belong in one."[2]

[2] Max Scheler, *Esencia y formas de la simpatía*, ed. Losada (Buenos Aires, 1943), p. 327.

His affirmation would be based on a precise and indubitable intuition: the awareness of a vacuum, of the non-existence of intentional acts toward another. Our forlorn Robinson longs for, without even knowing, that which is radically different from him, *the other*. This is because existence always turns toward the other; it is a hunger for the other, and when this other does not appear, one experiences the pain of a cruel mutilation.

We have seen that in the phenomenal world we can only find objects that point back to ourselves; we do not find in that world that which is radically different from us. In order to find that, it seems indispensable that we escape our own prison, that we break away from the enclosure of objectivity and that we find a tear in the dense fabric of phenomena. Is there such a tear through which we can reach the radically other? Can we transcend the phenomenal realm, the objective reality, in order to reach a reality that is no longer a lifeless mass just waiting for us to grant it meaning?

In order to solve this problem, we need to start from Gabriel Marcel's excellent analyses of objectivity and the person. In the way in which we relate to one another, Marcel distinguishes between a *you* and an *other*.[3] Let us take a closer look at this distinction. At first glance, the subject–object relation would seem to be constituted by two terms. In reality, there are three terms. The *object* is that element about which I can talk with an interlocutor—whether real or ideal. My interlocutor is always either myself or a *you*. The third term, the one about which I talk to this person, will be an *object* if I am talking about a thing or an *other* if it is a fellow man. The third term—regardless of whether it is a thing or an *other*—appears always as a simple source of information or a means of communication among the interlocutors.

Scientific knowledge is always a dialogue between the subject and himself. It would look as if the man of science interrogates the object, expecting it to answer. Yet there is no answer. The object is silent. In reality, the researcher proposes a question to himself, a hypothesis; he does not question the object, but rather asks himself *about the object*. The object, then, appears to the researcher as a mere source of information that, once its role is fulfilled, will be conveniently put aside. In separating, via electrolysis, water's two elements, the scientist is asking himself *about* the constitution of water. Those objects at his disposal during his experiment only serve him as sources of information.

The same happens when we address a person but treat him as an object. We get lost in a city and we ask the first person who crosses our path, "Where is the post office?" "Am I going the right way?" *The other* answers. But with that

---

[3] [Villoro writes "entre un *tú* y un *él*." We have translated *él* here as "other" to preserve the sense of what follows. It could be argued that *tú* refers to the Buberian sense of Thou. However, Villoro's *tú* is neither the formal thou of Buber, nor the absolute other of Marcel.—Editors.]

answer, his role in our life is exhausted; we have no more interest in him; *he* is but a report. As a matter of fact, we could have gotten this report from any object—a city guide, for example. *The other* is merely a catalogue, a file cabinet I check or fill, just as I do with any other object. As such, *he* can be judged by me. Judging always means that one classifies correctly; we place each item in its rightful category; we place each object in its box so that everything is in order and one does not constantly have to check the file. The technician, the one with objective knowledge, sees nature as a huge file cabinet that requires classification, an information desk with a wealth of knowledge. That is also how we usually treat our neighbors: as things that must fill out their particular skeletons before our very eyes, that include everything belonging to it. When I look at the other *as an other*, I am still within the plane of my objects. *The other* is but a point in a dialogue I carry on with myself.

But let us look at a different example, one that signals a very important step. While traveling, I strike up a conversation with a stranger. We talk about show businesss, current international events, and a thousand trivialities. In a short time, I get to know something about his life and his ideas. I say to myself that "he is a well-rounded individual, conservative, and a tad intense," thus characterizing him in an objective way. I am intrigued by some of his views, some of his political opinions, some of his experiences. I might even get something from him: new information, a point of view that to date I had not considered, or, simply, a momentary distraction. Until now, *he* is the third term, which I classify and clearly determine and which serves me as a source of information or amusement. But it could happen that little by little I begin to internalize myself in my interlocutor, that little by little I begin to take an interest in him, but not for his information or whatever lessons he may be able to teach me. I then notice that he begins to escape my classifications. He is not exactly "intense," nor does he fit the conservative type. His words and his actions do not exactly correspond to the motivations I had attributed to them, and through which I thought I could determine him. A gesture, a word, these no longer present themselves with the meanings I had given them. All of him escapes my conceptualizations and determinations; he becomes free right before my eyes. I can no longer delimit him and I have the feeling that he may surprise me. It is then that I begin to internalize myself in him as subject; before me, his status as an object starts to disappear. Through sympathy, I begin to understand his words and actions, not through what they mean in my world, or with a meaning I attribute to them, but with the meaning he gives them. I begin to understand his world as his, not mine. At the same time, his fate becomes mine; when I hear about his sorrows, I am moved to help him; when I hear about his joys, I share in them. At that moment, he is no longer the third element in my dialogue; on the contrary, he is that *with whom* I converse *about* a million different things. Everything around us becomes the third term, becomes terms of communication or information for *us*. My interlocutor, originally an *other*, has become a *you*.

But the *you* only gives itself before me in a relationship of sympathy or love. While human judgment always addresses an *anonymous other*, love always speaks of a *you*. I feel incapable of judging a *you*. I cannot classify a *you* because a *you* does not abide by my limitations. A *you* is not identical with the information it gives me, nor with its virtues or defects. I am no longer interested in the *you's* ability to answer to my questions, or whether a *you* can shine a light on my concerns. I am interested in the *you's* own and irreducible meaning. *I* and *you* form the permanent structure of *communion*. This structure is the original core of all authentic community.

I can determine the *other* with ease.[4] When I classify it, I hopelessly confine it; I imprison it in its own actions. Its future acts will not surprise me; I can know it perfectly, just as I know the way in which oxygen behaves in my laboratory. I know about its symptoms, its psychological reactions, and about its hidden complexes that I can file in their corresponding file. The *other* is a bundle of discreet and connected phenomena; as such, it can only demand from me dispassionate and generous treatment. The *you*, on the other hand, I find always unpredictable, and it is this everlasting capacity for the unexpected that I find fascinating. The being captured in friendship or love defies all judgment; I cannot characterize it, let alone define it. That is why that being is never confused with his concrete appearances; I cannot limit or reduce that being to its phenomenal psychic reactions. The being perceived through sympathy or love is not just the simple sum of its qualities, nor the succession of its reactions or complexes, as that is not what I love or understand through sympathy; it is the ground that is free and that sustains them. The key emerges here: while *the other* appears before me as a series of phenomena, the *you* appears before me as *freedom*.

The act of sympathy or love discovers the total transcendence of the person with regard to its concrete affective moods. The *you* transcends its apparent specifications; the *you* remains outside the ongoing surface appearances. I do not grasp the you as just another object of intuition, which stands there next to all other phenomena; if I did, I would turn the *you* into just another phenomenon. I grasp the *you* as a constant transcendence of all meanings I bestow upon him. The *you* appears to me as a constant absence of its own phenomenal manifestations. The person is not *there*, in that hand gesture or in that tone of voice; the person transcends these phenomena, she cannot be reduced to them. But only in *that* gesture and in *that* intonation does the *you* reveal itself as a *transcendence*

---

[4] [Up to this point, Villoro has been using *él* to denote the objective other; the other without a face, without language and without community, who is a mere *fact*. We thus have decided to translate *él* as "other" to denote this anonymity.—Editors]

of those concrete acts, as a negation of them both. The *you* appears to me in a twofold role: as the *negation* of its own external manifestations, and as the one that *bestows meaning*. I cannot limit *you* through my own concepts or meanings. The *you* gives me its own sense and its own meaning. Or, in other words, *you* is not like any other object, a satellite in my orbit; *you* does not need me to explain it; *you* is that which is *radically other to myself*.

Max Scheler has definitely established that the phenomena of love and sympathy do not give us the identity of persons. On the contrary, they are characterized by their ability to reveal the other's real diversity. "The function of genuine sympathy," he tells us (and this applies to love as well), "is that it suppresses the solipsistic illusion in order to grasp the reality of the *other qua other*."[5] Here we can introduce a distinction that, although some might consider it too academic, I think is extremely important. Both the *you* and the *Not-I* appear to me as my *other*. However, the alterity of both terms differs in essential ways, to the point that it seems like an equivocation. This table, the white paper I have in front of me, appear to me as strange. Their strangeness consists in having a being that is different from mine, one in which I will never be able to participate. That is why the only way to get to know them will be by including them in my own web of concepts and meanings. In their alterity, in their own way of being, independent from me, they will always remain hidden. In that way, they make up a circle of compactness that I encounter without being able to abandon my solitude. The *you* has nothing in his being that comes solely from me. He is an independent source of value and meaning that cannot be reduced to my *I*. The *you* is for that reason radically other to myself. While the intelligibility of the thing-in-itself depends on its relation to me, the intelligibility and meaning of the *you* is rooted in how it is distinct from me. But, paradoxically, in his manner of existing, the *you* is similar to me, since both he and I are sources of meaning. That is why, while it is the case that I cannot participate in the alterity of the thing-in-itself and can only know it by shaping it in my own image, I can participate in the *you* without having to transform it to my likeness. The *Not-"I"* is that which is silent and different from me in its way of being; the *you* is that which is loquacious and common in my way of being. While the world of objects is the strange, the world of the you is the *near* ... the *neighbor* [*el prómixo* ... *el prójimo*].[6] When I am among objects, I find myself in a strange and hostile world that becomes inhabitable only by sustaining it with my own meanings; which is why I find myself alone. On the other hand, in the *you* I perceive the shadow of my homeland,

[5] Max Scheler, *Esencia y formas de la simpatía*, ed. Losada (Buenos Aires, 1943), p. 97.

[6] Ancient languages possess different terms that we could use to designate these two kinds of alterities. *Alter*, ετεοος, would *approximately designate* the *you*'s alterity; *alius*, αλλος, that of the thing-in-itself.

which is why I can internalize myself in him. But—let us make this very clear—if this happens, it is precisely because the *you* is the only reality that is irreducible to me; the *you* alone I am unable to subject to my own "I"; I am unable to make him conform to my desires.

In grasping the other as other, we liberate ourselves from the prison of the ego. We are then able to pierce the fabric of objectivity. The *you* is that tear we were looking for in order to evade the phenomenal field. The *you* appears, indeed, as transcendental to the world of objects and phenomena. The clearest sign of this transcendence is the *you*'s liberation from the form itself that structures all other phenomena: space and time.

The *you* knows no distance. I can be infinitely separated from someone, even if she is by my side, and vice versa. The subject of our sympathy, however, is neither here nor there, but is always simply *present*. *Presence* is its way of being related to me, and through presence the transcendence of space-time manifests itself. When I say that my friend is *with* me in adversity, I am not saying that he is right in front of me, as a body among others; what I am trying to say is that I feel that he is with me. His presence is revealed to me in a gesture, a look, perhaps an understanding silence. This *with me* is neither close nor far; it is irreducible to a place; it simply *accompanies me*.

We have seen how we grasp the other's personhood as transcending his changing determinations and appearances. The *you* is something permanent that endures through feelings and actions. And the approach toward the other as permanence implies *fidelity*. But I can only be faithful to a reality that transcends fleeting instances. My unspoken vow of friendship or love is directed toward a reality that I know will last throughout time, because my loyalty is only possible as the background of the compromise of one permanent reality with another. We both live at the core of a reality that transcends our specific temporal instants. That reality is our communion, our mutual presence.[7]

It would appear, then, that in the *you* our solitude would have to definitively distance itself so as to give way to the security of the act in transcendence. This would seem to be our logical conclusion, since if we have indeed found the rupture that takes us toward the other, then it seems that we have overcome our solitude. Transcendence of the field of phenomena in the other, escape from the prison of my ego in the *you*, is likewise, according to good logic, the

---

[7] And does not the affirmation of our mutual presence presuppose that we affirm our victory over death? Dying consists in complete isolation, the rupture with all connection—all contact with beings. If death were shared with others, if after death the presence of the deceased lasted in the fidelity of the other, death would not be total isolation and, maybe, due to its communion with the other, the *I* would be reaffirmed. Thus, the other's transcendence is always revealed to me as a sign that points toward transcendence.

disappearance of my solitude. . . . Good logic, yes, but nonetheless, let us look at this a bit more closely.

Once we transcend time and space, we enter into a realm where familiar concepts of the understanding no longer appear applicable in a strict sense. The world of objects, with its perfectly defined entities, separated from each other by necessity, slowly begins to fade away before our eyes. Our usual categories, meant to be applied over a space-time that can be universally verified—categories meant to classify and divide, to generalize and determine objects—no longer work. We find ourselves in a realm deeper than science and logic, we enter the realm of the paradox and the conundrum.

We have said that through love I grasp what is other in its own meaning. This means that I grasp it in the authenticity and originality of its existence. Scheler claims that "the deeper we delve into a human being through a comprehensive way of knowing that is guided through our love for the person, the more incontrovertible, different, one of a kind, irreplaceable and unparalleled he becomes for us."[8] The other is entirely distinct from my own world, from everything that I know. Its meaning is different and strange; I cannot make the other thoroughly mine, because there is always something about it that escapes me. The other person always remains behind that which I grasp about him. And this is because I know him as freedom, and, as such, I can never determine him, fully predict his actions, capture him entirely in my significations. The other always subsists beyond all of this, as the permanent possibility of spontaneity, of the unexpected. Neither can I grasp the source itself; I cannot reach freedom in itself, from "within," so to speak, but only through its external manifestations, through its phenomena, as their simple *negation*. In this consists its radical alterity. And this alterity is irreducible; it always remains a force that rejects me, before which all my efforts to capture him fail. And it is precisely that irreducible alterity that we love. Here we find love's supreme paradox. It is this desire to thoroughly interiorize the other, to fully participate in him; it is the yearning to let go of one's own solitude to join the other in transcendence; the whole of existence becomes distended in this blind effort for participation. But this desire always—in every attempt it makes—finds an insurmountable limit to this unification; this desire runs into an irreducible reality that rejects it. And it is precisely this rejection that provokes love; the attraction is created by that which remains irreducible to the participation, because what sustains the attraction is the radically other. If everything in the person were given in the participation, he himself would become one more correlate of the "I", he would not have a meaning that is irreducible to mine; that which is radically other would disappear and we would relapse into that initial solitude. And just like solitude taken to its extreme limit

---

[8] Max Scheler, *Esencia y formas de la simpatía*, ed. Losada (Buenos Aires, 1943), p. 168.

revealed community to us, in that same way, if we were to take communion to its limit, we would relapse into solitude. Love aims to appropriate the other but, at the same time, it demands that the other remain independent, because if for a moment the other ceases to be irreducible, the loving relationship would disappear; there would not be two alterities facing each other, but one alterity in solitude. Similarly, the subject wishes to give himself thoroughly; however, only that originality that remains of him before the other sustains his love, only that impenetrable shelter, that intimacy; communion is sustained by that which remains in solitude. In this way, the most developed communion already carries within itself the most profound solitude.

"A magnet that repels by attracting" is what Antonio Machado said about love; and in those words he captured its essential paradox. By apprehending the *you*, I do not abandon my solitude, but affirm it before the other. And the more I am attracted to the loved one, the more he repels me; this because I think of him only as unique in solitude. Thus, two different solitudes, face to face, struggle in love: two solitudes that love each other as such, but remain in their solitude in a reciprocal way.

Struggling against every impulse to enslave the other, I keep him in his freedom. I want him in the solitary anxiety of his choice. Then my intervention in his action is transformed into a calling, an *invocation*. I can do nothing to determine the other; I cannot become an efficient motive in his action. His freedom remains intact, as he will have to choose between angst and absurdity. I can only encourage him, appeal to his freedom so that he responds. My encouragement will always be a calling to him to maintain his freedom, without alienating it, without avoiding it. That is why my calling will never determine his actions, as he can always ignore it, or reject it. That is why love does not do away with our angst; rather, it confirms us in it. Neither of us can force the other to act. The invocation invites the other to save himself, but to save himself freely, in solitude and angst. "Be more fully yourself; keep yourself irreducible, original, carry out your own salvation," silently implores this invocation. As such, beings that participate in communion mutually maintain themselves in a perpetual invocation.

If the totality of participation in the other were to transform itself into its opposite (i.e., solitude), then, in order to realize itself, communion would demand the permanent irreducibility of the terms in relation. This means that communion is sustained only in the constant failure of total unification toward which this relation naturally tends. Community is far from being the kind of situation that would deny once and for all my radical abandonment. Rather, it consists of that constant and insecure oscillation between a consciousness of my complete self-sufficiency and my humble attachment with the other. Communion is a bridge between my immanence and misery, on one side, and Absolute Transcendence, on the other—a bridge that will never be firmly secured on one or the other extreme. That opening that opens itself toward transcendence never gives us this firm security. The more reassured we become on the possibility of achieving it, the more persistently it escapes us. But the impulse never ceases; relentlessly, despite all its failures, existence persists in its desire, always pointing toward one extreme as its final objective: Absolute Transcendence. Moreover, and *hopefully*, we suspect that we might still find in Absolute Transcendence the synthesis of our essential paradox. Communion, community, aims to realize itself fully in hope. We have a feeling that there is a unity between those beings that appear distinct from one another but that indefinitely tend toward one another while maintaining their original difference; it is the nostalgia for the One, in which every being would find the definitive reconciliation of all of its opposites. But, while we are One in hope, we are different in reality.

Thus, communion puts in relief the constant tearing apart of existence itself. Suspended between two worlds, the human being sees herself thrown in the abandonment of her own fallen world; on the other hand, she feels the push to break free from her own confinement. But transcendence constantly escapes her and, as this becomes ever clearer, the more clearly she recognizes her own abandonment. But only in facing the infinite can existence affirm Absolute Transcendence as the final term of its love and of its faith.

Existence remains suspended between two abysses—one of misery, one of infinity—thus keeping itself in suspense about itself. Instability is its permanent condition, uncertainty its natural state. Perpetually oscillating between extreme and unattainable situations, man travels on, unable to steady itself, fearful and trembling. In fear and trembling, yes . . . but, also, in *faith* and *hope*?

CHAPTER 12

The Major Moments of Indigenism in Mexico

CONCLUSION (1950)

Luis Villoro

Translated by Kim Díaz

Let us briefly turn our attention to the journey we have traveled. From the beginning we alerted the reader that this is a unified path. Its slow and zigzagging course reveals itself as a dialectical process pointing toward a recovery and taking full ownership of what is Indigenous.[1]

The Conquest marks the decisive moment of doom and destruction of the pre-Conquest world. It is in this First Moment that what is Indigenous is negated and rejected and its reality appears destined for destruction. Nevertheless, the Indigenous element lives on. The entire Aztec universe continues to exist in the remnants of a culture that decays daily under the hands of the conquistador or the missionary. The Indigenous element continues to function, dragging its idolatry and shamelessly opposing the Good News. The Indigenous element is present and active. And precisely because of its proximity and effectiveness, our rejection of it is that much more explicit. The Indigenous element seems condemned to extermination. At this Moment, the Indigenous element appears as *near* and *negative*, but here begins the long journey that, despite its many deviations, will

---

[1] [Throughout *The Great Moments of Indigenism in Mexico*, Villoro is concerned with how and whether the Indigenist's consciousness accepts his or her own Indigenous element. Villoro uses the Spanish words *propio* and *propia*, which I have translated as "personally claimed" and "owned" in order to convey the sense of taking ownership for the Indigenous element in mestizos. I have translated *impropio/impropia* as "forsaken" to convey the sense of turning one's back upon, or not taking ownership of, the Indigenous element in mestizos.—Trans.]

take us toward recovery and definitive affirmation. This is because, since the conversion of the Indigenous people, the promise of reconciliation rises above the destroyed aboriginal world. In this Moment, this reconciliation is only that of the new man insofar as he denies his past; but the day will come when he will turn lovingly toward his lost world.

In the Second Moment, what is Indigenous becomes hopelessly distant, and we no longer feel it as an actual reality. Instead, we reduce it to a thing of the remote past. The Indigenous element no longer moves us and, instead, we find it ineffective and harmless. We have become *distant* from what once was *near* us. This distancing may seem to be our abandonment and denial; but this is far from the case, since our distancing actually constitutes the path to recovery. This is because as the Indigenous becomes distant from us, it is purified of its malignancy. Francisco Javier Clavijero and Fray Servando Teresa de Mier point to this revaluation, which would not be significant but for the ineffective distance at which the Indian is kept. We can most clearly distinguish this separation in Manuel Orozco y Berra. In him, the Indigenous is most certainly objectified. But it is due to this death that the Indigenous is fully purified of any demonic vestiges. It is at this Moment that the Indigenous acquires a positive value. And this is not because we feel close to the Indigenous element, but precisely the opposite: because we keep the Indigenous element distant. If in the previous Moment the Indigenous seemed *near* and *negative*, it now appears as *distant* and *positive*. The Second Moment becomes, then, the total negation of the First: we are now in the *Antithesis*.

The Third Moment emerges from the purification that has taken place over the distant past. This Moment does not even seem to keep any remnants of sin. It now becomes possible for us to move near to what is Indigenous. Given that the Indigenous element has now gained a positive value, it will not be dangerous for us to get closer; its positive value incites us to get closer. But this movement is not a simple return to the First Moment. This Third Moment denies the Second as we draw the previously distant Indigenous nearer to us. But the Second Moment is still affirmed insofar as we maintain the positive value of the Indigenous. It is not then a simple reversal of the Second Moment, but its overcoming. The Third Moment shows the Indian as *near* and *positive*; it then constitutes the *Synthesis* of the two previous Moments.

This is, broadly speaking, the process that Indigenism has followed. Each of the three Moments marks the essential points of recovery of the Indigenous. Despite its apparent independence, each Moment presupposes the previous one and emerges from it. But it is now necessary for us to describe this process carefully. In order to do this, we will consider three parallel facets in its evolution: the movement that Indigenism follows; the corresponding transformation that the Indian suffers; and the revelatory criteria responsible for said transformation.[2] Although the evolution is well understood, we draw distinctions only to help us present each Moment. It is the case that each of the three facets necessarily implies the other two, and it would be impossible for us to separate them.

> *First Moment*: It has been made sufficiently explicit already, so there is no
>   need to go over it again.
> *Second Moment*: It presupposes, as noted earlier, a distancing. But this
>   moving away is not done all at once, but rather in two successive stages.

First Stage (Clavijero, Fray Servando): a *distancing in time*. What is Indigenous is relegated to the *Ancient History of Mexico*. This distancing permits us, as we wrote earlier, a positive assessment of the Indigenous. Correspondingly, the Indigenous is revealed as "having been," that is, as a thing of the past—nevertheless, as a past that the criollo recognizes as his. The criollo accepts that this past constitutes part of his collective history, so much so that the Indigenous is the specific reality that makes the criollos unique vis-à-vis Europe. It is, then, *his own past*, insofar as the Indigenous element is accepted as constituting the criollo's history. However, the criollo does not completely claim what is Indigenous in him. This is the first step toward estrangement because insofar as what is Indigenous is accepted only as a thing of the past and not as something present, the Indigenous is taken to be an element that has definitively been overcome, as something that is ours but inactive. The claim of what is Indigenous in ourselves is then imperfect and it bears this contradiction. Because this claim is merely a "once was," it reveals itself as something we may *preserve*, but only insofar as we leave it in the past, insofar as it maintains its distance from us. Correspondingly, and finally, is the criterion that reveals why the Indigenous is placed at a distance: Universal Reason. Nevertheless, Universal Reason is taken into consideration insofar as it is used by the criollo. The criollo judges himself, from his context, applying this criterion (as an "instance"). It is therefore, a *personally claimed Reason*.

Second Stage (Orozco and Berra): The estrangement from what is Indigenous becomes accentuated until it reaches an end in all of its facets. Beyond the previous estrangement in time, a *contextual estrangement* now takes place. This is to say that, as a matter of fact, the Indigenous element is no longer interesting as the historian's own past. Indigenism is merely an interchangeable object. The historian becomes indifferent toward it. He considers it at the same distance as the Egyptian past or the past of the Norwegian because each has the same objectivity. The Indigenous is now a *forsaken past* insofar as it is not assumed

---

[2] [The revelatory criteria Villoro refers to are Providence, Reason, and Action. See Table 12.1.—Trans.]

to be a constitutive element of one's own context. The estrangement has a double potency: temporal and contextual. And thereby the estrangement of the Indigenous reaches its end, but also, with it, what is positive. The past, distant and estranged, may be *preserved*, even if at a complete distance. The "scientific" historian, just like the archaeologist, orders and classifies documents and rocks. Nothing should be lost; everything must be jealously guarded. The Indigenous reaches the limit of its purification and preservation. It is totally ineffective and harmless, so much so that it becomes absolute passivity before us, and in so becoming, lets itself be used by us as a tool. The Indigenous is absolutely positive: it does not harbor any evil . . . just as any other object. Correspondingly, the revelatory criterion becomes estranged. It is the same Reason, but now completely *impersonal* and *forsaken*. In the meantime, the historian wishes to reach a distant and impartial point of view, abandoning his own perspective and context in order to anonymously oversee things. In the whole of this Moment, we notice that Reason appears as precisely the right light that reveals the past as past, and at the same time purifies it of malice. It is ultimately Reason that is responsible for the estrangement and change of fate of the Indigenous element.

Third Moment: Just as the previous Moment assumed two stages of estrangement, likewise this one assumes two corresponding stages of approximation.

First Stage (Precursors of present-day Indigenism): Thanks to the positive assessment that came about through the previous Moment, it now becomes possible to overcome the estrangement. What takes place is an *approximation in time* but not in the actual situation. The repression of the estrangement is still partial. The Indian is seen as present and no longer as past. However, we think of him as being in a different context than our own. The "mestizo"[3] cannot claim the state of dejection and isolation in which the Indian finds himself. His situation is quite different. This is why, even if the Indigenous is a present element, it is still seen as remote and divided, as "Otherness." The Indigenous, then, is a *forsaken present*. Nevertheless, we conserve the positive assessment from this Moment. The Indian may be *preserved* to the extent that the "mestizo" needs him for his own ends. The mestizo becomes the Indian's ally because he protects him in order to affirm him. This approach is implied by the approximation of the revealing criterion, which will now be action—not ours proper, but that of the Other. What is now required is that the Indian be the one who recognizes the mestizo and reveals in the mestizo's actions the Indian's character. The "mestizo" does not

---

[3] [When Villoro writes "mestizo," he is referring to the group or class of people characterized by socioeconomic and political elements rather than racial ones.—Trans.]

want to become responsible for the exploited being that the Indian reveals, and the mestizo does not take ownership of his own choices as real manifestations of the exploitation of the Other. Rather, the mestizo waits exclusively for the Indian to reveal his own bondage through his behavior. It is then a *forsaken choice* in the sense that the mestizo does not accept it as his responsibility or as his personal choice.

Second Stage (present-day Indigenism): second level of approximation. Regarding the approximation in time, a *nearing in context* takes place. The movement is complete as it again reaches its end. We have called it *recovery*. This implies two things: appropriation and positive assessment. The *appropriation* is realized when we consider the Indigenous as an element of our own. The mestizo-Indigenist now considers himself as being in the same context as the Indian insofar as he accepts the Indian as an element of his social context and of his very own spirit. This then implies an *internalization* of the Indigenous because the Indigenous stops being the Other and becomes an element of the social and personal Self. But as the appropriation is taken to its limit, the Indigenous is projected into the future. We recognize ourselves as Indians in the past and the present and we repeat it in ourselves, re-creating and projecting it into what is to come. Only then can the past become fully ours without the weakening that results from estrangement. Through repetition, we turn the Indigenous into our permanent possibility and project it into the future. The Indigenous is then our *own present and future*. Moreover, the Indigenous is considered a fully positive element, capable of showing us our ideal target for action. However, we understand that present-day Indigenism only marks the beginning of a recovery, which will become completely realized only when it fulfills what this Indigenism postulates. Correspondingly, the revelatory criterion others use to judge him becomes internalized. Now *personal choice and love* are what reveal this criterion. While reason wards off its object, choice and love internalize theirs. And if that was the right sign to manifest the past as past, choice and love (and hence passion) are to deliver the present and future.

We can summarize the entire process by describing it in Table 12.1. We observe in this table that the dialectical movement caused by Indigenism appears in two correlative processes of internalization. The object of the Indigenist's consciousness becomes more and more internalized in said consciousness by way of the paradoxical and extreme estrangement of the disowned past. The internalization assumes two movements: from the past toward the future, and from the forsaken to the owned. Once realized, the full internalization is achieved in the final recovery. But it is also the internalization of the revelatory criterion in the Indigenist consciousness, through the same path of extreme estrangement of impersonal Reason, that leads at last to identify the criterion with concrete choice and personal love. Thus, at the end of the process, the Indigenous consciousness turns

Table 12.1 **The Three Major Moments of Indigenism in Mexico**

	Movement	*Being Indigenous*	*Revelatory Criterion*
First Moment	*Approximation* and *negative assessment*	*Present* and *forsaken*	*Providence*
Second Moment			
First Stage	*Estrangement over time* that permits a *positive assessment*	*Claimed past*, and thus, *preserved*	*Personal Reason (claimed)*
Second Stage	*Estrangement in a context* that permits *positive assessment*	*Forsaken past*, and thus, *preserved*	*Impersonal Reason (forsaken)*
Third Moment			
First Stage	*Positive assessment* that makes approximation *in time* possible	*Preserved*, and thus, *forsaken present*	*Estranged choice (forsaken)*
Second Stage	*Positive assessment* that permits *approximation in a context*	*Preserved*, and thus, *claimed present and future*	*Personal love and choice (claimed)*

on itself. Its object is able to constitute itself. Indigenism is focused on becoming conscious of itself, and this is only possible due to its long path.

Not one of the stages of Indigenous consciousness is closed off by itself. On the contrary, in each stage we are able to find elements of the other stages. What is more, the same fundamental categories that capture what is Indigenous appear in all of the stages. Despite the deviations and different nuances, the Indigenous Being is revealed in all stages with certain common characteristics. We shall try to enunciate the general characteristics that the Indigenous Being offers, along the different modalities of consciousness that manifest it.

First, what is Indigenous appears, above all else, as a reality that is always revealed and never revealing. Before the Indian stand "instances" of the European, criollo, and mestizo. But the Indian himself never assumes that role. Providence, Reason, choice, and love are some of the other criteria that illuminate and make manifest his being. However, the Indian never seems to bear any of these instances; he never makes use of them by, in turn, judging the Other. This is how we speak of the Indian: we measure and judge him, but we do not feel either measured or judged by him.

This feature takes on different nuances in different stages. It worsens in the complete estrangement of the Indian—it tends to disappear, without success, in its extreme approximation, but it always subsists. In its farthest point (Orozco and Berra) the Indian appears merely as an object, determined and regulated by us. We see him as pure facticity, with no depth to his being. In one degree less than extreme estrangement (Clavijero), we consider the Indian as a type of shapeless mass upon which we can register our possibilities. We try to read in him our own transcendence. In a first approximation (Precursors), we grant him the capacity for transcendence. We do not consider him an object-thing, but rather an object-person, given how we subjugate his autonomy to affirm our own. We know that the Indian is capable of judging us and we are interested in allowing him that capacity, but we ourselves determine what his judgment should be in each case, establishing his parameters in our own world. In this way we anticipate his transcendence, delimiting and determining from the outside his possibilities. The only thing that interests us from his undisclosed self is that he affirms his disclosed self. In the recovery (present-day Indigenism), we at last make him ours, but he always remains an undisclosed part of our being whom we try in vain to illuminate with our reflexive gaze. Even in our own selves, it is not he who illuminates, but rather, he depends on the light he receives as a reflection. The Indian can now recuperate his transcendence, but only within the transcendence of someone else. In order for the Indian to judge and measure, for him to surpass his possibilities, he must do this through another's bosom. The Indian's transcendence is either as a constitutive part of the mestizo (in the "spiritual recovery"), or as a constitutive part of the proletariat (in the "social recovery").

In short, it is always we who organize and constitute the world outside of him; this, despite the fact that we have the feeling that it should be he who should constitute and organize the world outside of us. And if we should ever feel that he is looking at us and judging us, this is because in our eyes, he no longer seems to be an Indian.

Second, the immediate consequence of this is that the Indian is subjected, in his own reality, to a strange process. His Being plays and is transformed by its passing from one hand to another. The Spaniard, criollo, and mestizo call on the Indian in their own struggles, but they do not wait for his answer; they each make him respond in the tone that each of them seeks. The Indian is molded into different forms depending on which group needs to use him. The Indian is given over to the Other; he is at their mercy. They dress him up from the outside, they arrange him and present him, they make him say public statements and take on roles. The Indian is involved in history without knowing it. Over there and from above, mestizos and criollos decide on his roles, distribute his performances, his historical situation. They name him their ally or their enemy, while the Indian is indifferent, ignorant of his own process, and continues to labor sadly, there below the process of history. In his own land, he has perhaps never been concerned with playing a historical role. But beyond where his performance comes to an end, where his situation becomes legitimate and his purposes become established, he has represented everything. This is how he ended up being the enemy of the Spaniard in light of Providence, the ally of the criollo in light of history, and of the mestizo in light of sociology. The Indian finds himself surrounded by a world that stalks him, that absolves or accuses him, and that determines his fate without him knowing it. And he can never access the same eyes that measure him, the judges who either save or condemn him. In order to make his opinion or his will reach them, his confession or his plea, he has only one intermediary: the mestizo. The mestizo is the only messenger capable of listening to him. But if the Indian wants to determine once and for all the world that judges and wraps him in its meshes, if he wants to escape the process that harasses him and face his judges, there is only one way: to renounce himself, to stop being an Indian in order to become a member of the same world that stalks him, to turn into a Westerner and mestizo.

Third, what is Indigenous appears also as a reality in which I can recognize myself, without this meaning that it must be different from me. It is alterity while pointing toward me. It is like a pond's surface, cloudy at times, but always allowing me to find the outline of my own reflection. What I seek to see in its surface is my own capacity for freedom and transcendence, even if the manifestation of this attempt varies in each case. In Calvijero I will find in the Indian the rupture of my estrangement by the Other and my freedom from the condemning foreign judgment by making the Indian out to be the "classic example." In the Precursors to the current Indigenism, I see my own recognition as an autonomous end. In the contemporary Indigenists, I find my own past and hidden self, which is reborn and recreated in the future.

Hence, sometimes the Indigenous appears as announcing my own coming and as an indication of my project. The project of my dominance over the Other (Precursors) or, inversely, the project of my liberation from the one who subjugates me (Clavijero and Fray Servando vis-à-vis the European, present-day Indigenism vis-à-vis the Oppressor). Because in the Indian I can only recognize myself as being outside myself. In the Indian I see *my* own transcendence turned into an external and visible reality. He is like a mirror in which, magically, I can see myself projecting myself *already* into the future.

Fourth, at other times, the Indigenous may appear as a reality that gives me consistency. The Indian substantiates me and makes me distinct. This takes place by countering the lucid contemplation with a reality that transcends it and that does not allow itself to be obviated. The contemplation that attempts to capture it may originate in the Other, in which case, the Indigenous appears as that reality that makes me distinct vis-à-vis him (Clavijero). Or it might be my own contemplation, in which case, the Indian appears as an obfuscated reality that individualizes me (present-day Indigenism).

Fifth, at last, the Indian is revealed as a reality of double depth. He is not a pure object, a simple facticity (except in the case of Orozco), but he is not recognized as a transcendence. He is a factual object, while also a never-realized capacity for transcendence. This is why he always seems—when we judge and determine him—as disguised and obfuscated. We realize that we never grasp him in his own being, that there is something about him that always eludes us. From here, his world is revealed as well—as often—in a double dimension: simultaneously determined from the outside, while also capable of his own meanings. From this perspective, we are both attracted and afraid of him, not because we know ourselves to be determined or dominated (estranged) by him, but rather because we can sense that in his depth, further from our judgments and lectures, a hidden reality is housed that we cannot reach and whose presence fascinates us. In the consciousness of this permanent background of his being, all of the descriptions of his reality arise, such as the conflict and clash between what is personal and free in his being and the parts of him that are shown before history (Bernardino de Sahagún, present-day Indigenism, etc.). Because every time, even if we illuminate him with our conscientious category, a personal sense remains, unknown and unrealized, in the face that he shows before us, his capacity for transcendence.

CHAPTER 13

Essay on an Ontology of the Mexican (1951)

Emilio Uranga

Translated by Carlos Alberto Sánchez

Emilio Uranga was born in Mexico City in 1921, where he died in 1988. A student of José Gaos and later a professor at the National University, Uranga became a founding member of the Hiperión group. Considered the most capable member of the group, "primus inter parus," he professed an interest in German. and French existential phenomenology, an influence that can be seen in his celebrated work Analysis of Mexican Being (Análisis del ser del mexicano, 1952). *The essay translated here for the first time, "Essay on the Ontology of the Mexican" anticipates that work. Other noteworthy works include* Literary Tricks (Austicias literarias, 1971), *and* Who Owns Philosophy? (¿De Quien es la filosofia? 1977), *works that testify to a struggle for and against the traditional postulates of philosophy and the philosophical life. "The Mexican and Humanism" has been translated into English in* The Modern Mexican Essay *(1965).*

Dr. Samuel Ramos dedicates a section in his book *Profile of Man and Culture in Mexico* to a "psychoanalysis of the Mexican character." In that essay, he writes:

> Others have spoken about the sense of inferiority of our race, but no one, as far as we know, has systematically used the idea to explain our character. For the first time, in this essay, we make methodological use of these old observations, rigorously applying [Alfred] Adler's psychological theories to the Mexican case. What must be presupposed is the existence of an inferiority complex in all those individuals who manifest an exaggerated preoccupation with affirming their personality; who take a strong interest in all things or situations that signify power, and who have an immoderate eagerness to dominate, to be the first in

everything. Adler affirms that the sense of inferiority appears in the child in realizing the insignificance of his strength in comparison with his parents. At its birth, Mexico found itself in the civilized world in the same way that a child finds itself with his elders. It appeared in history at a time when a mature civilization already prevailed, something that an infantile spirit can barely understand. From this disadvantageous situation emerges the sense of inferiority that is aggravated by the conquest, *mestizaje*, and even by the disproportionate magnitude of nature.

In a session at the Center for Philosophical Studies, held the previous year (1950), we proposed to Professor Ramos to substitute the concept of inferiority, which he applies to the Mexican individual, with that of insufficiency. In the case of the Conquest, we argued, we could certainly be talking about a relation of inferiority, similar to the relation between a father and a son, as Dr. Ramos proposes; but, in the case of Independence, the relation with the European was no longer one of father and son but, rather, one of teacher and student. We had, then, two "illustrations," which themselves expressed a difference between sufficiency and insufficiency, and no longer one between superiority and inferiority. We thus proposed a phenomenological analysis that would very precisely disentangle inferiority from insufficiency.

Inferiority is a modality of insufficiency, but it is not the only one. How does one go from a constitutional or ontological insufficiency to inferiority? Answering this question means giving an account of what Professor Ramos has called the Mexican's inferiority complex.

In the first place, in what sense should we understand, in an ontological manner, that the Mexican is insufficient? According to Dr. Ramos, the inferiority complex should serve to systematically explain "our character." But, what is our character?

When one considers their character, Mexicans are sentimental. At the core of this very particular human being, there is a strong emotive mixture, involving inactivity and the disposition to ruminate on each one of life's events. Mexican life is impregnated with a sentimental character and it can be said that the tone of that life sets up the play of the emotions, of inactivity, and of a tireless internal rumination.

Emotionality is a species of internal fragility; the Mexican feels weak or fragile inside. He has learned from infancy that his interiority is vulnerable and brittle, which gives rise to all the techniques for preservation and protection that the Mexican constructs in order to impede external forces from penetrating and injuring him. This helps explain his frailty, the elegance of his dealings, his avoidance of surprises, and his crude expressions. But it also explains that constant preoccupation with keeping a low profile, with being inconspicuous, and the impression he eventually gives of evading and hiding, of not allowing himself to be noticed, and finally, that sensation, so uncomfortable at times, of hiding one's person, of demureness, that almost borders on dissimulation and hypocrisy and that is ultimately nothing more than the conviction of an incurable fragility.

Fragility is the quality of always being threatened by nothingness, by the threat of falling into non-being. The Mexican's emotive life psychologically expresses or symbolizes this ontological condition. Whoever lives always threatened by destruction feels fragile, destructible, and tends either toward self-protection, if he values life, or opens himself to annihilation if, for instance, in the hurried-ness of a decision he chooses emptiness and nothingness. From there arises that characteristic contempt for human life attributed to the Mexican, as well as the familiar idea that the Mexican lives constantly ambushed by death. Mexican life is sensitive and delicate because the fundamental project of protecting a frag-ile being requires constructing the surrounding world as a practical system of resilient, elastic, and "soft" networks [*canales amortiguadores, elásticos, "algodono-sos"*]. But together with these protective networks, there is also a vast zone of brutal edges lying there as a threat. The contrast between brutality and fragility is as Mexican as the Mexican himself. Mexican life offers to emotive life compli-cated structures of preservation, species of Baroque altars in which thousands of twisted figures have been sculpted and from which one must skillfully pry oneself so as not be assaulted by the brutal and the grotesque.

Inactivity is the mark of the sentimental character. The various obstacles that oppose themselves to the various activities of the Mexican do not motivate him to grow or overcome those obstacles, but, rather, fold him over and drive him into himself [*lo replieguen y ensimisman*]. This is unwillingness [*desgana*] in all of its forms; it is to disconnect oneself from all tasks, to leave everything for "tomorrow." On the surface, to be unwilling is to be bored, since associations of unwillingness with boredom are always in abundance. When unwillingness dominates, human reality appears, from the outside, as if given over to an over-bearing boredom; however, deeper inspection removes that appearance, and we are confronted with aspects of human reality that are unrelated to boredom, pure and simple.

In unwillingness, our spirit colors itself with a particular repulsion for things, with a quiet repulsion for everything that surrounds us.[1] But, the unwilling man does not stop seeing a meaningful structure in the world (the world does not appear to him as it appears in [Sartre's] *Nausea*), as a copy of insignificant and gratuitous things. Rather, he sees a meaningful process that beckons his collabo-ration, his decision, his action, and that demands to be fulfilled by a *surplus* of determination. Unwillingness appears when life, soft and elastic, nevertheless

---

[1] Ramon López Velarde, in his poem *La Tejadora* ["The Weaver"], says that our spirit fills itself with "a tame disdain of things."

forces a decision. We are unwilling so as not to choose. In this sense, unwillingness is indifference before things, an unwillingness that could pass as contemplation if not for the obscure feeling of overindulgent irresponsibility that accompanies it. Being thus shows itself as a repertoire of meanings that wrap and bind us, and simultaneously as a structure of "supplicants" [*suplicantes*] whose lamentations have the precise sense of not being heard. Unwillingness is then indifference before a supplication; or, it is a resistance, if you prefer, against the spontaneous and originary voice of things or of others. When we are unwilling, the world sends us messages that arrive at an inattentive destination. And it is not to consciously cause harm that the calls go neglected, but rather because we have no desire to lend them our attention, because we decide not to move, to remain in inactivity (for instance, when we decide to let the phone ring rather than unplugging it). The unwilling individual lacks precisely the will to bestow sense. While he may feel in possession of a mechanism for sense bestowal, he will not act and will keep to himself the centrifugal impulse to attribute meanings.

Unwillingness is found in the opposite extremes [*antípodas*] of generosity. Generosity is, in effect, a determined choice to collaborate, a will to sympathize, to enter into auxiliary contact with things, with history, with social movements, of adding or synthesizing the capacity for teleological determination that emanates from freedom with the causality that weighs things down, with the dialectical course of the world that straightens itself toward a goal, but which without that *surplus* of determination can degrade or minimize itself into inadequate compromises. If history entails an essential indeterminateness, and freedom can force it to pass to a lesser degree of indetermination and toward greater precision and unity, then to not graft that degree of probability, to refuse to make history into a making that concerns us, is a lack of generosity, a lack of joy for an abundance that overflows, and that is precisely unwillingness.

In unwillingness there is disgust [*asco*] for the meaning that things have, for the sense that they contain. When it is said of something that it provokes disgust, we are not saying that we disapprove of the contingency of its being, of its stubborn lack of all sense or transcendence, but rather that as an indeterminate sense it calls on my collaboration while chaining me to a task that, as overdetermined, can only bring me closer to abjection. Unwillingness is precisely the disgust that overtakes us when we foresee that our action might contribute to a consolidation of the abject sense of things. All action is therefore valued, in unwillingness, within the horizon of its contribution to depravity and corruption [*podredumbre*]. It is thus conceivable that unwillingness emerges by the simple fact that one is Mexican. It is an attempt to dislodge oneself from that contingency, to uproot oneself from that facticity, an attempt to be disgusted with contingency and facticity. It is an unwillingness not to be otherwise, for our history not to be otherwise, for our customs not to be otherwise; unwillingness that prepares the choice for another that will be our savior or the choice of an inferiority complex. From there emerges that eagerness to see things as the outsider sees them, to allow ourselves to be justified by others.[2] From there emerges also "pochismo," "malinchismo," "Europeanism," and "indigenism."[3] With unwillingness, one of the modes of insufficiency, the Mexican flees from himself by choosing inferiority. Here we bear witness to how insufficiency transforms itself into inferiority by means of unwillingness—an inferiority that predisposes the Mexican to his sentimental character.

But inactivity also gives rise to other feelings that we will qualify as dignity. The Mexican lives in a constant state of indignation. Noticing that things begin to go badly, he is always prepared with a principle in accordance with which to condemn those things; however, he is also not disturbed by them going badly, and so he does not throw himself into action; all he does is protest, allowing free reign to his indignation. The obstacle, that is, does not redouble his activity. A task saturated with difficulties will not be incentive enough for the Mexican to redouble his efforts. Dignity resides in the will to stay clean, in the will to flee from any association or involvement with whatever is base. Being dignified is to make oneself immune to the wiles of irregularity, to keep oneself safe from suspect commitments. It corresponds very well to what Kant calls freedom in the negative sense, that is, the capacity for autonomy before inferior tendencies. A will to cleanliness, to rectitude and correctness, are aspects of the feeling of dignity. With a patience that ignores its origins, the dignified man surrenders to the decision to pass through life as cleanly as possible, to dedicate himself to causes that will not expose his vulnerabilities, and to avoid the paths that will make him a target.

What in the Spaniard shows itself as honor, in the Mexican appears as a proper sense of dignity. With this we touch upon the most profound layers of the different modes of being human. We touch upon the idea that freedom, which every human being represents, cannot be subjected to any law; it is unconditional. Because of freedom, the human being can be anything he wants in any given situation; he can be mean or noble, magnanimous or petty. In short, because of freedom, the individual enlightens the world with values and anti-values without

[2] "When I told him that we were foreigners [*extranjeros*], he stopped smiling, and looked at me with more respect. I had pronounced, without knowing, the sacred word: *extranjero* [foreigner], a word that in Mexico equates to a right of privilege, to Master of all things." J. Rubén Romero, *Apuntes de un lugareño*, p. 298.

[3] ["Pochismo" refers to the act of appropriating English words into Spanish, what we would today call "Spanglish"; "malinchismo" refers to giving preference to foreign ideas, tastes, or attitudes; "Europeanism" can be understood as a preference for European things and customs; and "indigenism" could refer to a cultural nostalgia regarding indigenous histories or cultures. All are typical criticisms of the Mexican character.—Trans.]

any sort of hindrance. This is what the Spanish drama of Don Juan very accurately represents. When the fair maiden has surrendered, when she has placed her life in his hands, she can no longer ask him to do what is right, to put things aside for a better time, for instance, for a time after the epithalamium sanctioned by human and divine laws. What is to be done is within the purview of Don Juan's unconditional freedom, and the only thing that matters is to appeal to his honor, to rest in his dignity which is a quality of freedom, a very peculiar coloring that always gives itself when one speaks of freedom. The French call this quality generosity, not honor or dignity. The free man is for the French the generous man, for the Spaniard the honorable man, and for the Mexican the dignified man. From a dignified man, likewise from an honorable or a generous man, we can expect anything, and can trust him with the most important and delicate situations, commitments, and so on, and trust him also with what is most disturbing, for which he will always respond . . . with dignity.

Dignity as a qualification of freedom is indefinable. It is impossible to convince someone of the meaning of dignity if he has not experienced it in the exercise of freedom. Here, as in every other case, understanding presupposes a previous grasping, comprehension. Dignity is, as we said before, a will to distance oneself from suspicious motivations having to do with our conduct. Every free act presupposes dignity, since the exercise of freedom is always preceded by an act through which the individual dislodges himself from a system of inferior motivations. But in the execution of the free act, such distancing is not enough. Escaping from the sensible while not morally determining oneself is a state of indifference that mirrors unwillingness and indecision. This is why dignity, unwillingness, and fragility are always tied together. Dignity needs the support of an active determination, or better yet, it is a virtue of inactivity and not of activity. As with honor, dignity has its advantages and its disadvantages.

A certain honesty bordering on arrogance comes with honor; a certain discretion bordering on immodesty accompanies dignity. The atmosphere that honor adds to our decision is one of clarity and warmth, while that which is added by dignity is nebulous and cold. The dignified man, through his decisions, allows a certain fragility to shine through, a certain incurable inconsistency. An internal rumination constitutes the third characteristic element of the sentimental man. Preserving our being means nothing else than allowing or bringing about an internal substitution of activity, allowing or bringing about a certain species of dreaming that involves reliving everything that has been lived, a going to and fro in interior life. Behind every face that evades activity and nausea we find an interior life, what every person has lived, his memories, his worries, his joys, a repertoire of facts that every Mexican cares about and continuously retells. The Mexican individual always gives the impression of having already lived, of carrying deep within his soul a world that has already been, and does so because its emotive weight was indelibly recorded.[4] On that our melancholy is grounded, as is the appearance of a man of bitter experience.

There is an almost supernatural correspondence between dignity and abruptness, an insight that our interior pains respond unequivocally to external obstacles, and that our timidity and our modesty are not only sources of dreams and worlds that deplete themselves in our heads but forebodings with hard external edges. The Mexican suffers and unravels; outsiders recommend that he reverse his marasmus, that he escape the asphyxiating ivy of his internal jungle, and do so with the sense of urgency that his surrounding world jealously awaits his awakening and his work. But as soon as that marasmus, those nightmares, are dissolved; as soon as the decision is made to consider the whole interior life as a macabre dance that will come to an end with the first ray of light; as soon as this is done and he throws himself courageously into the adventure, he is violently attacked, reviled, and reproached, maltreated, and humiliated. These are the oscillations, so familiar to Mexican existence, of a diligent enthusiasm, a hopeful deliverance to a movement that is followed almost immediately by a deep depression, by a falling once again into a hopeless dreaming.[5]

It is said in psychology that, as a means of coping, the introvert very carefully assumes the heaviness of those objects from which he flees. In a similar sense, we must keep in mind what we said before about dignity, namely, that it foresees those obstacles that externally oppose themselves to its intentions. Take the man who, from a sense of dignity, has retired from a corrupt business. This man later tries to convince himself that his scruples were based on unfounded apprehensions, and thus that he must return to the business. Very frequently, however, this man realizes that his apprehensions were not unfounded, that the warnings given to him by his sense of dignity corresponded to real difficulties, and that his tortured imaginings reflected, although in a twisted way, and obliquely, actual obstacles. This man soon realizes that it was his own cowardly nature that did not dare to see those obstacles for what they were, nakedly, directly, rightly, but rather allowed them to be expressed in the painful manipulations of his frustrated consciousness. The dreams of the melancholic, the doctors of old used to say, loosely represent in their scenes of horror the frightening struggle of his unruly humors.

The Mexican is a creature of melancholy, a sickness that belongs more to the imagination than to the body, but that expresses the human condition most

---

[4] The Mexican is "a man who constantly relives past adventures." José Gómez Robleda, *Imagen del mexicano*, p. 74.

[5] "Every time that I take flight to a height over all things, a sarcastic demon growls and brings me back to the mud." Ramón López Velarde, *Un lacónico grito*. [Included in Ramón López Velarde, *Obra Poética*, ed. José Luis Martínez (Paris: ALLCA XX, 1998), pp. 104–105.—Trans.]

acutely.[6] The Mexican is a groundless being [*un ser de infundio*], with all the nuances of dissimulation, concealment, falsehood, affectedness, and duplicity that belong to that word, but mainly with that characteristic of unfoundedness or ungraspability toward which the etymology of that word takes us. To be groundless is to lack a foundation, and only the human being can be the "groundless ground of value," which is ontological melancholy. Melancholy is the psychological reflection of our ontological constitution, of the precarious structure of our being, a being that is the ground of its own nothingness and not of its own being. Melancholy is more originary than anxiety, since, found in its ground, anxiety delivers us to the ecstasy of loss or care precisely because melancholy reveals us as groundless beings, as sick in our imagination. Melancholy also explains the motility of being, the transience of all things, the movement and becoming without hope of a future salvation in some foundational ground. With melancholy, the incurable motility of an entity can be seen and foreseen from the side of the object. In regard to values, freedom is the foundation without foundation, the fundamental groundlessness that infects us with melancholy. And in the Mexican this melancholy constitutes the groundless ground of his being, the nothingness in which he dwells.

Melancholy as a psychological phenomenon is possible only if we posit the human being as the ground of his own nothingness but not the ground of his own being, in other words, if we perceive that the human being is a being that dreams and imagines. The melancholy individual is trapped in his interior abode from whence he brings to the life of the imagination a thousand worlds to which he bestows value and sense while never losing sight of the fact that those worlds are grounded on nothingness, that they are suspended over nothingness, and this knowledge about the deception regarding the groundlessness of the world is precisely what we are apt to call melancholy.[7] Individuals who have projected a world, and who have realized it, eventually turn their gaze toward the foundations or grounds of those constructions, and upon finding them in the imagination are thrown into an incurable uneasiness, into an inevitable restlessness of finding the human edifice built on contemptible grounds. Individuals belonging to the greatest empires have thus been the most prone to melancholy. It is almost the national, imperial sentiment in the English; in the Roman it is enough to refer to the writings of Lucretius. All that is human rests in "nothings" [*naderias*], in cold or burning imaginings, and every image is a subtle secretion of that

---

[6] "Imagination is not a state; it is the very existence of humanity." William Blake, *Second Livre Prophetique*, trans. Pierre Berger (Paris: Rieder, 1930).

[7] "The Mexican flees from reality and shelters himself in dreams and fantasy." José Gómez Robledo, *Imagen del mexicano*, p. 74. [José Gómez Robleda, *Imagen del mexicano* (México: Secretaria de Educación Pública, 1948).—Trans.]

nothing which is the human being. The mystery of the imagination is contiguous with that of nothingness and this with that of the human. Melancholy expresses the intimate connection [*trabazón*] between the human being, nothingness, and sleep.

There exists for the Mexican the possibility, which is always open, that the world gives itself as "friend" or "enemy," as a danger or salvation, as threat or ally. These categories are especially valued in what is known as the political attitude. For the politician, being appears above all with a profile of neither friend nor enemy. Thus, Samuel Ramos infers an inferiority complex from the Mexican's interest in power. And it should not be surprising that the Mexican is interested in the constellations of power, since the world appears to him primarily in the background of the distinctions between friends and enemies, as with political Manichaeism.

That neutral state of being that does not show its destructible or resistant, fragile or vulnerable profile is only possible if the individual liberates herself from things in freedom and assumes the condition of "zozobra." "Zozobra" is the state in which we find ourselves when the world hides its fragility or destructibility; zozobra is the state in which we are not sure if, at any moment, a catastrophe will overwhelm us or if we will be secured in the safety of asylum. In zozobra we remain in suspense, in oscillation, as its etymology clearly announces (*sub-supra*; the world assumes a lack of definition and we assume indetermination). We are at the mercy of whatever may come, we are constitutively fragile, we have made ourselves fragile in choosing the world as insinuation, as threat, or as siege. By its very essence, destruction includes within itself the possibility of resistance; likewise, protection, the possibility of fragility. Being will appear as fragile for whoever seeks to protect it at all costs; it will appear as resistant for whoever seeks to destroy it. We must always know what we can count on, but the belief that we can never know what we can count on constitutes restlessness or zozobra. In destruction we approach being in order to reveal it as fragile or as resistant. But this fragility or resistance is forbidden to us. What is given appears to be first and foremost, and originally, in a state of expectant indifference. It is the state of the animal before jumping over a trench, the state of interest before situations of power, of interest before dominion. The Mexican is "introverted" [*huraño*], "withdrawn" [*retraído*], quick to jump or defend himself. Such an attitude is inexplicable if it is first not assumed that being appears as indifferent, and that only an unforeseen "accident" will bring about peace and confidence, on the one hand, or destruction and death, on the other. Confronted with the world, the Mexican stands as "friend" or "enemy," and does so in an unpredictable manner, in zozobra.

Questioning presupposes the intuition of non-being. Before questioning any existent being, there is always a prior familiarity with being and non-being.

Simply put, being-in-the-world is to be thrown simultaneously toward being and non-being. We are open to the entire field of experience and in that field we find spaces of non-being. Experience appears to us as neutral before being and non-being. Only further experience will reveal it to us as being or as non-being. This oscillation between being and non-being is what goes by the name of "accident." Being is always somewhat exposed, as is nothingness. But the accident hides and flees. We do not know what to depend on. This neutrality should not be threatening, but it is; this is because consciousness has previously been affected with fragility, has opened itself up to zozobra. Only when consciousness lives in zozobra can it fear that neutrality in such a way. In any other consciousness, one not qualified as fragile, neutrality is the condition of possibility for penetrating the real.

We have now arrived at an analysis of the characterological structure of the Mexican individual and her ontological constitution. Ontologically speaking, fragility and zozobra reveal us as accident. This is our inner constitution and it emerges likewise in that radical feeling of insecurity and evasion that affects all of our activities. Accidentality is insufficient before substance; it is precariousness before the massive and compact being of what subsists. It is what [Ramón] López Velarde indicates when he speaks about our "living today"— it is he who has placed zozobra and fragility at the center of his poetry. Thus, the analysis of our character has made unequivocally clear certain deficiencies and insufficiencies. But, what about inferiority? Is the insufficiency of accidentality already inferiority in some way? Inferiority presupposes insufficiency, but not the other way around. On the basis of insufficiency we can choose inferiority. Inferiority is one of the modalities of insufficiency—not the only one and of course not the possibility that Martin Heidegger would qualify as authentic.

Ontologically speaking, inferiority marks the project that involves being saved by others, of transferring onto others the task of justifying our existence, of unburdening us of zozobra, of allowing others to decide for us. So that such a project can be realized, it is necessary to have bestowed others with unlimited justification. And this is precisely what happens when we rely on the decisions of others. To allow our own life to become a project for others is to place in their hands every possible authenticating justification; it is to imagine that others always do the right thing, that they are closed off to the possibilities of accident, that they always know what to do. It is the "normal" situation of the child before his parents. This is why Samuel Ramos says that the inferiority complex that he attributes to the Mexican is acquired at the moment of the Conquest, since in the eyes of European culture we played the part of children. But that explanation does not satisfy us at all. There is a more profound dimension for the inferiority complex. Parents do not appear to their children as beings who are merely justified, but as beings who are absolutely justified. Jean-Paul Sartre has seen this clearly. Being absolutely justified can only be said of God, and in the inferiority complex, in the project of being saved by others, there is the transference of properties that only belong to being-for-itself, to anxiety, and to being-for-another.

Put in religious terms: in inferiority there is idolatry, a will to make the other an absolutely justified existence. According to Sartre, man fundamentally desires to be God. The transference of an intentional relation to the person of the other is precisely inferiority. One is inferior to the extent that one is idolatrous. The confusion between men and gods that we find at the origins of our Conquest already made it possible for us to easily accept an inferiority complex. If being itself is lacking, if it is unjustified, it becomes impossible that on its own it would generate or present justifications for itself; thus it would have to find in the other, or see the other, as a repository of being and, moreover, as its source. By definition, others have being. In analyzing myself, I can discover myself as accident, but I cannot speak of the other likewise as accident. No. The other is understood as massive consistency; the other is ripped away from zozobra and comfortably placed in subsistence. The individual who lacks the inferiority complex will not be able to say, as López Velarde writes, "our lives are pendulums," which means that he will not be able to take part in a unified project of zozobra. His life does not oscillate, but is rather frozen in the absolute justification of self-sufficiency [*aseidad*]; it is not accident, it is substance.

From the choice to be saved by others, a complex series of practices will emerge, aimed at promoting [*propiciar*] the giving away of the power of justification. Imitation, in particular, will be the ploy that will resemble original possession. A culture of imitation is a culture that rests in the fundamental project of being saved by others. Imitation is to appease [*propiciar*], to gain a favorable opinion. To the culture of imitation we oppose the culture of insufficiency, constitutive of those who have renounced the project of being saved by others and who risk the search for justification on their own terms.

If the Mexican as inferior is fundamentally an attempt to be saved by others, if he has chosen himself as accident, but one inevitably referred to as a self-sufficient being, if he has chosen himself as a contingency thrown against a necessity, an unjustified reality against a reality that has justified itself with reasons, then such a being will exist in a dialect driven by the search for that substance to which he has attributed the self-sufficiency that will save him. In this way, the Mexican has, of late, chosen himself as accident that refers itself to an indigenous substance. Indigenism is the latest of our projects involving an inferior mode of self-justification. When the European sees the mestizo, he stumbles over nothing, he crosses that space and only stops with the indigenous, which fascinates him.[8] The mestizo who has taken account of this situation has already arranged his affairs: he will approach the European gaze presenting only his indigenous side so as to be saved as the accident of that substance. The mestizo is an accident of the Indian, a nothingness attached to the being-in-itself of the Indian, who upon being loved, justified, by the European and the North American, will likewise gain its own justification. The mestizo claims the indigenous, he places it ahead of himself and chastises others whose perspectives presuppose anything else but the indigenous: he has learned to break away with the substance to which he would bind his fate. When indigenous relics seem to fascinate North Americans, the mestizo feels vindicated; it is then that he wishes that everything else could be transformed into an indigenous product, that life itself was transformed into an indigenous way of looking at the world. Every revolution carried out in the name of the Indian, artistic or political, has within it the unmentionable intention of saving the mestizo. In this way the indigenous serves as a means, as a substance that will reflect or radiate upon the mestizo its atmosphere of justification. Only the indigenous has been able to achieve universal worth; mestizo culture has not been able to go beyond its regional horizons. Thus we have the appeal to the indigenous as a reality that would come to save the mestizo; thus we have the perpetuation of the inferiority complex belonging to the mestizo when he becomes an indigenist. Just as frustrating as this project of salvation is the project of the "malinchista."[9] For the latter, the Spanish is the means to exclude accidentality. Recently, a friend proposed that an "accident," which occurred during a bull run, would not possibly happen in Spain. According to my friend, Spain represented the absolute exclusion of all accident; he felt with vigorous peculiarity that accidentality exists within us, and chose to transfer to Spain the absolute justification that excludes accident. Both the "indigenist" and the "malinchista" are mestizos who refuse to be alone, who throw upon the shoulders of another the task of justifying their own existence. But the mestizo must remain alone and, like Lopez Velarde writes, must open himself resolutely to the horizon of zozobra and accidentality.

Unwillingness, dignity, melancholy, and zozobra expose us to the field or, better yet, the abyss [el pozo] of our existential possibilities; they unmask and reveal us to our fundamental project, to the unprejudiced unity that we must attribute to things in the world, but not so as to blind us prematurely to the abyss, but in order to remain there, to tirelessly nurture ourselves from the wellspring of originary possibilities. The danger lies precisely in closing off the road toward the originary, in allowing a certain scarring to deceive us and conceal the living blood

---

[8] "Mexico becomes singular and individualizes itself *exclusively* for the Indian." José Gómez Robleda, *Imagen del mexicano*, p. 25.

[9] [See footnote 3, above.—Trans.]

that runs beneath, that moistens the bandages. The secret to a fundamental project lies precisely in repetition. To repeat is to reopen, in the sense in which it is said that one must "scratch" and reopen a scar that has inconveniently healed so as to allow the wound once again to exist in the play of its own possibilities. With this reopening we allow life itself, accidental and in zozobra, to remain immersed in its originary possibilities; we allow it to access its own sources and we keep it there, and there we nurture it. Inferiority is an insufficiency that has renounced its origins, that has lost itself and seeks to cover over the demands that its own decisions impose on us—rooted as they are in zozobra and accidentality. What will we do as beings in zozobra? How will we cover up our accidentality? How will we escape the proximity of death and zozobra? In maintaining oneself in the accidental, are we deprived of the possibilities for action? These questions no longer belong to ontology proper, but to morality. Now is not the time to answer them.

CHAPTER 14

Community, Greatness, and Misery in Mexican Life (1949)

Jorge Portilla

Translated by Carlos Alberto Sánchez

Jorge Portilla was born in Mexico City in 1919 and died there prematurely in 1963, at the age of 45. He was founding member of the Hiperión group (founded in 1947) and author of La fenomenología del relajo *(1966). Though he was a highly influential member of the Hiperión group, Portilla was not a prolific writer. The essay that follows is one of only a few published during his lifetime. Although he studied law and philosophy alongside other members of Hiperión and in various universities throughout the world, Portilla was not a professional philosopher. He avoided the academic life altogether. Nonetheless, his contributions to philosophy, and phenomenology in particular as evidenced by the few surviving texts, should make evident his profundity. His* Fenomenología del relajo *is available in English in Carlos Alberto Sánchez's* The Suspension of Seriousness *(2012).*

Introduction

This lecture series aims to disclose the levels of reflection that have been reached in Mexico regarding our own values, regardless of whether those reflections aim to fix or discover the "being" of the Mexican, or merely point to a psychological description of the Mexican character.

On this occasion, we do not intend, naturally, to offer a complete picture of Mexican reality. Rather, our aim is to offer an outline, perhaps of a mere idea, of a vast field of investigation that, we hope, might yield some unexpected results.

For now, we would like merely to point out a tendency in contemporary philosophy that we find most relevant for the unveiling of certain key characteristics required for the clarification of our particularity. By doing so, we are entrusting ourselves to the fundamental orientation that present thought exhibits in our country, one that has given itself to an energetic project of autognosis, which is, in the last analysis, the meaning of all authentic philosophizing from Socrates until today.

Existential and Phenomenological Conceptions of Community

Today it is evident that philosophical thought has begun to turn its attention from the individual to the community, or, at least, that it has modified its point of departure in such a way that it will make progress possible in this field, progress that evaded previous generations.

Gabriel Marcel opposes Hegel's absolute "I" with a religiously inspired philosophy of an absolute "Thou." Between these two essential dimensions of human existence, Martin Heidegger has demonstrated a certain "being-with-others" that betrays the active and gregarious spirit of his nationalism, while Jean-Paul Sartre has posited the gaze of the other as a ground of our pre-theoretical knowledge as well as an originary consciousness of our being in community, one that provokes inevitable conflicts in the sphere of concrete relations between man and man.[1] In his conception of concrete relations with the other, one can clearly read into the state of human relations in a society overrun by the most extreme individualism.

This tendency in contemporary philosophy appears to us so evident that it is surprising that a thinker such as Edmund Husserl—who, in one of the final passages of his *Cartesian Meditations*, affirms that the ground of all objectivity is a "transcendental intersubjectivity," which at times seems foundational and other times is confused with nothing less than "Being" itself—is thought to be the most typical representative of bourgeois individualism and is even accused of solipsism.

What Is Community?

Let us then point to some ideas regarding the forms of community that are found in Mexico, ideas that lend justification to certain aspects of the national character and to certain essential particularities belonging to *lo mexicano* [to *Mexicanness*].

But first, what is "community"?

---

[1] [I have translated *originario* as "originary" and not "original" because our aim is to situate Portilla within the phenomenological/existential tradition, to which he naturally belongs, and in which originary is rootedness and ownness, while original indicates novelty or simply origin; one is ontic (original), the other is ontological (originary).—Trans.]

At first glance, it seems that the answer to this question should be sought in sociology. This science, if we can call it a science, has lent a precise and technical sense to that term. In sociology, "community" is a term that designates a particular form of association. There is already the well-known distinction made by Ferdinand Tönnies between the concepts of "community" and "society," which he considers basic sociological categories.

Community represents a form of organic association into which the individual does not enter through a voluntary decision but in which he finds himself "always already," developing within it, tied to it by a solidarity of which he is not the author, moved by spontaneous impulses, by a species of essential will, that is, a will penetrated and determined by the unconscious emotional ground of all persons—a non-accidental will untouched by the considerations of a reflective calculus.

On the other hand, *society* is found to be freely constituted, by the free choice of the participating individuals, ordinarily realized by contractual procedures and in accordance with ends that the individual believes to be his own, but which coincide and concur with the ends of others, and in which he enters or exists voluntarily and deliberately.[2]

Typical cases of the first kind of association (i.e., of community) are the nation and the family; of the second, mercantile societies.

Max Weber calls community a social relation "if and when the attitude toward social action is inspired by the participants' subjective desires to form a whole." And he defines a society as "a social relation in which the attitude toward action is inspired by compensation of interests with rational motives or a union of interest with a common motivation."

Similarities between both conceptions are obvious. However, as far as we are concerned, highlighting the differences does not matter much.

It is important to note that we do not find this distinction in Anglo-Saxon sociological thinking. It is a distinction characteristic of German thought, corresponding to familiar German ideas regarding culture and civilization.

We have here two sociological conceptions of community, one founded on structural notions and the other on procedural notions, the details of which we need not analyze.

Everyday Conceptions of Community

These concepts and definitions of community, taken from sociology, are not useful for us. In the first place, they are overly general, referring to the most universal

---

[2] Cf. Luis Racasens Siches, *Principios de Sociología*.

forms of association, those we can find anywhere in the world. We would help ourselves very little if, for example, we were to offer abstractions regarding whether or not our community belongs to one of the types indicated by that science. Second, they are merely formal concepts, and our project could not be any more concrete: it is the project of determining, as clearly as possible, the specific structure of the Mexican community, making evident this structure as the ground of those superficial but visible manifestations that are the particular patrimony of our style of life.

Our point of departure cannot be, then, a concept of community forged by scientific thinking in accordance with its own methods and its own goals, but must be a concept that will benefit our purpose.

As a result, once we eliminate the sociological concept of community, we must return to our exposition and begin with the common, everyday, or pre-ontological concept of community. We must begin from that implicit conception of community that is at play when in everyday conversation we utter that word.

Community as Person

In its everydayness, we conceive of the community as a person, or as an entity that has, at the very least, one of the fundamental characteristics of the person, namely, being the ideal center, responsible for the performance of acts.

When we speak, for example, of US political influence in Latin America, we are taking the United States as an entity, as a "whole person" in Max Scheler's sense, to whom we attribute certain acts and purposes: those acts that reveal its politics in Latin America and those purposes that we guess lie behind them.

This same idea is in play when we speak of French history, of the destiny of a family, or of the financial situation of a corporation [*sociedad anonima*], and so on.

This is enough to affirm, even if vaguely, that the pre-ontological concept of community is none other than that of the person in its totality or as a collective, and that this common and vulgar representation makes possible an entire series of scientific and philosophical conceptions of community that are nothing else than attempts to unravel it.

Within the framework of its common meaning and its everyday expression other possibilities emerge, such as personal symbolic representations like that of "Uncle Sam," "John Bull," "the Russian Bear," and so on.

These common representations of community and society that we find in sociology, as well as those which are more respectable and ethereal, turn out to be nothing but this same vague concept of community, specified in accordance with the goals and the ideology of a thinker, who has imposed upon this imprecise and daily lived experience [*vivencia*] the unique mark of his particular reflection. Behind each of those representations lies the concept of community *vaguely considered as a person.*

Mexican Curious

Given this kind of objectivity, we can only speak of our own community if we place ourselves outside of it in the ideal, just as those historians from Renke's school pretended to do with their supposed scientific objectivity while facing the historical facts of their own nation. Today we know that this kind of stance is a movement in bad faith, as Edmundo O'Gorman has clearly demonstrated in his book *Crisis y porvenir de la Ciencia Histórica.*

We cannot, in any way, place ourselves outside of our national community, in the same way that we cannot truly situate ourselves outside of our own family community. To speak about Mexico from an external point of view can only be done by an outsider under whose watchful gaze we must become part of the community that has allowed us to exist as its members in some way or another (in our case, via our Mexican nationality) and that we constitute together with others (in this case, with our compatriots).

This means that, *from an external point of view*, the only thing we can affirm is that, with regard to Mexicans, we are co-responsible with all of our past and present compatriots for what Mexico is, and with our past, present, and future compatriots for what Mexico will be.

It may happen, as it has, that because of the radical insecurity of the values that are authentically rooted in our nationality, we assume that the gaze of the other captures us in the truth of our being. From there, we begin to believe that we are, for example, truly dissolute *charros* or sad Indians, deformed and false images of the Mexican not unlike certain representations on the movie screen, or on the painter's canvas, of forms or pseudo-forms of life torn from touristic retinas by a movie director or by the superficiality of some painter somewhere in his work.

All of this is *Mexican Curious*,[3] that is, the pure image or imagery of Mexicanness captured in the perspective of the stranger; it is the vulgar image of our "being for others" that turns us into a pure object of contemplation.

Naturally, we are tired of that image, and fortunately not all of our spiritual expressions can be reduced to those contained in it. To take an example from the art world, if Diego Rivera has painted what he believes is the Mexican seen from

---

[3] [This is in the original. This phrase is a derogatory way to refer to those fetishized products of Mexican culture reproduced for the consumer market.—Trans.]

the point of view of the North American, or seen from the point of view of the absolute "I" that dominates the perspective of universal history, there has also existed a José Clemente Orozco who has painted the world, including the North American world, and that has painted history, our history and universal history, seen from the point of view of the Mexican himself.

But even within this place prior to all reflection, we find another confused representation of the community, one that appears to us even more profound and that has not yet been explained in the objectivity of science with the same vigor and in the same measure as the previous representation.

Community as Horizon

In everyday life, that is, more in the life of "doing" than in the life of thought and language, there exists a manner of lived experience or a concept of community as horizon—more precisely, community as a horizon in which actions are articulated, or as the horizon for the comprehension of certain actions, and some would say for the majority of our human actions.

An example might clarify this idea. If on one of the days legally assigned we head to the nearest voting booth in our district to cast a vote in favor of a certain candidate or in favor of a certain political measure, we ourselves interpret our action within the horizon of our politically specified national community. The people who stand in line with us, the urn into which we deposit the piece of paper with such and such a sign, the delegates of the political parties that keep watch over the operation, and every other element that stands before us are articulated in our experience within and from the standpoint of that interpretive horizon, which likewise articulates the totality that is the Mexican nation in its political life. Here we have a transcendence common to all the voters and functionaries, characterized as national political transcendence, before which we are nothing but ephemeral personifications.

If suddenly a certain evil demon, playing a serious prank, were to conceal this horizon, we would suddenly find ourselves as if waking from a dream, incapable of understanding our very presence where we stand, incapable of understanding, moreover, any of the actions taking place in it. The scene would seem to us very strange. Perhaps we would retain a vague memory that our presence was not totality meaningless, but, lacking that memory, perhaps we would walk away holding tightly onto an incipient anxiety about the state of our mental faculties.

This example deals with the horizon of the national and the political community, but we also always live in a multiplicity of communal horizons that mix and weave with one another and that always remain potential or actual, depending on whether our *action* reveals or conceals them. We always live simultaneously immersed in a national community that can take various forms, ranging from the political to the aesthetic: in a professional community, a guild, a class, a family; even, perhaps, within the horizon of a human community overflowing with nature and the universal totality, in which we can also participate in certain forms of life belonging to the cosmic community, which is the ground for all kinds of pantheism, just as those other conceptions are the grounds for nationalism, for the feeling of class solidarity, what is called the spirit of a people, sectarianism, humanitarianism, and so on.

These horizons are critically important for human action. One of their primary functions is to serve as a wall against which the meaning of our actions bounces back like an echo. In this way, the echo of the act of voting may arrive with a certain distortion that indicates to us that in our national political horizon there exist certain mysterious peculiarities. The echo that bounces off our national community perhaps makes it evident that our vote did not have the exact meaning that we were giving to it.

The result is a weak political life with all of the consequences that entails and that we can clearly see: the bombastic ambiguity of the acts through which this life is manifested; the demagogic and hollow tone of the discourses, proclamations, bulletins, and so on; a general not-knowing what to depend on; the guessing game that serves as the criterion for deciding probabilities; rumors, and so forth.

This lack of horizon in action is that to which one refers when one says that one has lost one's "true north." The expression is appropriate since all action is performed always with the assumption that it will be accepted and that it will get a response from others or from the group, and when the response contradicts or offends what has been assumed, our situation is analogous to that of the explorer or sailor working with a broken compass. Her horizon, in this case a geographical horizon, has become confusing and more than likely threatening.

The Bribe and the Haggle

Very well, everything happens as if these structures of transcendence that we have named horizons of community in our country suffer from a sort of failure or inarticulateness such that they will determine our lives and our actions very weakly and secondarily. Perhaps this is the fact that will more strongly determine our national character.

This hypothesis would explain a set of typical and everyday facts with which every Mexican is familiar.

In the first place, we have the bribe [la mordida], that ghostly specter that we can blame for every one of our national embarrassments.

The monstrous development of bribery is possible because the functionary does not act as a representative of that communal transcendence that we call the State, but rather as a representative of his own personal interests.

Here we have a failure of that sentiment of solidarity that should have integrated this functionary into the total person of the State and under the watchful eye of the individual.

His community-State horizon disappears, and the only thing that remains is the sufficient means for his own relations with particular people to turn easily into personal relationships in which only personal interests are at play. His gaze has been displaced from a communal and objective transcendence and has fallen into a personal, subjective transcendence. Is this the immortality of the individual? Maybe not, but it is an alteration or weakness of the moral foundation which is the community.

Another phenomenon that grabs one's attention, especially the attention of the tourist, is the haggle. In haggling, the transcendence that regulates the actions of the buyers and sellers (i.e., the market), an objective determinant of price, is here a nonexistent horizon, and buyer and seller surrender themselves to a more or less skillful practice pertaining to each other's possibilities and necessities. In this game of cunning, in which he who knows more about his opponent's *personal* situation has the advantage, a price emerges, a price specific to each case, which is not purely numeric or quantifiable.

We could say the same thing about another very Mexican institution that we have baptized with a special name, a name that does not even allude to the juridical or moral issues that it raises, but rather to its significance for an individual's personal life, namely, the *casa chica*,[4] or "small house," a phenomenon that reveals the failure to actualize the family community as an entity that offers an aesthetic and legal horizon. It is a failure that translates to the search for illegitimate interpersonal relations outside the home.

Clearly, one might object that the acts discussed in this section are found elsewhere in the world and not just in Mexico, but what matters here is not the behavior as such—all human action is, as such, universal in a certain sense— what matters is the weight, the caliber, the reach, the evident importance that such acts have in Mexican life.

Emilio Uranga's Analysis

But the preceding is purely anecdotal, and we believe that the explanatory efficacy of our hypothesis reaches a more extensive and essential domain.

[4] [The "casa chica" refers to a "second family"—to an illegitimate family.—Trans.]

In his excellent "Essay on an Ontology of the Mexican," Emilio Uranga has highlighted essential aspects of the national character: an acute sense for the fragility of being, inactivity, and a tendency toward introversion, something like an interior rumination "internally substituting for activity, a species of daydreaming, of thinking and rethinking what has been lived," all aspects of a sentimental character.

It would seem, in effect, that the Mexican would not live in accordance with his being, and especially his own being, if it were endowed with a substantial consistency, but would live affected by the fragility of accidentality.[5] To be fragile, to be affected or transfixed by nothingness, or to be accidental—there lies the cornerstone on the basis of which an ontological description of the Mexican ought to be attempted.

In the categorical structure of the transcendental subject that would unify us as Mexicans, that is, in the being itself of the national consciousness, we find an emptiness. Lacking is the category of substance and, as an inevitable consequence, everything else that remains is affected by an incurable fragility or accidentality. Although it may seem strange, it might be said that we Mexicans are existentialists from birth.

We do not oppose Uranga's pronouncements. His descriptions seem to us to properly correspond to the way things currently stand.

Time and Mexican Being

Now, as Heidegger has demonstrated, the horizon for the intelligibility of being is time. Not astronomical or objective time, but human time, intersubjective time, inner time, Saint Augustine's distention of the soul, which for Heidegger contains our entire being and is the most profound stratum of our concrete existence, of our true reality. This originary and true time is described by Heidegger as a future that continuously becomes present in order to become past, as an "arriving presence that becomes a has been," according to Heidegger's own formula.

This real time on which our own existence rests runs counter to the derived, objective, and astronomical time of clocks or the planets. In it there is a foundation of the future.

On a concrete level, we construct our being from non-being; we construct our being out of a creation of possibilities whose foundations sink into the uncertainty of a future, of an arrival; we construct our being from

---

[5] [The notion of "accidentality" is crucial in Uranga's existential analysis. See Sánchez, *The Suspension of Seriousness* (2012) and *Contingency and Commitment* (2016).—Trans.]

an uncertain and empty temporal enclosure and through an act of *projection* that is the originary movement begetting human existence. Our existence is a project, in the double sense of scheme and thrownness, the first outline of which we trace in the non-being of the future. It is not strange, then, that human life, all human life, finds itself affected by an incurable nihilism, accidentality, or insubstantiality.

However, it is a fact that this particular specification for being human, so proximal and yet so confusing for us Mexicans, is intertwined in a special way with the lived experience of fragility and angst [*zozobra*] that Uranga has highlighted. How is this possible?

Certainly, projecting ourselves toward the future in search of our being does not consist merely in contemplating in advance an image of ourselves that would become real by an act of magic, but in an active projecting. Our being in potency becomes our actual being through an intermediary: action. We project toward the future actively, not contemplatively.

However, our action is not carried out in the middle of the desert, but in community. We cannot project any action whatsoever without counting on others, action that will be rejected or approved by others. Our action is inconceivable to ourselves if a somewhat precise halo is not attached to it, one of approval or reproach, of incentive or obstacle, whose source is the community, those "others." And if this communal horizon were to appear distant or unarticulated, how accurate will be the outline we attempt to sketch of our own being in time?

Before our own eyes, being in general, or our own being, will take on a weak, imprecise, and fragile character because the foundation of our action is itself weak, imprecise, and fragile; it does not offer sufficient resistance at certain points and is overly resistant at others. And action, every one of our acts, is a constitutive element of our being.

We can already see the foundation of inactivity, of inaction, of that leaving-everything-for-tomorrow that is today a common trait of our character.

The Notion of Embedded Action

In effect, if the community's reception or response in regard to our action cannot be determined with a certain amount of clarity, it is likely that we will indefinitely postpone the demanded action until the horizon clears up and, if this does not happen, we will carry it out only when the circumstances themselves turn it into a demand that cannot be postponed, and then it will probably carry within itself the mark of improvisation.

Nothing slows down the impetus toward action more than uncertainty concerning how the work will be done and received. Thus, in a community as fragmented as ours, the man of action, and even the intellectual, will find himself affected by a certain cynicism, which is nothing more than a defensive maneuver or a movement of self-affirmation, which can be described by the analogy of whistling or humming in the dark so as to forget one's fears.

This also explains how some people frequently find refuge in the embrace of small communities founded on interpersonal relations of friendship that determine and bestow a direction to politics and all other matters, even cultural life.

We do not know what to depend on in terms of our own place in the totality, but we know what to depend on within the small circle of friends, colleagues, and associates, more or less shut in.

The result is the periodic appearance in all areas of social life, with good or bad results, of groups or "cliques" that set themselves apart in respect to all matters, not so much because of the individual excellence of their members, but because they act over a ground of general inactivity.

Resignation and Fragility

To the sense of fragility and inactivity we add a third constitutive element of the sentimental character, according to Uranga, "an internal substitute for activity, a certain species of daydreaming that involves a re-living everything that has been lived, a going to and fro in interior life."

It is clear that a failed, unnatural, or badly interpreted action will turn us into introverts, melancholic and hopeless. Action becomes imaginary: everyday conversation in Mexico is filled with stories about men who attempted a noble act, who tried to realize a useful or noble endeavor, an act that was ultimately crushed by the harshness of the external world, or invalidated by collaborators who were inept or of bad faith. Stories that are accompanied by an expression of bitter experience: "You see, we all know that in Mexico you cannot do anything . . ." and so on, and so on.

We have no choice but to defend that fragile being that, upon its own emergence, appears vulnerable, threatened; we have no choice but to safeguard what we have already accomplished, to stabilize our situation, to conform ourselves to what we already have. "Defend the victories of the peasants," "Defend the victories of liberalism," "Defend the sacred relics of our tradition"—these are the fundamental *slogans*[6] of political life.

And all of that proclaimed, not before programs of concrete action, but before mysterious, unspeakable, yet contemptible, machinations of those "reactionary" or "militant" cliques that mysteriously remain as shadowy sources [*fuentes*

6 ["Slogans" is in the original.—Trans.]

tenebrosas]—in the political jargon there even exists the verb *tenebrosear* [to shadow]—and that threaten to put an end to the defense of our victories or our cultural relics.

From an external point of view, this state of things can be described as a state of the sub-integration of Mexican society, as a species of social malnutrition, that forms a thin yet suffocating spiritual atmosphere for whoever must form his personality within it. This is not the case, however, for those who have been formed in a super-integrated society. For the latter, this atmosphere seems to be a space of incredibly open opportunities for individual action, something like a paradise for the industrious man, a paradise that frequently transforms itself into the dominion of the predator.

The State of Sub-Integration

This state of things has yet another effect on individual life that matters greatly to the object of our study. The individual, prevented from securely founding his being on the web of human relations, finds himself painfully exposed to the cosmic vastness. We always live simultaneously entrenched in a human world and in a natural world, and if the human world denies us its accommodations to any extent, the natural world unleashes itself upon us with such a force so as to threaten the fragility of our connections. This would make some sense of the extreme importance given to landscape in Mexican art and the telluric character that fills everything from our painting to our novels and to our cinematography. But also, and above all else, this is what makes it possible that political life becomes polarized in parties that are not forms of rational association with concrete goals, but forms of association made up of believers who hold some particular conception of the world, which itself entails a divide whose profundity makes conflicting groups completely impermeable. It is thus that the turbulent and volcanic character of political change remains always already marked as such.

All that has been said will appear to be quite negative and lamentable. Without a doubt, the state of sub-integration of our society is an evil, but a greater evil can just as well be found in a state of super-integration. Nevertheless, there is no lack of testimony regarding the positive aspects that a situation like ours can offer. A few years ago, the German Hispanicist Karl Vossler summarized his experience on a trip to South America before the Bavarian academy with the following words: "Central Europeans of today, who are at the point of wrapping up our healthy members with a system of well-intentioned bandages and of making ourselves immobile by force of organization, can take example in the free spirit of independence of the Latin American."

Community as Coexistence

We have shown here that community in Mexico is lived at a distant and unarticulated horizon that does not offer a precise orientation or consistent support for individual action. By doing that, we have only achieved a negative characterization of the experience of community that seems to us specific to Mexico. Up to now, we have spoken only of two forms of understanding community: as person and as horizon, which are but two aspects of the same pre-ontological conception seen from either an objective or subjective position. There is still a third sense, a third pre-ontological or everyday form of understanding community, that will give us a clue to very important aspects of *lo mexicano*. But before expanding on that third sense, we must clarify a bit the scope of our investigation. We must first bring to light the existential foundation of the experience of community as person, horizon, and institution.

This foundation is nothing more than coexistence in the literal sense of this term. To exist is to coexist. The being of man is not just a "being there" or existence, but a "being-with-others" or coexistence, and this ontological structure is what makes possible our use of the word "us," which is something like the institution's guardian deity.

But let us look at this more closely.

In his analytic description of human existence [his existential analytic], Martin Heidegger takes as his guiding thread the unitary structure of "being-in-the-world." To be is to "be in the world." The entirety of his *Being and Time* is no more than an exposition of everything that this proposition implies.

The description of "world" in "being in the world"—characterized as the surrounding world—moves Heidegger to posit as constitutive elements of this world a plurality of existences that are coexistent with mine:

> The book I write, the field I cultivate, the car I drive, the suit I wear—
> objects of my surrounding world—are all equipment that refer to a plurality of existents who are readers, consumers, laborers, tailors. These
> are not far from me, but in my immediate world. The reader is in close
> proximity to the author, and if I am a laborer or a lawyer my clients are
> integrated in my surrounding world as well, as a priori schemas that are
> filled by concrete persons. Can one conceive of a doctor or a journalist by themselves without patients or readers? These occupations—we
> have already said—do not gain sense and reality otherwise than through
> others. But the others are not that part of humanity which remains outside of me. If that were so we would come to establish an illegitimate
> primacy of the "I," a solitude first established and then overcome. The

I does not have this kind of privilege. The others do not oppose themselves to the "I," to "me myself"; from them, at first glance, one does not distinguish oneself, amongst them I am also I. "With" and "also" are *existentiales*, that is, constitutive of the being of my existence. My being itself is a common existence with the other. The world I inhabit, I divide with him; it is a co-world, a world essentially shared. At bottom, the other is not "another I" but a "with me."

It is not a matter, then, of concluding the existence of the other beginning with ours, but rather that the other accompanies us in a world toward which we are inseparable.

With these facts we cannot oppose solitude, since there can be solitude only relative to the possible presence of the other. I can, on the other hand, be alone in the midst of the mass; proof enough that the presence of the other is not reducible to the fact of a mere material vicinity but rather that it is founded on that constitutive factor of existence which is being in common. Solitude will give itself, then, in accordance with a deficient mode of coexistence.[7]

As far as we are concerned, Jean-Paul Sartre criticizes the ontological reach of Heidegger's description of the existential structures of being, affirming that the experience of "us" is given only in the field of individual psychology and is only a symbol of the unity of transcendences; that is, "it is not in any way a real apprehension of subjectivities by a singular subjectivity; subjectivities remain really outside all reach and radically separated. They are things and bodies, the material paths of my transcendence that dispose me to apprehend this as prolonged and supported by other transcendences without having to leave myself. I recognize that I form a part of an 'us' because of the world." There is in the world an immeasurable number of formations that refer to me, that point to me, as "anyone whoever." In the first place there are the tools, the equipment, and the institutions. I am somebody who could manage them; I am any one of the voters in the polling booth; I am any one of the buyers in the market; I am any one of the spectators at a spectacle, and so on.[8] This is not the place to expound on the grounds or the justification of Sartre's objections to Heidegger's doctrine. For the sake of our task, it matters only to point out that the relation that unifies the individuals constituting an "us" is a mediated relation; it is always given through exterior events or things that point to or indicate a common transcendence. Through that, the experience of an "us" places us in an abstract and empty

[7] A. de Waehlens, *La filosofía de Martín Heidegger*, pp. 69, 93.
[8] *L'Etre et le Néant*, p. 498.

community whose witnesses are the things that point toward it. This is a species of an objective and purely material interweaving of solitudes. It is an opaque, one-dimensional, and dead community that translates the lived experience of man arm-in-arm with others into a mass or into the common subjective feeling that can unite slaves in their work, none of whom has any relation to the others. Each one of the others is here reduced to an abstraction without a face or name, to an "anyone," and the relation that unites them is a mere anonymous and blind contiguity.

This is the mode of "being with others" that presides over the life of the institutions and that is found behind every superstition and socializing hypocrisy like humanitarianism and beneficence.

We can do no more than agree with Sartre that through this lateral and mediated relation we cannot reach the being of man, but only the nothingness of man. The "us"-subject is simply announced; we sense him in the world of objects that allude to him more as an absence than as a presence. That is, presence is not given in the "us" but rather when this turns into an "us both." True community is not given except in an "us" that is an "us both," a "you and I" for whom the relation is immediate, without the interposition of any previous scheme, without any conceptual game or without an image.

Transcendent Personalities

Very well then, only within the field of this living and authentic relation does the Mexican search for the plentitude that has been denied him in the merely social dimension of his existence.

At first glance, this claim may not appear very clear and we do not have time to begin an analysis of certain everyday manifestations that would lend support to our thesis. But this fact has much broader implications, as it is also made clear to us in looking to the extensive stage of public life. There we clearly see how political action with a expansive reach is never the common projection of common associations but rather the galvanization of wills by the person of a certain party that assumes the risk of such action, and which is the only real power capable of overcoming the morbid equilibrium between hate and the politically perverse.

The communal instinct is here a desire for the world to meet us as a person, not as a collective person, veiled and always above its manifestations, but as such and such a person, with a face, with a proper name and with a concrete personal style—a person we can see and by whom we can be seen, whose hand we can grasp and with whom we can have a conversation. Our history is that of a few significant individualities that emerge from time to time over the still mire of deaf political conflicts. It is the history of the action of political leaders and their followers. We Mexicans do not believe so much in liberalism as we do in Juárez; we do not believe so much in order and progress as in Porfirio Díaz; we do not believe so much in agrarian reform and the workers' movement as in Zapata and Cárdenas; and liberalism, order, and progress, democracy, agrarian, and workers' reforms do not exist without Juárez, Díaz, Madero, Zapata, or Cárdenas. The truly serious political sin lies not so much in changing ideology or program as much as is personal infidelity to the military or *caudillo* [political leader].[9]

And let us not invoke, as proof to the contrary of what has been said, the analogy that may be found between Mexican *caudillism*, which I would call *caudillism* in good faith, and bad faith *caudillism*, which has long appeared in Europe. In Mexico, the military or *caudillo* responds personally, freely, for his action. He bases his politics on the contingent center of his person. His power, his prestige, and the reach of his action are not found disguised and suggested through the presentation of himself as a mere "embodiment" of a mythical and mystical power of blood, as in Germany, or of the historical past, as in Italy, or religious tradition, as in Spain. *In Mexico, loyalty to the caudillo is loyalty to a man and not a myth.*

What definitely counts is loyalty that is personal and free, that of friendship in all of its forms; it is that relation that can be captured, in the last analysis, by the words "you and I." In one of his novels, John Steinbeck highlights this fact, emphasizing that the word *amigo* is something like an *open sesame*, a magic word capable of toppling all barriers, of defeating all resistance. Public and private life unfold in a web of *inter-individual, personal* relations, which explains the palpable inequality between institutions and political reality.

Beyond Individualism and Collectivism

From antiquity, what has been said has been interpreted as the fruit of a regrettable individualism. Nothing is more erroneous. It must be kept in mind that the most individualistic societies on the planet, such as England and the United States, are precisely those in which the institution is given more weight. On the other hand, it is the abnormal growth of individualism that has driven Europe toward the threatening hypertrophy of collectivism.

No, the Mexican is not an individualist, but much less is he a collectivist. In our country, every collective tendency results from so obvious a falsehood as

[9] [We decided to leave *caudillo* in the original because, as the next paragraph suggests, it refers to a Mexican—and we would add, Latin American—phenomenon that defines the wars for independence as well as the nature of political life throughout the nineteenth century and, some would argue, continuing to the present.—Editors.]

the purported national indifference regarding all that which does not find itself supported by a real personality. On this basis we can characterize the Mexican as a man who instinctively distrusts both of these extremes [collectivists and individualists] and who searches for an authentic community. However, what we are saying is that he searches for it, not that he finds it, although he searches exactly where he might find it, namely, in the living and true relation between persons, in the relation between an "I" that directs himself to a "you" that responds.

To choose between individualism and collectivism seems strange and repugnant to us. Solitude breaks us and annihilates us in *zozobra*;[10] a society without a face or warmth makes us cold with distrust.

Wisely we refuse to choose between such alternatives, and in good time we throw ourselves into the third alternative, one of dialogue, that lies in between those extremes in which contemporary life finds itself. It is a third path that is not a mere intermediary path between those extremes, but rather a "fundamental fact of human life."

"The gorilla is also an individual," says Martin Buber, just as an anthill is a community, "but the I and Thou only give themselves in our world. What makes our human world singular is, above all, that in it something happens between being and being, something that does not happen in any other corner of nature. Language is nothing more than its sign and its medium; every spiritual work has been provoked by that something. Its roots are found in the search one being by another, both of whom are concrete, so as to communicate with each other in a sphere common to both but which surpasses the proper field of each one of them."[11] It is this sphere that Martin Buber calls the sphere of the "in-between" and which "constitutes a proto-category of human reality," where the Mexican finds his only communal dwelling.

Very well, then, a perfect community can only be that in which an "us" is sustained in its totality by a tight interlacing of personal relations; just as a perfect family is that in which the husband and wife, parents and children, are reciprocally bound within the relation "you and I," without either of the two finding the other as a mere "he" or "they" but always as an essential "Thou," and not merely a grammatical "you." It is that community in which the road from an "us" to a "you and I" will find itself paved rather than obstructed, in which the channels that make up both types of relations in a living totality are not found obstructed, but rather appear open in both directions.

There must exist the possibility of realizing with fullness an essential "us" where every "he" can be a "you" and where every "they" will become an "us"

---

[10] [For a fuller explanation of the significance of *zozobra*, the reader should refer to Uranga's "Essay on an Ontology of the Mexican" included in this volume.—Trans.]

[11] Martin Buber, *Que es el hombre?* Fondo de Cultura Economica, Mexico, 1949, p. 157.

in living and authentic communication. Only such a constellation deserves the name of community and our destiny as a nation depends on our capacity to realize it.

Melancholy and Community

Keyseling has said, someplace, that the Latin American's melancholy (and we can also add our experiences of our divided consciousness, of our fragility, of our *zozobra* and of our insufficiency) has its foundation in a feeling that the Spirit is absent. Nothing more true could be said, since the spirit demands a way to manifest itself and this cannot appear otherwise than in the bosom of a community.

It is probable that one day we find ourselves constituted by that great voice of the spirit, as Vasconcelos wished,[12] especially since today it seems that our community is finding itself in the trance of integration. But if one day the spirit's breath is to be felt in these latitudes, it will certainly not be due to the work of that dark, mystical land whose melancholy cannot be expressed even by the screaming lamentations of a [Pablo] Neruda. Neither will the spirit speak of race, since he who speaks of race speaks of blood, Aryan or otherwise, and any conception of nationality founded on blood or the mixture of blood cannot lead to anything else than this: more blood.

We do not carry the spirit within us like blood, but rather we are in it as the air that we breathe; the place of its manifestation is the "within" of a perfect community.

---

[12] [Here Portilla is referring to the motto of the National University, given to it by Vasconcelos, and which reads *por mi raza hablará el espíritu* ("The spirit shall speak for my race").—Editors.]

CHAPTER 15

Art or Monstrosity (1960)

◼

Edmundo O'Gorman
Translated by Cecilia Beristáin and
Robert Eli Sanchez, Jr.

Edmundo O'Gorman O'Gorman was born in Coyoacán, Mexico, in 1906 and died in Mexico City in 1995. He graduated with a law degree from the Free School of Law (Escuela Libre de Derecho) in 1928 before deciding to become a historian, first earning a master's degree in philosophy (1948) and then a PhD in History (1951) from the National University of Mexico, where he graduated summa cum laude. In 1964, he became a member of the Mexican Academy of History, and in 1969, a member of the Mexican Academy of Letters. Today O'Gorman is considered a pioneer in postcolonial studies, challenging a Eurocentric conception of "America," particularly as it is represented in phrases like "the discovery of America" and "the New World." In 1958 he published what may be his best-known work, La invención de América, which was translated into English and published in 1961. A shorter version, titled "America," is published in Major Trends of Mexican Philosophy.

This article contains a series of reflections, more or less connected, more or less sketchy, that are a first attempt to locate the general foundations that establish the type and manner of spiritual relation between the sensibility of contemporary Western man and the artistic world of the ancient Mexicans (or that part of it that has been revealed to us) and, in general, of all the American peoples in the period before their contact with the Europeans.

Strictly speaking, this essay only presents simple possibilities, barely made out, that with time and careful thought might be developed into something more solid. Together with other considerations, these [reflections] might replace the vague and insufficient cluster of notions that have satisfied those who have studied our ancient monuments so far, those who have done so from the point of view of their artistic content.

With great self-assurance and practically everywhere, we speak of Aztec *art*, of Mayan *art*, of Tarascan *art*, and so on. But, to the best of my knowledge, there are no studies that try to specify the meaning of such labels, because, it seems to me, they do not start by considering them as expressions of something problematic in itself. The first part of the paper begins with the latter consideration, and to that effect, I introduce a distinction between *critical historical contemplation* and *mere contemplation*, which considers the survival and contemporaneity of monuments and the works that motivate them. In the second part of the paper, I try to establish a general connection between very diverse historical expressions of artistic phenomena—such as Gothic, Aztec, and surrealist statues—linking them through the concept of *the monstrous*, derived from the mythical consciousness as an explanation of the necessary deformation involved in art [*de la necesidad deformativa implicada en el arte*].

The whole article is very hurried and perhaps bold to a fault. But if any value can be found in it, it is indebted to pointers from various readings, to the indelible impression that contemplating the colossal statue of Coatlicue in the National Museum of Mexico left on me, and to a conversation with the person to whom I dedicate these lines.

I

The general problems raised by the contemplation of a work of art are exacerbated when the work of art belongs to what we might call, somewhat vaguely, an exotic culture. Right away the analytic mind questions the legitimacy of characterizing the work as artistic. Clearly, if art were presented to us as necessary, that is, if human life could not but pick out the product of art [as artistic], this doubt would be resolved a priori. But a biological or sociological basis of art, which otherwise might be valid, is not enough [to resolve] the specific problem concerning the type or manner of relation between the subject and object of art, that is, the problem of contemplating art as such. *The important thing, then, from this point of view, is the scope and limit of the possibilities of our own sensibility* vis-à-vis *the artistic phenomena (or, in any case,* vis-à-vis *the phenomena that are presented to us as artistic) of a world that is, historically speaking, strange to us.*[1] Such is the most urgent question that both the art critic and the art historian run into when they purposefully confront so-called works of art from a culture untouched by their own.

An important distinction seems to impose itself, which we will try to explain. Pursuing the analysis to the outer limits indicated by the problem would lead us to historical results (in the sense of history as science), because its aim would be to fix, as the basis of a historical critique of art, the possibilities of our sensibility,

---

[1] [All long italics were originally emboldened.—Trans.]

first settling this other question: to what extent can our mind, conditioned by our history, conform to the manner and form of the mind of the creator of the work of art being examined? Thus, the work of art becomes the object of a very special kind of consideration, which begins with a kind of displacement of the subject who with effort—not just intellectual—undertakes a journey, leaving one's own historical position with the aim of annulling the differences in artistic sensibility between the creator's mind and one's own. Hence the art historian should avail himself of a wide range of knowledge and technique that is not immediately suggested by the work under consideration. This way of approaching the work, it seems to me, is the essential task of the art historian. Do not let it be said either that its essential artistic quality is violated because the critique is historical. Quite the contrary: only a historical examination of an exotic artistic world, or one simply bygone, can affirm in our mind the presence of that specific and inalienable quality if, in truth, the work possessed it. To contemplate a Greek statue from a position that, while not Greek, is more or less an approximation of the Greek spirit that created it cannot mean in any way that qualities that belonged to it are subtracted, if by "qualities" we understand the relation between the statue and the respective artistic sensibility of the historical period to which it belongs.

Now, it is possible that the results that are arrived at after a rigorous treatment of this kind differ greatly from the immediate meaning that the work has for us, situated in our world and historical moment—*so much so* that artistic content can be denied to something that for us has it to *a superior degree*. The art historian, therefore, should not examine the artistic sense and content of those things bequeathed to us by the past, things that *seem* to us expressions or objects of art, but should investigate, first, whether it has such *content*, and then, if it does, whether the expressions of it are specifically artistic. We can agree as much as we like, but that we agree that an object is a work of art is one of the results or aims of the investigation, *never its original intention*. The fact that the pictorial codices of the ancient Mexicans seem to us expressions of art, based on evidence that is *at bottom analogical*, does not authorize the *historian* of Aztec art, based on *her evidence, to develop an entire aesthetic theory and present it as a description of the specific artistic sensibilities belonging to the Aztecs.* We are led, then, to a vital problem of a history that, like ours, is in part rooted in an exotic past: the existence of the *artistic* spirit—in the Western sense of the term—of the world of the Ancient American peoples is brought into question. Even if this obstacle is overcome by means of psychological, sociological, or any kind of evidence other than historical, the main problem of *identifying*—by methods other than simple analogy—which objects are artistic remains. It is the problem of identifying *authentic expressions of art* even though they do not have an artistic quality to us. For there is always the possibility of thinking that the artistic spirit manifests and expresses itself in and through different media, which, although appropriate to art, might be foreign to and thus hidden from us—just as (as we know) the artistic spirit can manifest itself in a great variety of forms in the same medium. We cannot dismiss with a simple wave of the hand the possibility that the artistic feeling of the *Aztec soul might have found its highest, and perhaps only, expression in the form and style of war.* And if, in that case, it is asked what we should think of Aztec architecture, sculpture, pottery, ornamentation, it can be said that these relics are, without a doubt, artistic expressions. But that *they are for us,* for our sensibility, neither rules out nor confirms that they were also artistic expressions for the contemporaneous indigenous sensibility. Consider the possibility that in future centuries, a different historical mentality finds *today's mechanical-technical development an essential characteristic of our life.* In that case, the so-called industrial arts would occupy the highest place in our aesthetic appreciation, even though, if we were consulted, we would not agree with that interpretation at all.

From what we have presented, we would like to point out the following as essential: the art historian should try to reconstruct the mood of the creative spirit who produced the work. The fundamental thing is a subjective movement or process directed toward the contemporaneity of the objective, understanding by the latter, not this or that statue or painting, but, to use an expression of Simmel, the objectified spirit of a whole people or epoch.

But there is another way of contemplating a work of art, which constitutes the second term of the aforementioned distinction. Its foundation lies in the dual content of the artistic work, which is what *allows us to establish a connection to it despite and beyond its temporal distance or its exoticism,* with respect to the subject. Contrary to what happens in historical criticism, the subject does not try to annul spiritual differences between himself and the creative spirit in this kind of contemplation. *The subject establishes, or at least intends to, a dialogue, a relation to the object, but without abandoning his own historical position.* And the relation that is established is all the more valuable insofar as it is given as *an immediate experience in the consciousness of the subject.* If placed in front of one of the many ancient Mexican statues that the past has bequeathed to us, I receive (so to speak) a series of suggestions that touch my artistic sensibility; however historically inadequate they might be, *it is not possible to deny the evidence of a profound artistic experience, absolutely real and valid.* The object of exotic origin has been placed on equal footing with those that are broken off from the historical trunk from which the subject emerges. The considerations that could be offered regarding the origin of the object, that is, those that speak to the relation between that object and the spirit that created it, appear merely accidental, while from the point of view of historical criticism that accident is the essential thing.

The difference, then, between the two ways of thinking that we have been discussing can be expressed symbolically by saying that for historical criticism, the subject is incorporated into a historical world that the object belongs to, while for simple criticism, the object is incorporated into the culture of whoever makes it the object of contemplation. In the first case, it is a matter of bullfighting on the bull's turf; in the other, a matter of bullfighting on one's own. The question for both hangs on that delicate undertaking that is signified by the concept of *incorporation*. This last problem [of incorporation] is the subject matter, on the one hand, of the general theory of historical knowledge, and, on the other hand, of a theory of art concerned primarily with the content of artistic objects and their possibilities, which are certainly conditioned by history, but autonomous as artistic objects as such.

Of course, one might think that these two ways of contemplating the artistic object do not oppose or exclude each other. In truth, the duality is not irreducible because we are talking about two limiting positions of the same historical process: the contemplation of an artistic object—an observation that, as a phenomenon in itself, can be historicized. This, however, does not invalidate considering them independently, precisely because of their character and the conditions internal to the limiting forms and ways of contemplating a work of art.

The difference between these two limiting forms of contemplation has been established by emphasizing the opposition in the two ways in which the subject and object come together; but it could also be explained by introducing the volatile concept of *liberty*. In a certain sense the art historian's criticism involves a rigorous and concise treatment that presents it as less free than simple criticism. *The latter, in fact, can draw on, more or less consciously, considerations deduced from historical criticism; but—and this is the decisive thing—it also might not.* One consequence is that the art historian cannot legitimately distance himself from the many questions above, from whose examination, by contrast, the critic is exempt. He who as historian tries to say something about an ancient Greek statue (for example, about an Apollo) cannot do so adequately if he has not penetrated, among other things, the essential intimacy of the feeling of Greek religiosity. Such is not the case for the critic, who problematizes only the immediate relation between the statue, an object given artistic autonomy, and his own sensibility. It is obvious—and it almost does not need to be mentioned—that those two terms, artistic autonomy and sensibility, are not free-floating but are strictly historically conditioned.

Given these clarifications, it might make sense to say that the historical criticism of art problematizes the artistic content of the object, both what was intended and what was put there by the author unknowingly, paying close attention to the suppositions, prejudices, and historical limitations under which the art object could be created, while the other position problematizes the artistic content of the same object as it presented to the critic's sensibility. In sum, all this implies the idea that the artistic object, by the single fact of its survival and thus its contemporaneity with us, possesses something that is not the same as what it had for those who contemplated it in the period in which it was created, and, in the same way, that it will have something more [for those] who contemplate it in the future. If this is true, it is not conceptually empty to think about an artistic world, the brilliant creation of man, in which he can house his weary soul. And herein lies its most profound cultural meaning.

II

If we yield to the intense pressure, with or without our consent, that the luminous ideal of ancient beauty exercises on our spirit, as it is revealed to us in the formal perfection of its most representative statues, all of the great number of statues of other peoples and periods pale in comparison, and distance themselves from us so that we lose sight of them due to their crude lack of understanding.

That tiny ancient landscape, peopled with empty-eyed statues, tyrannizes us because nowhere else is the dictate of perfection so adequate. But the idea of perfection is paired with the distressing feeling of solitude. For me, solitude is the most impressive characteristic of the most beautiful Greek statues. They live in an eternal, absolute solitude, while they, immutable, accompany the highs and lows of our life from a distance. It is not an accident that the passionate love for a marble Venus, a symbolic expression of impossible love, is a relatively frequent literary motif. That height of perfection in the curve of human form seems to capture a tragic contradiction: our yearning to possess it is met by a smiling elusiveness.

The hermeticism of these perfect statues which otherwise, and fueling our desperation, we know have been inspired by men who nurtured petty hate and municipal rivalries, *challenges us to leave them in their rarified and solitary atmosphere*, interjecting between them and us a hatred that saves us. This is what the Middle Ages did, allowing time to bury the statues, decapitated and mutilated, condemning them to oblivion, and it did so as a full expression of pride. And all this is of an exemplary paradoxical nature: man is man's only and essential problem, and in the fine arts, the pursuit of maximum perfection in the human form, when reached, produces a portentous world that is so absolutely sufficient unto itself that it leaves one entirely empty-handed. And one has to begin again.

Perhaps this indicates the root of our artistic inclination toward imperfection that, like the tragic, implies the hidden existence of internal structural powers of destruction, of self-annihilation, as if we were searching in art for a glorification of our own impotence.

From this point of view, imperfection, judged in accordance with the living tradition of Greek antiquity, is related closely with ugliness, is presented as a value, as something positive, as something, in sum, that is not necessarily rejected by the spirit. On the contrary, ugliness can provide a favorable environment where the spirit finds a place of refuge that falls short of life [más allá o más acá de la vida].

Having been able to overcome, through art and in art, that ugliness is inherently negative, is an incalculable enrichment for Western man, because in some way it opened up the stream of mythic values that reason, so luminous, had concealed. Perhaps art is the clearest example of our mythic reality, where the most ancient enemy of reason, of seeking causes and first principles, still palpitates.

The meaning of ugliness, as has been suggested, that is, as something opposed to classical perfection, which fundamentally consists in the solitary perfection of the curve and proportions of the human body, could be elaborated in a concept that comes close to something like mythic beauty, as opposed to Beauty, and for which the natural curve is not a necessary limitation, since the mythic world has a fluidity that is essential to it and that authorizes all the bonds, insensible and gradual, between worlds that reason conceives of as distinct. Affirming the feeling of individuality leads to classical beauty, and solid proof of this is the Renaissance. It is not a coincidence that the men of that period could see only barbarity, a world of darkness, in the Middle Ages, because the Middle Ages are, in a certain sense, viewed as an age, after classical antiquity, that knew how to live the mythic destiny of being human intensely. Gothic art, with its chimeras, its gargoyles, its fantastical fauna and flora, is an art of ugliness, an art beautifully mythological.

When in the first third of the sixteenth century, the Europeans were able to gaze at the monumental statues of the ancient Mexicans, they could only be struck by their ugliness. The early chroniclers did not have another standard for them: as men of the Renaissance, they were unable to approach the mythical world populated by stone monsters. As a literary exercise—since a historian should not speculate—we might imagine what affinities the medieval European man would have found in Aztec statues, which, despite the great distance that separates them from Gothic statues, share in common that which we have called "ugliness," but which we could also characterize as "the monstrous."

In the concept of the monstrous, the fundamental key of ancient Mexican art and perhaps of art in general can be found. It seems to me that a careful reflection on that concept and the preceding application of it would be not only illustrative but also incalculably fruitful for efficiently and thoughtfully approaching that world which is so foreign and so distant in appearance. For us the monstrous has an immediate sense that comes close to ugliness: a sign of the highest degree that we are dominated by the definite and distinct standard [por el sentimiento perfilado y neto] of ancient beauty. But, strictly speaking, the primary significance of the monstrous is of the marvelous, of the prodigious, and fundamentally of what is outside the natural order. Something that is outside the natural order is a monstrosity; it is not necessarily something ugly, except for whom everything that is not within what they conceive of as the natural order is by definition ugly. *For classical Greek sculpture, the perfection* of form, with its maximal objectivity, and of the human form, with all that makes it exceptional, *is the eternal and immutable expression of the order of nature*, to such an extent that even the monstrous in classic Greece ceases to have a monstrous form. Think about the figure of the centaur or that of the siren, which are only pitiable false monsters, artificial, in which there exists no deep violation of the natural order, only a simple conglomeration of perfectly natural elements. There is nothing monstrous about the torsos, just as there is nothing monstrous in the bodies of horses and fish. By contrast, the statues of saints in the facades of the Gothic cathedrals, if we are to speak of them as human figures, *are*, with that intentional vertical deformation, monstrous. *In the latter case, there is an invasion of the natural order by the supernatural.*

Thus *there is a correlation between* the concept of *the monstrous* and an ordered and rational vision of nature, a vision that provides us with a *sense of security* based on the belief in a structure, more or less defined, that articulates in a coherent totality the diversity of planes or series that stand out with a certain individuality. Long before Aristotle's metaphysical foundation, a basic natural structure that identifies or separates the mineral, vegetable, and animal world was presented to man on his journey toward the concept of personality. As these planes are outlined with increasing sharpness, *any blurring is an extreme shock to consciousness*, and provokes *the terrible feeling of the portentous, of the monstrous.* But the mythical consciousness does not make these invasions. Primitive man, immersed in an environment of myth, not only hinders these invasions, but they do not even exist as such for him. And from the moment a fluid world is conceived—or perhaps it would be better to say, is lived—that which for good reason we call the monstrous ceases to be monstrous, and we enter the world of magic, *and touch perhaps the deepest strata of artistic phenomena.*

In the National Museum of Mexico,[2] there is a gigantic, monolithic statue that is indisputably of Aztec origin. It represents a dark god—the mother of the gods. It is Coatlicue, also called Cihuacoatl, which means "the female serpent." Contemplating this colossal statue stirs up a series of indescribable sensations that opens the path for reflection. But what first captivates the spirit with the force of the inevitable is its portentous monstrosity. *This Mexican monument is perhaps the most authentic representation of the monstrous, since it is not the result of what is called "creative imagination," a kind of idle intelligence; it is the result of a live and tragic synthesis of a duality of natures.* Never, I don't think, *has the fluidity of the world* been expressed so accurately—*the statue's only possible reason for being.* The spirit remains perplexed and in suspense. It is not possible to breathe the same

[2] [O'Gorman here is referring to the National Museum of Anthropology in Mexico City.—Trans.]

air as the monster that hides in its isolation, behind the rigidity of the rock, the impenetrable secret of its shameful nature. It is not a woman that has adorned herself with serpents; this would inevitably suggest the woman of the circus. Perhaps the dominant impression is of a multitude of serpents that, obeying the strange and astonishing power of an ancient spell, have been raised up into what one can only guess is a vague human form. Or perhaps it is a sketch of a human body that, infinitely unconscious of its own monstrosity, is emerging from, but still anchored in, the dark animal world. *But the fundamental thing is that there is not a simple superimposition, an aggregate of two natures. Coatlicue is an expression of the animal consubstantial with the human,* a being that has been captured in rock, capturing *the unthinkable and timeless moment of the intersection of two diverse natures* in a detached, autonomous, and [self-]sufficient form. Coatlicue is a crossroads that rides roughshod over the order that reason works so hard to construct, and that is only possible in the utterly indifferent fluidity of myth.

These considerations raise a question that, it seems to me, is central to art, although here it is only possible to hint at it as a possibility that requires rigorous thought. It is the problem of trying to approach the artistic phenomenon, drawing on the concept of the monstrous. With this concept, besides *opening the door to free us from the soft yoke of classical beauty, we might possess the key or term that links many different artistic expressions.* And perhaps, if we reflect on it even more thoroughly, we can arrive at *a mythical foundation of art.* The artistic world, like the mythical world, is not homogeneous, and both worlds fall short of reality. However, they are both worlds where *the spirit finds a kind of salvation, but a different kind from the salvation offered by a neat scientific point of view. Art is like the truth of our mythical background revealed.* All dislocations, disproportions, dissonances, stridencies, stylizations, and metaphors, in which we can recognize the creative genius specific to art, are other names that indicate the monstrous, that which is not natural, *what defies the order of nature according to our reason.* At the base of all this there is always an invasive movement that is provoked either by the desperate pursuit of a supernatural order, as in the monstrosity of Gothic art, or by weakness, by a resignation that gives into the biological inclination toward degradation, as in the monstrosities of surrealism, for which the invasion is between elements internal to one natural order, just as in the serpent-woman of the ancient Mexicans.

The essential thing about the phenomenon is the implicit principle of the being of monstrosity: an unlimited fluidity, a specific and characteristic trait of the mythical vision of the universe. Kant saw in art "a purposiveness without purpose"; this same formula has been employed to characterize the mythological. A theory of art carefully elaborated in the direction that has been indicated would lead to a surprising conclusion (among others): *a gigantic fraud can be discovered in the so-called "artistic" expressions of the ancient Greeks at their peak, since they represent the* greatest and most concealing disguise of the orderly and rational spirit, so characteristic of the Hellenistic mind. It is the disguise of reason that masks its own irrationality. It is "sophia" disguised as art, or, in the best case, it is wise art. But this last phrase contains a contradiction in terms. I read in something written by Chesterton that the most deceptive kind of lie is that which appears to be true; that is why it is not a coincidence that the fundamental theme of Greek statues is the mythological, although the figures, as forms, do not exhibit anything from mythology: they are absolutely natural men and women for whom the monstrous (mythology shaped into form), even in the case of the monsters themselves, is only a myth. In any case, Greek art and the forms of art that are inspired by it constitute, as contrived art, an exception within the artistic world, because they recognize the horror of deformation, the monstrous, as an internal fundamental principle.

Perhaps the great mystery of art can be found in the mythical; perhaps the mythical is not something like a phase that man has left behind in the distance in his accelerated march through History,[3] but rather a huge subterranean current inherent in his being that, as such, he has never abandoned. Art, with its necessary deformation, is the clearest manifestation of the validity and vigor of our mythical science.

[3] [This point might be read as a response to the Mexican positivist's view of history as proceeding in three stages or phases: the poetic (or mythological), the metaphysical, and the positive. Cf. Vasconcelos's "Gabino Barreda and Contemporary Ideas."—Editors.]

CHAPTER 16

On Feminine Culture (1950)

Rosario Castellanos
Translated by Carlos Alberto Sánchez

Rosario Castellanos Figueroa was born in Mexico City in 1925 and died in Tel Aviv, Israel, in 1974. Considered one of the most important Mexican female authors of the twentieth century, Castellanos was a diplomat, a poet, a fiction writer, and a philosopher. The text included here is from her master's thesis in philosophy, written when she was just twenty-five years old. Sobre cultura femenina would go on to become one of the most significant texts in Mexico's feminist movement of the second half of the twentieth century. Castellanos became ambassador to Israel in 1971, where she died after being accidentally electrocuted in her home. A Catholic, she was deeply invested in issues of social justice, including indigenous and women's rights. Her collected works span many volumes and have been translated into several languages. Some of her shorter works have been translated into English and are available in A Rosario Castellanos Reader: An Anthology of Her Poetry, Short Fiction, Essays, and Drama *(2010).*

Culture—and on this, historical testimony is irrefutable—has been created almost exclusively by men, by masculine characters. Among the imposing field of names, carried away by an avalanche of facts, confused, almost imperceptible, just a grain of sand on a mountainside, there one finds the work of women—a few women who stand out above the rest for their rarity, a miniscule "barely" that prevents culture from being the exclusive creation of men, of the masculine character. The discovery of their names, the rescue of their works, the possibility of distinguishing them from the fray would fill us with pride and joy if we had faced this problem as feminists did. Yet, after convincing ourselves that culture is a refuge for men, who have been denied the gift of maternity, after exalting maternity as a form of creation and perpetuation as legitimate and effective as any other, this "barely" does not bring us joy or pride. It troubles us. What is the value of the (few) exceptions to the rule that we have postulated? They merely served to prove the rule.

So as to be consistent, we propose a hypothesis that those isolated cultural attempts among women have their origins in the same endemic and systematic surges of cultural production among men and represent a similar reward. Culture is everywhere the refuge of those who have been exiled from maternity. For men that is natural, of course. But for women?

Nature takes care of the reproduction of its creatures. Within sexualized animal species, the excessive number of males—according to Lester F. Ward[1]—is a normative fact and a measure that makes it impossible for any of the females to remain infertile. Additionally, since males do not have any other end but procreation, once that end is met, they return to nature without much ado. But the higher we ascend on the zoological ladder, the proportional number of males becomes restricted based on the capacity of every male's ability to impregnate a greater number of females. On the other hand, the numerical proportion between males and females is closely related to the amount of food available to the species. Where there is more food, there are more females, and vice versa. This statistic is also applicable to the human species. This is not merely a supposition, but a theory proven in experience, which in tribal culture, where the conditions of life are more precarious, the human species nonetheless maintains an equilibrium between the number of women and the number of men that make up society. But as soon as those conditions become favorable, the equilibrium is broken. Beginning with the practice of agriculture, and from the change brought about from moving from a nomadic to a settled existence, where one remained in one determinate place, and finally, with the formation and growth of cities, there is a steady increase in the number of women until it ultimately surpasses that of men.

Very well, relations between the sexes have been codified by men who focus not so much on the good of the species or of the totality of individuals who comprise it, but on their own sentimental and economic interests. This is how, at least in the West, monogamy was instituted, which simultaneously allows for an easier and direct vigilance over women and, ultimately, greater security with regard to paternity (since, as Goethe says, paternity is in the last instance nothing more than a simple question of trust)[2] and which demands fewer expenditures for the maintenance of the family. But things arranged in this manner exclude thousands of women from their own ends, negated in their personality and in their mission, denied in their vocation. This problem, ongoing since time immemorial—Bucher affirms that during medieval times in Frankfurt, the number of women who lived alone represented one-sixth or more of its contributors

---

[1] Cited by André Gide in *Corydón*.

[2] This is a phrase of Goethe found in *Wilhelm Meister*, cited by August Bebel in his *La mujer en el pasado y el porvenir* (Editorial México, 1948).

(this statistic does not include the hundreds of nuns, monasteries, ministries, etc.)[3]—worsens as time passes. And not only in terms of quantity, which points to the growth of populated areas and consequently the rising number of women, but also because it now affects married as well as unmarried women. In effect, the insecurity of economic conditions, the constant threat of imminent war (and with it and its calamities the terrible conviction that life is not worth preserving and perpetuating in a world so stupidly cruel, one in which a son is no longer the link in an interminable temporal chain but merely flesh for cannons), the pursuit of pleasure (individual satisfaction needs to be a priority in a society that exalts individualism, and nothing opposes individualism more than maternity, the moment when a woman, rejecting her egoism, opens herself to the universe, recognizes her place in it and occupies it), and the disappearance of duty, of obligation, the suspension of morality, as well as scientific advancements in contraception that allows birth control—all these significantly lower the population indices that count women as members of national societies.

But the problem does not just affect women who do not have children, either because they cannot or because they refuse to; it also affects those for whom maternity has become a reality but who remain dissatisfied in a world where, by all accounts, the feminine principle, and all that it represents, has been devalued. This phenomenon, typical in hyper-intellectual societies as Brachfield notes,[4] is ultimately shared and accepted by those against whom the devalued feminine principles are exerted, determining in them a reaction, which is to imitate the masculine style, as well as a longing for the assimilation of the masculine qualities, a belief that only by fighting with the weapons of men can victory be won. This reaction is false, inauthentic, nocuous, but inevitable. Toward what mode of conduct can a woman aspire when she is ripped away from her peculiar ways of life, not only by circumstances, but worse, by the idea—so rooted in her that she does not recognize that it comes from without—that those forms have to be despised? She will aspire to those modes of conduct that everyone else exalts and that she makes herself (falsely) believe she admires.[5] If, as Boumier says, the gifts of women exist only in those of maternity, her way of being, loving, thinking, and suffering corresponds to an actual or virtual necessity of having to be

[3] A fact cited by Robert Arnold, *Cultura e ideales del Renacimiento* (México: Ediciones Monos, no date given).

[4] In his book *Los complejos de inferioridad de la mujer.*

[5] Someone might say that if women have allowed men to consider them inferior, it is because they are inferior. It is not about that. We have pointed out [elsewhere in *Feminine Culture*], that "a woman puts up with every kind of humiliation, every sort of condition, so long as she can, through them, become a mother." But when that humiliation consists in saying that the woman is not intelligent (when intelligence is not the usual goal of feminine ambition) and that she is weak (when this supposed weakness demands that she work in heavy and uncomfortable labor), she is told to accept what she is told without protest. But when to this humiliation is added the impossibility of

a mother; her inclinations, actions, and reactions, since infancy until old age, proceed from this maternal sentiment that is both respected and violated; and if society is organized in such a way that this sentiment, this necessity, and this satisfaction are systematically violated, we should strongly feel the consequences. And we feel them. That enormous charge of energy, of potency, of activity, that the woman represses as she goes against her natural end, or as she finds it not sufficiently satisfactory, has to find a way out. This is something demonstrated by Freud in his views about hysteria and culture, sickness and work. These are the terms of the dilemma. We do not refer here to hysteria and culture as accounting for everything and being exceedingly important so as to remain always on the horizon. The figure of the bitter and neurotic spinster is a cliché, and we should not insist on that figure. From the beginning, our intention has been to talk about the second set of terms, namely, sickness and work.

Work has had, in the vast majority of cases, the immediate purpose of resolving the most urgent economic problems. Women from every epoch (but especially since the Middle Ages) have had to confront the economic question in very unfavorable circumstances, since not only was common opinion hostile toward working women, but jobs were occupied mostly by men, and men had no intention of yielding their posts. (Perhaps common opinion was inclined toward hostility so as to devalue, and if possible, discourage competition in this area of life.) In spite of this, women slowly and imperceptibly entered into guilds, both those that were a bit less stringent and those that were impenetrable, and they came to occupy labor posts (manual posts, of course) and to dominate in them or achieve an equal status with their male counterparts. Some professions, such as the medical field of gynecology or obstetrics, became exclusively occupied by women, who practiced in great numbers (in German cities they came to account for up to 1,500 women doctors), and we suppose without any protest from their patients, since those professions still survive. Moreover, these female medics wrote popular treatises on these topics, the best known of which is the short treatise by Saint Hildegard of Bingen. Another occupation controlled and practiced exclusively by women was the field of cosmetics. (The care of the body has always occupied a post of primordial importance for women.)

---

fulfilling one's destiny, there is no such thing as passive acceptance. And if before one did not stop to reflect on masculine ideas, especially when it is clear that those ideas gravely affect women, now she begins to ponder and consider them. And to pretend to share them. If the condition necessary so as not to be rejected and unappreciated is to become strong intellectual beings, then that is what one must become. But here this adequacy with masculine concepts ceases to have use for women, since it consists in negating the notion that femininity and maternity are valuable. That old tactic turns out to be inadequate, since it is then that she begins, with men, to despise her own sex and to evade it so as to belong to the other.

Despite all of this, there still remained an indefinite number of women who were alone and had no means of supporting themselves. Many of them dedicated their lives to being vagabonds, or prostitutes, while others were taken in by the Church—an institution that has always worried much about the destiny of these beings who can easily become social parasites—which offered them refuge in the monasteries. (Thus, the Church has given shelter to an abundant number of Saints, some humble, others laborious with a great organizational capacity, the rest exalted visionaries.) But not all of them had a religious vocation or a desire to commit themselves to solemn and indissoluble vows. Thus, since the thirteenth century, a new form of community was born: the "Beguines," or sanatoriums, where women of different social classes and civil status associated with one another in order to run large centers dedicated, by and large, to the collection of pious donations to which they would quickly add their own earnings. The rule of these communities was very flexible: they were allowed to come and go freely and were also allowed to get married if they wanted and if they could.

The advent of new social conditions modified the situation of women but did not greatly improve it. In the last century we find women in England (and we mention this locale because it was there that our decisive battles for the emancipation of women took place) excluded from all well-paying professions and relegated to the most difficult and worst-paying jobs as factory workers. But, after the First World War, when men had to abandon their jobs to enlist as soldiers, we see women take over offices and professions, demand rights, boast equality with men, and practice their liberties. The figure of the woman is no longer strange in any area of labor. However, we should not forget the arduous battles that were fought for the conquest of this right to work for a living, the right to be like a man, a right that man himself made possible by making himself into a God while subjugating women, a right that today is widely recognized without much protest or without the presence of obstacles that are impossible to overcome. Again, the figure of the woman is no longer strange in any area of labor. Not even in creative labor.

Culture, as Freud says, is a sublimation of the instincts. Traditionally it was thought that this sublimation was impossible for women. But, in his *Civilized Sexual Morality and Modern Nervous Illness*, Freud himself showed that the insufficient development of the feminine personality, of her capacity to love and, even, her capacity for intellectual growth, is due to the inhibitions that dominate the knowledge and practice of sexuality. The sexual impulses could not be sublimated and transformed into cultural, moral, or artistic interests since women prematurely repressed everything that represented these instincts. This is not the case today. It is again Freud whom we should thank, or blame, for making us much more aware of sexuality, in its theoretical and practical aspects, which, as a consequence, makes it more susceptible to domination or transformation. Sublimation is now an experience shared by women. Culture will be its fruit.

Among the diverse cultural forms of creation there are some that require, in greater quantities than others, a special temperament (especially those that consist in a powerful capacity for abstraction, renunciation, and blindness to the well-being of the earth), a temperament that also requires elaborate and complicated techniques and which demands total domination and possession. These forms of cultural creation require special instruments, internal and external to the subject, to be realized. The orientation toward these cultural forms of creation is conditioned by an attitude of absolute belief in them, although their realization depends above all on learning, on practice. If we consider that traditionally and a priori women were considered outside the scope of these vocations—a common belief that their auditory capacities fail to register their call, thus through a fault of their perception, which is a symptom of their inferiority—and that consequently throughout the centuries women have been denied access to technical and instrumental training in these cultural forms, then it should not surprise us that among working women none will be found employed in these technical vocations. Instead, they will be displaced to other areas that are either less rigorous or more accessible.

Virginia Woolf writes that the only career that is permanently open to women is literature.[6] Since antiquity, the education given to family members has depended more or less on having certain accommodations or a certain level of prosperity; but even in a precarious living situation, the situation was never so bad that women were not at least taught how to read and write. (Although what they were made to read was only what their jealous guardians would qualify as innocent.) And if women wanted to write, they could, since it was never too difficult to get access to the right materials: paper, pen, wax and seal, or (if we are talking about antiquity) molding clay. On the other hand, if a woman wanted to paint or sculpt, she could not easily obtain the canvas and oils (these were not as easily available as they are today; moreover, mixing the right colors was a secret reserved for the master painters who experimented until getting the right color) or chisels and marble stones. Moreover, a woman could not enroll in institutions or workshops to learn artistic technique, nor was she allowed to have human models, especially if they were nude.

But those reasons that Virginia Woolf highlights are not the only reasons as to why literature is a much better path for women. It is also the case that certain artistic forms (such as science, philosophy, or religion) also have their own special language, their own esoteric symbols, which make them comprehensible

---

[6] In her book of essays, *Tres guineas*, translation by Román J. Jiménez (Buenos Aires: Ediciones Sur, 1941).

only to specialists. Moreover, initiation into those specialized fields is often long, difficult, and complicated. You do not find these difficulties (or at least they are not insisted upon) in the field of literature. In that field, the language employed is a common and simple language (or at least it appears so); it is the language everyone uses in daily life. Their words have the same sense, the same signification as those in the mouths of the ordinary person. And many times literary works tell us exactly the same thing as ordinary people do. They tell us, for instance, that some time ago the author met a young man who fell desperately and helplessly in love with his best friend's wife and ended up killing himself. Or the work describes cities and customs, or it captivates us with its fantasies in which strange or supernatural beings are described as real, concrete, and precisely, with a name and an almost palpable face. Or, it reveals the nature of and those hidden connections between objects and what they look like or resemble (which is the function of metaphor); or, the literary work talks about the primordial passions that we feel but are unable to articulate.

The reader who reads a novel or a poem for the first time has a greater chance of enjoying her experience than the unprepared reader who approaches, for the first time, a work of philosophy, a treatise in physics or mathematics. And so poems and novels are imitated. Women, who in their difference from animals and as an irrefutable fact of their superiority over them and their approximation to what is human, have crossed the Rubicon of the word. Women, who are capable of learning how to speak (and what is doubtful is whether they will be capable of stopping once they start) and of using language, turn out to be capable also of imitating literary works, of trying to write literature. History confirms this capacity as it records their attempts. Beginning with Sappho, and continuing to her most recent and most scandalous successor, it is in literature that we find in abundance the fruits of the feminine creative activity exiled from maternity. Simmel believes that in all of literature it is the genre of the novel that women find the most suitable mode of expression, if we think of the novel as Saint Real did, as a mirror placed before a path that it simply reflects. On the other hand, Federico de Onis believes that women find their best expression in lyric poetry because it is an immediate purging of one's emotions,[7] the immediate complaint of someone in pain or song when one is happy, all done without having to be conscious of one's particular emotional state, or without having to objectify it, or submit it to a more complex elaboration. Apart from the fact that lyric poetry requires less effort because it, in general, is less profound than the novel (in the sense of extension), it could still be that lyric poetry is a more suitable form of expression. Historically the appearance of lyric poetry comes before the

---

[7] In those parts that he dedicates to the poetry of Hispanic women in his *Antología de la poesía española e hispanoamericana* (Madrid: Revista de Filología Española, 1934).

appearance of the novel, as it was easier for primitive man to speak to children in verse rather than in prose.

Neither of these positions is right. Experience tells us that women have successfully attempted to write both novels and poetry (even if success has not been abundant). They are criticized for the poverty of their themes and the lack of originality in developing those themes; they are even criticized for the lack of generosity in their intent. That is, they are accused of mediocrity and told that their imitation of the work of men is not sophisticated enough. It is not about encouraging them, as with certain indigenous groups from the Caribbean, to develop their own idioms.[8] Rather, they are expected to acquire their own unmistakable style: a brand name. But this already exists! It is somewhat strange that those who demand a brand name fail to warn women that the brand name that already exists is a defect, which, given its consistency, invariability, and persistence across the written work of women, must be considered and admitted as a style, a distinctive and characteristic mode. This defect is narcissism.

One can approach literature as a long and winding road that leads whoever travels it far away from herself. Or, one can approach literature as a door through which one lives oneself more intimately, so as to transcend and rip open the iron bars of individuality, so as to force the serpent of our thinking, the serpent of our emotions and feelings, to stop biting its own tail. One can also approach literature as a mirror, but as the mirror of Saint-Real, located on the edges of the road that others travel, a road that disappears into the glass and duplicates itself in its happenings. Ultimately, we can say that literature is an image of the world, of a world that is "wide and strange."[9] Style, the unmistakable peculiar feature of each author, is also a point of view for the contemplation of her world, of whatever section of reality she captures, the environment she pictures. With what words. Through nouns she transforms objects, with adjectives she qualifies them, that is, points them out; with light, with color and hue, she illuminates them.

Here is where women come to literature, dragging their frustrated maternal feelings along, those feelings in the satisfaction of which they find immortality (the somatic immortality of which Weissmann speaks[10]) and in whose fruits, their children, they find, as Freud puts it,[11] a part of their own body as an exterior yet intimate object that is bound to them, that extends their own being and, moreover, to which they can devote a purely objectified love. When women come to literature they come not because they have lost the vigor of

---

[8] A custom noted by Pablo Kirsche in *El enigma del matriarcado*.

[9] This is the title of one of the novels of Ciro Alegría that I have seen but have never read.

[10] Cited by Freud in *Beyond the Pleasure Principle* (Vienna: Internationaler Psychoanalytischer Verlag, 1921).

[11] Cited by Freud in "Introduction to Narcissism," in *Jarbuch fur Psychoanalyze* (1914).

this feeling and the ways of expressing it, not because they have lost all respect for their corporality or because they value it less than before, but rather, for one reason or another, because they have not been able to channel that feeling in the right way. Finding themselves in need of letting themselves go, of transcendence, they encounter another channel, the literary, and it does not matter if it is adequate or not, so long as it is possible. And they pour themselves into it. And, depending on her social class (in general, the woman who writes belongs to the more privileged and elevated classes, those that have resolved the economic problem), if she possess a richer, varied, and complete language, she uses it. How? As men do? To broaden their limits, to conquer the land, to give nature an echo? None of that. She uses it in the opposite way: to set her limits, to affirm herself solidly within her individuality, to give herself her own echo. The mirror is removed from the road, denies its reflection to those who pass, and it comes to install itself, in most sad cases, in a flirtatious *boudoir*. No more scenes of the open country or of motley figures. The mirror faithfully copies a small visage, a body. It is inundated and overflowing with it. Here is where style intervenes: a point of view, a contemplated world, a section of reality, an ambience, the noun, an adjective, everything condensed in a single vernacular: I. And it is not an I do but an I think, I feel, I say. It is an I am; I am my body. And in some occasions, so as to mislead, I am you, them, and that place. But you, them, and that place, always in their relation to me. On rare occasions, the absolute, the divine. And this is the divine choosing me to reveal itself, making for itself a place in my body, resting in it, communing with it, marking it, and exalting it.

This style, if it does not create its own features, at least adopts and regularly cultivates a genre that can develop them better. This style is autobiography. Beginning with the Lady of the Renaissance to whom Arnold refers, who "narrates with an impressive realism the history of her own life and with more detail than that which belongs to feminine decorum,"[12] to the Countess of Noailles, women who have preferred to offer a portrait of themselves, perhaps out of fear, not fear that their biographers will see their qualities and demean them with notorious injustice, but rather out of the fear that those biographers will never exist. So as not to run the risk, they undertook this task for themselves and they did it with love, a kind of love that would embrace them entirely. The result is no longer comic, but pathetic. The belief about the value of her garments, of her attitudes, of her resolutions, is so integral, so naïve, so untroubled by doubt, that it can be no more than touching. However, what is bothersome is the false modesty that reveals itself at every step. For instance, there are instances between women when they do not dare to look each other in the face and talk, without insinuations but directly, about that which they have a passion for or that which

[12] Robert Arnold in *Cultura e ideales del Renacimiento*.

they find interesting, which is their own personality, choosing to talk instead about other things that merely point back to them. This is the case with some novels that seem to reflect a certain objectivity, which in reality they do not possess, so as to introduce a protagonist adorned with every splendor of beauty and virtue, a protagonist that is none other than the author herself. Also irritating is that class of lyric poetry which is a type of pseudo love poetry (or we could also say, a class of pseudo poetry) so cultivated by Hispanic-American women, in which feelings and their expression never abandon the expansive scope of individuality and describe, more than anything, internal physiological processes, phenomena whose relation with the outside world is always made to look nebulous, improbable (despite the fact that this relation is always highlighted or indicated), as if these processes neither have their origin in external stimuli nor owe their development to the external stimuli.

This aspect of narcissism, of uncompromising subjectivity, this fierce individuality so constant in the literary work of women, often hides behind a most refined language, but it never disappears. The capacity for abstraction, for objectivity, for projection toward that which one is not, for identifying with others through literary art, appears to be a gift denied to the woman writer [*parece ser un don negado a la mujer que escribe*]. Some, who with a more penetrating intuition, have recognized this limitation, have also sought to overcome it. Perhaps with a clear purpose, with discipline, the gift of objectivity may be conquered. This is an orientation that is a possibility for us. But what we ignore is whether or not it would be desirable. If it is essential that women write, we should at least expect that they do it by diving deeper each time into their own being, rather than making unfortunate, failed attempts to evade themselves (the very same literary profession is already an attempt at evasion), attempts that do not take her as far as she wants to be, but far enough so as to place her on false ground that she neither knows nor can control. What we can hope for, however, is that she inverts the direction of that movement (that is, if she is not going to invert the direction of that movement that separates her from her femininity, confining her to an imitation of the male), turning it toward her own being, and with such force that it may be able to overcome those immediate and fragile peripheries, and allow her to dive into those depths where she might reach her true and, until now, inviolable roots, pushing aside those conventional images of femininity that men have prepared for her, and thus she may form her own image, an image based on her personal, irreplaceable experience, an image that may or may not coincide with that other image. Moreover, once that depth has been plumbed (a depth that tradition either fails to recognize or considers false, which the usual concepts fail to reveal), the hope is that she may bring it to the surface and to consciousness, liberating it in the expression.

CHAPTER 17

Possibilities and Limitations
of the Mexican (1958)

José Revueltas

Translation by David W. Bird

José Revueltas Sánchez was born in Durango, Mexico, in 1914 and died in Mexico City in 1976. Revueltas was born into a family of artists and political activists. He was convicted of rebellion and sedition and was placed in reform school by the time he was fifteen years of age. He was a life-long leftist, communist, and provocateur, who found himself in prison on charges of subversion at the age of twenty. In the history of Mexican thought, he is remembered more as an exceptional writer of novels, theater, and short stories. In 1967, Revueltas received one of Mexico's highest literary awards, Premio Xavier Villaurrutia, for his Literary Corpus (Obra literaria). He was imprisoned again at the age of fifty-four for his involvement in the student movement of 1968, and remained in prison until 1971. Besides novels, theater, poetry, and essays, he was also a political philosopher and theorist. Revueltas was a prolific writer and social activist; his collected works fill twenty-six volumes.

I. The Mexican and His National Being

Posing problems in terms of "the Mexican" [*el Mexicano*], no matter what they are, implies, of course, an assumption that begs the question—that is, that "the Mexican" exists.[1] If we simply assume, as already agreed to without demonstration, that the Mexican exists, the direction of investigations into his problems totally lose their objective character, and are left at the mercy of the personal caprices and fantasies of the investigator. This explains, for instance, the surprising pronouncements that have been made, in which—without going into too much unnecessary detail about their development—one notices from the

[1] [Throughout this translation, I have translated *nación* and derivatives consistently as "nation," etc., and *país* as "country."—Trans.]

outset the propensity toward the facile and arbitrary. To speak of a particular "refinement" of the Mexican, or that the Mexican possesses a peculiar "feeling of rivalry," or in the same way a "voice, gesture, and silence" or an "amazement," or a way of feeling "the imaginary and the real," is to claim that certain invariant, universal phenomena are being expressed in an exclusive and differentiated way, due to who knows what mysterious factors, on a subject that in no way is or can be exclusive and differentiated.

To affirm a priori that the Mexican exists does not tell us much, or tells us very little, since such an affirmation leaves open the *why* and the *how* of that existence, and even the relative gradations of that existence. Only by beginning with these whys and hows of the Mexican's existence can we derive the other features, and then determine the particularity of these features.

Of course, to exist is not an abstract function. In other words, inasmuch as it cannot be other than a functional fact (since otherwise it would also fail to be an existence), it is produced and occurs in a concrete way, and in a concrete space and time. Thus, when we speak of the existence of the Mexican (which is just a form of the existence of man in general), we cannot conceive of this existence as being produced and occurring outside of a *praxis*, that is, outside of the relational reciprocity that the subject necessarily and unavoidably makes with his circumstances. It is abundantly clear that the relational reciprocity between the subject and his circumstances is never expressed passively; rather, the subject and the circumstances appear in continuous movement, mutually and ceaselessly conditioning each other, such that the subversion of the circumstances by the subject is resolved dialectically into a self-subversion of the subject himself.

Man appears within a *praxis* in his real, integral condition, in his continuous movement and development [*devenir*], not as a passive result of unconscious, blind nature, nor as a sum of conditioned reflexes, but rather as a *practical-critical* element, that is, a revolutionary.

> "Subject and object," according to the Italian Mondolfo, "exist only as terms in a necessarily reciprocal relation, whose reality lies in *praxis*; its opposition can only be the dialectical condition of its process of development, of its life. Therefore, the subject is not a passively receptive blank slate; it is (as is held by idealism) activity, which is then affirmed (and this runs counter to idealism) in human, subjective sensitivity or activity, which places, models or transforms the object, and in doing so forms itself."[2]

[2] Rodolfo Mondolfo, *Feuerbach y Marx*, ed. Claridad (Buenos Aires, n.d.), 18.

This subversive praxis, which seems to situate the individual as a relative, changing being, presupposes the existence of an objectively absolute human being, whose objective existence is absolute. Human history and societies have given us the Renaissance individual, the individual of the Middle Ages, bourgeois, feudal, and proletarian individuals, in the same way that more specific human communities have given us the German, French, and Mexican. But if we take all human beings together, leaving out the relativity to which they have been conditioned by history and societies that change, there remains an absolute constant, which is the human being himself as an objective truth.

The bourgeois or the proletarian, the Renaissance man or the caveman, the Swede or the Mexican, are individual men, but they are not Man [*son hombres, pero no son el hombre*]. For this reason, one cannot start the analysis of the relational, concrete individuals of some determinate society or country, within a local space and time, without referring to an absolute universal man [or human being], whose existence is absolute within universal time and space.

With all this in mind, the terms "the Mexican" [*el mexicano*] and "Mexicanness" [*lo mexicano*] acquire different meanings from their simple popular usage (or they ought to). If we observe the economic, sociological, and historical perspective of the country called Mexico, we see, for instance, that the Lacandón is not "the Mexican" or "Mexicanness," just as the Yaqui, the Cora, the Huichol, or the Otomí are not.[3] The reason why they are not can be found in the fact that their characteristics as human concrete communities have not been imposed on that other community of men, with their own characteristics and among whom they reside, who make up the rest of the country.

A human community becomes the National [*lo nacional*] of a given country when it creates the conditions to become it, and in no other circumstance; this does not mean, however, that one human community within a given country cannot be the National for itself: the Yaqui, the Cora, the Lacandón, and other linguistic minority groups are the National for themselves, regarding themselves, but they are not the National for the country, they are not the national being of Mexico. If any of these minorities could have created the economic, sociological, and historical conditions necessary for converting their own National into the National of the country, we would not be worrying about the problem of the Mexican, but in its place the problem of the Yaqui or the Cora or the Lacandón.

Thus we conclude that the problem of "the Mexican" is formulated to the degree that the Mexican, through a series of vicissitudes and circumstances

[3] [The Lacandón are an indigenous people related to the Maya that reside mostly in the Mexican state of Chiapas; the Yaqui, an indigenous group of Sonora; the Cora, of Nayarit; the Huichol, of the Sierra Madre Occidental; the Otomí, of the central Mexican altiplano. Revueltas is emphasizing the geographical diversity of these groups, whose homelands are within Mexico but far apart.—Trans.]

about which we will speak in a moment, has managed to make itself *the National* of a country, or more exactly, the *national* being of Mexico.

The reality of a country's national being, considered as *subject*—in our case the Mexican, the national being of Mexico—and the reality of its relations of interdependence and interaction with respect to the economy, society, and history of the country in question, these last considered as object, are rooted in *praxis*, which signifies therefore that *the National*, the *national being*, is nothing more than that universal process of transformation, integration, and disintegration of man, localized in a concrete point in space and time, which makes it possible for a community to formulate with respect to itself and to others the more or less absolute concept of "the French," "the English," "the Mexican," and so on. As a consequence of that universal process from which it cannot be separated, the concept of the National appears in the human brain as a *practically determined* form of the consciousness of being, of the consciousness of being human.

This consciousness of being human, in its *practically determined* form of the national being (just as in its form of the consciousness of class, and all its other forms), appears in the life of men as the result of a conjunction of economic, sociological, and historical phenomena, which have peculiar characteristics in each community despite the fact that the process of their appearance is regulated by unique universal laws. The road that was traveled by the French community in acquiring the consciousness of "the French" is quite different from the road traveled by the colonists of North America in acquiring the consciousness of "North American" [*lo norteamericano*], in arriving at the possible absolute of that consciousness. By "possible absolute" we understand the point at which the consciousness is realized, and at which, in realizing itself, it is transformed from consciousness of being into being itself. Regarding this, we have already said, referring to Mexico's linguistic minorities, that they are *the National* for themselves, but that this does not mean that they are the National for the country, though these minorities do possess a consciousness of their "I," of their national being. This is meant to show that the consciousness of the National, in the case of minorities of this kind, has not arrived at the point of its *possible absolute*, that is, of its economic, social, and historical realization, and which, therefore, is a stationary, passive consciousness.

A more precise characteristic of the national being of the Mexican is the fact that it cohabits as a national being with other nationalities within the limits of the same territory. The non-realization of the national consciousness of the linguistic minorities that cohabit with the Mexican constitutes, therefore, one of the basic antinomies that stand in the way of Mexican national being, conquering its possible absolute and realizing itself fully and in an integrated way. Nonetheless, the fact that the Mexican does not make up the entirety of Mexico's national being completely and totally does not mean that it does not take up the majority national being in the country, so that its character and its morphology are also in the majority.

But, then again, what is the Mexican?

Notwithstanding the fact that, as was said earlier, those universal phenomena that determine the Mexican are produced and developed with their own peculiar characteristics, this fact does not permit us to create an exclusive definition of the Mexican different from the one that exists, in order to establish the necessary conditions that must obtain for any human community, no matter which, to be considered as national *being*, as a nationality.

When intellectuals and professors try to define the Mexican by his sense of death, by his resentment, by his propensity for paradox and by his sexual inhibitions and elusiveness, they create nothing more than cheap drawing-room fables. The Mexican is not a single type for whom unique laws and definitions exist or ought to be invented, because such a type is to be found nowhere under any circumstances within the modern human conglomeration. The characteristics being passed off as unique to the Mexican (resentment, death consciousness, and so on) are features that have appeared and still appear among other peoples. Even more, these features, in the Mexican himself, are a changing surface, not only throughout history, but throughout a geographical range as well.

Humanity is made up of the world of human beings, and the material conditions of each life determine each consciousness, each social and political organization, each custom and each ideology. In this way, a correct analysis of the human being must unavoidably begin with the analysis of the material conditions of individual existence, which determine everything else. Just as in medicine the symptoms are not the disease, in human society determinate facts are not the human being, since the human being is constituted not just by what appears on the surface, but also and preponderantly by what is at the root, as the set of what determines individual human beings. The facts that determine the human being constitute an unstable set, which itself changes to the degree that it is determined by the facts. With regard to this permanence and instability of determining facts, these could be divided in quite a broad scale, but surely the facts of character and psychology are the most ephemeral, even if they are the favorites of those professors who love to weave empty hypotheses.

If we take a Mexican from Mexico City, specifically from the streets around San Juan de Letrán,[4] what we have for the most part is a blowhard, a sexual sadist who beats women, a grumbler and a cowardly bully, to mention just a few characteristics. But if we take another Mexican from the heart of Mexico City, say an intellectual, we find (with some exceptions) a complicated and astute being,

[4] [A central neighborhood of the Distrito Federal, known as a rough area in Revueltas's day, grouped around the main thoroughfare now named Eje Central Lázaro Cárdenas.—Trans.]

incredibly tortured by a hellish vanity, twisted, envious, and full of dark repressions. That is, between the San Juan pimp [*macró*] and the intellectual in the *Cabaret Leda*, we notice a difference immediately; that is to say, the determinate facts in these two types of Mexican fail to show a common magnitude or a common denominator. The difference is heightened if we take a Mexican from Monterrey, from Baja California, or from Nueva Rosita. Here we have a peaceful, sober, austere, cordial man, without any twisted complications. Nonetheless, the uselessness of these facts is obvious when we notice that neither the Mexicans of San Juan and the *Leda*, nor the Mexicans of Monterrey, Baja California, and Rosita, are really *the Mexican* proper, the national being of Mexico.

The national being of a human community cannot exist except on the condition that the community be united in itself by the same language, the same territory, the same economy, and the same culture. The absence of any of these factors causes the human community under discussion to lose its condition of national being. The Mexican is the national being of Mexico precisely because all of these factors are brought together in the community that it forms.

Nevertheless, over the course of history the Mexican has not always been the national being (i.e., the Mexican nationality). This means that Mexican national being has an origin and a development, and therefore must also have a culmination. The possibilities and limitations of the Mexican are only visible, then, in the light of the origin, development, and probable culmination of its national being.

II. The Mexican as the Fruit of Mestizaje

The pre-Hispanic society of Anáhuac[5] may well have been a homogenous state, but it was not a nationality. The nuclei that comprised the empire were linked among themselves by a common territory and common economic links, but they did not have the same language or culture. Thus the national origin of the Mexican cannot be found in the pre-Hispanic society of Anáhuac, because this society did not enjoy the conditions necessary for the constitution of a homogenous, stable nationality.

We can assume that without the factor of the Spanish Conquest, the Aztec Empire would have been dispersed into a series of autonomous states, each with its own nationality. The most important internal contradiction of the Aztec Empire, between the dominant Mexica and the other, dominated nationalities, was rooted in the lack of a common language and culture for all of its members. There was only one way out of this contradiction, which was the Mexicanization

---

[5] [*Anáhuac* is the old Aztec heartland, sometimes called the *Valle de México* in Spanish, and comprising roughly the area of the national capital Distrito Federal today.—Trans.]

of all the nationalities contained within the empire. Faced with the historical impossibility of such a Mexicanization, other conditions were created to resolve the problem, ultimately sowing the seeds for a violent revolutionary explosion against the oppressing nationality. This is demonstrated by the fact that the conquistadores found their best allies among the oppressed nationalities, without whose help the Spanish could never have been victorious.

It is hard to conceive of how any of the empire's constituent nationalities could have transformed itself into the national being of the country. As far as the oppressor nationality went, the Aztecs themselves were incapable of resolving the basic contradiction already discussed as the most important characteristic of the empire, and without which it was impossible for them to create a homogenous nationality. As far as other [viz., non-Aztec] nationalities go, it is inconceivable (taking into account their number and their territories) that they should have been more than a simple nationality for themselves, to have their own national being, but in no way could they be the national being of everyone else in the country.

The Spanish Conquest transformed ancient property relations and introduced new instruments of production, such as the horse, other beasts of burden, metal tools, and the wheel. This change in property relations brought along with it the suppression of class differences among the indigenous peoples [los aborígenes], and what is more important from our point of view, the suppression of national differences among them. Upon being despoiled and proletarianized by the Conquest, the indigenous peoples constituted in fact a more or less homogenous social class, one that shared the same economic interests.

In other historical conditions, these factors, that is, the transformation of property relations, the introduction of new productive instruments, and the almost total proletarianization of the indigenous population, might have meant a revolutionary, progressive phenomenon. That it was not so, indeed, that it was the opposite, is due to the fact that the conquistadores introduced a new fundamental contradiction, one which had barely existed before the destruction of the empire: the contradiction between property relations and forces of production.

In effect, as we have said, the most important contradiction in the Aztec Empire was of a more national than social kind. The nationalities oppressed by the Tenochca or Mexica, despite being internally structured in necessarily antagonistic social classes, seemed unified in their hatred and fear of the Aztecs; and the *macehuales* and *huehuetlacolli*, that is, the peasants and the slaves, seemed to have no consciousness of the need for a class struggle against their exploiters, and offered no sign that such a struggle would be forthcoming. Within the Mexica nationality itself, the lower classes stayed obedient, and showed no symptoms of rebellion. This forces us to think that the antagonism between property relations and forces of production had not arrived at that stage of maturity in which the exploited classes set themselves apart from national interests in order to struggle for their own interests.

At the same time that it was transforming property relations, the Conquest replaced the old indigenous masters with new Spanish masters. The consequence, as has been stated, was the liquidation of national contradictions among the indigenous peoples themselves, replaced in turn by the appearance of a new contradiction: on the one hand, the indigenous peoples taken together as forces of production, and on the other hand, the Spaniards, themselves understood as the expression of property relations. This phenomenon developed over three phases, in which it is possible to fix chronologically the moment at which appeared the economic factor that would later become the seed for a Mexican national being, the seed for the new nationality.

The first of these phases was the *encomienda de indios*. During this period the indigenous peoples were subject to servitude, but for the most part were not despoiled of their lands. The *calpullalli*[6] and the *tlamilpas*[7] were kept more or less unaltered, changing only the beneficiary of the tribute, who was now the Spaniards.

The second phase was the *repartimiento de indios*. Under the pretext of indoctrinating the Indians[8] in the Catholic faith, entire villages were turned over to the Spaniards, who exploited native labor power, especially in the mines. In this period the indigenous peoples were entirely despoiled, and the *calpullalli* disappeared. In place of the *calpullalli* the Indians were given meager lands as legal holdings, which is the village common.

The third phase was that of land grants. The Spanish kings granted lands to their vassals as a reward for services to the Crown, in order to promote the colonization of New Spain. The despoilment of the Indians thus acquired a legal character, and the Crown required the beneficiaries of this despoilment to reside in the granted lands for at least four years.

Of these three phases of the expression of the transformation of property relations and the consequent contradiction with the forces of production, the third is doubtless the most important, because it was in the third phase that the Crown forced the Spaniard to reside on the land. The residence requirement for the Spaniard necessarily brought along with it sexual commerce between Spaniards and indigenous women. To say this more clearly, this sexual commerce (which had previously been without economic content) now appears tied

[6] [*Calpullalli* is an instance of a system of unfree landholding that the Aztecs called generally *calpulli*. It somewhat resembles certain European feudal practices.—Trans.]

[7] [*Tlamilpa* is an inalienably owned piece of property devoted to in-kind production, whose produce was divided among the owners of alienable shares.—Trans.]

[8] [I am following Revueltas's usage generally, translating *indígenas* or *aborígenes* as "indigenous," but where he uses the term *indio* I will translate "Indian."—Trans.]

up with the holding of property in land. It is precisely here that mestizaje is born, no longer occasioned spontaneously and fortuitously, as it had been in the first periods, but rather under the imperative of an undeniable economic necessity. In sum, mestizaje appears in Mexican history not as a racial phenomenon, but as an economic phenomenon.

Defenders of Spanish domination praise the generosity of the Conquest, which took great care not to physically destroy the indigenous peoples of Anáhuac, as opposed to what the English emigrants who colonized North America did for their part. But if we analyze the problem more closely, we will see that the criterion of generosity, or the lack of generosity, simply has nothing to do with any of it.

The first period of Spanish domination is characterized by the purely extractive character of the economy. The Spaniards had no interest other than extracting from the land the largest possible quantity of precious metals. During this first period, the indigenous population, subjected to the ugliest jobs and deprivations, was reduced considerably in number, and would have disappeared (as happened in Cuba), if alongside the purely extractive economy a productive economy had not appeared, oriented to the exploitation of agriculture.

Beginning in this second period, then, the Spaniards attempted to ensure that the indigenous did not die out and vanish, because if the indigenous were to vanish, the Spaniards would lose the labor force indispensable for the exploitation of the land.

This obvious economic undertaking was dressed up in certain ideological forms. The Alexandrine Bulls,[9] which gave the Spanish monarchy the primacy in the West Indies on the pretext that Christendom would be extended throughout the world, is simply the juridical appearance under which Spain's imperial expansion appeared. Similarly, the *repartimiento* and *encomienda* of the Indians, which were nothing but the despoilment and exploitation of indigenous peoples, show up in turn in the form of a religious superstructure: the indoctrination of indigenous peoples in Catholicism.

It is clear that no serious analysis of the problem can be undertaken based on an acceptance of the generosity, gentlemanliness, or chivalry of the Spaniards, things that have no influence on the historical phenomenon. The archetype of Spanish virtue, Ruy Díaz de Vivar, exposes the real content of his deeds in these verses from the Cantar del Mío Cid, as Kurt Vossler quotes them:

Los moros e las moras vender non los podemos,
que los descabecemos nada non ganaremos;

---

[9] [The *Bulas Alejandrinas* (1492), the predecessor to the 1494 Treaty of Tordesillas, laid out the Spanish Pope Alexander VI's determination of where Spain's imperial expansion would be privileged, given a mission to "Christianize" the inhabitants of the New World.—Trans.]

cojámoslo de dentro, ca el señorío tenemos;
posaremos en sus casas y dellos nos serviremos.[10]

Little gentleness and little generosity is to be found in this most gentle and most chivalrous Spaniard of any age. He cannot sell the Moors or the Mooresses, and will gain nothing from their decapitation. The solution—perhaps more Phoenician than Spanish, or Phoenician because it is Spanish—is to be practical: he will take them as servants, and reside in their houses. As we see, there is little so-called poetry in the heroic attitude of the Cid.

The Spaniards of the Conquest and the colony did not think of the indigenous peoples of Anáhuac differently from the way that their ancestors had thought of the Moors in the time of the Cid. According to Vossler, referring to the Cid and the verses of the canto I transcribed in the preceding, "The knowledge that he is responsible for his followers' prosperity—and that these followers are a kind of business partners, gives this supposed forerunner of romanticism a format and a solidity of an economic kind, of a completely unliterary character." Vossler's words could refer, without changing a syllable, to Hernando Cortés and his followers. We could replace the word "unliterary," however, with "amoral."

Very often, social classes disguise their objectives under different appearances. Thus the Conquest is carried out not in order to increase Spain's economic power, but to bring into the Catholic religion thousands of souls otherwise condemned to hellfire. But the figure of the Cid, much like the cultural and historical figures of Cortés or Pizarro, have no need for the disguises that the ruling ideologies of their time had to dress them up with. However complicated these disguises may seem to us, it is always possible to discover what lies hidden beneath them.

The need to preserve and reproduce the labor force under the Spanish domination brought about, as a consequence, the appearance of mestizaje. We will now examine how that mestizaje began to constitute the seed of a new national being.

The Conquest destroyed any kind of historical possibility that any of the nationalities of Anáhuac would become the country's national being. As has been said, the Spanish Conquest and colonies annulled the indigenous peoples' national contradictions, turning them into a mass with shared economic interests, since in the new order of things they represented the force of production, in opposition to the property relations represented by the Spaniards.

---

[10] "The Moors and the Mooresses cannot be sold, / And we will gain nothing by cutting off their heads; / Let us take them inside [the conquered town] with us, since we have the lordship; / We shall quarter in their houses, and they shall serve us."

This heterogeneous mass achieved unity due to a shared economic tie—that of being the victims of Spanish exploitation—a shared religion, and a shared territory. In truth, the indigenous peoples appropriated the Catholicism of the conquerors as a resource for continuing to practice their old rites with impunity. But in order to become a nationality, this indigenous mass still lacked a shared language. The old pre-Conquest national languages could not serve as a shared linguistic tie, because none of them represented an instrument of economic relations, since all property was in foreign hands. The only shared language that the indigenous masses could appeal to was the conquerors' own language. In this way, impelled by economic forces, the indigenous mass (except for certain centers that have managed to avoid the phenomenon down to our own days) learned Spanish or was incorporated organically into this language by the mestizos. The result of this is that, together with the old nationalities of Anáhuac, which stands still and lacks historical perspective, and in opposition to the Spanish nationality, despoiler of the land and oppressor of other nationalities, a new nationality arose, a new being that, strictly speaking, can be called the Mexican.

Thus with regard to national characters, three main groups lived together in the colony: (1) the Spaniards (creoles and *peninsulares*[11]), (2) the Mexicans (Spanish-speaking mestizos and Indians), and (3) pure Indians, unincorporated into the Spanish language, divided up in turn into several nationalities.

As far as the society's economic scheme, the colony displays, in broad strokes, two fundamental groups: (1) the Spaniards and creoles, who determine the form of property relations, and (2) the rest of the population, which represents the force of production.

III. The First Great Mexican Revolution (1810)

After three centuries of the accumulation of forces, the moment arrives in which it is possible for the Mexican to begin a revolutionary transformation of property relations. The fight for the transformation of property relations coincides with the struggle against the oppressor nationality, the nationality which is, at the same time, the one that determines the character of these relations. For this reason, the revolution of 1810 shows up with a double character: as an agrarian revolution and as a national revolution.

We have already said that over the course of Spanish domination, an economic differentiation was produced within colonial society and colonial classes, which afterward determined the character of the groupings in respect to the

---

[11] [A *peninsular* is a Spaniard born in Spain, a creole [*criollo*] a person of entirely Spanish ancestry born in the Americas. Only *peninsulares* could hold certain government positions.—Trans.]

supporters of national realization, which is manifested first in the period around 1810 and then in the period around 1821.

On the side of the dominant sectors, this differentiation was expressed in an antagonism between Spanish *peninsulares* and Spanish creoles. The extent of the transformation of property relations that the creoles had in mind, the result of this antagonism, went no further than a simple displacement of the wealth of the Spanish *peninsulares* in their favor, with no notion that the feudal character of property should be changed in the least, and no notion that the weight of the exploitation of the land should be taken off the shoulders of the Indians and mestizos.

The creoles sought the juridical expression of this longing even in the colony's independence with respect to the metropolis, but this independence had nothing to do with the liberation of the Mexican nationality.

On the side of the oppressed sectors, this differentiation was expressed in the birth of a class of minor landholders and ranchers, along with the mestizo peasants and the landless Indians. Within these sectors, the natural antagonism that one would expect to exist between owners and proletarians was neutralized by the more important antagonism in society, between all the oppressed sectors taken as a whole versus the sector formed by the Spaniards and the creoles.

For the group of minor landholders—the ranchers, the Indians, and the landless mestizos—the colony's independence represented nothing more than a random consequence of the transformation of property relations. Father Hidalgo himself, in the beginning, urged loyalty to King Ferdinand VII of Spain. We should not see this attitude of Hidalgo's as some would have it, as an attitude of cowardice or confusion about objectives. Hidalgo had a clear consciousness of his historical task, and was by no means the stupid, lamentable old man whom reactionary historians present to us. Hidalgo was proposing a substantial transformation of New Spain's economy, and indeed trained the Indians in crops and industries that were prohibited by the Spanish Crown. The independence of the colony with respect to Spain did not have to mean the transformation of property relations, just as the transformation of property relations did not have to mean independence. But in any case, the transformation of property relations, with or without independence, necessarily meant the liberation of the Mexican nationality.

The insurgents ended up confusing the problem of Mexican national realization with the problem of political independence, and thus leaving the task of transforming property relation in the hands of Iturbide, who represented exactly those creoles who did not want any radical transformation of those relations, nor any integration of a Mexican nationality.

In this way the movement begun in 1810 as a revolutionary and nationalist movement degenerated in 1821 into a reactionary and anti-national movement.

As a consequence, the realization of the Mexican as the country's national being was postponed to the next historical period, the period we know as Independent Mexico.

IV. Independent Mexico and Nationality

The revolution of Ayutla and the Reformation[12] represent a great step forward in the realization of the Mexican as the country's national being, in that they meant the historic defeat of the feudal landowners (including the Church), the inheritors of the counterrevolution of 1821.

Nonetheless, the transformation of property relations that Ayutla and the Reformation implied was incapable (because it was insufficient) of creating the conditions for a thorough, full integration of the Mexican nationality.

We have stated that within the nucleus of classes oppressed by colonial domination (that is, the small landowners, ranchers, Indians, and mestizos), there was a latent antagonism that could not manifest itself before the more powerful antagonism that existed between this nucleus, taken together, and the nucleus comprising the Spaniards and the creoles. This latent antagonism would manifest itself later, when this neutralizing factor ceased to exist. This was the moment following the triumph of Ayutla and the Reformation, and the defeat of the Second Empire, when the classes who had benefited from the Spanish domination were definitively swept off the stage of history.

The transformation in property relations that the Reformation brought about was expressed legally in the expropriation laws. This expropriation was translated into the economic strengthening of small landowners and ranchers, who suddenly became new feudal landowners. Add to this that the expropriation included indigenous peoples' common lands, such that the problem of the contradiction between the force of production and the new property relations was considerably aggravated. In this way, the mestizos and Spanish-speaking Indians, called upon to be the integrators of a liberated Mexican nationality, could not do so, impeded as they were by the feudal trappings of their society. From this perspective we can explain why it is that the regimes of Juárez and Porfirio Díaz [el juarismo y el porfirismo] fought so heatedly against the indigenous masses.

In the period that we know under the name of independent Mexico, there are two great national uprisings that appear to have succeeded. Two different nationalities: the Maya, in the Yucatán Peninsula, and the Huichol in the western

---

[12] [The Revolution of Ayutla and the Reformation are the names given to the plan and subsequent war to dethrone Santa Anna as the dictator of Mexico in the 1850s. After overthrowing him, it established a liberal constitution in 1857.—Trans.]

mountains of Nayarit, rose up in arms to struggle for their national independence. Neither of these rebellious nationalities, neither the Maya nor the Huichol, attempted to become the country's national being; they wanted simply to be national beings for themselves, free in their own territory. Mexico's dominant classes smashed these rebellions with fire and blood, something that was avoidable, or could have been channeled toward the integration of the Mexican nationality, had the property relations not been as they were.

The struggle against the indigenous peoples during the Reformation and the regime of Porfirio Díaz can be explained by the fact that the dominant nucleus, constituted by the new landowners, transformed into a nucleus just as anti-national as the anti-national classes inherited from the colony over which it triumphed.

Unable to transform property relations in a way that would break up very large landholdings, this dominant nucleus unraveled under the same conditions that made it possible for the dominant classes of the colony to make themselves the most significant obstacle for the realization of a new nationality.

During the last stage of the Díaz regime, a new phenomenon appeared in the world: the appearance of economic imperialism of monopolist capital. The owner classes of the Díaz regime, created by the Reformation, having at this point lost the national spirit that had nourished them from the beginning, did not hesitate to open the country's doors to imperialist encroachment.

The integration of the Mexican as the national being of the country, a task that the Reformation carried halfway through, only to the degree that it struggled against the most reactionary and anti-national classes of its time, was postponed once again until the historical period that would follow it.

This period was that of the Revolution of 1910. This revolution, in contemplating the transformation of those feudal property rights inherited from the Reformation and the Díaz regime, simultaneously contemplated an anti-imperialist revolution. In the realization of this task, the Revolution of 1910 therefore involved two classes newly interested in the realization of the Mexican as the national being of the country. These two new classes are the bourgeoisie and the proletariat.

V. Bourgeoisie, Proletariat, and Peasants: Nationalist Classes

The revolutionary movement of 1910 fundamentally transformed the feudal relations of property in land, and thereby created the economic conditions for the integration of a Mexican nationality, almost four centuries after this nationality began to gestate with the appearance of the mestizo. Modern Mexico's linguistic minorities, having acquired land as a result of the 1910 revolution, ceased to be oppressed nationalities. The education that was provided to them in their native languages, conveniently systematized for writing, and as a resource for assimilating them to the economically dominant language, would eventually cause them to be incorporated into the sole and homogenous nationality that Mexico would become in the future.

After this examination, in which we have seen the circumstances and trials through which the Mexican has been able to become the National [*lo nacional*] for Mexico, what remains for us is to reflect on the peculiar contradictions that this process of integration has carried with it, contradictions that seemingly comprise that which gives the Mexican his own physiognomy.

These contradictions can be grouped as follows:

First: The conquest of Anáhuac is not the imposition of one nation on another, but rather the practical dispersion and dissolution of a combination of autochthonous nationalities, which in fact vanish under the weight of a new social organization that has superior resources of production and oppression. As a consequence, the impossibility of drawing upon their own heritage of tradition, culture, and language in order to regroup into a nucleus capable of reacquiring a national being, pushes the dispersed autochthonous nationalities to take up the conqueror's own weapons: the Catholic religion and the language.

Second: The new Mexican nationality, product of the use of the foreign religion and language, united to the community of economic and territorial ties, ultimately appears, is born into existence as an oppressed nationality, with an imperfect tradition that is reduced to a hazy collective memory of something that existed very imprecisely in the past, whose traces survive in the linguistic quirks [*giros*] with which Spanish is adopted and the pagan forms in which Catholicism is practiced. As a consequence, the new nationality does not feel linked in an organic way either to its indigenous past, which is in general a multinational and heterogeneous past, or to the Spanish tradition, which represents foreignness and oppression.

Third: The Mexican nationality is born under the weight of a doubly adverse condition, which, on the one hand, consists of Spanish oppression and, on the other, in the existence of great national states, which have been able to arise in the world thanks to the abolition of feudalism. Later the Mexican nationality develops and attempts to become the national being of Mexico, not only when national states had already been constituted, but when they moved from mercantile capitalism to factory capitalism [*capitalismo manufacturero*], and when the majority of them had already had their bourgeois revolutions. As a consequence, the Mexican nationality is born and develops with a considerable historical delay. This delay forces it to consider, along with the tasks of its national realization, other greater tasks (such as the bourgeois revolution, for example) that do not fit well with the state of development of its economic infrastructure.

Fourth: The Mexican nationality, finally, becomes the national being of Mexico in a world where two phenomena coexist that had not existed in earlier periods: imperialism and socialism. As a consequence, the Mexican nationality considers the problem of its [historical] culmination (or its disappearance) as a problem of choosing between the two horns of a historical dilemma: either socialism and survival or imperialism and extinction.

These four contradictions are reflected in every aspect of Mexican life. It is natural, for example, that the Mexican's Catholic religion should be a melancholic religion, heartbreaking and full of nostalgia, since it is a religion meant to stand in for something that has been lost, something that is now unknown. Another characteristic of the Mexican is his feeling of dispossession. This is, of course, the origin of his attitude toward life and death, his largesse, and the little importance he gives to the fact of disappearing. All these characteristics, however, originate in circumstances of economic, sociological, and historical character, and are subject to transformation.

We could discuss many other psychological features of the Mexican that are a product of the economic and social contradictions that we have seen; but what is important to emphasize here, as our main object, are the possibilities and limitations of the Mexican.

The limitations of the Mexican, as we have said, are entirely the consequence of his historical delay. Nonetheless, within the Mexican's limitations are also his possibilities.

In 1810, for instance, one insuperable limitation was that the Mexican needed to consider the problems of a bourgeois transformation of society and the problems of his national being at the same time, and do so without even having a class adequate to the task of putting into practice the ideology of the time. But now things have changed.

With the existence of socialism in the world, the contradiction between the ideological, cultural, and political superstructure and the economic infrastructure has ceased to be an impermeable barrier for peoples. Non-secular peoples, such as the Chinese people, have managed to place themselves, despite their backwardness, at the height of the most advanced forms of political organization. The Mexican is not a unique case in the global panorama. Despite whatever historical backwardness he may face, the conquests of science and culture are within his reach. Even more, despite his historical delay, the Mexican can add new notions and contributions to universal culture. That

Mexico which almost vanished in 1847 and 1862, the revolutionary Mexico of today, which managed to integrate itself in 1910 and carry out its social reforms at the same time, will be the same Mexico that flourishes without limits, as a national being within the universal being of man in the socialist world of tomorrow.

CHAPTER 18

The X on the Brow

SOME REFLECTIONS ON MEXICO (1952)

Alfonso Reyes

Translated by Roberto Cantú

Alfonso Reyes Ochoa was born in Monterrey, Nuevo León, in 1889 and died in Mexico City in 1959. Reyes was a member of the Ateneo de la juventud *and has been referred to as Mexico's most perfect example of the man of letters. Primarily an essayist, Reyes was also widely known for his literary criticism, philosophy, journalism, historical analyses, poetry, storytelling, and for his contributions to aesthetics. In 1911, at the age of twenty-one, he published his first book,* Aesthetic Questions (Questiones estéticas). *Though Reyes committed much of his intellectual effort to reflecting on his native Mexico, he was also remembered for his encyclopedic knowledge and universal interests, living the middle third of his life outside Mexico. He lived in Spain from 1914 to 1924 and in Paris from 1924 to 1927, serving in diplomatic posts, and was ambassador to Argentina (1927–1930) and Brazil (1930–1935 and 1938), before finally returning home in 1939, at which time he organized the House of Spain (Casa de España), now the College of Mexico (Colegio de México). Among his many writings on Mexico, the following are translated into English:* The Position of America and Other Essays *(1950) and* Mexico in a Nutshell and Other Essays *(1964).*

On the Mexican

I. ALPHABET, BREAD, AND SOAP

Appearance is not to be disdained.[1] Even when deceived, one is given a clue. Whether we accept it or wish to rectify it, it is in the appearance that knowledge

---

[1] [The translator has chosen to translate from *The Complete Works of Alfonso Reyes* (*Obras completas de Alfonso Reyes*), a multivolume edition published by UNAM, so that interested readers who also

grounds itself. To allow oneself to be guided by visual perception is not a bad method, on the condition that one remain alert. At first sight, what is most noticeable and impressionable about Mexicans is their widespread poverty. Perhaps this is our quintessential misfortune. If only it were possible to distribute money throughout the country as one sprinkles salt on one's favorite dish! And if only this were enough to improve the nation's economy!

Unfortunately, even such a prospect, worthy of a tale from *A Thousand and One Nights*, would not solve the problem. It is like the physicist's paradox: if suddenly the size of what can be measured in the universe were to be increased a hundredfold, nothing would change and we would not even notice.

The example set by political leaders proves that allowing money to spread is only for show and of limited reach. It also proves, however, that the relief this brings provokes a national optimism never seen before. Fleeting moments of joy, of inebriation, of a day! How to stop and hold, oh Faust, the ever-fleeting instant of happiness: "Stand still . . . you are so beautiful!"

There are fruitful sorrows; there are bitter moments that drown, only to rebound, or regrow [*rebotar, o rebrotar*] human virtue from the abyss. Poverty itself, the "loyal companion of Greece" according to the ancients, illustrates our national attributes. The toil against sterile environments engenders the stimulus of great civilizations more so than the luxuriant plenitude of earthly paradises. However, if scarcity or obstacles annihilate opportunity and human hope, then nations lose their inner sap and begin to wane.

That leavening agent of optimism that only rises and swells when it reaches a certain level of well-being seems indispensable for the virtues of nations to ascend and prosper. When the daily exertion is vital and harsh, when the available money is in the hands of governments, and men contend anxiously over public posts as the only means to obtain food and respect, where are we to find the undeveloped merits? The results are the claw and the fang, and not the intelligence and social conduct. Samuel Ramos, my admired and beloved friend, is this *The Profile of the Mexican Man*? We shall have a clear view of him when we nourish him, when we reconcile him with his existence, when he is able to enjoy a certain degree of sovereignty.

So, which profile will it be? What will our people bring forth after resolving and creating their source of sustenance? I have dreamed of that possible Mexico, not necessarily joyful because it would be too much to ask, and even

read in Spanish will be able to locate the lengthier versions of these essays. All subsequent footnotes are the translator's and provide the relevant bibliographic information. This particular selections of essays, however, was published in 1952 under the preceding title as the first volume in a collection of short works about Mexican identity. That series was published by Porrúa y Obregón in 1952–1955 and was directed by Leopoldo Zea, who published his own *Conciencia y posibilidad del mexicano* (Knowledge and Possibilities of the Mexican) in the same year.—Editors.]

impossible: but let us dream of what we can. To this day, all of us live in Mexico in a daily stumble, and lucky are the few of us who can really call ourselves privileged. We bear, however, the face of a bad conscience. We know there is a skeleton in our closet. When we reflect on the nation, our subconscious points vaguely to immense areas in which entire populations barely exist in subhuman conditions. What will these people be once they can access Humanity itself? At that point, and only then, shall we know what our people are able to produce.

The alphabet, yes! Bread of the soul! Our president said it best in one of his declarations, which more than a decree seems to be a human cry. But, running parallel and as a prerequisite, bread for the body; a bit of well-being, a bite of happiness in one's daily physical existence. The one goes with the other, and given that well-being does not fall from heaven, one must solicit and seek it from one's land by means of techniques and skills stemming from the Alphabet. "Alphabet and soap," demanded José Vasconcelos years ago, thinking of the necessity to reconstruct biologically and culturally our human substance. Let us say instead "alphabet, bread, and soap." All the rest will come as icing on the cake.

II. CONTEMPORARY AND FUTURE CHARACTERISTICS

In our country, as everywhere else, one finds apparent characteristics and possible or latent qualities not yet fully revealed through the intimate circumstances of vital anguish in which we ourselves unfold up to the present day.

About those characteristics that manifest themselves, enough has been said. For instance, courtesy—the gentle restraint on man's animal inclinations, and the practical school of humanization for Man—has been the topic of eloquent and scholarly treatises. Ruiz de Alarcón, Mme. Calderón de la Barca, and other testimonies have been recited on the subject. Some have explained, reasonably well, that certain rude behaviors—under which one can detect the provincial and vernacular origins of gentle manners—are the result, on the one hand, of transitory social turbulences that naturally distort genuine social conditions (since it is not possible, in the midst of a civil war and with a pistol under one's belt, to continue being who we once were); and, on the other hand, that such rude behaviors are the result of the world's general evolution. Today's societies gallop, so to speak, at a fast-moving stride and thus with no time for caution. While we search for a new equilibrium between celerity and ceremony, everywhere people will continue to be somewhat rude.

Enough has been said as well about the Mexican's artistic talents. Clay, glass, straw, feather, silver, gold, other popular crafts, and our magnificent paintings; our musical and lyrical abilities, progressively displaced by the demand of new industries (radio, cinema), an overwhelming demand that turns our song into a monotonous moan or a tremulous and ridiculous recital, the product of mass production and, one can only hope, condemned to disappear. The artistic talents of the Mexican have never been questioned. But art, like love, is another sacred dimension in one's life, aloof and enduring, and compatible even with social vexations and with institutional turmoil. It is also a valve for the release of pain, our retaliation against a bitter existence.

In between the apparent characteristics and our latent virtues, there is an intermediate range of indications that allow us to anticipate certain future developments in our people that will take place in conditions of well-being.

Our point of reference is that aptitude toward discretion which, in poetry and criticism, has been called the "twilight mood": the aversion to garish notes (naturally, except in exceptional cases) that I, fearing associations with "decadence" or "swooning" that the word "twilight" suggests, have preferred to call a tendency toward classical restraint and solemnity. These appear to be, in fact, the norms—or better yet—the forms in which the Mexican soul is wrought.

Viewed from another side, one notices in all peoples of the Americas—in spite of the appearances and the displaced appreciation that our internal turmoil could have provoked in those who continue to ignore us—the Mexican is the least "tropical," by which is understood the brash and heedless, the trusting candor, the excess in sentimental expression, and the empty chatter. The Mexican is reserved and sober to the point that peoples from other Latin American nations appear to us as eccentric and deluded (this said without malice), including people of the United States, such affable charlatans; Argentines, so easily satisfied; then there are the Chileans themselves, who claim to be the Scandinavians of the South.

Well then, this reserve, that restraint, the mistrust, and such a constant need to doubt and to prove, make of the Mexicans something like the immediate disciples of the *Discourse on Method*, native Cartesians, predisposing them—when the day of well-being arrives, with his political participation, and the resulting development of faculties currently dormant—to be a scientific people par excellence.

This does not mean that other interior virtues, superior in inspiration, will be lost, nor will we lose our recollection or our metaphysical depth. Our children, or the children of our children, will be witnesses to this.[2]

México, September 1944

México's Three Kingdoms

Common wisdom counsels to be wary of appearances. There is no worse and mistaken advice, given that we live in the midst of appearances, like those

---

[2] [Selected from "Los trabajos y los días," *Obras completas de Alfonso Reyes*, Vol. IX (México: Fondo de Cultura Económica, 1959): 421–424.]

prisoners in Plato's cave who were only allowed to contemplate the shadows of objects. To trust appearances, to submerge oneself in them, and to inquire what they are is the only possible path to knowledge, be it religious, philosophical, ethical, artistic, or scientific.

The first impressions received through our senses are sacred. It matters little if afterward one must rectify or reinterpret them. Vision is a precious faculty; light, a divine gift, without which it would be impossible to find delight in the "twenty atmospheres" condensed—according to Gautier—in the background of the *Meninas* by Velázquez. It would also be impossible for us to represent to ourselves the contours of the universe, be it in the old image by Newton, or in the modern one by Einstein.

Geometry was created by the eyes and, according to Santayana's apt expression, air itself is architecture. When the ancient fable takes sight away from the sage, it feels obligated, as a form of compensation, to endow him with clairvoyance, as happened with Tiresias and with Homer. Only prophecy or poetry can compensate us for such a loss. The terrible sanctity of the Stoic screams through Quevedo's voice: "I lost my eyesight! I missed the opportunity to go astray!" It could well turn into its opposite: "I lost the opportunity to save myself!"

The admirable photography of George Hoyningen-Huene, even in its sufficient mutism—unhindered by legends or announcements that always distract from the candor and proximity of details—achieves the ultimate work of charity: to restore sight to the blind.[3] There is no sociological treatise, and no economic statistics when studying a people, that will replace the intuitive depth of a photo album, the register of static appearances through which Mexico's face is revealed in the plenitude of its gestures, its sensibility, its poignancy, its melancholy, or its subtle cheerfulness.

When the illustrious teacher of Hispanic criticism, Marcelino Menéndez y Pelayo, examined for the first time the spectacle of Mexican poetry, he recommended that one seek the foundations of its originality—above all and preferentially—in the effect of the landscape on the imagination. Jaime Torres Bodet added that the problem of the landscape diminishes in importance as it merges into the larger problem of a national literature. Whoever mentions the word "literature" alludes to the fundamental expression of a people's soul. Without light—light and shadow—one would not understand certain paradoxical distancing effects ("aloofness," according to Coleridge) often found in poetry. For example, our Modernist poets would often close their eyes to the native imagery of our America. The self-same negation of the environment reveals, however, the environment that one intends to exclude.

---

[3] [See Alfonso Reyes, *México eterno: tres panoramas* (México: Editorial Atlante, 1946).]

This complicated framework of influences called Human Geography, without which History is incomprehensible, is none other than the reaction, the response of our will in the face of the natural and telluric system that surrounds us: whether one conceives of Egypt, like Herodotus, as a gift of the Nile; or, like Toynbee, as a response to a challenge made by the Nile. The Colombian Germán Arciniégas proposed this incisive argument: "If a spirited inquirer chose to reconstruct the history of light in America, the canvas would be filled with landscapes unknown to us, such as the Conquest, the Colonial Era, the Wars of Independence, and the nineteenth century. One cannot explain the behavior of peoples if one does not first attempt the recreation of an atmosphere."

As a contribution to this future work, Hoyningen-Huene's *Mexican Album* is of immense value. On other occasions I have attempted to forge a path in that direction, describing ancient Mexico's plateau as "the atmosphere's most transparent region" (Alfonso Reyes, *Visión de Anáhuac* [1915]).[4]

Dissimulated, and sometimes incorporated into the features of a natural physiognomy, one always feels the presence of ancient gods. Something akin to a sacred breathing sprouts from the tree and the stone. Our remote ancestors, who centuries ago treaded on Mexico's soil, attributed—as ancient peoples always do—a divine circulation to the animated land that enclosed them: a kind of hieroglyphic decipherment that man's consciousness always attempts to apply to the surrounding world from which he must orient his conduct.

In a long intellectual process, our grandfathers avoided a mere mimetic representation, perhaps because their technical possibilities did not predispose them in that direction (luckily!). They created an art abounding with symbols, thus to be interpreted as writing.

The contortions and monumental flights of Mexican archaeology—inspired by religious impulses—correspond to a reading of the universe that specifically attempts to merge with ambient appearances, and to understand them from a human point of view.

This is a human approach radically different from our own. It is a human approach, however, that one can understand only if one confronts the texts read by the ancient Mexican (the landscape and the environment: a section of this album) with the interpretation obtained from the same texts: namely, the archaeological documents.

---

[4] [This phrase in Reyes's *Visión de Anáhuac* inspired the title of Carlos Fuentes's novel *La región más transparente* (1958). Reyes appropriated this phrase as an homage to Alexander von Humboldt's *Political Essay on the Kingdom of New Spain* (1808–1811) in which Humboldt refers to Mexico's atmosphere as "et plus rare et plus transparent." See Rex Clark and Oliver Lubrich (editors), *Cosmos and Colonialism: Alexander von Humboldt in Cultural Criticism* (New York: Berghahn Books, 2012), 7.]

Art would have no meaning without this game of actions and reactions: the riddle of the world and man's response—it must be said—at times reveals itself to be a second-order question given that the riddle is far from resolved. To the enigma of the environment, of the natural forms, of the landscape that encloses, caresses, or tortures us, corresponds the enigma of artistic expression: to the Mexican landscape—in its own terrible and transcendental manner—Mexican archaeology is the answer.

On top of this original stratum, an indigenous layer, will later cascade another civilization, flowing with Spanish conquistadors, driven also by a religious purpose. The Christian cross will soar over the ruins of the Aztec temple. Over time, and over the same indigenous soil, a second human echelon will be transformed into another civilization.

Landscape, Mexican archaeology, and Mexican colonial art compose the present album, like three indispensable phases of a process. The modern age is cosmopolitan and bland—in other words, neutral and devoid of a national expression. It is something we can dispense with. A noble scruple to flee from the ordinary and misleading temptations of the "tourist's documentation" have charged the author of this album of photographs with the aesthetic bravura of removing the human figure. Man makes his appearance only in our eyes—in other words, in contemplation. A miniature god has completed his work and turns to witness his creation. It is well done! Our history has no regrets.

In addition to the material enticements and the desire to discover paradises of gold (the emperor Montezuma removed his robes in front of the conquistador Hernán Cortés as evidence that he was not made of the precious metal!), the Spaniards who thrived throughout our land were soldiers of Christ, knights of a new Crusade. This means that their first churches were also fortifications and garrisons. The sword carried a cross on its grip.

No doubt they were also stirred by a craving to behold marvels. That same insatiable curiosity swept Alexander—in spite of the many protests of his warriors—beyond the known limits of the world, knowing that his distracted expedition lacked any strategic or political purpose. This image, however, must not be exaggerated because the Spanish sense of realism has in great measure rectified all proclivities toward fantasy, the madwoman of the house.

In the end, it cannot be denied that in all the heroic deeds of discovery and conquest of America, the driving force was the utopian inspiration, the hope that better lands for adventure and other forms of human happiness could be discovered.

During its Colonial Era, Mexico slowly acquires its historical physiognomy. The tumults of conquest are relaxed and from the amalgamation of bloods emerges a ceremonious and courteous people, whose provincial timbre emphasizes and accentuates an affected sovereignty and aristocratic airs.

This is revealed in the plays of Juan Ruiz de Alarcón, the first universal writer born in Mexico. It is also revealed in the extremes of the "Mexican Baroque," where the Hispanic arrogance mingles with the convulsive inspirations of indigenous art.

Afterward . . . the land tends toward uniformity. Peoples decide on different influences. Independences become interdependences (which is not the same as dependences). Nations are bound to each other with economic ties made of steel. One can only hope that from it will rise a new dawn of human fraternity, transcending borders, former "autarchies," and outdated imperialisms.[5]

Assorted Fragments

I

I dream—I was telling you—of writing a series of essays with the following theme: "In search of the national soul." A first chapter could be my essay *Visión de Anáhuac* (1915), followed by interpretations from which to draw the moral of our terrible historical fable: to feel the pulse of the nation in all men and in all moments in which our history seems to have intensified; to demand from the brutality of events their spiritual meaning; to discover the mission of the *Mexican man* on earth, stubbornly questioning all the phantoms and the stones on our nation's tombs and monuments. A country redeems itself when it is able to glimpse the message that it must bring to the world: when it is able to electrify itself toward one pole, be it real or imaginary, because life is woven with the threads of reality and the imagination. Creation is not an idle activity; all crafts hide a secret eloquence, and it must be passionately wrung for it to release its hieroglyphic truth. In search of the national soul! This would be my constant preaching to the youth of my country. This disinterested concern alone can provide us with advantages and counsel us as to our nation's political conduct. I refuse to see history as the overlapping process of a mute fate. There is a voice that surges from the depths of our former pains; there is an invisible bird of bad omen that continues to sing: *tihuic, tihuic,* beyond the chaos of our rancor. Who will be able to hear the solitary solidarity, the muffled oracle that has resonated from one century to the next, with mysterious conjugations of sounds and concepts telling us where we can find the remedy to our disputes, the answer to our questions, the key to our national coexistence!

[5] [From *Obras completas de Alfonso Reyes*, Vol. VIII (México: Fondo de Cultura Económica, 1958): 105–109.]

And you, my friend Antonio, who has deeply felt and sung the portent of the Spanish might spilling on our land, you said to me:

> It is true. We have not yet broken the code, the unity of our soul. We rest satisfied in knowing that we are the children of two conflict-ridden races. Like the biblical woman, we can tell our country: "Two nations rest in your breast." We hear of the political redemption of the Indian more so than of his spiritual redemption. I mean: more so than of his integration, explained and accepted, as a formative element of our modern soul. This is an indispensable and necessary task prior to the political question, much as the idea is prior to action. All those dark voices of our Indian grandfathers, who weep in our hearts, have not known a moment of rest. Perhaps the first part of the project consists in recovering Indian traditions, as they have reached us in tales and proverbs that long ago uplifted our young imagination.

And at this point you began to narrate to me. . . .[6]

II

. . . But I should also declare, in order for it to serve as a lesson to those more fortunate than myself, that my Mexican courtesy has often hindered me in Europe—where communication, in general, is more direct and curt—when I speak with concierges, janitors, and the like. And this has happened not only to me. One day our countryman Carlos Pereyra approached a female porter and, adopting a custom perhaps imported from Switzerland or Belgium, but in accordance with his Mexican temperament, he courteously took off his hat before asking, "Good morning, lady porter, will you allow me to take the elevator so I can ascend to Mr. So-and-So's floor?" He then had to listen, from the lips of the porter, the following oracle: "Since you ask permission, it must be due to the fact that you have no right to use the elevator; therefore, you must climb the stairs belonging to the servants" (this case happened in Madrid).[7]

III

The deep-rooted background, unconscious and involuntary, determines who I am as a Mexican: this is a fact, not a virtue. It has been a cause not only for

---

[6] [Selected from "Carta a Antonio Mediz-Bolio (August 5, 1922)" *Obras completas de Alfonso Reyes*, Vol. IV (México: Fondo de Cultura Económica, 1956): 421–422.]

[7] [Selected from "Un recuerdo de año nuevo," *obras completas de Alfonso Reyes*, Vol. IV (México: Fondo de Cultura Económica, 1956): 397.]

happiness, but also of bloody tears. No need to invoke its causes in each written page for the comfort of fools, nor do I find pleasure in conceding to a patriotic fraud the compensation for my modest work. Without my own effort and thus with no personal merit, this is revealed in the sum of my books, drenching all of my thoughts with its vegetative humidity. It takes care of itself. On my part, I do not desire the weight of any limited tradition. Mine is the worldwide heritage by right of love, and because of my zeal toward study and work, the only authentic entitlements.[8]

IV

Worthy task for the educator of tomorrow who shall resolutely abandon exotic influences that took root in Mexico and that were never well acclimated; who repudiates contemptible pedagogies that produce surgeons by correspondence; who saves the everlasting scientific riches that Gabino Barreda's great educational reform brought to our culture; and, lastly, who will rescue the forgotten treasures of a tradition that has begun to lose traits beneficial to the soul of Mexicans! To return to ourselves, to our tradition. To seize as our own and to spread that secret stemming from the humanities that for a long time has sought refuge in defeated political classes! How many university people in Mexico know the history of scientific efforts by Mexicans? And why do references to a "Mexican science" sound like a paradox? How many are aware of the impressive expansion of studies in Latin that the expulsion of the Jesuits, during the reign of Charles III, suddenly terminated? Where can one study, in Mexico, the history of Mexican culture? Where is the surgeon—apart from those who are self-taught—who knows of the attempts and ardor behind Mexican medicine, or who has acquired in special courses the secrets of the indigenous pharmacology, a science frequently taught to us by foreigners, as happens for example with *peyote*? What do names such as Cristóbal de Ojeda, Cristóbal Méndez, and Pedro López tell us beyond the fact that they were surgeons in New Spain at the end of the sixteenth century? And what about Fray Lucas de Almodóvar, who had the gift to cure others and whose death, according to Mendieta, was heralded by omens? Tell me of the mining engineer who has found an academic source dedicated to the forerunners of Mexico's mining and chemistry? Is there one of our lawyers who has felt the need to know the background of Mariano Otero and where he acquired the idea of a writ of *amparo*, a Mexican legal procedure? I do not claim that the preceding is totally ignored: my argument is that it is not cultivated as a

---

[8] [Selected from "Pueblo americano," *Obras completas de Alfonso Reyes*, Vol. XXIV (México: Fondo de Cultura Económica, 1990): 362.]

general obligation and as part of university expertise. Only those obsessed with erudition know about the chapters written by Icazbalceta about the origins of our industrial sciences. We are doing well, at least in principle, in rural schools, rudimentary, popular, and basic vocations; however, we still need to invigorate the core—the heart itself—of instruction, an organ whose function is to pump blood to the entire body.

And to claim that these matters are not the concern of the people is as foolish as to wish once again that science be the privilege of a priestly cast; or to hope that people learn without teachers who will be in charge of instruction; or to pretend that people forget their vital needs so they can invent culture on their own; or to dream that the important trends of the nation shall trickle to the masses from the summit of a fabulous Sinai, without the work of researchers who will devote their time to inquire and question in their studies, during their vigils, and throughout their lives.

The autochthonous, from which the educational system of my era unconsciously alienated us—without realizing it—can be approached from two perspectives. Sometimes it is an intuitive force, so evident that any attempt to defend it with sophistry only brings ruin to it, whereas any hope to ground it in abstract models removes its best attribute: spontaneity. He who says, "I shall be instinctive," cannot be. He who says, "I will create art unconsciously," is lost and has no idea of what he or she is talking about. The originality of the autochthonous is so spontaneous and even unavoidable that oftentimes it operates against the conscious intentions of the artist. Latin American Modernists openly embraced the influences of French Symbolism. Nonetheless—and often without expecting it—it produced an original and most unusual creation, thus renewing (after a few inevitable errors) the richness of our sensibility and of our poetic language.

In a more concrete and therefore more consciously accessible sense, our American culture is an enormous mine of raw materials, of objects, forms, colors, and sounds, that should be incorporated and dissolved in the sap of our Mexican culture, thus transmitting its nutritive substance in motley and succulent spices. To this day, the only waves that have reached our shores—influenced and tinted by Spanish historical currents—are Latin tides. We do not possess a moral representation of the pre-Cortesian world, only a fragmentary vision with no more value than the one inspired by curiosity and archaeology: an absolute past. Today no one feels inclined toward the sacrifice of smoldering hearts upon the hearth of ferocious divinities, daubing one's hair with blood and dancing to the rhythm of hollow lumber. Since these cultural practices are no longer acceptable—nor the view of human life that they presuppose—we should no longer deceive ourselves or disturb people with pernicious deceptions: the

Mexican spirit glories in the hue that it took from Latin waves that reached our ancestral beaches, bathing its sands and the red clay of our land.

Human intercommunication is increasingly a daily fact. Man is the great leveler of geography, and it seems that his prime task in the world is to polish and smooth the billiard ball that is our planet. "The Pyrenees are no more!" is our heart's howl. The ideal of the human race—conscious of etymologies and with no imposed ecclesiastical intention—is a catholic ideal, that is, universal. All isolated groups, differences, and frontiers seem to be mere necessities enforced by economic laws, by the gravity of social masses, and by the laws of labor interests. In terms of craft industries and regional curiosities—such as *sarapes*, feather embroidery, colorful exquisiteness, and what a daring Mexican painter once called *el jicarismo* (the art of making drinking bowls)—one feels inclined to favor the development of the local nuance given that lovely adornments are what Mexican culture wears proudly. However, when one considers the true ideals of culture, who will argue that our scientific truth is different from that of another nation? What would Plato say of the Mexican who inquires into the moral good only applicable to Mexicans? Poetry, so sensitive to the contingencies of the moment, does not reach its plenitude when it halts at the brink of the differences in humor. "What do my handkerchiefs soaked with my blood—said Stevenson—matter to posterity!" The highest poetry is that which contemplates man in the abstract, more so than the accident that we are, or the archetype we would like to be. The same fine arts, bound by necessity to the immediate enchantments of matter, are in search—hieroglyphically—of a satisfaction of a moral order in manifestations of clay or marble, iron, cement, oil, and water: be it utility, contentment, or mere enthusiasm.[9]

[9] [Selected from "Discurso por Virgilio," *Obras completas de Alfonso Reyes*, Vol. XI (México: Fondo de Cultura Económica, 1960): 159–160, 161, 170.]

CHAPTER 19

The Problem of Truth (1960)

Abelardo Villegas

Translated by Carlos Alberto Sánchez

Abelardo Villegas was born in 1934 in Mexico City and died in Helsinki, Finland, in 2001. Villegas was the first of Leopoldo Zea's students to receive his doctoral degree under his guidance. Nonetheless, in his first book, The Philosophy of lo mexicano *(La filosofía de lo mexicano, 1960), Villegas presents himself as one of Zea's most unapologetic critics. Villegas was a great historian of Mexican philosophy, who, like his teacher, aimed to ground ideas in their social and political reality. He is the author of* Philosophy in the Political History of Mexico *(La filosofía en la historia política de México, 1966) and* Mexican Thought in the 20th Century *(El pensamiento mexicano en el siglo XX, 1993).*

1. The Philosophy of Perspectivism

Is a philosophy of *lo mexicano* possible? We must now answer this question. However, before we do that, we must summarize what we have gained from our investigation in order to know the effective reach of the question. It will be noticed that our investigation has not examined every opinion offered on the subject of the philosophy of *lo mexicano*; but our purpose has never been to carry out an exhaustive investigation, which coincidentally is not needed; rather, we have aimed to review, if not every opinion, at least all of the different positions that have been adopted around that problem.[1]

[1] Some of those familiar with the philosophy of *lo mexicano* will certainly admonish me for not having made a more thorough study of Octavio Paz's book, *El laberinto de la soledad* (Cuadernos Americanos, Mexico, 1950). I insist, however, that the present study does not aim to be exhaustive, but rather problematic. It is about resolving a question and not about doing history. Paz's book posits precisely, although inconsequentially, the problem that we have been treating in this work. His inspiration is, without a doubt, Samuel Ramos's *El perfil del hombre y cultura en México* (1934). Similar to our present investigation, there we find a characterology and an interpretation of the history of

It may be rightly objected that we have not made explicit mention of, nor paused to reflect on, the ideas of Dr. José Gaos, who has carefully examined the problems in the philosophy of *lo mexicano*. However, his position is already implicitly analyzed in [what came before], and in addition we have made use of a number of his ideas in order to criticize the essentialism of Emilio Uranga. And to these ideas we can add the following: to the criticism that the phenomenology

lo mexicano. And just as Ramos analyzes the "peladito," Paz does the same with the "pachuco." With an abundance of objectivity, Ramos tries to uncover the psychological foundation of a number of the *pelado*'s profane linguistic insults. Paz, with much less objectivity and with a brilliant literary style, does the exact same thing. Ultimately, if our work were historical, we would run the risk of monotony.

Adding to the length of this note, I will say a few things about how the problem of the particularity and universality of the Mexican is posited in Paz's book. Octavio Paz says that "[t]he Mexican and Mexicanness are defined by rupture and negation. And, simultaneously, as a search, as a will to transcend that state of exile. In sum, as a living consciousness of solitude, historical and personal" (p. 89). Very well, then, "feeling alone has a double significance: on the one hand, it consists in having consciousness of oneself; on the other, in a desire to escape the self" (p. 173). Solitude, then, is originary consciousness, but at the same time, a desire to commune with others. "This will to return," writes Paz, "is an effect of solitude and communion, of reunion and separation that appears to preside over our historical life" (p. 144).

The Mexican has realized that dialectic, having been at times original and at times trying to live as others live. The greater part of our ideologies—Scholastic, Enlightenment, Liberalism, Positivism—are nothing more than the result of that trying to live as others live; they are, as Octavio Paz puts it, "masks" that hide our solitude, our originality. Within this dialectic, the Revolution represents a turn to originality. "The Revolution was a discovery of our very selves and a return to our origins, first; then, a search and a hesitation for synthesis, aborted various times, incapable of assimilating our traditions and offering us a new saving project" (p. 164). That is, it has not been capable of realizing a second movement in that dialectic.

In accordance with the preceding, the philosophy of *lo mexicano* must recover a consciousness of our mode of being. "So far as being an examination of our tradition, it will be a philosophy of the history of Mexico and a history of Mexican ideas. But, our history is nothing more than a fragment of Universal History. That is, always, except at the time of the Revolution, we have lived our history as an episode of the entire world. Our ideas, in themselves, have never been entirely our ideas, but an inheritance or a conquest of that engendered by Europe. A philosophy of the history of México will not be, then, but a reflection on the attitudes that we have assumed before those themes that Universal History has given us. Counter-reformation, rationalism, positivism, socialism. In sum, the historical meditation will lead us to answer the question: how have Mexicans lived universal ideas?" (p. 165)

Well, now we ask, what constitutes our originality and our solitude? It is evident that the second moment of our dialectic, i.e., of communion, is sufficiently clear; we have been rationalist, positivists, etc., in our eagerness to live as others live. But, in what does *lo mexicano*, our solitude, our originality, consist? Paz's response is: "Mexicanness will be a mask that, upon falling, will finally let us see a man" (p. 167). After an enthusiastic search for *lo mexicano*, Paz emphasizes excitedly: "solitude, the feeling and knowing oneself to be alone, released from the world and alienated from oneself, separated in oneself, is not characteristically or exclusively Mexican . . . solitude is the ultimate foundation of the human condition" (p. 173).

Finally, there is one problem: when we are rationalists or positivists, we live like others live; when we feel alone, we are also living like others live. Then, why are we in angst and why do we despair? What happens is that Octavio Paz falls into a paralogism: he quietly introduces a third term into the of the Mexican and phenomenology in general fall into a vicious circle when they attempt to determine their object of knowledge, José Gaos adds that the "aporia of the essence of the exemplary fact" is not resolved. That is, the phenomenology of the Mexican fails to decide whether there is such a thing as an exemplary Mexican man, one who is more Mexican than other Mexicans, one who would embody better than anyone else the essence of the Mexican. And if ever such a distinction is made, the criterion that serves to effect it will not be explained or justified.

Very well then, we say that Gaos's position is already implicitly examined by us because his reflections set up the problem that we will treat in this chapter: the problem of historicity and the objectivity of philosophical truth. For the reasons provided earlier and given his historicist criterion, Gaos denies the essentialism of the philosophy of *lo mexicano* in the following way: "In sum, the historicity of the human being appears to oppose itself to the existence of an essence in him. . . . Conclusion: the possibility of a philosophy of the essence of Mexicanness, and more still of the Mexican, is at the very least very problematic," since "there should not be an essence of things which are purely historical, which is why these should not be defined, but historicized."

We would have to add to a phenomenological philosophy of the Mexican a historical description. But, I insist, such a move does not solve the problem, but rather aggravates it, since "after all, history cannot be written without a good dose of terms expressing 'essences,' some concrete, some abstract." That is, according to Gaos, certain generic terms that designate characteristics of units or totalities belong to all historical description. For example, consider the following lines from Justo Sierra: "the *rural multitudes,* abandoning their harvest and their homes followed him as a *Messiah*; the cry of 'Long live our Virgin Lady of Guadalupe and death to the evil government' (or death to the *gachupines,* as they were called), the *conjuration* of Querétaro had become an *immense popular uprising.* It was the *insurrection.*" With this we see that men cannot think in purely concrete terms, but need to think "eidetically," even if this eidetic thinking is part of the historical process. [. . .]

Gaos concludes by stating, "*historicism stumbles over* essential *limits*" (see his *En torno a la filosofía Mexicana*).

This means that not only can we not speak without essences, but neither is historical development nor the Science of History possible without the existence of

dialectic of universal solitude and communion, one that he is unable to explain: *the Mexican.* In the first part of his book, the Mexican is alone when he feels Mexican, indigenous, or Zapatista; he feels in communion when he feels European, positivist, or rationalist. Then, when it comes time to explain what the Mexican is, he cannot, so he removes him; what he ends up with is simply man, and with that Paz obtains a reputation of being a profound philosopher.

certain universal elements. We ask, in what does human historicity consist? The question arises because Gaos's conclusion is contradictory, or at least it is not sufficiently explained. Thus, we ask José Gaos: how do we reconcile the historically singular with the universal in man? Or, better yet, understood as the science that studies universal objects on the one hand and the Mexican as a historical entity on the other, how is a philosophy of *lo mexicano* possible?

In order to answer such a question, we have to take stock of what we have so far discovered and confront it directly. In the previous chapter we spoke about our particular perspective when confronted with the philosophies of Antonio Caso and José Vasconcelos. We saw them through a historical lens, as philosophers who do the history of thought, concerned more with comprehending it than criticizing it, concerned more with making a history than with deconstructing it [*deshacerla*]. But this did not commit us to looking for the same historical approach in other philosophies. We faced those without prejudice, allowing them to convince us as to whether or not they were telling us the truth and we were ready to criticize them if we found them in error. But it turns out that critical truth is that which places complexes of rigorous ideas in opposition to one another, which means that criticism can only be carried out with criteria that, from a certain point of view, are founded on solid ground. But facing the edifice of historicism we found ourselves unprepared. Why? Well, because ultimately we attached ourselves neither intellectually nor emotionally to approaches, complete and elaborated, that would have opposed both historicism and existentialism. We did not examine historicism and existentialism with the help of elaborated critical criteria because that is precisely that for which we are searching. The ultimate goal of this essay is to find that criteria and demand a firm stance within the panorama of philosophical ideas. This is our imperative.

Do we find ourselves, then, at a loss before these philosophical tendencies [viz., historicism and existentialism]? No. If we were at a loss, we would not have tried to write a word about them. From the vast archive of the philosophical tradition we chose a logical principle that in its simplicity and clarity could serve as foundational in the recognition of the error [in the philosophy of *lo mexicano*]. We already referred to the logical principle of non-contradiction, so abused since Hegel and even by our own philosophy professors [*en la Facultad de Filosofía y Letras*]. Clearly a theory cannot be formulated without scrupulously respecting this principle. A philosophy cannot say that truth is history and then declare that some truths are universal without canceling itself out, without both propositions mutually annulling each other. Without respecting the principle of non-contradiction, no theory is possible. Of course, neither should we concede to it unlimited value, since while it is one of the conditions of truth, it is not the only one, since truth depends not only on formal rules, but also on content, although, in this case, respecting the formal imperative is the first step required to reach it.

Clearly, this is not the only notion to which we have appealed, but we highlighted it because, as we saw, there is a notable contradiction at the foundations of Mexican historicism. With that we confronted the problems of the philosophy of *lo mexicano*. We saw, in the first instance, that that to which that name refers can rightly be designated as the philosophy of the Mexican individual [*el hombre mexicano*]. Gaos has spoken about the philosophy of *lo mexicano* when treating of Mexican individuals and things, but, since the latter are always placed at the service of the former, reflection always turns to the individual. Very well then, the basic point of this philosophy of *lo mexicano* is the conviction that all philosophical truth is a historical truth. If the Mexican is a historical entity as the person that he or she is, then one can correctly speak of a philosophy of *lo mexicano*. The problem lies, however, in the *concept of philosophical truth*. If truth is historical and relates only to that which is temporal or historical, then obviously there can be a philosophy of *lo mexicano*; if not, then we have to reconsider everything once again. This is what we are trying to clarify, not something else. To discuss whether the Mexican suffers from an inferiority complex, if he is capable of being a part of a supposed cosmic race,[2] is to go backward not forward. If we disagree with Uranga regarding the aspect of accidentality he attributes to the Mexican and if we do not discuss the presuppositions of his question, we are implicitly accepting those presuppositions. This is why it is necessary to ask the question regarding philosophical truth with as much rigor as possible.

Historicist and existentialist vitalism is a current of thought developed as a critique of intellectualism which, since Descartes until the late nineteenth century, dominated the European philosophical landscape. Heidegger, for instance, seems to have had Hegel's *Logic* on his table when he was writing *Being and Time*, but only to criticize it; and Ortega y Gasset, in *The Modern Theme*, makes some profound objections against rationalism, aiming to reveal its marginality and its limits. Very well, then, the peculiarity of rationalism, especially in the systems of Kant and Hegel, is that it is built upon an analysis of reason, that is, on an examination of cognition and truth, since they both affirm that it is not possible to do philosophy without knowing the structure of reason, the conditions for the possibility of truth. In contrast, the vitalists, historicists, and existentialists proceed differently; as their name indicates, they build systems on an analysis of life, of history, or of human existence. They do not see the human being through the lens of reason, or the necessary forms of knowledge, but rather see reason and knowledge as functions of life, and life as a condition for their possibility. This touches on our theme, because when we speak of the concept of truth as it appears in such philosophical positions, we are unable abstract from

---

[2] [Villegas is here referring to Samuel Ramos's *Profile of Man and Culture in Mexico* (1934) and to José Vasconcelos's *Cosmic Race* (1925), respectively.—Editors]

them the concept of life or human existence that is said, rightly, to be its ground. Historicism and existentialism want to be, at bottom, in close proximity to concrete human existence, leaving behind abstractions such as "consciousness in general" in order to substitute them for concepts such as the consciousness of man, who is oneself "in each case," as Heidegger graphically illustrates.

In order to begin the analysis of life without having to derive it from an analysis of the structure of cognition, as the idealist objection would demand, historicism and existentialism avail themselves to a method that is fundamentally descriptive and indicative [mostrativo]. Phenomenology, as Heidegger conceives it, is precisely an example of that. Heidegger does not *demonstrate* the temporality that is constitutive and absolute in human life; he simply *indicates* it. A great deal of Greek philosophy held that reason in its demonstrative work could not comprehend absolute movement or temporality, but Heidegger's phenomenology does what Crito would have done, that is, Plato's teacher, who, facing the impossibility of reducing becoming to mere concepts, had renounced speaking and limited himself only to pointing with his finger. Phenomenology is an intellectual pointing. If the object to which it is directed, in this case human existence, is presented as absolute temporality, it delimits itself in indicating it and limits itself to a shrugging of the shoulders. Phenomenology ends up as skeptical as Crito.

What is the result of the analysis of life? In order to answer, we have to look at Ortega y Gasset, since he has been the most influential among Mexican historicists and because, in terms of substance, he shares some conclusions with Heidegger (whom we might have occasion to discuss at a later time). For Ortega, man is a perspective, that is, situated in a corner of the world where he himself is, and each man is a part of the world in such a way that history is only the succession of unique and non-transferable perspectives. Whether these perspectives belong only to one man or are shared by an entire generation is something that Ortega never fully clarified. What is clear is that, for our purposes, such a clarification is secondary, since what is important is that the world of each man or generation is what he calls his "circumstance." Men are their circumstance and from that circumstance they contemplate the universe.

Here we come across the problem of truth. Truth is considered as a function of life and, as such, turns out to be as limited and circumstantial as man himself. But let us look at this more closely. Neither philosophy, nor any other science, nor any kind of human segregation, can reach an absolute truth in its traditional sense, that is, a truth for any possible world. However, we are not faced with any sort of relativism; Ortega's fundamental idea is that relativism only appears when someone believes in the existence of absolutes, in the existence of an absolute reality. Relativism is the incomplete knowledge of the absolute. But if we deny the existence of an absolute reality, insofar as an absolute reality can in no way appear to us, then relativism disappears and knowledge becomes a perspective, a point of view.[3] "A perspective," writes Ortega, "is the order and form that reality takes for the individual who contemplates it. If the place occupied by the one contemplating changes, so too does the perspective. On the other hand, if someone else substitutes the one contemplating, taking his place, the perspective remains identical. Obviously, if there is no subject that contemplates, one to whom reality appears, there is no perspective."[4] A perspective is not a deformation of reality, but its organization before a subject that contemplates it. "Cosmic reality is such that it can only be seen through a determinate perspective."[5] Moreover, all we have in the universe is a series of perspectives, mere points of view. Every person, every people, every epoch has its own perspective on the universe, its own truth. Ultimately, no one can take the place of anyone. *"Each life is a point of view on the universe,"* says Ortega, *"strictly speaking, what that life sees cannot be seen by another."*[6] [. . .]

What we reject outright is that man is a perspective, a point of view, a circumstance—at least in the sense previously described. And we hold this view because we find an incongruity between the *factum* of knowledge and the description of the man that produces it. The man-perspective, man as monad and solipsist, cannot produce or organize a science as commonly understood, that is, essentially communicable, essentially evolutionary. Natural sciences, which are progressive, and the sciences of the spirit, which are fundamentally comprehensive, cannot have as their base an entity that is constantly prohibited from communicating with others. Ortega says that the humanity inherited by man is an old humanity. And in that he is right. But understood as an irreplaceable perspective, unique and absolute, blind to other things, it turns out that humanity is an always-trying-on-new-perspectives, a having to forget what others have done.

Certainly, it is the concept of man that founds the concept or theory of knowledge, and also science itself, but there is always, there must always be, a relation of congruence between what is founded and the foundation. If truth is made by and for man, and is, moreover, objective and communicable, this cannot be a matter of pure perspective; it must contain a structure that makes possible such objectivity. We find ourselves once again facing the problem that Ortega introduced, namely, the problem of historicism: the problem of reconciling subjectivity and objectivity, the problem of reconciling the subject with culture, man with himself.

---

[3] *El tema de nuestro tiempo* (Madrid: Espasa-Calpe, 1923), p. 219.

[4] Ibid., p. 227.

[5] Ibid., p. 114.

[6] Ibid., p. 151.

2. The Individual as an Object of History

Is man a historical being? And if he is historical, do we understand by history the succession of closed perspectives that Ortega and historicism have popularized? We must answer in the affirmative to the first question. Man is historical to the extent that he is time itself; each man is, in effect, irreplaceable, unique, and, above all, ephemeral—ephemeral, however, only to a certain point, to which we will allude momentarily. This observation would be worthless if philosophy would have already discovered, and also justified, the existence of an a-temporal, omnipresent element in human evolution. But Spirit, Absolute Reason, God himself, are concepts that cannot be proven rationally. In this sense we adhere to that aspect of contemporary philosophy that places metaphysics in crisis. Heidegger himself, who asks about being in general and, in the last instance, God, has been unable to answer his own question. And it is natural to ask, if we think of man as temporal, and if man himself is a world: how would an element which is absolute and a-temporal fit within him? Experience, Kant would say, never gives us totality or necessity, but always gives us that which is finite and contingent; the only necessity is the a priori structure of the understanding, of the will, and of the senses. The first part of that proposition is true, the other part is false. Contemporary critical idealism has recognized it as such. Citing a Mexican example, we reproduce the following lines of Francisco Larroyo: "what we understand by nature is something static and absolute; it is the existence of things insofar as we understand existence as determinate, as Kant said at one point, but arranged according to laws, to concepts that the man of science conceives of in order to interpret the phenomena. *But the fundamental laws or categories of natural science are not, as Kant had it, absolute principles, but concepts in in a cycle of reiterated overcoming.*"[7] That is to say, the self-same categories of the understanding, which are also those of nature, are historical; they find themselves reiterated in overcoming. The historical structure of man also affects the structure of a priori categories. Thus, the first proposition that philosophy must investigate for the sake of understanding truth is the proposition regarding human historicity.

Again, by "historicity" we do not mean perspectivism. The phrase "each life is a point of view on the universe. Strictly speaking, what that point of view sees cannot be seen by another point of view" makes history an atomistic or discontinuous succession of points of view, heterogeneous and irreducible in themselves, and it breaks with the continuity of history so as to enclose each person—or each generation, which is the same—in a capsule of his own life. Historicism could thus be called historical monadism. Understood in this way,

[7] *Los principios de la etica social* (Mexico: Editorial Porrua, S.A., 1946), p. 112.

historicism [as perspectivism] does not explain the relations of comprehension between diverse points of view, between diverse individuals. Because, in effect, if what I see cannot be seen by anyone else—if what my generation sees cannot be seen by any other generation—and if I cannot see what others see, then why should the life of another matter to me? Why make history if in choosing the theme, as Edmundo O'Gorman says, all I am doing is betraying the situation of my own life, a situation that, in the last instance, I am already living? The other's point of view, insofar as it is another's, can very well be individual and unique, but not so much that I cannot say of another that he is an *other like me*, not so much that I am unable to identify myself with him. The past is heterogeneous to my present, but not sufficiently so that I am unable to say that it is *my* past. Clearly, historicism says that the past is *our* past, but it does not say that in the same sense in which we are saying it. Historicism as perspectivism[8] is a version of solipsism, since if the past is ours *we* give it life in the present, we make it speak. The past, on its own, neither speaks nor lives. The themes of history, which are only reflections of the historian's vital situation, make of the past an image and likeness of the present. At bottom, historicism as perspectivism suppresses the past so as to remain with the pure present. But since there are as many presents as there are individuals, human life is a series of monologues that have meaning only to whoever is speaking.

When we say that we can identify with the past, we are obviously referring to ourselves as living today, but also to the nature of the past itself. The past is to a certain extent independent of the present; it is independent in the sense that it is not the present that makes it real, or in the sense that it makes itself real. We do not make of the past an image and likeness of ourselves, but rather the past is that which *allows itself* to be identified with the present. That is, we cannot do with the lives of others as we wish, since every human life is sufficiently individual to resist the imposition of concepts that are not adequate to it.

Let us make this clearer.

All philosophy that speculates about history, or simply put, every investigator who decides to know history, will face the necessity of having to find—to quote Arnold Toynbee—a "unity of historical style." Thus, for example, Toynbee himself defines this unity with the term "civilization." Spengler denominates it in the same way, although with a different meaning. Ortega y Gasset talks about "circumstance." When we are talking about the positivist science of history, the unity is constituted by a determinate lapse and a portion of space in which action takes place. For Carlyle, finally, the unity is the successful, heroic individual, around whom figures can be formed. What is certain is that this unity of historical study is what gives meaning to the facts happening within it; the

---

[8] [For instance, in the work of José Ortega y Gasset.—Editors]

appearance of the bourgeoisie, for example, can only be explained within the framework of Western civilization, and not by the elements in Muslim society. The unity of historical study, while it sufficiently explains a series of facts, lends them individuality. It characterizes them in a certain way so that they may not be confused for others. But this necessity to establish a unity, be it individual, circumstantial, or civilizing, comes not only from a necessity of the science of history, but also from the very same object with which it occupies itself, namely, the human being.

We could say that a person is such insofar as he is an individual, insofar as he determines himself before others as individual, as original, and as distinct. If we were to find two individuals, alike in every way as two drops of water, and we were obligated to relate their lives, we would have to either describe only one or confuse them both, without discerning which would be the particular characters of each one of them. Their identical structures would make it necessary to suppress the existence of one of them, or we would have to consider both as one individuality, that is, we would have to suppress them both. That is why, in a certain way, individuality is existence; the less individuality an individual may possess, the less existence. What is the origin of individuality? Undisputedly, the origins lie in the creative capacity, which every individual possesses in more or less quantities. The creative capacity is manifested in the self-determination of each existence before manifesting itself in objective creation. Each individual, to the extent that he exists, is self-determining. History occupies itself with those who are more individualistic, with those who more forcefully stand out from the crowd, although each one of us possesses this capacity. When we examine a photograph of a group of men unknown to everyone, this photograph tells us nothing, unless there are some in the group who stand out in their appearance. On the other hand, when within that group we find a person we recognize, he is immediately picked out from the crowd because we take notice of his concrete existence, of his individuality; his appearance may not differ from the rest in the photograph, but we know that it belongs to that life. The people in our family or in our circle of relatives are not perfectly individual because we know in what ways they have created themselves, which means that they have a concrete individuality and existence within an anonymous mass.

But if every human being has the capacity for creation and individuality, then why does history not occupy itself with them all? The reason is that there is gradation in these individualities. It is true that if we compare a man in our family to an unknown man in the street, we will find the man in our family perfectly individual, but if we compare him to the type of man who is in style in our epoch, then perhaps we will not find so many differences. A contemporary middle-class Mexican will not call the attention of history if he does not possess determinate characteristics that will distinguish him in his class. History occupies itself with those individuals who, within that unity of historical study of which we have spoken, are distinguished as original existences, that is, as creative existences. The more vigorous and original they are, the more they will attract the attention of history. Within the very same generation, for instance, the generation of the Mexican Revolution, we can perfectly observe the gradation of original existences. Thus we find figures of first-order importance: Madero, Carranza, Zapata, Obregon, Calles, and so on; then, those of the second order, like Cabrera, Huerta, Villa perhaps, De la Huerta, Múgica, and so on and so on, until we find ourselves face to face with the regular person, one who can easily blend into the popular mass, and who is only mentioned when he stakes a specific and distinct attitude within the normal modes of appearance.

Very well then, when we say that history must deal with the most original individualities, we are not following a similar conception to that of Carlyle, since when we speak of original existences we are referring not only to persons, but also to their culture, and their works. The history of a culture reproduces novel scientific, political, and artistic creations. The key moments in that history are the blossoming of consciousness that constitute original contributions in a particular field. It does not deal, however, with those cultural products that due to their absolute lack of originality are confused with others. Between these and the former there is an immense difference in gradation in terms of originality.

We see, then, that history is about human existence insofar as that existence is more human, more original, more creative. If we look at this closely, we can see that historical development involves persons and things, and their relationships, in a process of repetitive novelty. But more extraordinarily still is that what is new to historical development, namely, individual lives themselves, transcend the circumstances in which they were given, and reach us. If we conceive of time as an absolute development, as a "passing of things and men," historical individualities are, to a certain extent, atemporal insofar as they do not completely pass, insofar as they transcend their moment and arrive at ours. The truth of some individuals in a particular circumstance is not only valid for that circumstance, but it reaches us and competes with our truths. When Ortega says that "the divergence between worlds does not imply the falsity of one of them," what he tries to make understood is that, although the truth of an Athenian of the fourth century B.C. might contradict mine, both are equally true insofar as each one is rooted in its circumstance; I cannot say that the Athenian's is false, nor can the Athenian say that mine is false. But such a conception destroys science itself since in that view the truths of the past are not left for us as truths, but as mere narrations, pure fiction. I cannot say, for example, that the adventures of Julian Sorel, the protagonist of *Red and Black*, are false, since Stendhal did not write them thinking that the reader would take them as truths. When we deal with a novel, we suspend the criterion of truth, but this cannot be done with something like Ptolemy's physics. In comparing it with Newton's or Einstein's, we have to err on the side of one of them or we will be dealing with pure literature. The dialogues of Plato's or Aristotle's contemporaries have as their ground the fact that their truths are not true only for their world, but are also true for ours; they reach us, not as narration that requires us to suspend all considerations of their truth, but, rather, *as truths* that are debatable insofar as they aim to be truths. This is why, from the point of view of its truth or falsity, Stendhal's *Red and Black* is not open for dispute.

Historicism could object that it is not that those truths are still valid, but that we, in discussing them from our circumstance, make them valid. Correct: of course, all truth is [valid] for whoever thinks it, but that does not mean that the category of truth for a proposition must have a foundation only in my thinking. We have already said that we can discuss Ptolemy's theory so long as it was formulated with a pretention to truth, but we cannot say the same thing with Odysseus' adventures in the Isle of the Cyclops. In other words, the quality of truth for a series of propositions not only emanates from the fact that my thinking considers it such, but also from the structure with which it was formulated.

And this because for the historicist the past lacks sense on its own; it is the historian who gives it sense and makes it speak. But with that we arrive at the conclusion that the past will have the sense that the historian wants to give it, and it will speak what the historian wants it to speak. Certainly, it is clear that one event can be the subject of various interpretations, even some that are opposed to one another, but we cannot infer, in a rigorous way, that the variety of interpretations emerges only from the diverse points of view of the historians, but rather that it also has a grounding in the variety of aspects presented by the historical phenomenon itself. Due to the singularity or the individuality of the historical event, we can say that it speaks for itself and has its own sense; the best proof of this is that although a multitude of interpretations may fit a certain event, we can easily find the limit of those things that can be predicated on that event. Thus, for instance, we cannot say in any way that the conquest of indigenous Mexico was carried out by Anglo-Saxons. A multitude of interpretations fit into the significance of the Spanish conquest, but not so many as to bring me toward those that would explain the Anglo-Saxon conquest of Mexico. This evidently demonstrates how the historical event, in itself, has a particular constitution, a particular determination or individuality that does not allow every kind of predication; *that is, it gives us a margin of error.* The perspectival and fictional interpretation of history cannot explain the error because it does not lend the historical event its own proper constitution, but merely has borrowed from the historian, the forger of worlds. Only when we consider man as enclosed in his own life, in his own circumstance, can we say that the past does not speak for itself, which is when we can endow it with every predication imaginable.

In sum, the particularity and individuality of the historical phenomenon that transcends "its own moment" determine, in the last instance, those judgments that can be made about it, that is, so long as it resists determinate types of predications that stand on the margins of truth or error. In this way, we can explain those concepts that historicism has been unable to justify. Such "transcendence of its own moment," belonging to the historical phenomenon, also explains objectivity and subjectivity. It explains the continuity of history and makes science possible. Only historical monadism, or solipsism, ends up utterly ignorant.

3. The Philosophy of *lo mexicano*

We asked ourselves at the start of this final part of our work about philosophical truth and about the philosophy of *lo mexicano*. In the previous paragraph we attempted to give an answer to the first question, although the reader will note that we have talked instead about truth in general more than we have spoken about philosophical truth. With that we assume the same theoretical attitude as Ortega. In *The Modern Theme*, Ortega does not refer to philosophical truth, but to truth in general. He tries to explain its structure and its possibility. We differ on this specific point of his problematic, but coincide in the idea that fundamental philosophical truth does not really consist in any determinate concrete proposition, but, rather, in the explication of the structure and possibility of all truth.

Moreover, this investigation also deals with the elucidation of human historicity, since, at bottom, to clarify this is to explain the structure and the possibility of which we speak. The philosophy of *lo mexicano*, especially the kind promoted by Leopoldo Zea, has recognized this; however, Ramos, Uranga, and to a certain extent O'Gorman, in speaking about objective values, the being of the Mexican, or the being of America, maintain that such values and beings can be the proper object of philosophical truth. Our analysis has demonstrated, however, that such objectives are purely historical—O'Gorman, for his part, also seems to affirm this. Values cannot exist independent of human life, nor can there be such a being of the Mexican. Thus, our investigation has subscribed itself to the note of historicity predicated on all humanity.

Ortega y Gasset has said that human historicity, understood as perspectivism, grounds all possible truth. We are in agreement with that view, except in our understanding of historicity as perspectivism. The essential object of philosophy has thus been delimited: while it consists in the explication of the structure and possibility of truth in general, it also consists in an explication of the structure of human life; *science* and *life* are concepts that complement and reciprocally need each other. This is why it is necessary that we avoid being radically Heideggerian.

Heidegger wants to place existence as the ground of science, but, as previously noted, we correct a deficient concept of existence by appealing to the essential structure of science. Science presented itself to us as fundamentally objective, communicable, and existence appeared as monadic, closed. The particular structure of the former forced us to open our eyes before the particular structure of the latter. Science and existence cannot both be monadic because such a proposition would annul itself, so we had to find them communicable with each other, open, and reciprocally influential.

We saw that of all human acts, the only ones that transcend their historical moment, that moment in which they give themselves, are the most individualistic, the most original, and the most creative. This is why history seems to us the search for the novel and the innovative. I insist, originality—creativity and individuality—are particular to each person, as each person creates and makes distinct her own life; as a matter of fact, that is the distinct feature of humanity each person possesses. This feature appears in gradations, as some persons are more creative and individual than others, which makes it possible that those gradations in creativity can be the ground for a possible axiological scale. History, then, concedes a greater importance to those human phenomena that are more individualistic, and its interest decreases as the particularity of this is de-emphasized. It occupies itself with the common person, with the person in the mass, only when this person assumes a distinct, new attitude in relation to his habitual modes of comportment. Very well then, this individual phenomenon, this object of history, to a certain extent determines the possible predicates that can be affirmed in relation to that person; precisely because of his particular individuality, he resists certain judgments and interpretations. This shows that it is not the historian who gives sense and voice to the historical event or fact, but rather that this event or fact already possesses a particular structure prior to judgment, and that, we must insist, this structure only manifests itself in judgment. Such an appraisal of the structure itself of the historical event is necessary if we want to explain how true or false judgments are possible. If the event does not speak for itself, it would be at the mercy of the historian, who could construct interpretations based on his own tastes.

In sum, when we affirm the individuality and singularity of the human phenomenon, we aim to refute the absolute theoretical validity of logical formalism. A judgment over a historical fact indubitably has its form, but its quality of true judgment comes not only from that form, but also from its content, its matter, and this is because we find relations within not only the judgment but also the intervention of irreplaceable individuals. When we affirm that the individual human phenomenon transcends the moment in which it is given, we aim to ground the communicability and the objectivity of science.

Precisely because those truths that men of science formulate regarding themselves and their circumstance transcend that circumstance, we can discuss those truths as truths, as objectively valid (so long as objectivity is understood as the openness to discussion of a truth as such). And finally, with the affirmation that individual, cultural, and historical phenomena pose in themselves a particular structure that limits the judgments that can be predicated upon them, we aim to explain truth and falsehood, those fundamental categories of knowledge itself. Such is our position before these fundamental problems of human existence and science.

Now, what do we understand by the philosophy of *lo mexicano*? The philosophy of *lo mexicano* will be those analyses of the Mexican that have as their ground the ideas previously noted. That is, knowing that the human phenomenon is individual, and that it transcends its moment the more individual and original it is, the philosophy of *lo mexicano* will consist in a type of analysis that will inform us as to the particularity that the Mexican possesses in relation to other peoples. We can see, in effect, what it is that we have in common with other peoples—which can be many different things—but only so as to distinguish that originality that we can offer other peoples, namely, a historical and cultural experience that they may not have. Every individual or every determinate group of individuals, as far as their particularities, can contribute original experiences via some suitable expression. Human inequality consists in that some do this while others do not, and that inequality, added to the levels of individuality observed in history, constitute a valuation on human existence. Since the individual historical phenomenon endures much longer than the chronological moment in which it is given, each man or nation has the duty to contribute his own creations to the common archive of humanity. He has the duty to create, to invent, as Caso and Vasconcelos rightly pointed out. When first Sierra and then Caso and Vasconcelos realized that it was necessary to invent solutions abstracted from a specifically Mexican circumstance, they were proposing the necessity for men in our country to be more human. When Leopoldo Zea insists on Mexico's or America's responsibility toward the world, he is expressing that same necessity, the necessity that we must make our own solutions and our own existence.

To return to the individual, to the most characteristic that we possess, is not to fall once again into narcissism, into a solipsism or a closed nationalism; on the contrary, it is to contribute to human experience. Only he who clings to what is common, only he who does not make of himself an individual, who does not invent, reduces his own humanity. From the point of view of philosophical anthropology, he is less human than the rest; from the point of view of morality, he is more egoistic than the rest.

Only thus is the philosophy of *lo mexicano* justified. Only thus is it possible.

BIBLIOGRAPHY

Bartra, Roger. *La jaula de melancolía*. New Brunswick, NJ: Rutgers University Press, 1992.

Bassols, Alejandro Tomasini. "Luis Villoro, the *Tractatus*, and Analytical Philosophy in Mexico." *APA Newsletter on Hispanic/Latino Issues in Philosophy* 14, no. 1 (2014): 4–9.

Bondy, Augusto Salazar. *Sentido y problema del pensamiento filosofico hispanoamericano (with English translation)*. Lawrence: The University of Kansas Press, 1969.

Caponigri, A. Robert, trans. *Major Trends in Mexican Philosophy*. Notre Dame, IN: University of Notre Dame Press, 1966.

Carnap, Rudolph. "Notes and News." *The Journal of Philosophy* 67, no. 24 (1970): 1026–1029.

Carrion, Jorge. *Mito y magia del mexicano*. México, DF: Porrua y Obregon, 1952.

Caso, Antonio. *Discursos a la nación mexicana*. México, DF: Robredo, 1922.

Caso, Antonio. *El problema de México y la ideología nacional*. México, DF: Editorial Cultura, 1924.

Clark, Meri L. "The Emergence and Transformation of Positivism." In *A Companion to Latin American Philosophy*, edited by Susana Nuccetelli, Ofelia Schutte, and Otavio Bueno, 53–67. Malden, MA: Blackwell, 2010.

Clemente Orozco, José. *An Autobiography*. Translated by Robert C. Stephenson. Austin: University of Texas Press, 1962.

Flower, Elizabeth. "The Mexican Revolt against Positivism." *Journal of the History of Ideas* 10, no. 1 (1949): 115–129.

Frondizi, Risieri. "A Study in Recent Mexican Thought." *The Review of Metaphysics* 9, no. 1 (1955): 112–116.

Gaos, José. *Filosofía de la filosofía e Historia de la filosofía*. México, DF: Editorial Stylo, 1947.

Gaos, José. *Filosofía mexicana de nuestros dias*. México, DF: Imprenta Universitaria, 1954.

Gaos, José. *Introducción a El Ser y el Tiempo de Martin Heidegger*. México, DF: Fondo de Cultura Económica, 1971.

Garizurieta, César. *Isagoge sobre lo mexicano*. México: Porrua y Obregon, 1952.

Gracia, Jorge J. E. *Latinos in America: Philosophy and Social Identity*. Malden, MA: Blackwell, 2008.

Gracia, Jorge J. E., and Elizabeth Millán-Zaibert, eds. *Latin American Philosophy for the 21st Century: The Human Condition, Values, and the Search for Identity*. Amherst, NY: Prometheus Books, 2004 (1969).

Guerra, Ricardo. "Jean Paul Sartre, filosofo de la libertad." *Filosofía y Letras* 16, no. 32 (1948): 295–308.

Guerra, Ricardo. "Una historia del Hiperión," *Los Universitarios* 18 (1984): 1–10.

Haddox, John H. "The Aesthetic Philosophy of José Vasconcelos." *International Philosophical Quarterly* 4, no. 2 (1964): 283–296.

Haddox, John H. *Antonio Caso: Philosopher of Mexico*. Austin: University of Texas Press, 1971.

Haddox, John H. "Philosophy with a Mexican Perspective." *Philosophy and Phenomenological Research* 24, no. 4 (1964): 580–586.

Haddox, John H. *Vasconcelos of Mexico: Philosopher and Prophet*. Austin: University of Texas Press, 1961.

Hurtado, Guillermo. "The Anti-Positivist Movement in Mexico." In *A Companion to Latin American Thought*, edited by Susana Nuccetelli, Ofelia Schutte, and Otávio Bueno, 82–94. Malden, MA: Wiley-Blackwell, 2010.

Hurtado, Guillermo. *El Buho y la Serpiente: Ensayos sobre la filosofía de México del siglo xx*. México, DF: UNAM, 2007.

Hurtado, Guillermo. "Dos mitos de la mexicanidad." *Diánoia* 40 (1994): 263–293.

Hurtado, Guillermo. *El Hiperión*. México: UNAM, 2006.

Hurtado, Guillermo. "Paths of Ontology." *APA Newsletter on Hispanic/Latino Issues in Philosophy* 10, no. 2 (2011): 17–21.

Hurtado, Guillermo. "Portraits of Luis Villoro." Translated by Kim Díaz. *APA Newsletter on Hispanic/Latino Issues in Philosophy* 15, no. 1 (2015): 24–27.

Hurtado, Guillermo. *La revolucion creadora. Antonio Caso y José Vasconcelos en la revolución mexicana*. Mexico: UNAM, 2016.

Ibargüengoitia, Antonio. *Filosofia Mexicana: En sus hombres y en sus textos*. México, DF: Editorial Porrua, S.A., 1967.

Joseph, Gilbert M., and Timothy J. Henderson, eds. *The Mexico Reader: History, Culture, Politics*. Durham, NC: Duke University Press, 2002.

Krauze, Rosa. "Sobre la *Fenomenoloogía del relajo*." *Revista de la Universidad de México* 20, no. 8 (1966): 1–11.

Kubitz, O. A. "Humanism in Mexico." *Philosophy and Phenomenological Research* 2, no. 2 (1941): 211–218.

León-Portilla, Miguel. *Aztec Thought and Culture: A Study of the Ancient Nahuatl Mind*. Translated by Jack Emory Davis. Norman: University of Oklahoma Press, 1963.

Lipp, Solomon. *Leopoldo Zea: From Mexicanidad to a Philosophy of History*. Waterloo, ON: Wilfried Laurier University Press, 1980.

Lomnitz, Claudio. *Exits from the Labyrinths: Culture and Ideology in the Mexican National Space*. Berkeley: University of California Press, 1992.

MacGrégor, Joaquín Sánchez. "¿Hay una moral existencialista?" *Filosofía y Letras* 16, no. 32 (1948): 267–278.

Maffie, James. *Aztec Philosophy: Understanding a World in Motion*. Boulder: University Press of Colorado, 2014.

Martí, Oscar. "Early Critics of Positivism." In *A Companion to Latin American Philosophy*, edited by Susana Nuccetelli, Ofelia Schutte, and Otávio Bueno, 68–81. Malden, MA: Wiley-Blackwell, 2009.

Martínez, José Luis, ed. *The Modern Mexican Essay*. Translated by H. W. Hilborn. Toronto: University of Toronto Press, 1965.

Michael, Christopher Domínguez. "¿El existencialismo fue un relajo?" *Tinta Seca* 25 (1996): 7–10.

Michael, Christopher Domínguez. *Octavio Paz en su siglo*. México, DF: Aguilar, 2014.

Millon, Robert Paul. *Mexican Marxist: Vicente Lombardo Toledano*. Chapel Hill: University of North Carolina Press, 1966.

O'Gorman, Edmundo. "El arte o de la monstruosidad." In *Seis estudios historicos sobre tema mexicano*, 41–55. México: Universidad Veracruzana, Jalapa, 1960.

Oliver, Amy. "Values in Modern Mexican Thought." *The Journal of Value Inquiry* 27, no. 2 (1993): 215–230.

Ortega Esquivel, Aureliano. "Thinking about the Mexican Revolution: Philosophy, Culture, and Politics in Mexico: 1910–1934." *Pupkatha Journal on Interdisciplinary Studies in Humanities* 2, no. 3 (2010): 247–255.

Ortega Esquivel, Aureliano, and Javier Corona Fernandez, eds. *Ensayos sobre el pensamieno mexicano*. México, DF: Universidad de Guanajuato, 2014.

Ortega y Gasset, José. *Meditations on Quixote*. Translated by Evelyn Rugg and Diego Marin. Champlain: University of Illinois Press, 2000.

Paz, Octavio. *The Labyrinth of Solitude*. Translated by Lysander Kemp. New York: Grove Press, 1985.

Pereda, Carlos. *La filosofía en México en el siglo XX. Apuntes de un participante*. México, DF: Consejo Nacional para la Cultura y las Artes, 2013.

Pereda, Carlos. "Latin American Philosophy: Some Vices." *Journal of Speculative Philosophy* 20, no. 3 (2006): 192–203.

Pilcher, Jeffrey M. *Cantinflas and the Chaos of Mexican Modernity*. Wilmington, DE: Scholarly Sources, 2001.

Pilcher, Jeffrey M. *¡Que vivan los tamales! Food and the Making of Mexican Identity*. Albuguerque: University of New Mexico Press, 1998.

Ponce, Armando. "El grupo Hiperion." *El processo*. April 2, 2005: 1–2.

Portilla, Jorge. "La Crisis Espiritual de los Estados Unidos." *Cuadernos Americanos*, 65, no. 5 (1952): 69–86.

Portilla, Jorge. *Fenomenología del relajo*. México, DF: Fondo de Cultura Económica, 1984.

Portilla, Jorge. "La Nausea y El Humanismo." *Filosofía y Letras* 16, no. 32 (1948): 243–265.

Ramirez, Mario Teodoro, ed. *Filosofía de la cultura en México*. México, DF: Plaza y Valdez Editores, 1997.

Ramos, Samuel. *Profile of Culture and Man in Mexico*. Translated by Peter Earle. Austin: University of Texas Press, 1962.

Reyes, Alfonso. *La X en la frente*. México, DF: Porrrua y Obregon, 1952.

Reyes, Alfonso. *Mexico in a Nutshell and Other Essays*. Translated by Charles Ramsdell. Berkeley: University of California Press, 1964.

Reyes, Alfonso. *The Position of America and Other Essays*. Translated by Federico de Onís. New York: Alfred A. Knopf, 1950.

Reyes, Juan José. "Jorge Portilla, por los caminos de la libertad." *Crónica de Hoy* (2003). Accessed April 4, 2016. http://www.cronica.com.mx/nota.php?id_nota=99164.

Reyes, Juan José. *El péndulo y el pozo: El mexicano visto por Emilio Uranga y Jorge Portilla*. México, DF: Ediciones Sin Nombre, 2004.

Romanell, Patrick. "The Background of Contemporary Mexican Thought." *Philosophy and Phenomenological Research* 8, no. 2 (1947): 256–265.

Romanell, Patrick. "Bergson in Mexico: A Tribute to José Vasconcelos." *Philosophy and Phenomenological Research* 21, no. 21 (1961): 501–513.

Romanell, Patrick. *The Making of the Mexican Mind: A Study in Recent Mexican Thought*. Lincoln: University of Nebraska Press, 1952.

Romanell, Patrick. "Samuel Ramos on the Philosophy of Mexican Culture: Ortega and Unamuno in Mexico." *Latin American Research Review* 10, no. 3 (1975): 81–101.

Ruanova, Oswaldo Diaz. *Los existencialistas Mexicanos*. México, DF: Editorial Rafael Gimenez Siles, S.A. de C.V., 1982.

Russel, Bertrand. *The History of Western Philosophy*. New York: Simon & Schuster, 1945.

Sáenz, Mario. *The Identity of Liberation in Latin American Thought: Latin American Historicism and the Phenomenology of Leopoldo Zea*. Lanham, MD: Lexington Books, 1999.

Salmerón, Fernando. "Una imagen del mexicano." *Revista de Filosofía y Letras* 21, no. 41–42 (1951): 175–188.

Sánchez, Carlos Alberto. *Contingency and Commitment: Mexican Existentialism and the Place of Philosophy*. Albany: State University of New York Press, 2016.

Sánchez, Carlos Alberto. "Heidegger in Mexico: Emilio Uranga's Ontological Hermeneutic." *Continental Philosophy Review* 41, no. 4 (2008): 441–461.

Sánchez, Carlos Alberto. "Jorge Portilla's Phenomenology: *Relajo, Gelassenheit*, and Liberation." *APA Newsletter on Hispanic/Latino Issues in Philosophy* 6, no. 2 (2007): 1–7.

Sánchez, Carlos Alberto. *The Suspension of Seriousness: On the Phenomenology of Jorge Portilla*. Albany: State University of New York Press, 2012.

Sarita Gaytán, Marie. *¡Tequila! Distilling the Spirit of Mexico*. Stanford, CA: Stanford University Press, 2014.

Schmidt, Henry C. "Antecedents to Samuel Ramos: Mexicanist Thought in the 1920s." *Journal of Interamerican Studies and World Affairs* 18, no. 2 (1976): 179–202.

Schmidt, Henry, C. *The Roots of Lo Mexicano: Self and Society in Mexican Thought 1900–1934*. College Station: Texas A&M University Press, 2000.

Sierra, Justo. *The Political Evolution of the Mexican People*. Translated by Charles Ramsdell. Austin: University of Texas Press, 1969.

Sobrevilla, David. "Phenomenology and Existentialism in Latin America." *Philosophical Forum* 20, no. 1–2 (1989): 85–113.

Stabb, Martin S. *In Quest of Identity: Patterns in the Spanish American Essay of Ideas, 1890–1930*. Chapel Hill: University of North Carolina Press, 1967.

Stehn, Alexander V. "From Positivism to 'Anti-Positivism' in Mexico: Some Notable Continuities." In *Latin American Positivism: New Historical and Philosophic Essays*, edited by Gregory D. Gilson and Irving W. Levinson, 49–81. Lanham, MD: Lexington Books, 2012.

Valero, Aurelia, ed. *Filosofía y vocación: Seminario de filosofía moderna de José Gaos*. México, DF: Fondo de Cultura Económica, 2012.

Vasconcelos, José. *The Cosmic Race/La raza cósmica (Race in the Americas)*. Translated by Didier T. Jaén. Baltimore, MD: Johns Hopkins University Press, 1997.

Vasconcelos, José. *A Mexican Ulysses: An Autobiography*. Translated by W. Rex Crawford. Bloomington: Indiana University Press, 1963.

Vásquez, Francisco H. "Philosophy in Mexico: The Opium of the Intellectuals or a Prophetic Insight." *Canadian Journal of Political and Social Theory* 4, no. 3 (1981): 27–41.

Vieyra, Jaime. "La ambiguedad insuperable de la condición humana (La lectura sobre Merleau-Ponty del joven Emilio Uranga)." In *Merleau-Ponty Viviente*, edited by Mario Teodoro Ramírez, 66–73. Barcelona: Anthropos Editorial, 2012.

Villegas, Abelardo. *La filosofía de lo mexicano*. México, DF: UNAM, 1979.

Villoro, Luis. "La cultura mexicana de 1910 a 1960." *Historia Mexicana* 10, no. 2 (1960): 196–219.

Villoro, Luis. "Genesis y proyecto del existencialismo en México." *Filosofía y Letras*, 18, no. 36 (1949): 233–244.

Villoro, Luis. "La reflexion sobre el ser de Gabriel Marcel." *Filosofía y Letra* 32, no. 16 (1948): 279–294.

Weinstein, Michael A. *The Polarity of Mexican Thought: Instrumetalism and Finalism*. University Park: Pennsylvania State University Press, 1976.

Wimer, Javier. "La Muerte de un filósofo." *Revista de la Universidad de México*, 17 (2005): 27–33.

Uranga, Emilio. *Análisis del ser del mexicano*. México, DF: Porrua y Obregon, S.A., 1952.

Uranga, Emilio. *Análisis del ser del mexicano y otros escritos sobre la filosfofia de lo mexicano (1949–1952)*. México, DF: Bonilla Artigas Editores, 2013.

Uranga, Emilio. *¿De quién es la filosofía?* Guanajuato: Gobierno del estado de Guanajuato, 1990.

Uranga, Emilio. "Dialogo con Maurice Merleau-Ponty." *México en la cultura*. March 13, 1949: 3–4.

Uranga, Emilio. "Dos existencialismos." *Mexico en la Cultura*. August 14, 1949: 3–4.

Uranga, Emilio. "Ensayo de una ontología del mexicano." In *Análisis del ser del mexicano y otros escritos sobre la filosofía de lo mexicano (1949–1952)*, edited by Guillermo Hurtado. México, DF: Bonilla Artigas Editores, S.A. de C.V., 2013.

Uranga, Emilio. "Maurice Merleau-Ponty: Fenomenologia y existencialismo." *Filosofía y Letras* 15, no. 30 (1948): 219–241.

Uranga, Emilio. "Notas para un estudio del Mexicano." *Cuadernos Americanos* 10, no. 3 (1951): 114–128.

Uranga, Emilio. "Untitled." *México en la Cultura*. September 11, 1949.

Zea, Leopoldo. "El existencialismo como filosofía de la responsabilidad." *El Nacional*. June 5, 1949: 3.

Zea, Leopoldo. *La filosofía americana como filosofía sin más*. México, DF: Siglo XXI Editores, S.A. de C.V., 1969.

Zea, Leopoldo. *La filosofía como compromiso y otros ensayos.* México, DF: Fondo de Cultura Económica, 1952.

Zea, Leopoldo. "Positivism and Porfirism in Mexico." In *Latin American Philosophy: An Introduction with Readings,* edited by Susana Nuccetelli and Gary Seay, 198–218. London: Pearson, 2003.

Zea, Leopoldo. *Positivism in Mexico.* Translated by Josephine H. Schulte. Austin: University of Texas Press, 1974.

Zea, Leopoldo. *The Role of the Americas in History.* Edited by Amy Oliver. Translated by Sonja Karsen. New York: Rowman & Littlefield, 1992.

Zea, Leopoldo, and David R. Maciel. "An Interview with Leopoldo Zea." *The Hispanic American Historical Review* 65, no. 1 (1985): 1–20.

Zirión Quijano, Antonio. *Historia de la Fenomenología en México.* Morelia: Jitanjáfora, 2004.

Zirión Quijano, Antonio. "Phenomenology in Mexico: A Historical Profile." *Continental Philosophy Review* 33, no. 75 (2000): 75–92.

INDEX